Engendering Violence
in Papua New Guinea

Engendering Violence in Papua New Guinea

Edited by Margaret Jolly and Christine Stewart
with Carolyn Brewer

Australian
National
University

E PRESS

Published by ANU E Press
The Australian National University
Canberra ACT 0200, Australia
Email: anuepress@anu.edu.au
This title is also available online at http://epress.anu.edu.au

National Library of Australia Cataloguing-in-Publication entry

Title: Engendering violence in Papua New Guinea / edited by Margaret Jolly and
                 Christine Stewart ; with Carolyn Brewer.

ISBN: 9781921862854 (pbk.) 9781921862861 (ebook)

Notes: Includes bibliographical references.

Subjects: Family violence--Papua New Guinea.
                 Social psychology--Papua New Guinea.
                 Social adjustment--Papua New Guinea.
                 Papua New Guinea--Social conditions.

Other Authors/Contributors:
                 Jolly, Margaret 1949-
                 Stewart, Christine.
                 Brewer, Carolyn.

Dewey Number: 362.829209953

Cover design and layout by ANU E Press

Contents

Preface xi
   Christine Stewart

Acknowledgements xiii

Abbreviations and Acronyms xv

Prologue: The Place of Papua New Guinea in Contours of
   Gender Violence xvii
   Margaret Jolly

Introduction— Engendering Violence in Papua New Guinea:
   Persons, Power and Perilous Transformations 1
   Margaret Jolly

1. Black and Blue: Shades of Violence in West New Britain, PNG 47
   Naomi McPherson

2. Troubled Masculinities and Gender Violence in Melanesia 73
   Laura Zimmer-Tamakoshi

3. Engendered Violence and Witch-killing in Simbu 107
   Philip Gibbs

4. Becoming Mary: Marian Devotion as a Solution to
   Gender-based Violence in Urban PNG 137
   Anna-Karina Hermkens

5. Engendering Violence in the Papua New Guinea Courts:
   Sentencing in Rape Trials 163
   Jean G. Zorn

6. Conversations with Convicted Rapists 197
   Fiona Hukula

7. 'Crime to be a Woman?': Engendering Violence against
   Female Sex Workers in Port Moresby, Papua New Guinea . . 213
   Christine Stewart

8. Gender Violence in Melanesia and the Problem of
   Millennium Development Goal No. 3 239
   Martha Macintyre

Contributors 267

Index 271

Maps

Map 1.   General map of PNG showing the sites of research included   xxiv
in this volume

Map 2.   Gende villages are located in a mountainous region of the   74
Madang Province which borders Simbu Province

Illustrations

Figure 1.   *Meri Ikirap Sapotim*. Some women, like members of this   xviii
NGO, wear striking uniforms during the March against
Gender Violence, Port Moresby, 2006

Figure 2.   'Hey, men, we are not your pigs or dogs. Please think   xviii
about that, and don't treat us badly.' Handmade banner
proudly displayed during the March against Gender
Violence, Port Moresby, 2006

Figure 3.   Dame Carol Kidu MP in the midst of the huge crowd   xix
gathered at Tabari Place, Port Moresby, 2006

Figure 4.   Laura Zimmer-Tamakoshi instructing her field assistants   77
on how to do the Yandera household survey, 2007

Figure 5.   Yandera men working at Marengo's core shed, 2009   78

Figure 6.   Young men playing cards in Yandera in 1982   93

Figure 7.   Legionaries in Madang preparing for a meeting, placing   148
their leader the 'Immaculate Conception' on a make-shift
altar, 2006

Figure 8.   Typical club, Port Moresby, 25 January 2006   214

Figure 9.   The NGO, 'Women Arise', demonstrating support for   257
women's rights, Port Moresby, 2006

Tables

Table 1.   Use of three terms in the *Post-Courier* and the *National*   109
Daily Newspapers, Jan. to Dec. 2008

Table 2.   Data from the Kundiawa Police, Hospital and Surgical Ward   125
Records

Table 3.   Highest educational attainment of the sexual offenders   200
interviewed for this study

Table 4.   Place of origin and where the interviewed offenders grew up   201

For Dorothy Counts and Dame Carol Kidu

Preface

Christine Stewart

It all began early in 2004, when I had just started my PhD program at The Australian National University, Canberra. Suddenly, stories of the Three-Mile Guesthouse Raid burst into cyberspace. The emails started flying, the hidden tales were posted online, email discussion lists picked up the issue, lawyers dissected the police case, distressed anthropologists and social workers tried to understand. On ASAONET, the discussion list of the Association for Social Anthropology in Oceania (ASAO), someone asked: why the violence? Others contributed their thoughts, observations and theories to the discussion. Someone suggested that it would make a good session topic for ASAO's annual meeting.

For two weeks, I was glued to my keyboard, frantically networking, fielding questions to which I had only partial answers. This was my place, my territory, my work. I had lived, studied and worked in PNG for more than half my adult life. I had been involved in the later stages of the Law Reform Commission's initiative on domestic violence of the 1980s and 1990s. I had drafted PNG's HIV management law, just a couple of years previously, constructing it as far as possible so as to render HIV stigma and discrimination unlawful, and ensuring that sexual minorities were included in the protection afforded by the law.

Now, I was appalled at and perplexed by the total abjection of the helpless women caught up in the raid. How could anyone be treated so shamefully and brutally in public, in the nation's capital? Who was protesting? Hardly anyone, it seemed at the time.

When the ASAO session was suggested, I waited anxiously. Nobody volunteered to facilitate. Then Dorothy Counts chimed in with a query about the original news item. At the time, Dorothy was only a famous name to me: editor and driving force behind two books and a special journal edition devoted to domestic violence in cross-cultural perspective. Was she going to take charge again? Perfect, I thought, and contacted her. No, she replied, she would not take on the task, but she offered me every assistance if I would.

Do it, said my long-time friend and former UPNG law teacher Jean Zorn, now far away in the USA. Do it, said Margaret Jolly, head of what was then the ANU Gender Relations Centre. And so this volume was born, initially christened 'Gender Violence in Oceania' and developed into its present form through sessions at ASAO annual meetings in Hawai'i, California, Virginia and

Canberra. My first thanks must therefore go to ASAO and its cheery band of itinerant anthropologists, who welcomed me into their ranks and supported me throughout.

Many potential contributors arrived to join the session. Some left, and their founding work does not appear here. I want to thank Lawrence Hammar, Vicky Lockwood, Abby McLeod, Marta Rohatynskyj, Paige West and 'the two Christines', Christine Salomon and Christine Hamelin, for their enthusiastic participation and fascinating contributions in the early stages of our work together. I also make special acknowledgement of Phineas Hartson, prevented from attending his first (or any) meeting by USA immigration requirements, simply because he had once been arrested for participating in a gay rights protest in Australia—gender abuse of a slightly different kind?

An even bigger thankyou goes to those who stayed the course, crafted their papers, willingly joined in the round robins of commenting on each others' work—even, in several cases, completely re-writing and shifting ground as we progressed. The results of their labours make up this volume.

A special huge thanks goes to my supervisor, professor and mentor Margaret Jolly who on several occasions and in various ways rescued me, my PhD and the entire Engendering Violence project from total oblivion. All we asked her to do, really, was to become our lead discussant, but ultimately she did far more. It was Margaret too who enlisted the assistance of Carolyn Brewer, *rédactrice par excellence*, who skilfully crafted our simple texts into professional online book form. Thanks also to The Australian National University, to its newly established Gender Institute, and especially to the Australian Research Council, which in funding the Discovery Project *Oceanic Encounters* and the Laureate Project *Engendering Persons, Transforming Things* has made the resources available to bring this important project to fruition.

Most of all, I thank Dorothy Counts. She retired from active participation after the Engendering Violence project was safely under way, but she was always there for us, if not in person then in spirit.

Tenkyu tru, bosmeri, yu bin halivim long givim nek long husat oli bin pilim pen bilong dispela pasin nogut long daunim ol meri.

Acknowledgements

Apart from the individual thanks offered by our several contributors, we as editors must acknowledge the support of Gender and Cultural Studies and Pacific Studies in the School of Culture, History and Language at The Australian National University and the Australian Research Council, in funding the Discovery Project *Oceanic Encounters* and the Laureate Project *Engendering Persons, Transforming Things*. We are also grateful for the assistance given by Professor Stewart Firth as head of the Pacific Editorial Board of ANU E Press.

We especially thank the two readers of this book, whose constructive suggestions made a good book even better.

Finally our thanks to the editors of both *Oceania* and *Catalyst* for permission to republish previously published work:

Philip Gibbs, Witchkilling and engendered violence in Simbu, in *Catalyst* 40 (2010): 24–64, and Anna-Karina Hermkens, Josephine's journey, *Oceania* 78(2) (July 2008):151–67.

Margaret Jolly
Christine Stewart
Carolyn Brewer
March 2012

Abbreviations and Acronyms

Note on language: In this text, all foreign words are italicised and the relevant language is noted by the use of the following abbreviations:

B	Bariai
BIS	Bislama
G	Gende
H	Huli
L	Lihir
K	Kuman
S	Simbu
TP	Tok Pisin

Other abbreviations and acronyms

AIDS	Acquired Immunity Deficiency Syndrome
AusAID	Australian Agency for International Development
CAD	Canadian dollars
FSW	female sex worker
HIV	Human Immunodeficiency Virus
ICRAF	Individual and Community Rights Forum
MSM	males who have sex with males / men who have sex with men
NCD	National Capital District
NGO	non-government organisation
PacLII	Pacific Legal Information Institute
PNG	Papua New Guinea
PSP	Poro Sapot Project
RPNG	Royal Papua New Guinea Constabulary
SPC	Secretariat of the Pacific Community
STI	sexually transmitted infection
VCT	voluntary counselling and testing

Prologue: The Place of Papua New Guinea in Contours of Gender Violence

Margaret Jolly

Friday 24 March 2006. Port Moresby, Papua New Guinea. A large group of women and some men are gathering at Jack Pidik Park at Five-Mile to march to Tabari Place in Boroko. The women are of diverse generations but most of them are residents of Port Moresby. Some wear casual clothes, some are more formally dressed, some wear the striking uniforms of their professions, the women's and church groups they belong to or the NGOs they work for. Many are carrying *bilums* (string bags) which suggest both their national identity as citizens of Papua New Guinea (PNG) and their diverse ethnic origins (from the Sepik, from the Highlands, from the Gulf ...). They carry banners and posters, some professionally printed, some handmade on cardboard, which echo the language of protest against gender violence in many countries of the world. Some are in English: STOP the Violence against Women; No Means No; Say No to Incest; Respect Human Rights. Some are partially or wholly translated, vernacularised into Papua New Guinea's lingua franca of Tok Pisin: *Meri Ikirap Sapotim* Education for Good Governance, Active Citizenship and Women's Rights (Women Arise Support Them:[1] Education for Good Governance, Active Citizenship and Women's Rights), *Hei Ol Man Mipela ino Pik o Dog Bilong Yupela* (Hey men, We are not your pigs or dogs)[2] and *Lukautim yu yet long AIDS* (Protect yourself from AIDS). The banners protest gender violence, they call for stronger penalties against rapists and they affirm the importance of human rights in PNG. Street marches are part of the global vocabulary of politics and protest against gender violence along with Thursdays in Black and White Ribbon campaigns (see Merry 2006). For many Papua New Guineans, gender violence is a pervasive and intractable problem—in the home, on the streets, in the marketplaces, in the towns and villages of the nation. The women and their male supporters march from Five-Mile along the main highway to throng Tabari Place in Boroko, where the sole woman in the PNG Parliament then as now, Dame Carol Kidu, MP, a tireless advocate for women, human rights and HIV awareness in PNG, addresses the crowd. The scene is captured in a series of photographs taken by my co-editor Christine Stewart, some of which appear on the cover of this volume and in subsequent pages.[3]

---

1   *Meri Ikirap Sapotim* is variously known as just Women Arise or Women Arise Support Them. It is an NGO led by Sarah Garap (personal communication Katherine Lepani and Nicole Haley 26 January 2012). Its logo can be seen on their banner in the photo (see Figure 1).
2   This hand-made banner signs off more breezily with *Luv Mipela*, Love from us (see Figure 2).
3   I thank Christine Stewart for her description of this event of which she was a witness.

Figure 1. *Meri Ikirap Sapotim.* **Some women, like members of this NGO, wear striking uniforms during the March against Gender Violence, Port Moresby, 2006.**

Photograph by Christine Stewart.

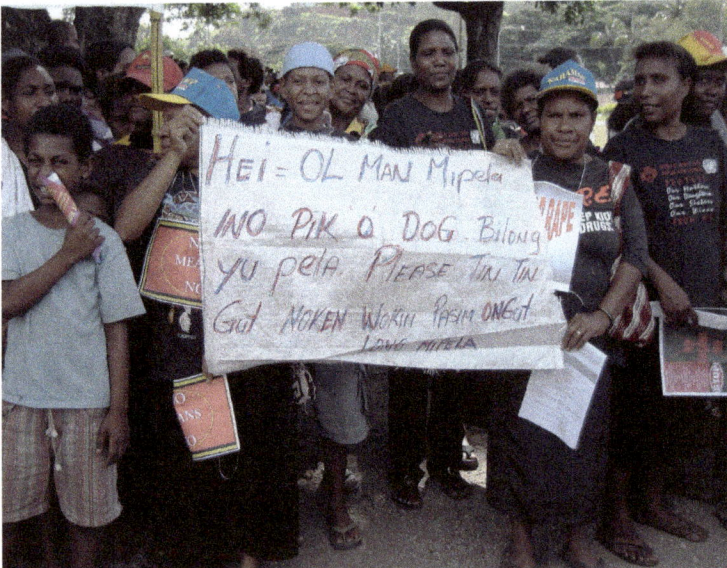

Figure 2. 'Hey, men, we are not your pigs or dogs. Please think about that, and don't treat us badly.' Handmade banner proudly displayed during the March against Gender Violence, Port Moresby, 2006.

Photograph by Christine Stewart.

Figure 3. Dame Carol Kidu MP in the midst of the huge crowd gathered at Tabari Place, Port Moresby, 2006.

Photograph by Christine Stewart.

This march and a multitude of other public protests and workshops in the towns and villages of Papua New Guinea in the last decade suggest that gender violence is increasingly being seen as an important problem by many Papua New Guineans and that it is possible to mobilise large congregations of women and men in protest and to increase the visibility of gender violence as a national political issue. The shape of this march also suggests the huge ethnic diversity of PNG, the particular place of educated and urban people in such struggles, the respective roles of the state, police, churches and NGOs in combating gender violence and the ways in which such movements connect to global agendas and foreign aid.

Little over thirty years before this march, in September 1975, PNG gained independence from the erstwhile colonial power, Australia. Several authors (Wolfers 1975; Nelson 1977, 1982; Waiko 1993; Moore 2003) have told the complex story of European exploration and exploitation of this vast territory, started in earnest from the mid-nineteenth century by Germany in the north (German New Guinea) and Britain in the south (British New Guinea, later Papua). The British presence was primarily promoted by Australian interests in Queensland. The colonial fate of the country was intimately entangled with the two world wars between the rival imperial powers of Europe and Asia. Australian troops occupied German New Guinea in World War I and administered the north first as a mandated territory and then, after brutal battles in the Pacific, including at Rabaul, the Bismarck Sea, Kokoda, Milne Bay and many other sites during World War II, as a United Nations Trust Territory (see Nelson 2006). Following World War II the two territories which had been administered separately were conjoined as a single administrative and judicial system: the Territory of Papua and New Guinea.

The unity of a state was thus imposed on indigenous peoples of enormous diversity. PNG still boasts about 800 indigenous languages (*tok ples*) spoken by the current population of six and a half million people, alongside the lingua franca Tok Pisin and English. Its overwhelmingly indigenous inhabitants derive from two distinct migrations: ancestors of those who speak Papuan languages from around 50–60,000 BP and the ancestors of those who speak Austronesian languages from c. 4000 BP. Of these two distinct language families, the former are concentrated in the interior mountainous regions called the Highlands and the latter in the coastal and insular regions, but this is not an exclusive or rigid configuration. There has been much intermingling of diverse languages and cultures, occasioned both by indigenous patterns of exchange, trade, conquest and movement and processes originating in the colonial period: the circuits of Christian missions, schools, and hospitals, the predominantly male migrant labour to plantations and mines both within the territories and overseas and, increasingly, from the 1960s and especially after Independence in 1975, when freedom of movement was guaranteed by the new constitution, processes of migration to urban centres engaging women as well as men (see Moore 2003).

The remote valleys of the Highlands, though settled earlier by indigenous inhabitants (where the origins of agriculture can be traced to 50,000 BP), were the last region to encounter *ol wait man* (TP: white men) in the 1930s (see Connolly and Anderson 1983, 1988; Bonnemère and Lemonnier 2009). Coastal and insular regions such as the Sepik and the Massim had a far deeper experience of the several agents of European colonialism dating back to the mid-nineteenth century: explorers, Christian missionaries, planters and traders, and officials of colonial states. The Australian colonial state was arguably more successful in the promotion of its blatantly commercial goals through the establishment of private expatriate plantations and mines than in the cultural and political goals of bringing 'civilisation' and modern political and legal structures. Ted Wolfers (1977), Bill Gammage (1999) and Sinclair Dinnen (2001) and others have stressed the draconian, racialised character of Australian administration in its laws enforcing spatial segregation, sartorial differentiation, curfews and ordinances protecting white women from the perceived threat of sexualised violence from black men (see Inglis 1974). The independent state is still often seen today as a foreign, remote and ineffectual entity by many Papua New Guineans. Christian missions were far more successful than secular political institutions in gaining indigenous legitimacy and adherents. Today 96 per cent of Papua New Guineans identify as Christian following either the mainstream denominations introduced early in the colonial period (Catholic, Anglican, Lutheran, Methodist/ Congregationalist—the latter two now amalgamated as the United Church), a burgeoning variety of evangelical churches (Baptist, Seventh Day Adventist, Mormon, Assemblies of God) and an ever-increasing number of independent, charismatic, fundamentalist and Pentecostal churches (see Gibbs 2004; Jebens 2005).

The independent state has not fulfilled the more optimistic hopes of its founders and the nationalist aspirations of the first generation of leaders, intellectuals and artists. The huge wealth generated from the profitable extractive industries of mining and logging has too often benefitted primarily expatriate owners and multinational corporations, national and local politicians, and a minority of primarily male landowners (Filer 2001, Filer and Macintyre 2006). Bougainvillean attempts to secede from the independent state of PNG in the context of a controversial mine at Panguna morphed into a complex and bloody civil war which lasted a decade and engaged PNG national troops on one side of this divisive conflict (Saovana-Spriggs 2007; Regan 2010). Poverty, at least as defined by a commodity economy, is palpably worsening both in some remote regions and in the squatter settlements of towns (Allen, Bourke and Gibson 2005; Cammack 2007). The state of education and health is parlous especially in the rural regions of the country and some PNG citizens look back on the colonial period with nostalgia as a time when schools and universities, clinics and hospitals were better resourced and administered. Malaria, TB and various STIs continue to be endemic diseases while HIV has been pronounced a generalised epidemic (Luker and Dinnen 2010; Lepani 2012). There are major problems of law and order in urban centres like Port Moresby, Mt Hagen and Goroka and on major roads like the Highlands Highway where *raskol* gangs combine theft with murder and rape. Police responses tend to be as draconian and violent as those in the colonial period (Dinnen 2001). The national parliament continues to be dominated by men, with a sole woman representative, Dame Carol Kidu, MP, who has announced she will not stand at the next election in July 2012. As I began writing this Prologue, the Government of the new Prime Minister Peter O'Neill was promising to endorse the proposal espoused by Dame Carol Kidu and many others, that twenty-two seats in the National Parliament be reserved for women. The first stage of this process was achieved in November 2011, when Parliament passed enabling legislation. But an ongoing leadership dispute between O'Neill and previous Prime Minister Somare creates a strong possibility that necessary constitutional amendments may not be approved before Parliament is prorogued and the nation goes to fresh elections scheduled for 2012. Dame Carol Kidu remains confident, saying that progress has been made, and whatever happens, the legislation sets the foundation upon which to build after 2012 (Tiwari 2012).[4]

These persisting problems in PNG have occasioned negative media both within PNG and beyond, most especially in the erstwhile colonial power, Australia. There have been several versions of doomsday foreign policy rhetoric, portraying PNG as a 'failed state' or as a crucial point in an 'arc of instability' which curves around the region embracing Solomons, Fiji and even Vanuatu (May ed. 2003; Jolly 2007; Fry and Kabataulaka 2008). Such dystopian discourses are fuelled by the fact that Australian aid to PNG consumes the largest part of its aid and development budget ($436.5 million in 2011–12).[5] Such expenditure on programs to assist education, health, justice and good governance, to promote gender equality and combat HIV and gender violence are seen by some to be 'wasting' the money of Australian taxpayers, especially if inefficacy, extravagance or corruption can be detected. This has led to successive controversies and standoffs around the tension between the sovereignty of PNG as an independent state and how Australia perpetuates its 'special relationship' with PNG through various forms of tied or conditional aid or by sending Australians to be line managers and executives in its state bureaucracy.

Clearly any analysis of the pervasiveness of gender violence in PNG must perforce contribute to the negativity of its national portrait. This is patent in any website search and especially from the salience of gender violence in PNG in the web presence of major NGOs such as Amnesty International, International Women's Development Agency, Save the Children, Caritas Australia, Human Rights Watch and Medicins Sans Frontiers. The contributors to this volume, all long-term residents or scholars of PNG, are painfully aware of this fact. But it must be acknowledged that there was recognition of the problem of gender violence by the independent state in the early 1980s and indeed a series of studies and reports emanating from the Law Reform Commission which still constitute some of the most comprehensive studies of the problem in PNG. But, as a series of subsequent reports has suggested, successive governments have failed to implement recommendations fully and indeed some initiatives such as public awareness programs or attempts to change the perceptions and practices of the police have failed (see Introduction).[6]

4　I thank Christine Stewart for the wording of the four preceding sentences. There is now a striking difference between the several independent and predominantly Anglophone states of PNG, Solomons, Vanuatu and Fiji where there are very few women in national parliaments and the Francophone territories of New Caledonia and French Polynesia where the French metropolitan laws on 'parity' have been recently mandated and have in general been highly successful in bringing women into the formal political system. Despite some caveats expressed about the possibility of similar legislation elsewhere in the Western Pacific, Jon Fraenkel (2006) Nicole George (2011) and others support the enormous potential of such moves to break the perduring male domination of legislative politics in countries of the western Pacific.

5　This is the amount directly from AusAID. The total from all Australian government departments was $482.3 million (Papua New Guinea. *Australian Government AusAID* 2012)

6　I thank Martha Macintyre for the wording of the two preceding sentences.

The way in which current debates about gender violence articulate with fraught colonial histories both in settler states like Australia, New Caledonia and Hawai'i and sovereign states like PNG, Vanuatu, Solomons and Fiji is worthy of a broader comparative study (see Merry 2000; Merry and Brenneis 2004). Writing from Australia in 2011 it is impossible not to mention the salience of gender violence and the sexual abuse of children in legitimating the bipartisan political support of the national government's 'intervention' in the indigenous communities of Northern Australia, even though that has been hotly contested and critiqued by both indigenous and non-indigenous Australians (Altman and Hinkson 2009). Yet it is a complete dead end to blame *either* indigenous 'culture' *or* the devastating dispossession and emasculating effects of colonialism for such contemporary configurations of gender violence. The pervasiveness and complexity of the problem require more than such black *or* white solutions. To name and to analyse indigenous gender violence is fraught, especially for indigenous women, and is too often portrayed as a betrayal of racial or ethnic solidarity. As the brilliant Kanak author, feminist and independence activist and now Deputy President of New Caledonia, Déwé Gorodé, suggests in her incendiary novel *The Wreck*, there is a complicity between the gender violence of indigenous patriarchal forms in New Caledonia, perpetrated in *la coutume* (custom) over generations and the violence of colonial possession of the land and gendered violence against its peoples, including the capitalist commodification of women's bodies.[7] The same might be said of PNG.

This then is the complex historical and contemporary context for the essays in this volume. The chapters traverse the diversity of the country from the remote rural regions of the islands (West New Britain, Ch. 1) and the Highlands (Simbu, Gende, Chs 2 and 3) to the towns of Madang (Ch. 4), Port Moresby (Chs 5 and 7) and Bomana Prison on Moresby's outskirts (Ch. 6) (see Map 1). We approach the problem from diverse vantage points complementing the particularities of localised research done in indigenous languages in villages and mine sites, with a national perspective viewed from the courts, police stations, jails, government suites, NGO offices, and guesthouses of the towns and a global perspective on how gender violence in PNG is situated in the complex networks of foreign aid, development assistance and international agendas (Introduction and Ch. 8). We trust this volume contributes not just to enhanced understandings but to strategies for effecting change so that the pervasive and perduring problem of gender violence in PNG can be ameliorated.

---

7   The novel, while it celebrates the joy of sexual desire and heterosexual union, depicts intergenerational practices of older Kanak men coercing younger women into incestuous relations and the horrors of a gruesome pack rape and murder of a wilful woman. Her editors comment on the multilayered character of her view of gender violence and its perduring perversity: 'Moving edgily between a critique of the violence of colonization, a protest against the global exploitation of women's bodies and an uncompromising gaze at the underside of Custom, Gorodé's novel attempts to mitigate the impact of its revelations by showing that its criticism of violence against women is both anchored in particular historical and social contexts and resonates beyond Kanak society. In fact perplexing many of her readers, Gorodé's fiction leaves the question of the origin of violence against women open, partially undecideable' (Walker-Morrison and Ramsay 2011: xii).

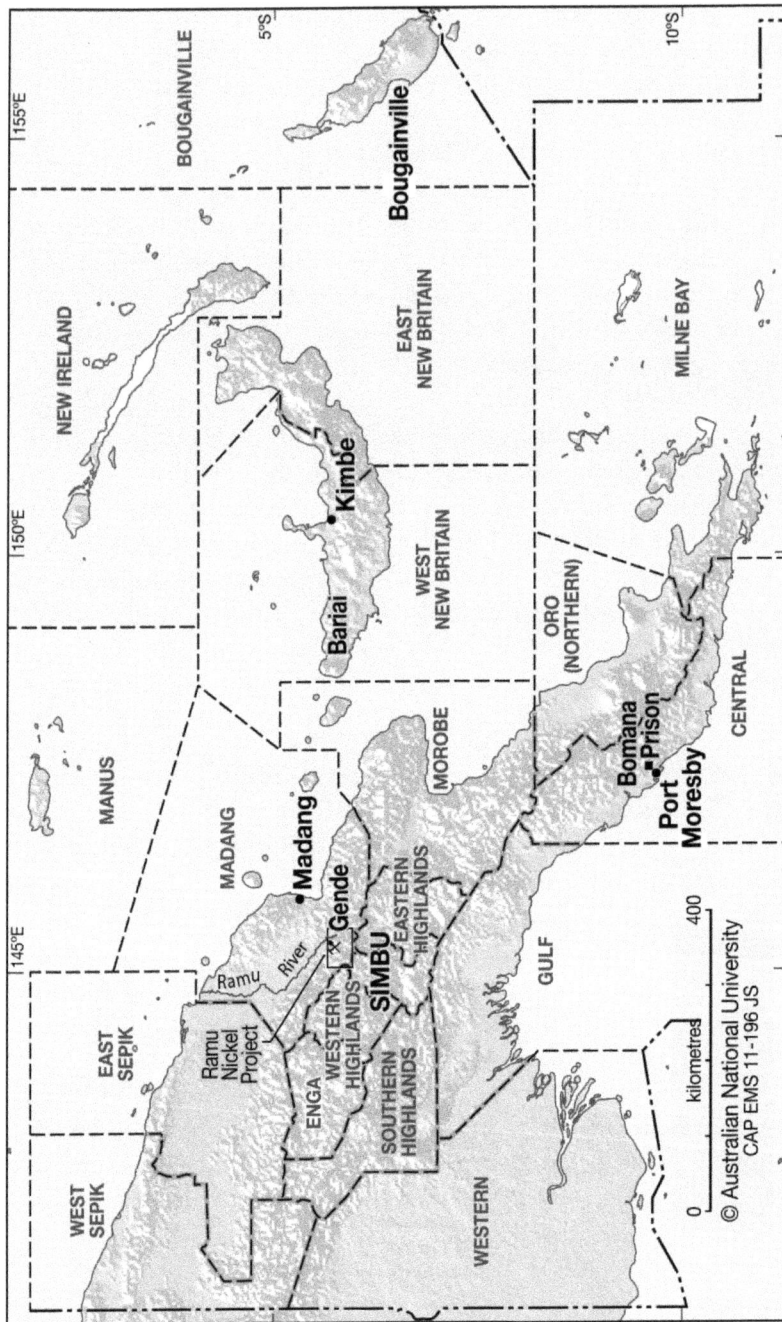

Map 1. General map of PNG showing the sites of research included in this volume. Map production by Education and Multimedia Services, College of Asia and the Pacific, The Australian National University.

Acknowledgements

Heartfelt thanks to contributors and cherished colleagues, Christine Stewart, Martha Macintyre and Katherine Lepani for excellent comments, criticisms and suggestions under intense time pressure. All errors and infelicities remaining are mine.

References

Allen, Bryant, R. Michael Bourke, and John Gibson, 2005. Poor rural places in Papua New Guinea. *Asia Pacific Viewpoint* 24(2): 201–17.

Altman, Jon and Melinda Hinkson, eds, 2009. *Culture Crisis: Anthropology and Politics in Aboriginal Australia*. Sydney: UNSW Press.

AusAID, 2012. Papua New Guinea. *Australian Government AusAID*. Online: http://ausaid.gov.au/country/papua.cfm. Accessed January 20, 2012.

Bonnemère, Pascale and Pierre Lemonnier, 2009. A measure of violence: forty years of first contact among the Ankave-Anga of Papua New Guinea. In *Oceanic Encounters: Exchange. Desire, Violence*, ed. Margaret Jolly, Serge Tcherkézoff and Darrell Tryon, 295–333. Canberra: ANU E Press.

Cammack, Diana, 2007. Chronic poverty in Papua New Guinea. Background paper for the the *Chronic Poverty Report 2008-09: Escaping Poverty Traps*. Chronic Poverty Research Centre. Online: http://www.chronicpoverty.org/publications/details/chronic-poverty-in-papua-new-guinea/ss. Accessed 23 February 2012.

Connolly, Bob and Robin Anderson, 1983. *First Contact*. Documentary film. Ronin Films.

--------1988. *First Contact: New Guinea's Highlanders Encounter the Outside World*. New York: Viking Press.

Dinnen, Sinclair, 2001. *Law and Order in a Weak State: Crime and Politics in Papua New Guinea*. Honolulu: University of Hawai'i Press.

Filer, Colin, 2001. Between a rock and a hard place: mining projects, indigenous communities, and Melanesian states. In *Mining in Papua New Guinea: Analysis and Policy Implications*, ed. B.Y. Imbun, P.A. McGavin, pp. 7–23. Waigani, Papua New Guinea: University of Papua New Guinea Press.

Filer, Colin and Martha Macintyre, 2006. Grass roots and deep holes: community responses to mining in Melanesia. *The Contemporary Pacific* 18(2): 215–31.

Fraenkel, Jon, 2006. The impact of electoral systems on women's representation in Pacific Parliaments. In *A Woman's Place is in the House – the House of Parliament*. Research to Advance Women's Political Representation in Forum Island Countries. Suva: Pacific Islands Forum Secretariat.

Fry, Gregory and Kabutaulaka Tarcissius Tara, eds, 2008. *Intervention and State-Building in the Pacific*. Manchester: Manchester University Press.

Gammage, Bill, 1998. *The Sky Travellers: Journeys in New Guinea 1938–1939*. Melbourne: Melbourne University.

--------1999. Review of August Ibrum K. Kituai. *My Gun, My Brother. The World of the Papua New Guinea Colonial Police 1920–1960*. In *Oceania* 70(2): 193–94.

George, Nicole, 2011. Pacific women are quietly making their mark on male politics. *The Conversation*. Online: http://theconversation.edu.au/pacific-islands-women-are-quietly-making-their-mark-on-male-politics-3297. Accessed 24 January 2012.

Gibbs, Philip, 2004. Growth, decline and confusion: church affiliation in Papua New Guinea. *Catalyst* 34(2): 164–84.

Gorodé, Déwé, 2011. *The Wreck*. Translated and with critical introduction by Deborah Walker-Morrison and Raylene Ramsay. Auckland: little island press limited.

Inglis, Amirah, 1974. *'Not a White Woman Safe': Sexual Anxiety and Politics in Port Moresby, 1920–1934*. Canberra: Australian National University Press.

Jebens, Holger, 2005. *Pathways to Heaven: Contesting Mainline and Fundamentalist Christianity in Papua New Guinea*. New York, NY: Berghahn Books.

Jolly, Margaret, 2007. Imagining Oceania: indigenous and foreign representations of a sea of islands. *The Contemporary Pacific* 19(2): 508–45.

Lepani, Katherine, 2012. *Islands of Love, Islands of Risk. Culture and HIV in the Trobriands*. Nashville Tennessee: Vanderbilt University Press.

Luker, Vicki, and Sinclair Dinnen, eds, 2010. *Civic Insecurity: Law, Order and HIV in Papua New Guinea*. State, Society and Governance in Melanesia Program, Studies in State and Society in the Pacific, No. 6. Canberra: ANU E Press. Online: http://epress.anu.edu.au/?s=Civil+Insecurity. Accessed 23 February 2012.

May, Ronald J. ed., 2003. *'Arc of Instability'?: Melanesia in the Early 2000s*. (Occasional Paper No 4). Co-published by State, Society and Governance in Melanesia Project, Canberra and MacMillan Brown Centre for Pacific Studies, Christchurch NZ.

Merry, Sally Engle, 2000. *Colonizing Hawai'i: The Cultural Power of Law*. Princeton Studies in Culture/Power/History. Princeton, New Jersey: Princeton University Press.

-------- 2006. *Human Rights and Gender Violence: Translating International Law into Local Justice*. Chicago and London: University of Chicago Press.

Merry, Sally Engle and Don Brenneis, eds, 2004. *Law and Empire: Fiji and Hawai'i*. Santa Fe, New Mexico: School of American Research Press/Oxford: James Currey.

Moore, Clive, 2003. *New Guinea: Crossing Boundaries and History*. Honolulu: University of Hawai'i Press.

Nelson, Hank, 1977. *Black, White and Gold: Goldmining in Papua New Guinea 1878–1930*. Canberra: Australian National University Press.

-------- 1982. *Taim Bilong Masta: The Australian Involvement with Papua New Guinea*. Sydney: Australian Broadcasting Commission.

-------- 2006. *The Pacific War in Papua New Guinea. Memories and Realities*. Tokyo: Rikkyo University Japan, Centre for Asia Area Studies.

Regan, Anthony J., 2010. *Light Intervention: Lessons from Bougainville*. Washington: Institute of Peace Press.

Saovana-Spriggs, Ruth, 2007. Gender and peace: Bougainvillean women, matriliny and the peace process. PhD thesis, Canberra: The Australian National University.

Tiwari, Sally, 2012. Last chance for women seats. In *National*, 9 January. Online: http://www.thenational.com.pg/?q=node/27587. Accessed 10 February 2012.

Waiko, John, 1993. *A Short History of Papua New Guinea*. Oxford: Oxford University Press.

Walker-Morrison, Deborah and Raylene Ramsay, 2011. Introduction. In *The Wreck*. Déwé Gorodé. Translated and Critical Introduction by Deborah-Walker Morrison and Raylene Ramsay. Auckland: little island press, pp. v–xxxi.

Wolfers, E.W., 1975. *Race Relations and Colonial Rule in Papua New Guinea*. Sydney: Australia and New Zealand Book Co. Pty Ltd.

Introduction—Engendering Violence in Papua New Guinea: Persons, Power and Perilous Transformations

Margaret Jolly

First thoughts, which words?

> Gender violence is not a new problem. It takes place in virtually all societies around the world, but only in the last thirty years has it become visible as a social issue.

> Understanding gender violence requires looking both at the intimate details of family life and at geopolitical considerations of power and warfare. In order to understand gender violence it is necessary to understand the world (Merry 2009: 1, 19).

Violence: Acts and states, facts and values

Gender violence poses a classic anthropological dilemma apropos human universals versus culturally relative concepts and values. But, both in research and in policy and associated programs of prevention and intervention, we need to try to move beyond this impasse, looking at the interaction and translation of local and global meanings in the transnational relations of our world and at the dynamic and complex historical processes which ground how gender violence has been named as a problem by national and international agencies and social movements (see Merry 2006, 2009). Naming is not just a matter of dry scholarly definition and debate but of vigorous and sometimes heated political contest.

In many recent conceptions (e.g. in the United Nations Millennium Development Goals), violence refers not only to violent physical acts against persons—beating, wounding, torturing, killing—but also to emotional violence, psychological harassment, sexual abuse, financial violence, neglect and coercion. It embraces acts between intimate partners, known kin or acquaintances and strangers; it can occur in contexts which stretch from households, through public locations to the physical, and even the virtual, battlefields of war. Increasingly, it also refers to 'structures' or 'states' of violence, routine forms of coercion or threats of violence inherent in systems of deprivation, exploitation, slavery or oppression (see Chs 1, 2, 4 and 8 this volume; Merry 2009: 4–5).[1]

This is a very expansive definition, but it must be stretched yet further to accommodate some cultural practices and beliefs whose reality is contested or which entail hidden or invisible agencies, such as those of witchcraft and sorcery, pervasive in Papua New Guinea (PNG) (see Chs 1, 2 and 3). As Philip Gibbs shows (Ch. 3), the violence recognised by Papua New Guineans (and in his case, Simbu)[2] is not just the violence involved in the torture and killing of witches and sorcerers (which foreigners likely privilege) but the violence of the original act imputed to the witch or the sorcerer: the ruining of bodies through sickness and death, the destruction of crops and pigs, misfortunes which are imputed to be caused by the witch. In Gibbs' view there are, thus, 'divergent opinions as to just who are the "victims" ... those who suffered the direct effect of acts of witchcraft ... [or] those who have been accused of being witches.'

As his case studies show, the first are predominantly male, the second, those accused, are predominantly female, or men who are connected to the women accused and/or elderly or marginalised. Women accused are more likely to be tortured and killed than men who are usually only ostracised. But women also provoke harm to other women by accusing them of being witches. Gibbs suggests that accusations of witchcraft or sorcery are often deployed in situations of conflict to legitimate violent assaults, torture and even murder of the accused. Killing witches is thus seen as meritorious and protective of the community: '[t]he apparent moral propriety of the act would lead many to consider it acceptable and legitimate' (Ch. 3; cf. Haley 2010; see Zorn 2006).[3] Zimmer-Tamakoshi (Ch. 2) also highlights the way in which witchcraft and sorcery accusations figure in violence *between* men, as younger men accuse their fathers and uncles for instance. The violence of witchcraft thus poses both an epistemological and an ethical challenge for us.[4]

---

1   Sally Engle Merry powerfully plots the difficulties of definition:

Violence, like gender, is a deceivingly simple concept. Although it seems to be a straightforward category of injury, pain and death, it is very much shaped by cultural meanings. Some forms of pain are erotic, some heroic, and some abusive, depending on the social and cultural context of the event. Cultural meanings and context differentiate consensual or playful eroticized forms of pain from those of a manhood ritual and those from a cigarette burn on a disobedient wife (2009: 4).

2   These people were previously called Chimbu. However, Philip Gibbs notes that 'the Provincial Government now uses the term Simbu, which is becoming the accepted form' (Ch. 3).

3   Nicole Haley suggests the horrific recent torture and killing of witches among the Duna is not seen as continuous with past practices and is far more contested. These acts, typically by young men fuelled both by marijuana and guns, are expressly deplored by many older male community leaders who say neither they nor state forces can control them (2010: 230).

4   These epistemological and ethical challenges were vigorously debated by the contributors to this volume at discussions at ASAO panel sessions and subsequently on email. Gibbs notes the view of a PNG Justice George Manuhu that the time has come to regard 'murder as murder' and the establishment in April 2009 of a

Clearly then naming an act as 'violence' entails adjudications of both facts and values and these are intimately entangled. This is nowhere clearer than in those instances where acts adjudged as illegitimate violence by the terms of international conventions and protocols (such as the United Nations Convention for the Elimination all Forms of Discrimination Against Women or the Millennium Development Goals) are accorded national or local legitimacy.[5] The third Millennium Development Goal which aims to promote gender equality and empower women includes as its seventh strategic priority 'Combat violence against girls or women' (Grown, Gupta and Kes 2005: 3; see Ch. 8). This expressly includes the violence of 'genital cutting' and the stoning of women for adultery in parts of Africa and the Middle East where gender violence is normal and indeed legal according to Sharia law.

We have a similar problem with the widespread *legitimacy* of violence in general and gender violence in particular in the Pacific. The pervasive legitimacy of gender violence in PNG has been acknowledged from the foundational studies of the Law Reform Commission in the 1980s to the present (Toft 1985; Toft and Bonnell 1985; Counts 1990, 1992; Zimmer 1990; Zimmer-Tamakoshi 1993a, 1997; Dinnen and Ley 2000; Borrey 2000; Bradley 1994a and b, 2001; Eves 2006). As Fiona Hukula (Ch. 6) suggests, gender violence is often seen as a customary, collective practice in PNG – *em pasin blo ol* – (TP: that's their way) and as normal – *em nomol ya* – (TP: that's normal).

For the Bariai of West New Britain, Naomi McPherson (Ch. 1) consummately shows how girls and boys are, from an early age, socialised not only to *expect* but to *accept* violence, and especially that violence which accompanies hierarchies of power, of adults over children and of men over women. Origin myths relate how men violently stole sacra and spiritual power from women; women have persisting fears of rape and murder if they transgress men's sacred spaces. The patriarchal authority of ancestral religion and charismatic Catholicism here combine to legitimate gender violence, 'to make violence look, even feel right'

---

working committee by the Constitutional and Law Reform Commission to review the law on sorcery and related killings in PNG. We have to acknowledge apropos witchcraft that what is perceived as violence, legitimate and illegitimate, is not just culturally specific but historically changing. So, from the medieval period through the so called 'Enlightenment', the reality of witchcraft and sorcery was assumed in most of Europe. Accusations swirled around Europe's villages and towns in the *longue durée* of the so-called 'witchcraze', supported both by the authority of Christian churches and of emergent secular states. As Mary Douglas (1970) showed long ago, this violent history shaped attitudes by many European colonisers to such occult violence in Africa and Melanesia and moulded the approaches of several Western colonial agents: missionaries, police, judges, doctors and anthropologists. Even as indigenous people converted to Christianity and tried to eschew such practices as satanic they reinforced the reality of such nefarious powers exercised by the living as the work of the Devil. Even as laws were introduced in attempts to outlaw and eliminate witchcraft and sorcery practices, accusations and punishments, they paradoxically reinforced beliefs in their reality and efficacy (see Aleck 1996; Forsyth 2006; Stewart 2010; Zorn 2006).

5   Merry (2009) observes how CEDAW did not originally include references to gender violence but that these were added as part of later protocols.

(Galtung 1990, cited in Ch. 1). Yet, as McPherson insists, Bariai men are not 'monsters' and Bariai are not an especially violent people. Despite such local or national caveats, the overwhelming impression from the papers in this volume is that PNG *is* a country where violence in general and gender violence in particular is both expected and accepted by women and men alike. Susan Toft writing for the Law Reform Commission (1985: 14) estimated that around 67 per cent of rural women and 56 per cent of urban women had experienced a beating at the hands of their husbands. Sixteen years later Christine Bradley reported that most adult women in PNG had been either assaulted or raped by their husbands or other men (2001: 2). Collective representations of gender violence as typical of PNG pervade media representations, in national newspapers (see Chs 3 and 7) and overseas media, especially in Australia (see Ginau and Papoutsaki 2007; Duffield, Papoutsaki and Watson 2008),[6] and in the global print and web-based campaigns conducted by influential NGOs such as Amnesty International (2006), the International Women's Development Agency and Médecins Sans Frontières.

Most of these studies conclude that the victims are predominantly women. But they also reveal that such violence is gendered in another sense, in terms of its legitimacy. Thus, an assault by a man on his wife is typically accorded greater reason and justice than that by a woman on her husband. As Martha Macintyre and Jean Zorn (Chs 5 and 8) both demonstrate, men are more often seen to be entitled, to have the *rait* (TP: right, authority) to violence, to express 'righteous indignation' and to be acting reasonably while violent women are viewed as lacking such entitlement, as subversive of legitimate male authority and to be acting irrationally or emotionally. McPherson (Ch. 1) further suggests that Bariai women are seen as emotional, uncontrolled and weak in will and body, so that when they resort to violence, they must use those weapons at hand, from metal spoons to machetes. Their violence is often ridiculed and rarely condoned. Men by contrast are thought strong in will and body and should use only their bodies to bash or kick (although several of McPherson's case studies suggest they frequently resort to machetes and axes). Their anger is serious, feared and legitimised (see Ch. 3 for similar ideas of male and female difference in Simbu). In West New Britain, as in much of PNG, violence by a husband is thought justified if a wife refuses sex, if he suspects her of infidelity, if she secretly uses contraception, if she fails to adequately nurture their children or look after him

---

6   Ginau and Papoutsaki (2007) discern both ignorance and undue negativity in Australian journalists' representations of PNG, focusing on violent crime, corruption, HIV and problems with Australian aid. Duffield, Papoutsaki and Watson (2008) in an analysis primarily of ABC and SBS broadcast and online media found a more balanced and mixed reportage in March 2008, at the time of Rudd's visit to PNG as Prime Minister. This no doubt caused a spike in interest, but significantly much of the optimism in these stories focused on the figure of Rudd, an older statesman view of Somare and privileged sites for Australian war memory like Kokoda and the promise of a more collaborative rather than a 'Big Brother' approach in foreign policy.

by gardening, cooking and cleaning, if she fails to graciously accept co-wives, if she scolds him for his laziness or drunkenness, or if she disobeys his edicts (Ch. 1). Violence by husbands is the most common form of gender violence but women are also legitimately beaten by their fathers and brothers if they become pregnant outside marriage and sometimes even if they are victims of rape. And many chapters evidence the gender violence of younger, unmarried men, either singly or collectively (Chs 2, 3, 5 and 6).

Engendering violence? Children, men and same-sex violence

Contested concepts of violence and its widespread frequency and legitimacy in PNG thus pose big problems for all the contributors to this volume. But what then of that other term in our title: *Engendering*? In contemporary English this word has a productive double meaning, signifying both the idea of giving rise to, precipitating, even begetting but also endowing with gender. I here conceive gender not just as the relations between actual women and men, but gender as a cultural code signifying masculine and feminine. This engages a profound debate about how we can best conceive of gender in Melanesia, a debate haunted by Marilyn Strathern's brilliant and provocative study *The Gender of the Gift* (1988). Simply put, this propounds the idea that in PNG as in the rest of Melanesia we cannot readily distinguish between the 'nature' of sexed bodies as a deep biological substratum and 'culture' as a more superficial layer.[7] Nor can we simply conceive of female and male persons on the model of Western individuals (see also Butler 1990, 1995; Thèry 2008). Strathern rather posits the person in PNG not as a bounded autonomous individual but as a locus of relations, as permeable and partible. She sees gender not in terms of sexed bodies nor merely as relations between the sexes, albeit opposed or the same, but as a dominant cultural code, even perhaps *the* dominant code for talking about human beings in general, and especially about the relations between persons and things. Her approach has proved influential in the ethnography of gender in PNG but has long been critiqued for its failure to acknowledge male domination and gender violence and to address social transformations in both colonial and independent epochs and radical changes in gender relations, even perhaps in models of the person (see Jolly 1992a; Macintyre 1995; Wardlow 2006).

---

7   McPherson (Ch. 1) deploys this binary in her cogent argument against a universal account of male violence as a 'biologically determined and evolutionarily honed human (genetic) trait' suggesting rather that violence is a cultural trait, 'engendered and embodied' in the course of socialisation. See also Merry (2006: 8–15) for a succinct exposition of fundamental shifts in the study of gender in the last two decades: the shift from sex to gender, from rigid roles to fluid performances for diverse audiences and from essentialist to intersectional analysis of gender identities.

So how does this relate to the approach we espouse in this volume? Why do we use the phrase *engendering* violence rather than *violence against women* or *domestic violence*? Although crucially important in early transnational feminist alliances, and as a credo for ongoing global campaigns, *violence against women* excludes those victims of violence who are children and men. Although in the many situations depicted in these chapters women are the predominant, or the primary victims (see AusAID 2007), we cannot occlude the fact that children are also often victims of violence perpetrated by adults (see Human Rights Watch 2005) and that men *may* be victims of violence, from women or other men, as well as its perpetrators.

Domestic violence is also a problematic term insofar as it presumes a domain distinction between domestic and public life, another Eurocentric binary akin to nature/culture which is hard to sustain in PNG (Strathern 1988). In much early research and writing on violence in PNG and Melanesia more generally there was often a distinction made between so called 'domestic violence', the violence enacted between close kin in households versus 'tribal fighting', the public violence of *raskol* (TP: rascal, criminal) gangs and increasingly the violence unleashed in electoral combats (see Garap 2000, 2004; cf. Jolly 2000a). But how do we draw this line? Many intimate disputes, between married couples for example, resonate with violent clashes between clans and lineages in 'tribal fighting'. Throughout the Highlands of PNG, wives usually come to their husband's place from neighbouring groups, who are often enemies, and a dispute between them can implicate a broader battle (although in the past women could also act as mediators between groups, see Strathern 1972).[8] Moreover, as Zimmer-Tamakoshi shows for the Gende of the PNG Highlands (Ch. 2), violent relations between men, of different generations and different locales, often swirl around economic disparities in access to land and labour and around contested exchange relations, frequently engaging disputes about women and bride price. The wives and children of enemies are crucial sources of economic and cultural value to men and are as much potential victims as male combatants.

The concept of 'sexual antagonism' in early Highlands ethnography was seen to implicate both avoidances and conflicts pertaining between men and women as intimate partners and the solidarity of 'men in groups' engaged in deadly battles over land, resources, exchanges and often women (Langness 1967, 1999;

---

8   This capacity for women to mediate is perhaps reduced in the present, as Wardlow suggests for the Huli that women are no longer 'in between' their natal and affinal kin, as men invest less time in extended kinship relations and working men in particular show a 'withdrawal from relationality' (2006: 23). Macintyre suggests that Marilyn Strathern's 1972 ethnography dates from a period when pacification was strictly enforced and there was a lull in fighting which necessitated novel modes of dispute settlement (pers. comm. 18 January 2011). Macintyre also reminds me the Kup Women for Peace Initiative required not only women who were from fighting clans but neutral women (see Garap 2000, 2004). Rumsey's (2000) depiction of women's extraordinary mediation in the Nebilyer Valley shows how they deployed modern identifications of their power as Christians and citizens of the PNG state to stop tribal fighting.

Read 1982; Herdt and Poole 1982; see Strathern 1988 for a consummate critique; and Ch. 3). Women who moved at marriage to enemy groups were thus more vulnerable to the collective violence not just of their husbands and agnates, including accusations of treacherous witchcraft and gang rape, which was used to silence or intimidate recalcitrant wives (Ch. 3). In violent political struggles between ethnic groups in Highlands PNG the rape and sexual torture of women accompanied the murder and mutilation of combatants and civilians, men and women, in patterns very similar to those reported in European wars, such as those in Eastern Europe in the 1990s, Hindu-Muslim conflicts in India and the genocide in Rwanda in 2004 (Merry 2009: 156–71).

Insofar as it does not presume women are always the victims, nor distinguish unduly between domestic and public violence, *gender violence* has become the preferred concept in both global research and programs of intervention in recent time. Sally Engle Merry defines gender violence as 'violence whose meaning depends on the gendered identities of the parties. It is an interpretation of violence through gender' (Merry 2009: 3).[9] For the most part this is the concept we deploy in this volume. And we use the title *engendering violence* to signal the process whereby contemporary gender violence in PNG is situated in the context of massive social transformations which are provoking new forms of conflict and novel understandings of such violence. But what does this change of name actually mean in practice? As in many areas of aid and development, gender has too often become synonymous with women. And this is at odds with the need to see gender as a relation, between women and men, but also between women and between men. We need to bring into the frame not just the female victims of violence but its male perpetrators, to engage men as, for example, Fiona Hukula and her colleagues at the National Research Institute have done in 'conversations with convicted rapists' (Ch. 6). Many chapters in this volume relate gender violence to changing masculinities in contemporary PNG (see also Eves 2006; Jolly 2008; Taylor 2008a and b), and most perceive the profound social transformations of the last decades as provoking dangerous uncertainties and contests in models of masculinity. We can witness how changing gender relations have, in many parts of PNG, generated a sense (if not the reality), of a diminution of male power and laments for the younger generations of

---

9   Merry elaborates, showing how gender violence can occur in opposite sex and same-sex relationships and in heterosexual and homosexual partnerships. The meaning of the violence might also be filtered through racial or national difference.

> For example when a blow is understood as a man's right to discipline his wife, it is gender violence. When a mob lynches an African American man for allegedly raping a white woman, the violence is defined through gender and race.... These relationships are used to explain and even justify the violence. For example, a man may justify hitting his wife because she was disobedient. A prisoner may explain his anal rape of a fellow prisoner by saying that the victim is less than a man because he was a sexual predator against children. A soldier can explain raping an enemy woman as a way to dishonor his enemy (2009: 3).

'shrinking men' with the seemingly inexorable progress of modernity (see the early essays by Clark 1989; Meggitt 1989; Clark 1997). In a controversial book Donald Tuzin (1997) expressly joined such lamentations, proclaiming 'the death of masculinity,' suggesting that the destruction of the male cult of the Ilahita Arapesh with their secondary conversion to a more evangelical Christianity entailed not just cultural evisceration but emasculation (cf. Knauft 1997, 1999). Yet masculinity has not so much died as been reborn with Christian conversion.

Moreover, as Naomi McPherson argues (Ch. 1), such male cults previously prevalent in the Sepik, the Highlands and the Gulf regions of PNG entailed violence on young boys—thrashings, abrasion with nettles, swallowing canes, cicatrisation, genital cutting, food deprivation and terrorisation—in order to transform the boys from gentle children to violent martial men. In some cults the stress was on removing polluting female blood, in others the emphasis was on the ingestion of semen through fellatio or anal sex with older men; both were enjoined to make boys into men (Allen 1967, 2000; Herdt 1981, 1982; Godelier 1986; Godelier and Strathern 1991; Bonnemère 1996). Everywhere the power of older over younger men was powerfully articulated with the power of men over women (see Ch. 2). Thus, we might also conceive the activities of these erstwhile cults as manifesting gender violence as well as evincing forms of desire, initially called 'ritual homosexuality' (Herdt 1981, 1982).

Some Christian women, like those in the Sepik depicted by Tuzin, may celebrate the end of male cults and enjoy an enhanced status in the new spiritual domain of Christian and evangelical churches. But, as McPherson (Ch. 1) and Anna-Karina Hermkens (Ch. 4) argue, conversion to Christianity can also *re*masculate men and reinscribe patriarchal authority, as introduced forms of 'spiritual violence' (McPherson's telling phrase) eclipse indigenous forms (see also Hammar 2010). Many women conform to the combined customary and Christian pressures to be good women and wives, subject to the authority and the violent rage of their husbands (see Chs 1 and 4). But other women are 'wayward' (Wardlow 2006), trying to evade such violent subjection either by not marrying (Spark 2011), by desertion or divorce, by transactional sex rather than conjugal sex or by their own violent resistance, which can occasion yet more violent male retribution (see Chs 7 and 8).

Gibbs (Ch. 3) also depicts threats to male dominance among the Simbu since younger women can do much that their mothers could not: deliver public speeches, drive cars and run businesses. Many men now allow their wives to handle family finances since they are better at budgeting. But young men, and especially those who are uneducated, unemployed and unmarried, express feelings of frustration, envy and humiliation, particularly if women desire only men with cash. Such young men resort to alcohol and drugs and vent their anger in violence towards others, especially women and girls. This parallels Holly

Wardlow's chilling portrait of Huli men and the pervasiveness of *madane* (Huli) an emotional state she translates as bitter resentment and disappointed rage and which proves crucial to her understanding of the fraught, often violent, relations of Huli men and women (2005, 2006). This suggests that although the concept of 'sexual antagonism' is no longer valid as a way of linking intimate relations between men and women, male cults and tribal fighting, relations between men and women in the Highlands are still agonistic, even if that antagonism is fuelled by novel, modern tensions (see Josephides 1985; Hammar 2010).[10]

And in many places the agonistic relations between men and women are linked to generational differences and conflicts between older men and younger men. Younger men figure prominently in many of the cases of gender violence discussed in this volume (Chs. 2, 3 and 6). Hukula (Ch. 6) notes the prevalence of young men amongst convicted rapists, especially those involved in *lainup* (TP: pack rape); Gibbs (Ch. 3) notes the prevalence of young men implicated in gender violence in Simbu, while Zimmer-Tamakoshi (Ch. 2) sees the gender violence in Gende, both between men and women and between men, as intimately linked to patterns of marriage and bride price. Generational conflicts between older men and younger men have ensued because older men earlier dominated access to women as wives and tried, but ultimately failed, to monopolise wealth from mining. Physical violence and related sorcery attacks and accusations have developed from such generational conflicts between frustrated younger men and older men.

Rising rates of gender violence? Continuities and ruptures

We often hear claims that gender violence is increasing in PNG with the pressures of modernity and urbanisation. And yet this is nearly impossible to gauge. Even in rich countries like Australia or America, statistics of gender violence are notoriously difficult to collect and the records of both police and hospitals and even 'victimisation' surveys are commonly adjudged to be inaccurate indices of the actual rates, and to be skewed by race, nationality and class (Merry 2009: 20–22, 104–16). In PNG many such acts of violence go unreported and, even if victims go to the police, charges may be dropped for various reasons. Macintyre (Ch. 8) reports that even those policemen who have attended awareness workshops and can speak eloquently about why gender violence is illegal, criminal behaviour, often try to dissuade wives from pursuing charges against their husbands in the interests of domestic and wider social harmony. It seems

---

10 I thank Martha Macintyre for discussion on continuity and rupture apropos 'sexual antagonism' in Highlands PNG.

many police are reluctant to implement the law, partly because of their own perceptions of the legitimacy of gender violence and partly since many women later drop charges (often due to pressure from husbands and other male kin). In PNG the customary justice system of compensation and reconciliation is often preferred by men while the very process of the state-based system of laying criminal charges and pursuing a court case has in PNG, like many countries, often proved a site of secondary violence for the victim (see Zorn 2010 and Ch. 5 on rape cases).

It is impossible then to credibly speculate in a country like PNG whether rates of gender violence have been increasing or decreasing since, for example, the period of the work of the Law Reform Commission in the 1980s (Macintyre 2006). It would take a huge and expensive national research program to begin to answer this question. For the more specific act of rape, Jean Zorn notes very high per capita rates and an extremely high incidence of pack rape (in comparison to Britain at least). But, as to whether the more general rates of gender violence are increasing or decreasing, I endorse Martha Macintyre's stance (Ch. 8). She suggests that the need for 'thorough research' to underpin programs of intervention by agencies such as AusAID has 'finally been recognised' but that the time and costs of procuring such data for 'robust and consistent analysis have not' (Ch. 8). She concludes: 'The research required to establish a base-line for prevalence would be costly, time-consuming and invasive of privacy' (Ch 8). From the viewpoint of those struggling to reduce gender violence there is already far too much, so there is little point in such an expensive research exercise (see AusAUD 2007 for a cogent smaller study).

But the important fact remains, that there is public rhetoric, in the national media of newspapers, radio and television, and often in more local fora, about an *alleged* rise in gender violence, and this typically gets linked to broader concerns about modernity, laments about lost 'traditions' and the way in which both alcohol and marijuana are implicated in a loss of discipline and contemporary masculine cultures of intoxication. In such discussions, the frequency and legitimacy of gender violence in the past is often occluded. In some of the more romantic assessments of restorative justice there is a tendency to downplay the violence inherent in pre-colonial dispute resolution and punishment, not just the violence of tribal warfare and frequent village relocations due to violent fissions or sorcery accusations but those more intimate acts of gender violence: the gang rape of recalcitrant women, the violent punishment of women who had been unfaithful wives (but not their male lovers, even if they themselves are husbands) and the rape and murder of those women who intruded into men's secret, sacred spaces.

Thus, it is important not to underestimate the gender violence of the past and indeed the violence of much 'restorative' justice (Ch. 8). It was often more important to restore relations between powerful men rather than to redress the wrong done to a woman who had been raped or beaten. As Sinclair Dinnen suggests: '"restoring" relations may simply serve to reinforce those underlying inequities' (2002: 11). This is why so many indigenous women at a Port Vila conference in 2000—including Ruth Saovana-Spriggs from Bougainville, Rita Naiviti from Vanuatu and Alimita Duratalo from Fiji—called for 'transformative' rather than 'restorative' justice (see Dinnen 2002; Jolly 2003a, 2011; and Forsyth 2009 on the relation of customary and state justice in Vanuatu).

In the broader literature on PNG some privilege continuity while others privilege rupture in the history of gender violence. In a number of important early papers Zimmer-Tamakoshi (1993a and b, 1997, and, writing as Zimmer, 1990) stressed the continuities with past practices of gender violence, such as the gang rape of women in warfare and patterns of torture of both rebellious women and those accused of being witches in the Gende context. But, writing of PNG more broadly, she also highlighted the ways in which such violent patterns of control over women were being modernised, in narratives about nationalism and sexuality for example, given the way in which the sexuality of educated or urban women was being linked to the mobility and alleged 'looseness' of western women and contrasted with the controlled and demure sexuality of village woman. Zorn (Ch. 5) also notes how judicial opinions articulated by both Australian and indigenous male judges in those cases of rape brought to courts in PNG have tended to rely on such caricatures of 'good', controlled village women versus 'bad', uncontrolled urban women (see also Ch. 7). Other authors such as Banks (2000: 95) have stressed how violence against women is more likely when 'men perceive they have lost control over women' (see Ch. 4). Several chapters in this volume suggest that even in rural regions men perceive their control over women to be less than that of their fathers or grandfathers (see also Wardlow 2006). Often this is linked with a sense of diminished power in the world at large, as the values of modernity, Christianity and commodity economy eclipse the more certain controls of ancestral gender hierarchies and past male cults. Thus it is not a question of continuity *or* rupture but both. Gender violence persists but often in new contexts, in new forms and with novel meanings.

Engendered social transformations on four dimensions

Although it is difficult, and likely not worthwhile, to try to calculate how far rates of gender violence have increased from past to present, the chapters in this volume powerfully reveal how the engendered violence we witness in contemporary PNG is linked to those broader but frequently disarticulated and divergent social transformations which have been collectively labelled 'modernisation'.[11] This is a conclusion which emerges from all the chapters in this volume, although they focus on four different dimensions of such transformations: (1) the impact of commoditisation and especially of extractive industries like mining and logging; (2) the transformation of forms of 'spiritual violence' entailed in conversions to Christianity; (3) the 'implanting' of Western modes of justice and the law and (4) the impact of the HIV epidemic and the broader introduction of biomedicine. Across these four dimensions I highlight the tension between more relational and more individuated notions of gendered persons, a problem to which I return in the concluding sections of this introduction on the challenges for aid programs dedicated to combating violence in PNG and questions of women's empowerment, agency and human rights.

1. Commodity economics, extractive industries and masculine 'landowners'

First, the economic transformations which are a part of a process of uneven capitalist development grounded in extractive industries like mining and logging have enriched certain people (usually men) and certain regions while leaving others (and especially women) marooned in increasing poverty and isolation (see Filer and Macintyre 2006). These processes are not only fuelling emergent class and regional divisions but conflicts between generations and genders.

This is most graphically revealed in Laura Zimmer-Tamakoshi's chapter on Gende, which focuses on the radical changes she has witnessed over the last decade with the development of mining in this region. Two major mining operations have rapidly moved into this part of southern Madang Province: Ramu Nickel (previously Highlands Gold but run by the Chinese Metallurgical Construction Company since 2005) and Marengo Mining Limited, a small Australian company which in 2005 took over control of a project at Yandera also initiated by Highlands Gold.

She stresses that it is important not to talk about all men versus all women, but to see gender as imbricated with relations of generations. She reveals how older and younger men were and are in relations of both conflict and complicity

---

11 It is beyond the scope of this Introduction to consider this much-debated concept (see Jolly 1998; and Knauft 1997, 1999). Suffice it to say that I eschew any notion of a homogenous and teleological process, stressing not just the pluralities and diversities of global experience but the way in which the oppositions of tradition and modernity have become reified, rhetorical concepts both in scholarly theory and some indigenous philosophies (see Jolly 1992b).

in local systems of alliance, exchange and bride wealth, competing for wives but also allied in their violent control of women. Whereas in the 1980–1990s she witnessed the 'bachelorisation' of Gende society whereby old men were commandeering women as wives and young men were unable to attract wives, that situation has been dramatically reversed with the flow of new wealth from the mine and its anticipated increase to a torrent in the future. Polygyny has ceased to be the privilege of old men and is now eagerly sought by young men. The Gende had been relatively impoverished in relation to Simbu, but now people are trying to pursue claims of attachment to those parts of Gende territory where the mines are concentrated. Gende are returning from town and from Simbu territory to be registered as 'landowners', and this is fuelling violent conflicts (including many accusations of sorcery culminating in violent murder of those accused).

As elsewhere in mining and logging developments there is a stark gendering of the benefits both of land compensation and of employment associated with the mine. The novel notion of the 'landowner' entails not only more capitalist concepts of land as property rather than a personified place over which people are collective custodians, but increasingly masculinist ideas of control over the use and transmission of land (see Macintyre 2002, 2003; Filer 1997). Although women may be 'landowners' by law they are typically marginalised by male-dominated landowner associations. Macintyre has demonstrated this more broadly in the context of mining in the region (see Lahiri-Dutt and Macintyre 2006). In her chapter in this volume Macintyre shows that even in a matrilineal society, such as Lihir, the previous influence which women exerted over land and its transmission has been diminished by men's greater access to registering land titles and their increasing domination of the negotiations of local landowner associations, such that women, even articulate, well-educated women, are denied a public voice. We can hear from Macintyre (Ch. 8) how Lihirian women were rudely silenced and humiliated by furious men who, while acknowledging matriliny, simultaneously insisted that women speaking in public was against *kastam* (TP: culture, tradition).

Zimmer-Tamakoshi relates how Gende women have pursued more violent direct action to gain employment in mining sites and camps as laundry assistants, cooks and secretaries. Although women are in general losing power in these developments and will likely continue to do so as men dominate the emergent landowner associations, certain women are assuming positions of leadership. A spectacular example is a young woman, the daughter of a local Gende Big Man, who became so successful as a business entrepreneur that her father called himself her *boi* (TP: employee, mimicking the infantilising language used by colonial bosses for indigenous male workers). Women who are successful in the modernist enterprises of business and education regularly attract the accusation of being *bikhet* (TP: big-headed, impertinent, obstinate). In this case the woman's father was killed by a group of young men, although it is unclear how far their resentment of this woman's success was a factor in his murder as well as disputes over land and compensation payments. Those women who are successful in more local ways seem to attract less opprobrium. Gende women can achieve power locally by hard work and fulfilling their exchange obligations, but women's capacity to do so and repay their bride price has been diminished by development, especially for the younger generation. But those older Gende women who repaid their bride price long ago are still proudly planting gardens and nurturing pigs so they can complete funerary payments for their dead husbands and contribute to their sons' marriage payments. Zimmer-Tamakoshi dubs them 'merry' widows (Ch. 2); they seem to have secured some happiness and well-being despite the challenges of the profound social transformations wrought by mining development.

As well as precipitating competition and conflict between men and women in accessing the new wealth emanating from mining, such developments in the commodity economies of extraction are entangled with the gendering of broader hopes and fears about modernity. Zimmer-Tamakoshi suggests that 'researchers focus on both men's uneasy confrontation with modernity and *kastam* and women's efforts at achieving a semblance of agency and personal security in the midst of deeply challenging economic, cultural and social changes' (Ch 2).

The effects of commodity economics are most dramatically charted for the Gende, but several other chapters allude to how transformations in material life have increased gendered tensions and violence. For Simbu, Gibbs links the pervasive emotional state of *jelas* (TP: dangerous feeling of desire, envy, see also Wardlow 2006: 30ff) to transformations in the material basis of existence. Such feelings are fuelled by the increasing scarcity of good land and gardens given the burgeoning population and the differential opportunities to pursue education and *bisnis* (TP: business). Moreover, he suggests there are important economic dimensions to witchcraft accusations: not only is divination well-paid work (mainly for men) but the land and the possessions of the accused are often plundered by the accusers and the alleged victims of witches. As Gibbs observes (Ch. 3), most of those accused are women, and in particular elderly women who married in from elsewhere, who are perceived as physically weaker and socially inferior, especially if they lack influential husbands or brothers and strong sons. Plundering their flourishing gardens or thriving pigs proves relatively easy.

2. Gendered conversions: Christianities and 'spiritual violence'

Second, there have been dramatic transformations in gender relations and engendered violence which have accompanied conversion to Christianity. As Hermkens (Ch. 4) argues, the influence of Christianity in contemporary PNG is profound, not only as proclaimed in the rhetoric of the state's independent constitution, or in political and popular discourse but as practised by the overwhelming majority of its citizens, 96 per cent of whom adhere to one of the many Christian denominations or independent churches (Gibbs 2004).[12] Many have recently reconverted from the more mainstream denominations introduced during the colonial era—Catholicism, Anglicanism, Lutheranism, Methodism— to more evangelical or charismatic forms and independent local churches (see Barker 2001; Eves 2003, 2008; Gibbs 2004; and Robbins 2004). Christian conversion has been canonically associated with the coming of the light and of peace, although colonial state violence was indubitably as important as Christian ideals in the incomplete process of what has been paradoxically called 'pacification' in PNG. This was articulated with the parallel demise or wilful termination of male cults, which in many regions of the country were linked to warrior modes of masculinity (cf. Jolly 1994). The message of Christian peace has surely not resounded loudly enough in several valleys of Highlands PNG where tribal fighting persists and/or has been recently revived with more deadly weapons like guns and automatic rifles, including M16s, AR15s and SLRs (also used by *raskol* gangs who intimidate travellers on the highways of the region and in urban centres: see Dinnen and Thomson 2004; Macintyre 2008). But, even in those parts of coastal and insular PNG where warfare has been banished to *taim bilong daknes* (TP: time of darkness, heathen past) parallel calls for peace in Christian households and families have not been similarly heeded.

McPherson (Ch. 1) offers a compelling example of how the 'spiritual violence' of past and present has creolised among the Bariai. Although the Bariai lacked the male cults typical of Highlands, Sepik and Gulf regions of PNG, key myths of primordial origins explained how men violently dispossessed women of the sacred Bullroarer and access to spiritual powers through the murder of all adult women, sparing only suckling infants who would have no knowledge of what was lost. Women were forbidden access to men's houses and witnessed their sacra on penalty of gang rape and murder. Other myths explain the distribution of Bariai people as the result of the primal violence of an old man whose virility and hence masculinity was threatened. Contemporary women are still fearful of the vengeful power of ancestral spiritual beings and of living men. McPherson

---

12   Gibbs' estimate (2004) is based on official census figures from July 2000 and some non-official figures from the National Statistics Office. This paper offers a consummate survey of the 200 Christian churches, the diversity of beliefs and practices and changing patterns of religious affiliation a decade ago.

recounts two incidents in the 1980s, one involving a female visitor and another, an elderly woman, who were proximate to a men's house and might have witnessed male sacra. These both occasioned tense discussions as to whether these women should be killed; they were eventually spared. But, even in those contexts where men have relaxed the spiritual segregations of the ancestral religion, women still articulate discomfort, even terror.

McPherson describes how conversion to Catholicism has entailed the end of men's houses and associated patterns of male homosociality, but also how the movement of men to live with their wives and children in women's houses, in patterns more approximating a nuclear family, has also engendered more intimate, quotidian violence. Men now exert a daily and punitive control over the household, asserting their rights as 'head' of the family as enshrined in Catholic doctrine. This extends to their close surveillance of their wives' fertility, which is seen as a sign of their virility. Post-partum taboos which entailed birth intervals of about four years have lapsed since the 1980s and have not been replaced by indigenous abortifacients or introduced contraceptives, largely because of the Catholic ban on such birth control: women who use contraception are thought destined for Hell. Women are thus denied condoms either to control their reproduction or as protection against HIV, and are consequently bearing as many as ten children, exponentially increasing their load in garden work, carrying wood and water, child care, cooking, cleaning and laundry (see Jolly 2001b).

Paradoxically, while the Catholic ban on such birth control is closely policed by catechists and husbands alike, edicts against polygyny are flouted with impunity, as young men increasingly marry second and even third wives (see also Ch. 2). Sexual jealousies, regularly a source of violent conflicts in marriages in the first few years, are compounded by this revival of polygyny. As in those Biblical stories which implicate Eve as the origin of carnal knowledge, women are cast as lustful and uncontrolled, who through their eternal sexual allure (and novel provocations such as wearing wide-legged pocket trousers!) arouse men and are thus the 'true cause' of men's insatiable desires (see Cummings 2008; McDougall 2003). The Bible is frequently used to justify the patriarchal power of the husband and father as head of the family (as Christ is head of the church) and to legitimate men's violent disciplining of women, canonically wives, but also daughters and sisters.

So, alongside the legitimation of violence through resort to ideas of ancestral practice or contemporary *kastam*, Christian doctrines can justify not just gender inequality but the gendered violence which accompanies it. Apropos Catholic women in Madang, Hermkens concludes: 'This union of Christian and cultural values results in a powerful doctrine of submission' (Hermkens Ch. 4). And, she suggests, in some Christian traditions this is developed into a theology which celebrates female suffering and endurance as the path to personal transformation.

Hermkens recounts the gruelling detail of Alice's story, to show how The Legion of Mary in Madang and in particular the late Father Golly, the Legion's local and national director, promoted the Virgin Mary as a 'role model' (see Hermkens 2007, 2008, Ch. 4). Alice and many other women who have been the victims of violence and sexual abuse from their husbands are being enjoined not to resist, but to be patient, to endure, to survive and to hope, through their female submission, to transform their husbands' hearts and vitiate their violence. As the story of Alice graphically reveals, this ethic of submission is extended to their daughters even when *raskol* gangs, rape and HIV coalesce to form the fearful spectre of a modern dystopia.

As Hermkens reveals, women's power to survive and even hopefully transform men is drawn from mimetic, embodied identification with the figure of Mary, a model of humility, simplicity and obedience. They aspire not just to copy her outer form, through dressing in blue and engaging in perpetual prayer, but her inner virtues and particularly those of patience and submission—*daunpasin* (TP: humility). There is also a martial aspect to Marian devotion since her followers are cast as warriors in her service as she crushes the several heads of the serpent of Satan. But they are ultimately enjoined to be obedient slaves to her and to their husbands. According to the edicts of the late Father Golly, a wife should not leave her husband, even if his violence persists unabated and, even if he is having extra-marital affairs and she fears contracting HIV, she should never use condoms as protection (see below).[13]

Hermkens stresses how Marian devotion is thought to occasion a highly personalised self-transformation. This process is both painful and paradoxical. It entails hard daily discipline and great strength to wrench peace from the emotional turmoil of abuse by a husband. And ultimately this self-fashioning is also a triumph over the many heads of the serpent of the self: self-exaltation, self-seeking, self-sufficiency, self-love, and self-satisfaction etc. As Hermkens (Ch. 4) sagely observes: '[t]his Christian rhetoric which calls for the denial of the self also emphasises the self.'

Her chapter raises some fascinating questions about contesting models of relational and individuated persons and ideas of empowerment and agency (see

---

13   Gibbs offers an alternative suggestion that such women's prayer groups can also be a way for women to distance themselves from their husband's control (including violence and sex), in local idiom 'getting out from under the legs of men' (pers. comm. by email 20/01/11; see Gibbs and Mondu 2010). It will be interesting to see what the effect of the 2010 announcement of Pope Benedict XVI relaxing the Catholic policy on condoms in relation to HIV will be in PNG. (On the limitations of the Pope's pronouncement on the use (or non-use) of condoms see Ch. 4, note 12.)

below). Apropos the recent debates in the anthropology of Christianity in PNG, and especially that between Joel Robbins (2010) and Mark Mosko (2010a and b) she suggests that conversion to Christianity has entailed neither the radical rupture to a more individuated self which Robbins claims for the Urapmin (2005) nor the persistence of Strathern's 'dividual' persons, engaged in spiritual as well as material transactions, as Mosko claims for the Mekeo (2010a). She considers both representations of personhood, individual and relational are co-existing 'albeit sometimes conflicting' (Hermkens Ch. 4: 116; see Wardlow 2006: 19–20).

3. Implanting western justice and law

Third, I ponder the transformations of engendered violence which have accompanied what Jean Zorn (Ch. 5) calls the 'implanting' of western modes of justice and the law.[14] I here briefly distil the connected insights of Zorn's chapter and those of Fiona Hukula and Christine Stewart.

Zorn's (2010, Ch. 5) extraordinary review of cases of rape heard in the PNG courts by both expatriate Australian and Papua New Guinean judges certainly makes for disturbing and depressing reading (see Ch. 8). Her chapter subverts the hopes of those who see western-style policing and courts as likely to deliver more justice to women who are victims of such violence. She shows how rather than evincing the legal ideals of cool reason, the decisions made by male judges in these cases are, for the most part, an extraordinary concoction of emotion and masculinist presumption about victims of rape in particular and women in general. Many of the notorious myths of rape which circulate in contexts in Australia and America are revivified in fresh milieu: that it is primarily an act of strangers, that women consented if they did not shout out, physically resist or immediately report the rape; that women's uncorroborated testimony is untrustworthy in general and especially about rape; and that women who drink and have sex are 'bad' women who don't deserve to be seen as victims of rape. In a recent paper (Zorn 2010), she shows how judicial suspicions about women's uncorroborated testimony have persisted in PNG long after they have been cogently critiqued and dispatched in many other common law countries through processes of legal reform.

Zorn (Ch. 5) traces the sexism of many judges in PNG to three sources: the indigenous pre-colonial cultures of PNG, the cultures of the colonisers, Britain, Germany and Australia and the rapid and uneven development which characterises PNG's post-colonial history. Moreover she discerns sexism in the prevailing sub-culture in which judges are educated, which privileges reason and logic (deemed masculine) over emotion and unreason (deemed feminine; see

---

14 Apropos similar processes in the dispersal of law and international protocols, Sally Engle Merry (2006) speaks of 'transplants'.

Lloyd 1984). The masculinist predisposition of the law results in adjudications whereby the physical injury of the victim is seen as more real or tangible than her emotional injury. She suggests that male judges find it hard to empathise with the female victims' emotional pain. Even when rape cases are reported in such graphic detail as to constitute pornography, the protected anonymity of the victim together with the use of first person affidavits generates a curiously hybrid genre: eliciting sexual excitation while simultaneously detaching the reader from embodied identification with the person who suffered (see also Zorn 2010 for a detailed analysis of narrative identification in judgements of rape cases in PNG).

Some judges, both Australian and indigenous, are starting to break free from such judicial sexism in sentencing, partly because of changing attitudes but also in response to the gravity of rape in PNG. According to Zorn rapes per capita in PNG are high and increasing and there is an alarming prevalence of violent pack rapes, typically occurring in the wake of household or automobile robberies. In response to this, PNG's judges first devised sentencing guidelines, which increased the 'starting point' for sentences to around eight years (many were under five years prior to 1987) and added more years for 'aggravating factors' including undue or extreme violence, acts of 'sexual perversion' (such as anal rape or rape with objects), if the victim was very old or very young, or if the rapist was in a position of trust or authority. The *Criminal Code (Sexual Offences and Crimes Against Children) Act*, passed in 2002, was designed to raise the 'starting point' to fifteen years for non-aggravated rape, but some judges have disregarded this Act in their judgements, ignoring its existence, disingenuously misinterpreting or manipulating the wording of the Act to award sentences even lighter than those suggested by the earlier guidelines, and in some cases even claiming its unconstitutionality (without warrant). The same judges (particularly Justices Cannings, Sevua, Lenalia) are using conservative legal arguments to challenge a 'quantum leap' in sentences. These judges, claims Zorn, are the very judges whose judgements evince an incapacity to empathise with the female victims of rape.

By contrast those who have manifested such empathy in their judgements are more likely to use the 2002 Act to impose far tougher sentences on rapists and to cite the PNG Constitution to declare women's equal humanity with men and their rights to travel freely without the threat of rape and gender violence (Justices Injia and Kandakasi are named as exemplary). Still, in some of the recent judgements even of these more empathetic jurists, there is a tendency to show differential empathy to women on the basis of ethnicity, locale and education. Whereas in the past white women who were victims were often treated more generously than indigenous women (see Zorn 2010), now it seems that the most deserving victims are those good village women, who are portrayed as innocent and naïve, in contrast to more educated urban women (Zorn, Ch. 5; see also Zimmer-Tamakoshi 1993a, 1993b).

Fiona Hukula's 'Conversations with Convicted Rapists' (Ch. 6) offers a fascinating counterpoint to Zorn's, from the perspective of the men who perpetrated such acts of rape, incest and indecent assault. Fifty men, all incarcerated as prisoners in Bomana Prison outside Port Moresby, were interviewed by Thomas Semo and Hukula, on a project initiated at the National Research Institute (NRI). Hukula suggests that as a woman her interviews were less successful, because she was bound by cultural protocols of not discussing sex with men and because she was mistakenly thought to be a lawyer intent on lengthening their sentences. By contrast, in interviews with Semo, inmates comfortably offered frank perceptions and retrospections on their acts of rape. Semo also conducted interviews with male Correctional Service officers employed to guard these men and with whom they had close daily contact.

Hukula's chapter underlines how frank these inmates were about their actions (see also Ch. 8, about men's disarming honesty apropos their gender violence). Moreover, their retrospective accounts as to why they raped yield some unexpected, if gruesome, insights into changing masculinities in PNG. Some explanations of their acts are expected and stereotypical: claims of the irresistible 'nature' of male sexual desire (see Ch. 5),[15] claims of the inexorable allure of certain women, claims of sexual frustration due to being denied sex by partners or to being unmarried, claims to be under the influence of alcohol, claims that male friends or kin pressured them into gang rape. Some explanations are rather less expected for those who live beyond PNG. Many such accounts highlight desires for revenge and retribution not just against the individual female victim but her family. There are stories of prior thefts, of unreciprocated debts, of previous killings through witchcraft, of pre-existing tense group relations, of humiliation occasioned by the victim or her family. A common refrain is that the offender was 'set up' or even coerced into the act of rape: by his brothers, by his wife's first husband, by the victim's family and/or the victim herself, even by the 'inevitable' consequences of watching pornography. Significantly for those who have argued that female consent is not so much an issue for rapes in PNG as her male kin's rights in her person (e.g. Borrey 2000), several rapists exculpated their acts by insisting that the women consented (sometimes allegedly under

---

15　This claim about the irresistible 'nature' of male sexual desire is significantly at odds with prior practices of sexual restraint after the birth of children or prolonged periods of ritual celibacy in many parts of PNG, practices which were thought rather to increase men's strength and status, often because sexual contact with women was thought to pollute or emasculate men (see Herdt 1981; Jolly 2001a). In some parts of PNG men were thought to be less troubled by sexual desire than women. Wardlow (2006) reports that the ideal Huli man was cool, reasonable and not very desirous while woman were thought hot and emotional with undisciplined sexual desire. Christianity might be doubly implicated here both in the termination of such practices and in the ideology that husbands have conjugal rights to have regular sex with their wives (see Chs 1, 4).

the influence of alcohol) but then later recanted, and with the assistance of their families, charged them with rape. In many of these retrospective accounts men insist they were not so much the perpetrators of rape as themselves victims: of desperate or unfortunate circumstances or of being 'set up' by the machinations or coercions of others. There is a clear deflection of individual responsibility here, perhaps through a stress on relational personhood, as well as 'disarming honesty'.

These individual, even idiosyncratic, stories might be counterposed with what Hukula alludes to at the beginning of her chapter, those generalised explanations of gendered violence in PNG as due to shared 'culture' or reified social norms. The NRI research project was designed rather to explore the specificities of the individual experience of these rapists, according to their age, region, marital status, education and economic situation. Her chapter suggests that explanations which only address the specificities of the embodied power relation between the individual man who rapes and his female victim fail to address the wider social context in which rape occurs in PNG. Although ultimately adjudged in the courts in terms of individuated models of consent and coercion, rapes clearly implicate broader questions not just of unequal gendered power (see Ch. 5) but the perils of profound social transformations in PNG. This chapter thus offers a distinctive and unusual perspective which reveals much about men who rape and about what has been dubbed 'embattled' or 'troubled' masculinities in the context of encroaching modernities in PNG (see Ch. 2; Jolly 2000).

The final chapter in this trio is that by Christine Stewart (Ch. 7), a confronting analysis of the extreme violence of the police raid on the Three Mile Guesthouse in Port Moresby in 2004. Police raids on sites of alleged *raskols* in settlements and prostitutes in 'brothels' are not unusual in PNG, perpetuating a colonial pattern of violent frontier pacification into the present (Dinnen 1998a: 260–61, 1998b). But this raid proved exceptional in many ways. That extraordinary event involved not only the brutal arrests of many women alleged to be selling sex but, initially, a number of men. Some of these were likely customers in the bar as were the women; some were perhaps clients of those women who were selling sex. But, they too were accused, alongside the women, of selling sex.

In the police violence which ensued, which involved physical beatings, rapes, (one with an air freshener can), forced fellatio and the forcible ingestion of condoms and a humiliating parade at gunpoint down the streets of Port Moresby, the women were subject to a level of sexualised violence which far exceeded that meted out to the men. Women were charged and kept in prison for days without food, washing facilities or medical attention while the forty men caught up in the raid were swiftly released. Three weeks later all charges of 'living on the earnings of prostitution' were dropped in the absence of proper search warrants.[16] But in the ensuing media frenzy, which inaccurately perpetuated the myth that the men were prostitutes too, the ideal of gender equality was paradoxically and, perhaps cynically, used to argue that the men should have been treated just as badly.

Stewart (Ch. 7) thus reveals the fragility of the discourse of human rights in PNG and how it can be too readily dismissed as a set of foreign values funded by foreign aid donors (see below) or, as in this case, used by some lawyers and commentators to perversely argue that gender equality should have meant equal violence and humiliation for men. In PNG, men who were alleged to have sold sex to other men have typically been charged with the more serious crime of sodomy (Stewart 2008). Stewart demonstrates how the violent and criminalising forces of the law have conjoined with ancestral and Christian ideals of wanton, polluting women in the moral panics around the figure of the *pamuk meri* (TP: prostitute, harlot, a woman who sells sex). And, as is clear from that powerful image of the ingested condom, HIV is also focal in this narrative of fear, pollution and retribution.

4. HIV and introduced biomedical models

So, finally let me highlight the importance of the HIV epidemic in reconfiguring relations between men and women in PNG and in the broader debates about gender, modernity and violence. This is not the specific subject of any particular paper in this volume although it has been the focus of much excellent recent research and practice by Lawrence Hammar (2008, 2010) and Elizabeth Reid nationally (e.g. 2010a, b, c, d and e), by Katherine Lepani both nationally and in the Trobriands (2007, 2008a, 2008b, 2010), by Nicole Haley in Duna country (2010), by Naomi McPherson and Richard Eves in New Britain and New Ireland and by several other ethnographers in collections edited by Alison Dundon and Charles Wilde (2007), Richard Eves and Leslie Butt (2008) and Vicki Luker and Sinclair Dinnen (2010). The reality of HIV and the spectre of AIDS resurfaces in many of these papers: it haunts Philip Gibbs' depiction of Simbu (see Ch. 3 and Gibbs 2009, Gibbs and Mondu 2010); it frames the stories of Alice and Julie as told by Hermkens (Ch. 4) and it is focal to Christine Stewart's story of the Three Mile Guest House raid (Ch. 7).

Gibbs reports a pervasive stigma about HIV in Simbu: if a family member is suspected of dying from AIDS, they are buried quickly so as to preclude

---

16 See Stewart (2011) for a persuasive assessment of how police and judges have both thwarted the intent of the new law on 'prostitution' which was to criminalise not those selling sex but those who were living off their earnings, such as pimps or owners of brothels.

the possibility of diagnosis of witchcraft. Alice's story as told by Hermkens graphically reveals the intimate relation between gender violence and HIV. When Alice's daughter is gang raped Alice is afraid that she has contracted AIDS. She is also fearful for herself given her ex-husband's affairs and his violent abuse of her, including his coercive insistence on conjugal sex. Given her strong Catholic commitment as a follower of the Legion of Mary she refuses to use condoms but relies on God for protection. Both Alice and her daughter tested negative, a fact she construes not as their good fortune but as God's divine will. Catholics oppose condoms not only because they are seen to interfere with God's plan but also because they are thought to encourage sexual promiscuity and hence the spread of AIDS. The late Father Golly, at the time national spiritual director of the Legion of Mary, advised his followers to avoid AIDS by advocating not the government mantra of ABC 'abstinence, be faithful, condoms' but ABBA: 'abstinence, be faithful, be faithful and abstinence'. Both Alice and Anna, who works as a nurse at Madang hospital, are caught in a dilemma, between the government program of promoting condoms as part of the ABC policy and their Catholic faith. They usually choose the latter, telling both clients and patients that they should adhere to God's will and refuse condoms (see Wardlow 2008). Only if they are undisciplined 'like animals' should they resort to condoms.

Such images of sinful sex and of moral decay which suffuse the responses of various churches to HIV appear to have far more effect on popular perceptions than government poster campaigns and public health awareness programs (the messages of which have been regularly interpreted in ways different to those intended, see McPherson 2008). Hermkens (Ch. 4) reports on healing ministries and pamphlets which promise that faith in God will cure AIDS (along with 'family violence'). And, as other research has revealed (Eves 2003, 2008), the apocalyptic visions of an evangelical Christianity have often converged with the public health panics about the 'end times'. These 'end times' are distinctly gendered since undue blame is being given to women as source and vector of the disease, as witches (see Haley 2010) or *pamuk meri*, while men are usually exempted from blame.

This is dramatically revealed in the chapter by Stewart. The excessive police violence which occasioned the raid on the Three Mile Guesthouse was patently licensed by the spectre of AIDS. The Metropolitan Police Superintendent said that the 'raid had been conducted to prevent sex workers from contracting and spreading HIV' (Ch. 7). This intimate connection between sex work and HIV is distilled in the material sign of the condom: simultaneously seen as enabling and even promoting sexual promiscuity and 'prostitution' and as the means, though contested, for protection against HIV. In one of the newspaper editorials cited by Stewart the spread of the virus is likened to a 'bushfire', searing young girls. The poverty and desperation of those women who sell sex is acknowledged but this newspaper editor indulges in predictions that they will perforce all fall victim to HIV and be 'among those anonymous carcasses to be bulldozed into the mass burial pit of Bomana cemetery' (Ch. 7). And so the stigma of the disease and the threat of death are congealed in the bodies of its unnamed, depersonalised victims (paralleling Zorn's insights on the anonymity of female rape victims).

Stewart situates this stigma in the long history of how women (and especially 'prostitutes') rather than their male partners were perceived as the source of sexually transmitted diseases since nineteenth-century laws in both France and Britain tried to monitor and control 'contagious diseases'. The British laws had long-distance implications with the establishment of lock hospitals and surveillance measures in the colonies of India and Africa and the British territory of Papua (see Lepani 2008b, 2012; Reed 1997). She connects this history to the more recent transplantation of the global HIV discourse to PNG and shows how this has often exacerbated local stigma, focused as it is on isolating 'high risk' groups which are labelled by a plethora of acronyms: MSM (men who have sex with men), FSW (female sex workers), and so on. Hammar (2008, 2010) and others have queried this fixation in public health discourse and suggested that those most at risk are likely to be those wives with unfaithful husbands who, unlike most sex workers, are not using condoms. Lepani (2008a, 2008b, 2008c, 2012) has eloquently demonstrated the negative effects of this global language of risk and death and how it has been localised both in the specific context of the Trobriands and more broadly across the nation. She has also demonstrated the limits of the individualist biomedical model for a country like PNG where relational concepts of the person still prevail over more individuated models. Inappropriate models are surely also apparent in the typification of the women who sell sex as 'prostitutes' or 'sex workers', as if their lives as mothers, sisters, daughters, partners and wives are irrelevant (see Wardlow 2004; Ch. 7; Lepani 2012; Stewart 2011 for compelling examinations of labelling the selling of sex, including the phrase 'transactional sex').

Stewart's argument that global HIV discourse, an introduced criminal legal system, Christian moralism and middle-class exclusionism have congealed to form the scar of stigma of HIV in PNG is compelling. Such stigma not only hampers diagnosis, prevention and care of those with HIV but generates fear, lack of empathy and even releases the blood of torture and death for those suffering, or suspected to be suffering, from AIDS. This is patent in several witch-killings in the Highlands (Haley 2010). But the spectre of AIDS is also used to justify, as in the Three Mile Guesthouse raid, violence against *pamuk meri*, and seemingly, by analogical reasoning, all women who are thought wayward or eluding the control of men.

Combating violence? Translating research into policy and practice

As a totality, this book thus focuses our attention on how patterns of gender violence in PNG are intimately imbricated with major ongoing social transformations in that country. It is not just a matter of understanding the proximate causes to the vast array of individual acts which constitute gender violence but the structures which predispose and enable that violence. Gender inequality is a crucial enabling structure, but though some have seen this as so pervasive and persistent as to be part of PNG 'culture' (see Macintyre 1998 for an overview; Macintyre 1987; and Lepani 2008c on the Massim), the character and dimensions of gender inequality have changed dramatically in alignment with the huge social changes depicted in this volume: the combined influences of commodity economics, Christian conversion and the introduced regimes of law and biomedicine in the context of the HIV epidemic. The gendered culture of PNG's modernity is thus as much implicated as the gendered culture of tradition (see Merry 2006: 12ff, 2009: 2).

Major social transformations in PNG have yielded a surfeit of combustible material which is often concentrated and even fuelled through the prism of gender. Women, and especially powerful, wayward or resistant women, are often blamed for those negative consequences of social change which occasion inequalities and resentments. But, given this, how might we then address the question of how our research connects to policy and practice, to past and future attempts to combat violence? Does the evidence assembled in this volume suggest a new approach?

Macintyre (Ch. 8) stresses that many of the aid and development programs initiated to combat gender violence are relatively innocent of, and even ignorant of, the rich anthropological and legal research in PNG to date, and the huge burgeoning global literature on gender violence from the perspectives of the diverse disciplines of anthropology, psychology, medicine and the law. Research has rarely been well articulated with programs and practice despite the huge efforts of many organisations such as UNIFEM, the World Bank, Amnesty International and especially AusAID (but see AusAID 2009). And, as Richard Eves (2006) suggests in his comprehensive report for Caritas Australia, large-scale public programs to promote awareness of gender violence and to reduce its incidence have to date proved relatively ineffective in PNG (as elsewhere, see Merry 2009: 2). Like the carefully designed and expensive posters to combat AIDS, they have often been subject to creative interpretations wildly at variance from the intentions of their creators. The work of awareness-raising through theatre groups has had rather mixed, even negative, results. As Naomi McPherson (2008) has shown for West New Britain, local theatre performances can reinforce gendered caricatures about good faithful village wives versus *pamuk meri* and portray the latter, rather than men, as the main source of HIV. Eves (2006) recommends shifting the focus of intervention from women to men, and from mass public campaigns to small awareness-raising groups. He advocates small, all-male groups with male facilitators as the most successful mode of raising awareness of gender violence and changing men's attitudes, in accord with models deployed in overseas countries. This has been initiated by Philip Gibbs and others working for the Catholic Church and Caritas Australia.

The evidence we have from Macintyre's experience over four decades as both an anthropologist and a consultant to AusAID in PNG on programs dedicated to improving the awareness of police and promoting a human rights approach to gender violence is that awareness-raising and dedicated programs may have little effect and indeed can sometimes prove counterproductive (Ch. 8). A woman who participated in one of Macintyre's workshops, and was thus made newly aware of her rights, challenged her violent husband only to be beaten up even more violently. She suggests that direct programs expressly designed to reduce gender violence may be less successful than broader projects of women's economic and social empowerment.

Macintyre (Ch. 8) cites the well-known example of how reduced population growth in countries like India has been achieved less through the direct methods of family planning, contraception, safe abortion and campaigns for women's reproductive rights and more through improving education and economic conditions for women (Sen 1990; Macintyre Ch. 8). She advocates a similar indirection in relation to gender violence.

'Considering what might hasten or alter the gender inequalities that underpin violence, I think that the Millennium Development goals aimed at empowering women more generally necessarily have to precede campaigns that aim to combat violence' (Ch. 8). And yet, as we have seen from several chapters in this book, including Macintyre's own, those few PNG women who have benefited from being well educated and/or have succeeded in business or government employment have also been subject to punitive gender violence, like the majority of their poorer fellow female citizens living in the towns and villages of PNG.

Macintyre also suggests that the very mode of engagement of foreign donors and the neoliberal precepts which have suffused aid and development programs in recent time are part of the problem. Like most global agencies, government and non-government, AusAID the major donor for development in PNG has been heavily influenced by economic rationalism and the technocratic modes of 'audit culture' (see Strathern 2000). AusAID outsources most of its programs to commercial companies through contracts which place high priority on processes of monitoring, auditing and evaluation and 'deliverables': the numerous reviews and reports mandated at each stage of a project. Macintyre estimates that in her work as a consultant in PNG, about 60 per cent of her time was spent reporting on what she was doing rather than doing it. The arcane, technical requirements of many projects are completed by foreign experts rather than Papua New Guineans, resulting in what has been called 'boomerang aid' (where most money is spent on Australian consultants) and novel forms of tied aid, shaped by the moral imperative of 'accountability' to taxpayers and donors rather than to the recipients of aid (Kilby 2010). Unequal and dependent relations between donor and recipient countries and their nationals persist despite all the public relations patina of partnership and collaborative research. Like much of the rhetoric about diversity and equality, Macintyre sees this as empty talk.

Empowerment and agency: Changing persons in the era of human rights?

> If one accepts that these dual modes of personhood [relational and individual] can coexist, if in highly contested ways, then a variety of questions emerge. For one, might a transformation be occurring with more individualistic expressions of agency coming to the fore?... And if 'modernity' had something to do with an increase in individualism, what is it about modernity that has this effect? Further, how might the expression of a more individualized sensibility be gendered? (Wardlow 2006: 20).

Empowering women, as many have suggested, is a curious concept. It seems to simultaneously imply that women's power is there to be revealed *and* that it needs to be animated or even endowed by others. The cruel reality is that power often has to be wrested from men, who are violently resisting challenges to their control. As Martha Macintyre stresses (Ch. 8), if women are to be 'empowered' to resist or reduce violence, men are going to have to be disempowered. The promotion of human *raits* (TP: rights) implies the erosion of the *rait* (TP: right, authority) of men to rape, beat, maim and murder women. As Macintyre insists, it is a romance to presume this is a 'win-win' situation, in which both women and men will benefit.

There are several examples in this book of the hazards of women's empowerment in individuated acts of resistance to gender violence. Wives who resist their husbands' beatings with their own violence or with righteous words about their 'rights' as equal citizens or Christians risk even more violence in retribution (see Chs 4 and 8). In a compelling examination of women's 'negative agency' among the Huli, Wardlow (2006: 72–8) shows how wives can deploy more subtle subversions, by 'forgetting' their husband's edicts, neglecting to garden or cook, declining sex or even being careless about their menstrual blood. This can sap the husband's will and undermine his collective projects. In Wardlow's view (2006: 75) it inherently entails a more individualised expression of self. Ultimately this risks vilification and further violence. Such extremities cause many women and especially wives to self-harm, to lop off their fingers or even to hang or drown themselves. Rates of suicide among Huli women are extremely high (see also Counts 1993). The woman is typically blamed and the husband interprets this as an attack on himself, depriving him of her work and thus 'throwing away his bridewealth'. Thus, even this most extreme and desperate form of women's individual negative agency is ultimately encompassed by male agency and masculinist values.

More collective acts on the part of women to stop tribal fighting in the Highlands of PNG (see Garap 2000, 2004; Rumsey 2000) or to secure their share of employment in mining ventures (Ch. 2) may have proved more effective, but they are rare. Clearly the exercise of 'agency' is not just restricted to individual women, but male-dominated structures often inhibit their collective action (see Wardlow 2006: 69–72). We cannot optimistically imagine collective solidarity between women in PNG to redress men's power given the way in which they are routinely and powerfully divided by kinship, generation, language, religion, ethnicity and class. In matrilineal parts of PNG there were traditions of female collectivity associated with the reproductive power and regenerativity of matriclans and the influence women exerted over the transmission of land and leadership (see Lepani 2008c on the Trobriands; Macintyre 1987 on Tubetube; Saovana-Spriggs 2007 on Bougainville). But in much of PNG, the main contexts for women's solidarity have been the Christian churches, where the most efficacious expressions of women's collective agency have flourished in various women's groups (see Douglas 2003; Jolly 2003b). So what chance is there that, rather than being places where women are encouraged to submit to male authority, moralise about sinful *pamuk meri*, or suffer violence patiently, Christian churches and women's groups might become sites for combating gender violence and contribute to that broader economic and political empowerment which Macintyre perceives as a necessary predicate?

In an earlier paper on questions of 'domestic violence' and human rights I suggested (2000 [1996]) that some ni-Vanuatu women were resisting masculinist interpretations of the Bible, and transforming earlier missionary models of 'uplifting' indigenous women through their own appropriation of ideas of 'bringing the light' into their lives. I argued that there was a universalism in the rhetoric of such Christian women which emphasised the transnational similarities of women despite their differences (cf. Robbins 2004). I concluded that these indigenous Christian ideas were important in laying the historical foundations for the acceptance and promulgation of more secular notions of human rights by some ni-Vanuatu women (especially by the late Grace Mera Molisa and particularly in the capital of Port Vila; Jolly 1997, 2005; but see Patterson 2001 on the rural context of North Ambrym). Since the time of my writing, this 'vernacularisation' of human rights in Vanuatu has been challenged by men, including a backlash movement on Espiritu Santo, which called itself 'Violence Against Men'. As John Taylor has shown (2008b), this movement was especially opposed to proposed new legislation apropos marriage and the foreign funding of NGOs working to protect women who were victims of gender violence. They challenged human or women's *raets* (BIS: rights) with the notion of male *raet* (BIS: right).

The context of gender violence in PNG is different and evinces a divergent scale of complexity and diversity. The effects of commodity economy in terms of extractive industries, the importance of male wage labour and nationalist consumption patterns are far greater (see Filer and Macintyre 2006; Foster 2002). But here too we can discern how such gendered conflicts can reanimate reified divisions between a male-defined *kastam* and introduced ideas espoused by women which are reviled as 'foreign'. It is often claimed that the universalist values of human rights and the claims of 'culture' or the national sovereignty of countries like PNG are essentially opposed. Indeed in two chapters in this volume we hear opinions expressed in these terms: a PNG man adjudges that human rights will never become 'popular' in PNG and that it will take fifty to one hundred years to stop men beating their wives (Ch. 8) and that the 'lofty ideals' of international human rights discourse sit uneasily with popular discourses in PNG which are accepting of gender violence and gender inequality and which blame victims (Ch. 7).[17]

But how far can we accept this dichotomy, seeing the 'culture' of PNG as necessarily opposed to the universal aspirations of human rights? And who is speaking for culture? Merry (2006) has persuasively argued that there is a problem with the 'culture' concept in debates about human rights. The problem is also a paradox. At the same time as older conceptions of 'culture' as shared norms, enduring traditions or national essences, have been extensively challenged, especially by anthropologists, and have given way to views of culture as contested, changing and permeable, 'culture' has too often been used in the human rights context, as in many development arenas, in a reified and ultimately a sexist and racist way (Merry 2006: 10–16; see also Lepani 2010). Patriarchal traditions in Pakistan are labelled 'culture' but those challenging such traditions are excluded from 'culture'. Genital cutting in Africa and the Middle East is seen as cultural and labelled 'mutilation' but genital reconstructive surgery in the United States is construed as an individual choice (Merry 2006: 7ff).

---

17   We should note however the way in which both the PNG Constitution of 1975 and later human rights protocols have been cited by some indigenous judges in cases of rape (see Zorn Ch. 5).

As this volume shows, although gender violence in contemporary PNG is grounded in past practices, its forms and meanings have changed with the profound social transformations engendered over the last few decades. It has assumed new shapes in the diverse and dynamic cultures of Papua New Guinean modernity. Moreover, although human rights may be dismissed by its opponents in PNG as something 'foreign', western, even Australian, the global evidence is rather that human rights discourse has multiple origins and that it is being locally appropriated and vernacularised in many parts of the world (see Hilsdon *et al.* 2000; Grimshaw *et al.* 2001; Merry 2006, 2009). Although the genealogy of human rights discourse is typically plotted back to the individualist and masculinist models of the European Enlightenment, given its transnational articulations over the last thirty years, this is increasingly looking like a dubious origin myth.

It is true as Merry acknowledges that

> Human rights promote ideas of individual autonomy, equality, choice, and secularism even when these ideas differ from prevailing cultural norms and practices. Human rights ideas displace alternative visions of social justice that are less individualistic and more focused on communities and responsibilities, possibly contributing to the cultural homogenization of local communities (Merry 2009: 4).

But Merry's books are also replete with examples of how, as human rights discourse is translated and vernacularised, it has assumed not just the local inflections of different languages but absorbed some of the influences of divergent social philosophies and notions of the person. Moreover, as has been often argued, the individualist and liberal emphasis of European models of rights has been complemented with more collectivist ideas of 'rights' as in movements for the rights of indigenous peoples, workers, migrants, refugees, sexual minorities and even 'women' (see Dickson-Waiko 2001; Merry 2006).[18]

How then might we bring these insights back to the disturbing and depressing portrayal of gender violence in PNG presented between the covers of this book? In reading and thinking and dreaming about these chapters, I have often been haunted by those twin recurring figures in contemporary PNG culture: the good Christian wife and the bad wayward woman, if not a *pamuk meri* then a

---

18   The recognition of women's rights as human rights was a protracted and difficult struggle (see Merry 2006, 2009). The international human rights machinery was initially established, in the wake of the Holocaust to deal with violations of human rights by states, and the canonical figure of someone whose human rights had been violated was the victim of genocide, state torture or political imprisonment. And yet Amnesty International, one of the major organisations which dealt with political prisoners, also took up the cause to argue that women's rights are human rights. Moreover, as Merry suggests, 'In the 1990s, gender violence was defined as an important human rights violation for the first time. Now it is considered the centerpiece of women's human rights' (2009: 1).

woman who eludes male control. They seem to embody hypostatised visions of the relational versus the individuated person. But, as Holly Wardlow (2006) perceptively suggests in the quote that heralds this section, in practice these two figures, these rival models of persons, though conflicting can also co-exist. This is clear in those alleged transformations from relational to individual persons along the four dimensions of social change discussed above. Like Wardlow, in any discussion of 'incipient individualism', I consider it crucial to connect conversion to Christianity with changes in material life, especially the commoditisation of economy (see also LiPuma 1998; Foster 2002), and the introduction of novel legal and biomedical regimes.[19]

It is very hard to be optimistic about significant reductions in patterns of gender violence in PNG in the near future. Dedicated small group work with men as proposed by Eves (2006) and broader programs of economic and social empowerment for women as envisioned by Macintyre (Ch. 8) are both excellent suggestions from long-term observers of PNG. Zimmer-Tamakoshi (Ch 2) makes important suggestions about potential transformation to the bride price system such that it is 'curtailed and cut off from local and global market forces' and that there is a more equitable distribution of mining wealth to 'landowners' across generations and genders. The innovative methodologies of 'community conversations' deployed by Elizabeth Reid and the team of the Papua New Guinean Sustainable Development Program offer a promising path for social transformation in villages in several provinces, which should not only increase HIV awareness, prevention and care but redress gender violence. But I also hazard a final suggestion that the Christian churches might be crucial in many such efforts. Efforts to work with men in small groups associated with churches along the lines of Christian women's groups might be a better place to start than more secular state-sponsored workshops. Such groups have already been initiated by Philip Gibbs, one of our contributors, over the last five years in the Western Province.[20] And although we have heard the dismal litanies of many Christians who legitimise gender inequality and even gender violence and espouse the values of submissive domesticated wives, there is an alternative voice to be heard in Christianity; a voice which promotes gender equality and peace, and even the projects of women's empowerment through education and public leadership. Let us hope such submerged voices might be articulated more powerfully in the future and let us hope they are heard.

---

19   This is the basis of a five-year Laureate project for which I have been funded by the Australian Research Council, called *Engendering persons, transforming things: Christianities, commodities and individualism in Oceania* (FL 100100196).

20   Gibbs notes that these 'men's matters' workshops, of about forty men from across the Western Province, have met annually for a week at the invitation of Bishop Cote of Kiunga, and that this has been 'an interesting and productive experience'. They were in part a follow up to Eves' report for Caritas Australia, and Gibbs hopes to write about them in the near future (pers. comm. by email 20/01/11).

Acknowledgements

I especially thank Christine Stewart for the invitation to act as a discussant at the panel of the Association for Social Anthropology in Oceania in 2009 and then to convert those comments into an Introduction and to co-edit this volume. It has grown exponentially in that process and also hopefully matured! Thanks to all the contributors for their feedback on earlier drafts and to several of them and in particular Martha Macintyre, Christine Stewart and Carolyn Brewer for very close readings of the final draft, which improved both substance and style. All remaining errors of fact and interpretation are my own. I thank both The Australian National University and the Australian Research Council for support of my work over several years, and especially the latter for the Laureate Fellowship, *Engendering persons, transforming things: Christianities, commodities and individualism in Oceania* FL100100196 which has supported the publication of this volume.

References

Aleck, Jonathan, 1996. Law and sorcery in Papua New Guinea. PhD thesis. Canberra: The Australian National University.

Allen, Michael, 1967. *Male Cults and Secret Initiations in Melanesia*. Melbourne: Melbourne University Press.

-------- 2000.Male cults revisited: the politics of blood versus semen. In *Ritual, Power and Gender. Explorations in the Ethnography of Vanuatu, Nepal and Ireland*, by Michael Allen, 137–57. Sydney Studies in Society and Culture. Leichhardt and New Delhi: Manohar Publishers.

Amnesty International, 2006. *Papua New Guinea: Violence Against Women. Not Inevitable, Never Acceptable*. AI Index: ASA 34/002/2006.

AusAID, 2007. *Violence Against Women in Melanesia and East Timor: Building on Global and Regional Promising Approaches*. Canberra: AusAID Office of Development Effectiveness, Australian Government. Online: http://www.ode.ausaid.gov.au/publications/pdf/vaw_cs_full_report.pdf. Accessed 21 November 2011.

-------- 2009. *Responding to Violence Against Women in Melanesia and East Timor: Australia's Response to the ODE Report*. Canberra: Australian Agency for International Development (AusAID). Online: http://www.ausaid.gov.au/publications/pdf/ResVAW.pdf. Accessed 21 November 2011.

-------- 2011. *Eliminating Violence against Women* (25 November). Canberra: Australian Agency for International Development (AusAID). Online: http://www.ausaid.gov.au/keyaid/gender_approach.cfm. Accessed 29 November 2011.

Banks, Cyndi, 2000. Contextualising sexual violence: rape and carnal knowledge in Papua New Guinea. In *Reflections on Violence in Melanesia*, ed. Sinclair Dinnen and Allison Ley, 83–104. Sydney: Hawkins Press and Asia Pacific Press.

Barker, John, 2001. Afterword. In *Charismatic and Pentecostal Christianity in Oceania*, ed. Joel Robbins, Pamela Stewart and Andrew Strathern. *Journal of Ritual Studies* 15: 105–7.

Bonnemère, Pascale, 1996. *Le pandanus rouge. Corps, différence des sexes et parenté chez les Ankave-Anga*. Paris: CNRS Éditions, Éditions des Sciences de l'Homme.

Bradley, Christine, 1994a. *Why Male Violence Against Women?: Methodological and Personal Perspectives*. London: Sage Publications.

-------- 1994b. Why male violence against women is a development issue: reflections from Papua New Guinea. In *Women and Violence*, ed. Miranda Davies, 10–27. London: Zed Books.

-------- 2001. *Family and Sexual Violence in Papua New Guinea: An Integrated Long-term Strategy*. Report to the family action committee of the consultative implementation and monitoring council. Waigani: Institute of National Affairs.

Borrey, Anou, 2000. Sexual violence in perspective: the case of Papua New Guinea. In *Reflections on Violence in Melanesia*, ed. Sinclair Dinnen and Allison Ley, 105–18. Sydney: Hawkins Press and Asia Pacific Press.

Butler, Judith, 1990. *Gender Trouble: Feminism and the Subversion of Identity*. New York: Routledge.

-------- 1995. *Bodies that Matter*. Berkeley and Los Angeles: University of California Press.

Butt, Leslie and Richard Eves, eds, 2008. *Making Sense of AIDS: Culture, Sexuality and Power in Melanesia*. Hawai'i: University of Hawai'i Press.

Clark, Jeffrey, 1989. Gods, ghosts and people: Christianity and social organisation among Takuru Wiru. In *Family and Gender in the Pacific: Domestic Contradictions and the Colonial Impact*, ed. Margaret Jolly and Martha Macintyre, 170–92. Cambridge: Cambridge University Press.

-------- 1997. State of desire: transformations in Huli sexuality. In *Sites of Desire, Economies of Pleasure: Sexualities in Asia and the Pacific*, ed. Lenore Manderson and Margaret Jolly, 191–211. Chicago: Chicago University Press.

Counts, Dorothy Ayers, 1990. Domestic violence in Oceania. Conclusion. *Pacific Studies* 13(3): 225–54.

-------- 1992. 'All men do it': wife-beating in Kaliai, Papua New Guinea. In *Sanctions and Sanctuary: Cultural Perspectives on the Beating of Wives*, ed. Dorothy Ayers Counts, Judith K. Brown and Jacquelyn C. Campbell, 63–76. Boulder and Oxford: Westview Press.

-------- 1993. The fist, the stick and the bottle of bleach: wife bashing and female suicide in a Papua New Guinea Society. In *Contemporary Pacific Societies: Studies in Development and Change*, ed. Victoria S. Lockwood, Tom G. Harding and Ben J. Wallace, 249–59. New Jersey: Prentice Hall.

Cummings, Maggie, 2008. The trouble with trousers: gossip, *kastom* and sexual culture in Vanuatu. In *Making Sense of AIDS: Culture, Sexuality and Power in Melanesia*, ed. Leslie Butt and Richard Eves, 133–49. Honolulu: University of Hawai'i Press.

Dickson-Waiko, Anne, 2001.Women, individual human rights, community rights: tensions within the Papua New Guinea State. In *Women's Rights and Human Rights: International Historical Perspectives*, ed. Patricia Grimshaw, Katie Holmes and Marilyn Lake, 49–70. London and New York: Palgrave.

Dinnen, Sinclair, 1998a. Criminal justice reform in Papua New Guinea. In *Governance and Reform in the South Pacific*, ed. Peter Larmour, 253–72. Canberra: National Centre for Development Studies, The Australian National University.

-------- 1998b. Law, order and the state. In *Modern Papua New Guinea*, ed. Laura Zimmer-Tamakoshi, 333–50. Kirkson Missouri: Thomas Jefferson Press.

-------- 2002. Building bridges: law and justice reform in Papua New Guinea. Discussion Paper 2002/2. State, Society and Governance in Melanesia Project, Research School of Pacific and Asian Studies Canberra: The Australian National University.

Dinnen, Sinclair and Allison Ley, eds, 2000. *Reflections on Violence in Melanesia*. Sydney: Hawkins Press and Asia Pacific Press.

Dinnen, Sinclair and Edwina Thomson, 2004. Gender and small arms violence in Papua New Guinea. Discussion Paper 2004/8. State, Society and Governance in Melanesia Project, Research School of Pacific and Asian Studies. Canberra: The Australian National University.

Douglas, Bronwen, 2003. Christianity, tradition, and everyday modernity: towards an anatomy of women's groupings in Melanesia. *Oceania* 74(1&2): 6–23.

Douglas, Bronwen, ed., 2003. *Women's Groups and Everyday Modernity in Melanesia.* Special issue of *Oceania* 74(1&2).

Douglas, Mary, 1970. *Witchcraft: Confessions and Accusations.* Association of Social Anthropology Monographs No 9. London: Tavistock.

Duffield, Lee, Evangelica Papoutsaki and Amanda Watson, 2008. Australian broadcast media coverage of PNG: not nasty but not enough. *Australian Journalism Review* 30(2): 111–24.

Dundon, Alison and Charles Wilde, eds, 2007. *HIV/AIDS in Rural Papua New Guinea.* Special issue of *Oceania* 77(1).

Eves, Richard, 2003. Aids and apocalypticism: interpretations of the epidemic from Papua New Guinea. *Culture, Health and Sexuality* 5(3): 249–64.

-------- 2006. *Exploring the Role of Men and Masculinities in Papua New Guinea in the 21st Century: How to address violence in ways that generate empowerment for both men and women.* Report for Caritas Australia. Online: http://www.baha.com.pg/downloads/Masculinity%20and%20Violence%20in%20PNG.pdf. Accessed 28 November 2010.

-------- 2008. Moral reform and miraculous cures: Christian healing and AIDS in New Ireland, Papua New Guinea. In *Making Sense of AIDS. Culture, Sexuality and Power in Melanesia,* ed. Leslie Butt and Richard Eves, 303–25. Honolulu: University of Hawai'i Press.

Filer, Colin, 1997. Resource rents: distribution and sustainability. In *Papua New Guinea: A 20/20 Vision,* ed. Ila Temu, 220–60. Pacific Policy Paper 20, National Centre for Development Studies. Canberra: The Australian National University.

Filer, Colin and Martha Macintyre, 2006. Grass roots and deep holes: community responses to mining in Melanesia. In *Melanesian Mining Modernities: Past, Present, and Future,* ed. Paige West and Martha Macintyre. Special issue of *The Contemporary Pacific* 18(2): 215–31.

Forsyth, Miranda, 2006. Sorcery and the criminal law in Vanuatu. *LAWASIA Journal*, 1–27.

-------- 2009. *A Bird that Flies with Two Wings: Kastom and State Justice Systems in Vanuatu*. Canberra: ANU E Press. Online: http://epress.anu.edu.au/kastom_citation.html. Accessed 2 February 2011.

Foster, Robert, 2002. *Materializing the Nation: Commodities, Consumption, and Media in Papua New Guinea*. Bloomington: Indiana University Press.

Galtung, John, 1990. Cultural violence. *Journal of Peace Research* 27(3): 291–305.

Garap, Sarah, 2000. Struggles of women and girls – Simbu Province, Papua New Guinea. In *Reflections on Violence in Melanesia*, ed. Sinclair Dinnen and Allison Ley, 159–71. Sydney: Hawkins Press and Asia Pacific Press.

-------- 2004. Kup Women for Peace: Women taking action to build peace and influence community decision-making. Discussion Paper. 2004/4. State Society and Governance in Melanesia Project. Research School of Pacific and Asian Studies. Canberra: The Australian National University.

Gibbs, Philip, 2004. Growth, decline and confusion: church affiliation in Papua New Guinea. *Catalyst* 34(2): 164–84.

-------- 2009. Sorcery and AIDS in Simbu, East Sepik and Enga. Occasional Paper No. 2. Port Moresby: National Research Institute.

Gibbs, Philip and Marie Mondu, 2010. *Sik Nogut o Nomol Sik. A Study into the Socio-cultural Factors Contributing to Sexual Health in the Southern Highlands and Simbu Provinces, Papua New Guinea*. Sydney: Caritas Australia.

Ginau, Martha and Evangelia Papoutsaki, 2007. Image of a nation: Australian press coverage of PNG. *Australian Journalism Review* 29(1): 127–40.

Godelier, Maurice, 1986 [1982]. *The Making of Great Men: Male Domination and Power among the New Guinea Baruya*. Cambridge and Paris: Cambridge University Press and Maison des Sciences de l'Homme.

Godelier, Maurice and Marilyn Strathern, eds, 1991. *Big Men and Great Men: Personifications of Power in Melanesia*. Cambridge: Cambridge University Press.

Grimshaw, Patricia, Katie Holmes and Marilyn Lake, eds, 2001. *Women's Rights and Human Rights: International Historical Perspectives*. London and New York: Palgrave.

Grown, Caren, Geeta Rao Gupta and Aslihan Kes, 2005. *Taking Action: Achieving Gender Equality and Empowering Women*. London and Sterling VA: Earthscan.

Haley, Nicole, 2008a. Sung adornment: changing masculinities at Lake Kopiago, Papua New Guinea. In *Changing Pacific Masculinities*, ed. John P. Taylor. Special issue of *The Australian Journal of Anthropology* 19(2): 213–29.

-------- 2008b. When there's no accessing basic health care: local politics and responses to HIV/AIDS at Lake Kopiago, Papua New Guinea. In *MakingSense of AIDS: Culture Sexuality and Power in Melanesia*, ed. Leslie Butt and Richard Eves, 24–40. Honolulu: University of Hawai'i Press.

-------- 2010. Witchcraft, torture and HIV. In *Civic Insecurity: Law, Order and HIV in Papua New Guinea*, ed. Vicki Luker and Sinclair Dinnen, 219–35. Canberra: ANU E Press. Online: http://epress.anu.edu.au/apps/bookworm/view/Civic+Insecurity%3A+Law,+Order+and+HIV+in+Papua+New+Guinea/2551/upfront.xhtml. Accessed 2 February 2011.

Hammar, Lawrence, 2008. Fear and loathing in Papua New Guinea: sexual health in a nation under siege. In *Making Sense of AIDS: Culture, Sexuality and Power in Melanesia*, ed. Leslie Butt and Richard Eves, 60–79. Honolulu: University of Hawai'i Press.

-------- 2010. *Sin, Sex and Stigma: A Pacific Response to HIV/AIDS*. Wantage, UK: Sean Kingston Publishing.

Herdt, Gilbert, 1981. *Guardians of the Flutes: Idioms of Masculinity*. New York: McGraw Hill.

Herdt, Gilbert, ed., 1982. *Rituals of Manhood: Male Initiation in Papua New Guinea*. Berkeley: University of California Press.

Herdt, Gilbert and Fitz John Porter Poole, 1982. 'Sexual antagonism': the intellectual history of a concept in New Guinea anthropology. In *Sexual Antagonism, Gender, and Social Change in Papua New Guinea*, ed. Fitz John Porter Poole and Gilbert Herdt. Special issue of *Social Analysis* 12: 3–28.

Hermkens, Anna-Karina, 2007. The power of Mary in Papua New Guinea. *Anthropology Today* 23(2): 4–8.

-------- 2008. Josephine's journey: gender-based violence and Marian devotion in urban Papua New Guinea. *Oceania* 78(2): 151–67.

Hilsdon, Anne-Marie, Martha Macintyre, Vera Mackie and Maila Stivens, eds, 2000. *Human Rights and Gender Politics: Asia-Pacific Perspectives*. London and New York: Routledge.

Human Rights Watch (Coursen-Neff, Zama), 2005. Making their own rules: police beatings, rape and torture of children in Papua New Guinea. *Human Rights Watch* (30 August). Online: http://www.hrw.org/en/reports/2005/08/30/making-their-own-rules-0. Accessed 7 February 2011.

Jolly, Margaret, 1992a. Partible persons and multiple authors (contribution to Book Review Forum on Marilyn Strathern's *The Gender of the Gift*). *Pacific Studies* 15(1): 137–49.

-------- 1992b. Specters of inauthenticity. *The Contemporary Pacific* 4(1): 49–72.

-------- 1994. *Women of the Place:* Kastom, *Colonialism and Gender in Vanuatu*. Chur and Reading: Harwood Academic Publishers.

-------- 1998. Introduction: colonial and postcolonial plots in histories of maternities and modernities. In *Maternities and Modernities: Colonial and Postcolonial Experiences in Asia and the Pacific*, ed. Kalpana Ram and Margaret Jolly, 1–25. Cambridge: Cambridge University Press.

-------- 2000a. Epilogue: further reflections on violence in Melanesia. In *Reflections on Violence in Melanesia*, ed. Sinclair Dinnen and Allison Ley, 305–24. Sydney: Hawkins Press and Asia Pacific Press.

-------- 2000b (2006). *Woman Ikat Raet Long Human Raet O No?* Women's rights, human rights and domestic violence in Vanuatu. In *Human Rights and Gender Politics: Asia-Pacific Perspectives*, ed. Anne-Marie Hilsdon, Martha Macintyre, Vera Mackie and Maila Stivens, 124–46. London and New York: Routledge. Updated and expanded version of article first published in *Feminist Review* 52: 169–90 (1996).

-------- 2001a. Damming the rivers of milk? Fertility, sexuality, and modernity in Melanesia and Amazonia. In *Gender in Amazonia and Melanesia: An Exploration of the Comparative Method*, ed. Tom Gregor and Donald Tuzin, 175–206. Berkeley: University of California Press.

-------- 2001b. Infertile states: person and collectivity, region and nation in the rhetoric of Pacific population. In *Borders of Being: Citizenship, Fertility, and Sexuality in Asia and the Pacific*, ed. Margaret Jolly and Kalpana Ram, 262–306. Ann Arbor: University of Michigan Press.

-------- 2003a. Epilogue – some thoughts on restorative justice and gender. In *A Kind of Mending: Restorative Justice in the Pacific Islands,* ed. Sinclair Dinnen, 265–74. Canberra: Pandanus Books.

-------- 2003b Epilogue. In *Women's Groups and Everyday Modernity in Melanesia*, ed. Bronwen Douglas, 134–47. Special issue of *Oceania* 74(1&2).

-------- 2005. Beyond the horizon? Nationalisms, feminisms, and globalization in the Pacific. In *Outside Gods: History Making in the Pacific*, ed. Martha Kaplan. Special issue of *Ethnohistory* 52(1): 137–66.

-------- 2011. Flying with two wings?: Justice and gender in Vanuatu. Review article of Miranda Forsyth *A Bird that Flies with Two Wings:* Kastom *and State Justice Systems in Vanuatu.* ANU E Press, 2009. In *The Asia Pacific Journal of Anthropology* 12(2): 195–201.

Jolly, Margaret, ed., 2008. *Re-membering Oceanic Masculinities.* Special issue of *The Contemporary Pacific* 20(1).

Josephides, Lisette, 1985. *The Production of Inequality: Gender and Exchange among the Kewa.* London and New York: Tavistock.

Kilby, Patrick, 2010. *NGOs in India. The Challenges of Women's Empowerment and Accountability.* Milton Park and New York: Routledge.

Knauft, Bruce, 1997. Gender identity, political economy and modernity in Melanesia and Amazonia. *Journal of the Royal Anthropological Institute* 3(2): 233–59.

-------- 1999. *From Primitive to Postcolonial in Melanesia and Anthropology.* Ann Arbor, Michigan: the University of Michigan Press.

Lahiri-Dutt, Kuntala and Martha Macintyre, eds, 2006. *Women Miners in Developing Countries.* Burlington VT: Ashgate Publishing Company.

Langness, Lewis L., 1967. Sexual antagonism in the New Guinea Highlands. A Bena Bena example. *Oceania* 37: 161–77.

-------- 1999. *Men and 'Woman' in Papua New Guinea.* Novato, California: Chandler and Sharo.

Lepani, Katherine, 2007. *Sovasova* and the problem of sameness. Converging interpretive frameworks for making sense of HIV and AIDS in the Trobriand Islands. In *HIV/AIDS in Rural Papua New Guinea*, ed. Alison Dundon and Charles Wilde. Special issue of *Oceania* 77(1): 12–28.

-------- 2008a. Mobility, violence and the gendering of HIV in Papua New Guinea. In *Changing Pacific Masculinities*, ed. John P. Taylor. Special issue of *The Australian Journal of Anthropology* 19(2): 150–64.

-------- 2008b. In the process of knowing: Making sense of HIV and AIDS in the Trobriand Islands of Papua New Guinea. PhD thesis Anthropology. Canberra: The Australian National University.

-------- 2008c. Fitting condoms on culture. Rethinking approaches to HIV prevention in the Trobriand Islands of Papua New Guinea. In *Making Sense of AIDS: Culture, Sexuality and Power in Melanesia*, ed. Leslie Butt and Richard Eves, 246–66. Honolulu: University of Hawai'i Press.

-------- 2010. 'Steady with custom': mediating HIV prevention in the Trobriand Islands, Papua New Guinea. In *Plagues and Epidemics: Infected Spaces Past and Present*, ed. D. Ann Herring and Alan C. Swedlund, 305–22. Wenner-Gren Foundation Monograph Series. Oxford: Berg Publishers.

-------- 2012. *Islands of Love/Islands of Risk: Culture and HIV in the Trobriands*. Nashville: Vanderbilt University Press.

LiPuma, Edward, 1998. Modernity and forms of personhood in Melanesia. In *Bodies and Persons: Comparative Perspectives from Africa and Melanesia*, ed. M. Lambek and Andrew Strathern, 53–79. Cambridge: Cambridge University Press.

Lloyd, Genevieve, 1984. *The Man of Reason: 'Male' and 'Female' in Western Philosophy*. London: Methuen.

Macintyre, Martha, 1987. Flying witches and leaping warriors: supernatural origins of power and matrilineal authority in Tubetube Society. In *Dealing with Inequality: Analysing Gender Relations in Melanesia and Beyond*, ed. Marilyn Strathern, 207–28. Cambridge: Cambridge University Press.

-------- 1995. Violent bodies and vicious exchanges: objectification and personification in the Massim. In *Bodies, Selves, Emotions*. Special issue of *Social Analysis* 37: 29–43.

-------- 1998. The persistence of inequality: Women in Papua New Guinea since independence. In *Modern Papua New Guinea*, ed. Laura Zimmer-Tamakoshi, 211–31. Missouri: Thomas Jefferson University Press.

-------- 2000. 'Hear us, women of Papua New Guinea': Melanesian women and human rights. In *Human Rights and Gender Politics: Perspectives in the Asia-Pacific Region*, ed. Anne-Marie Hilsdon, Martha Macintyre, Vera Mackie and Maila Stivens, 147–71. London and New York: Routledge.

-------- 2002. Women and mining projects in Papua New Guinea: problems of consultation, representation and women's rights. In *Tunnel Vision: Women, Mining and Communities*, ed. Ingrid MacDonald and Claire Rowland, 26–29. Melbourne: Oxfam–Community Aid Abroad.

-------- 2003. Petztorme women: responding to change in Lihir, Papua New Guinea. *Oceania* 74 (1-2): 120–33.

-------- 2006. Indicators of violence against women. *Development Bulletin* 71: 61–3.

-------- 2008. Police and thieves, gunmen and drunks: problems with men and problems with society in Papua New Guinea. In *Changing Pacific Masculinities*, ed. John P. Taylor. Special issue of *The Australian Journal of Anthropology* 19(2): 179–93.

McDougall, Debra, 2003. Fellowship and citizenship as models of national community: United Church Women's Fellowship in Rannonga, Solomon Islands. In *Women's Groups and Everyday Modernity in Melanesia*, ed. Bronwen Douglas. Special issue of *Oceania* 74(1–2): 61–80.

McPherson, Naomi, 2008. *SikAIDS*: deconstructing the awareness campaign in rural West New Britain, Papua New Guinea. In *Making Sense of AIDS: Culture, Sexuality and Power in Melanesia*, ed. Leslie Butt and Richard Eves, 328–54. Honolulu: University of Hawai'i Press.

Meggitt, Mervyn, 1989. Women in contemporary Central Enga society. In *Family and Gender in the Pacific: Domestic Contradictions and the Colonial Impact*, ed. Margaret Jolly and Martha Macintyre, 135–55. Cambridge: Cambridge University Press. Digital reprint 2010.

Merry, Sally Engle, 2006. *Human Rights and Gender Violence: Translating International Law into Local Justice*. Chicago and London: University of Chicago Press.

-------- 2009. *Gender Violence: A Cultural Perspective*. Introductions to Engaged Anthropology Series 1. Chichester, UK: Wiley-Blackwell.

Mosko, Mark, 2010a. Partible penitents: dividual personhood and Christian practice in Melanesia and the West. *Journal of the Royal Anthropological Institute* 15(2): 215–40.

-------- 2010b. Partible penitents: a response to comments. *Journal of the Royal Anthropological Institute* 16(2): 253–59.

Patterson, Mary, 2001. Breaking the stones: ritual, gender and modernity in North Ambrym, Vanuatu. In *Anthropological Forum* 11(1): 39–54.

Ram, Kalpana and Margaret Jolly, eds, 1998. *Maternities and Modernities: Colonial and Postcolonial Experiences in Asia and the Pacific*. Cambridge: Cambridge University Press.

Read, Kenneth, 1982. Male-female relationships among the Gahuku-Gama: 1950 and 1981. In *Sexual Antagonism, Gender, and Social Change in Papua New Guinea*, ed. Fitz John Porter Poole and Gilbert H. Herdt, 66–78. Special issue of *Social Analysis* 12.

Reed, Adam, 1997. Contested images and common strategies: early colonial sexual politics in the Massim. In *Sites of Desire, Economies of Pleasure: Sexualities in Asia and the Pacific*, ed. Lenore Manderson and Margaret Jolly, 48–71. Chicago: Chicago University Press.

Reid, Elizabeth, 2010a. Reading as a woman: understanding generalised HIV epidemics. *South Pacific Journal of Philosophy and Culture* 10: 35–58.

-------- 2010b. Putting values into practice in PNG: the Poro Sapot Project and aid effectiveness. In *Pacificurrents. E Journal of the Australian Association for the Advancement of Pacific Studies (AAAP)*, 1.2 and 2.1 (April 2010). Online: http://intersections.anu.edu.au/pacificurrents/reid.htm. Accessed 21 February 2012.

-------- 2010c. Rethinking human rights and the HIV epidemic: a reflection on power and goodness. In *Civic Insecurity: Law, Order and HIV in Papua New Guinea*, ed. Vicki Luker and Sinclair Dinnen, Canberra: ANU E Press. Online: http://epress.anu.edu.au?p=94091. Accessed 21 February 2012.

-------- 2010d. Ela's Question. In *Civil Insecurity: Law, Order and HIV in Papua New Guinea*, ed. Vicki Luker and Sinclair Dinnen. Canberra: ANU E Press. Online: http://epress.anu.edu.au?p=94091. Accessed 1 March 2012.

-------- 2010e. Developing good HIV practices in PNG: the Serendipity Educational Endowment Fund (SEEF). *HIV Australia* 8(2): 24–27. Also online: http://www.afao.org.au/library/hiv-australia/volume-8/hiv-and-png/serendipity-educational-endowment-fund. Accessed 1 March 2012.

Robbins, Joel, 2004. *Becoming Sinners: Christianity and Moral Torment in a Papua New Guinea Society*. Berkeley: University of California Press.

-------- 2005. The humiliation of sin: Christianity and the modernization of the subject among the Urapmin. In *The Making of Global and Local Modernities in Melanesia: Humiliation, Transformation and the Nature of Cultural Change*, ed. Joel Robbins and Holly Wardlow, 43–56. Hampshire, Burlington: Ashgate Publishing.

-------- 2010. Melanesia, Christianity, and cultural change: a comment on Mosko's 'Partible penitents'. *Journal of the Royal Anthropological Institute* 16(2): 241–43.

Rumsey, Alan, 2000. Women as peacemakers: a case from the Nebilyer Valley, Western Highlands, Papua New Guinea. In *Reflections on Violence in Melanesia*, ed. Sinclair Dinnen and Allison Ley, 139–55. Sydney: Hawkins Press and Asia Pacific Press.

Saovana-Spriggs, Ruth, 2008. Gender and peace: Bougainvillean women, matriliny and the peace process. PhD thesis Politics. Canberra: The Australian National University.

Sen, Amartya, 1990. More than 100 million women are missing. *New York Review of Books*, December 1990.

Spark, Ceridwen, 2011. Gender trouble in town: educated women eluding male domination, gender violence and marriage in PNG. *The Asia Pacific Journal of Anthropology* 12(2): 164–79.

Stewart Christine, 2008. Men behaving badly: sodomy cases in the colonial courts of Papua New Guinea. *The Journal of Pacific History* 43(1): 77–93.

———— 2010. The courts, the churches, the witches and their killers. Paper presented at Conference Law and Culture: Meaningful Legal Pluralism in the Pacific and Beyond. USP School of Law, Port Vila, Vanuatu, 30 Aug–1 Sep 2010.

———— 2011. *Pamuk na Poofta*: criminalising consensual sex in Papua New Guinea. PhD thesis. Canberra: The Australian National University.

Strathern, Marilyn, 1972. *Women in Between. Female Roles in a Male World*. Mount Hagen, New Guinea. London and New York: Seminar Press.

———— 1988. *The Gender of the Gift: Problems with Women and Problems with Society in Melanesia*. Studies in Melanesian Anthropology, No. 6. Berkeley and Los Angeles: University of California Press.

———— 2000. *Audit Cultures: Anthropological Studies in Accountability, Ethics and the Academy*. London and New York: Routledge.

Taylor, John P., ed., 2008a. *Changing Pacific Masculinities*. Special issue of *The Australian Journal of Anthropology* 19(2).

———— 2008b. The social life of rights: 'gender antagonism', modernity and *raet* in Vanuatu. In *Changing Pacific Masculinities*, ed. John P. Taylor. Special issue of *The Australian Journal of Anthropology* 19(2): 165–78.

Théry, Irène, 2008. Pour une anthropologie comparative de la distinction de sexe. In *Ce Que Le Genre Fait Aux Personnes*, ed. Irène Théry and Pascale Bonnemère, 15–43. Paris: Éditions de L'École des Hautes Études en Sciences Sociales.

Toft, Susan, ed., 1985. *Domestic Violence in Papua New Guinea*. Monograph No. 3. Law Reform Commission, Papua New Guinea.

-------- 1986. *Domestic Violence in Urban Papua New Guinea*. Occasional Paper, No. 19. Law Reform Commission, Papua New Guinea.

Toft, Susan and Susanne Bonnell, 1985. *Marriage and Domestic Violence in Rural Papua New Guinea: Results of a Research Project Conducted by the Law Reform Commission and Administrative College of Papua New Guinea*. Port Moresby: Papua New Guinea Law Reform Commission.

Tuzin, Donald, 1997. *The Cassowary's Revenge: The Life and Death of Masculinity in a New Guinea Society*. Chicago and London: University of Chicago Press.

Wardlow, Holly, 2002. Headless ghosts and roaming women: specters of modernity in Papua New Guinea. *American Ethnologist* 29(1): 5–32.

-------- 2004. Anger, economy and female agency: problematizing 'prostitution' and 'sex work' among the Huli of Papua New Guinea. *Signs* 29: 1017–39.

-------- 2005. Transformations of desire: envy and resentment among the Huli of Papua New Guinea. In *The Making of Global and Local Modernities in Melanesia*, ed. Joel Robbins and Holly Wardlow, 57–72. Aldershot, Hampshire: Ashgate Press.

-------- 2006. *Wayward Women: Sexuality and Agency in a New Guinea Society*. Berkeley: University of California Press.

-------- 2008. 'You have to understand: some of us are glad AIDS has arrived': Christianity and condoms among the Huli. In *Making Sense of AIDS. Culture, Sexuality and Power in Melanesia*, ed. Leslie Butt and Richard Eves, 187–205. Honolulu: University of Hawai'i Press.

Zimmer, Laura J., 1990. Sexual exploitation and male dominance in Papua New Guinea. In *Human Sexuality in Melanesian Cultures*, ed. Joel Ingebrittson, 250–67. *Point*, Series No 14. Goroka, PNG: Melanesian Institute.

Zimmer-Tamakoshi, Laura J., 1993a. Nationalism and sexuality in Papua New Guinea. *Pacific Studies*. 16(4): 61–97.

-------- 1993b. Bachelors, spinsters, and *Pamuk Meris*. In *The Business of Marriage: Transformations in Oceanic Matrimony*, ed. Richard A. Marksbury, 83–104. Pittsburgh and London: University of Pittsburgh Press.

-------- 1997. 'Wild pigs and dog men': rape and domestic violence as 'women's issues' in Papua New Guinea. In *Gender in Cross-Cultural Perspective*, ed. Carolyn Brettel and Caroline Sargent, 538–53. Englewood Cliffs, New Jersey: Prentice-Hall.

Zorn, Jean, 2006. Women and witchcraft: positivist, prelapsarian, and post-modern judicial interpretations in Papua New Guinea. In *Mixed Blessings: Laws, Religions and Women's Rights in the Asia-Pacific Region*, ed. Amanda Whiting and Carolyn Evans, 61–99. Leiden: Martinus Nijhoff Publishers.

-------- 2010. The paradoxes of sexism: proving rape in the Papua New Guinea Courts. *LAWASIA Journal*, 17–58.

1. Black and Blue: Shades of Violence in West New Britain, PNG

Naomi McPherson

Abstract

In this chapter, I am concerned to take up what Galtung argues are the two problems to be dealt with in violence research: 'the use of violence and the legitimation of that use' especially 'those aspects of a culture that serve to justify and legitimize violence' (1990: 291). I begin with a brief discussion of Bariai cosmology to provide background to Bariai concepts of gender and how the enculturation process engenders men, women and children. This is followed by a consideration of violence experienced by women as women, spouses, school girls, and as members of their faith within a changing cosmology manifested most recently by a shift to fundamentalist charismatic Catholicism. My basis for this discussion assumes violence is about power differences and power inequities are a necessary and sufficient condition for violence, and my primary goal is to delineate those aspects of Bariai culture that make 'violence look, even feel right—or at least not wrong' (Galtung 1990: 291).

Introduction

The May 1986 'Seville Statement on Violence' (in Hussey 2003: 355–57) debunks essentialist, biologically reductionist explanations for human violence. In statements that begin 'It is scientifically incorrect' the authors point out that (1) humans have not inherited violent tendencies from our primate ancestors; (2) violent behaviour is not genetically inherited; (3) aggression was not selected for in human evolutionary history; (4) human neurophysiology does not compel us to violence; and, (5) violence is not instinctual in humans. While certainly capable of violence, the notion that violence is a biologically determined and evolutionarily honed human (genetic) trait needs to be vigorously critiqued and ruled out (see McCaughey 2008; also Tracy and Crawford 1992). It has been estimated that 67 per cent of gender violence in Papua New Guinea (PNG) is husbands abusing their wives and that 'men are far more likely to be the perpetrators of violence, regardless of the sex of the victim. Masculinity, thus, has a role in promoting and legitimising the use of violence; in many prevailing models of masculinity, violence is seen as a normal and entirely justified way of resolving conflict or expressing anger' (Eves 2006: 15). But we cannot argue that males perpetrate violence against females because they are biologically bigger and stronger, or because they are hormonally predisposed to be aggressive. To accept this is to accept the worst form of biological reductionism and gender essentialism, and leaves no options for change (except perhaps through genetic manipulation). We need to consider that violence is not a human genetic trait, that it may very well be a cultural trait, learned, practised, and integral to cultural concepts of gender. My objective in this chapter is to explore how violence is engendered and embodied in a West New Britain society.

For decades, anthropologists have documented male socialisation and cultural concepts of masculinity as an essential part of the 'rituals of manhood' in many Papua New Guinea societies (Herdt 1982; Gewertz and Errington 1991: 58–100; Tuzin 1997; Zimmer-Tamakoshi 2001). Generally, in these male initiation rites, boys are taught cultural concepts of male privilege, superiority, and dominance over women and youth. The rites themselves more often than not include some form of physical violence (e.g., thrashing, deprivations, cicatrisation, cane swallowing, abrasion with stinging nettles) inflicted by adult kinsmen on boys to eliminate female essences from their bodies in order to re-create (rebirth) those boys as strong men and members of their kin groups. During male initiation rituals, John Fitz Porter Poole reports that Bimin-Kuskusmin boys 'are negatively identified with female characteristics ... [and] are physically controlled, harangued and abused with respect to their female substance, food, and behaviour' (1982: 117). Thus, by purging them of female essences, initiation rites 'transform gentle boys into warriors capable of killing rage, stealthy murder, and bravery' (Keesing 1982: 3), men who are taught to fear 'the dangers *to men* which are posed by women's natures' (Hays and Hays 1982: 206).[1] In this way, an aggressive, violent culture of masculinity is literally inscribed on young, male bodies and when this culture of gender is perpetuated within changing social and economic structures, we have, as Laura Zimmer-Tamakoshi puts it, 'troubled masculinities' and increased violence (Ch. 2: 58). One aspect of this chapter is to show how children in a PNG society, which does not practise any violent form of male initiation, learn to be violent in their interactions with one another and with adults and how, as boys and girls grow into men and women, violence becomes an embodied aspect of their personality and their gender identity.

---

1   It is interesting to note that Melanesian masculinity is seen as so connected to culture, as in learned not biological; whereas femininity is considered to be an essential feature of female 'nature'. There has been a theoretical disjuncture in discussions of gender in Melanesia which has overlooked how females learn their culturally approved femininity.

Despite recent efforts to theorise a cultural concept of violence (Riches 1986; Krohn-Hansen 1994; Dinnen and Ley 2000; Stewart and Strathern 2002), what constitutes 'violence' is a contested issue. The contributors in Sinclair Dinnen and Allison Ley (2000) speak to the variety and complexity of different types of violence in contemporary Melanesian cultures. There, violence ranges from actual physical violence characteristic of spousal abuse to metaphorical rhetorical violence, for example, when a transnational company talks about 'driving a spear of development into the heart of Irian Jaya' (Banks 2000: 254). My basic premise here is that violence, like gender relations, is always about relations of power, more specifically, 'power over' in the sense of both structural violence, where violence is based on inequality—economic, political, social, religious—and cultural violence where individuals are enculturated to a system of beliefs that hold violence to be legitimate and normal. Thus, violence—whether physical, psychological, verbal, spiritual—is, broadly, acts against another who consequently suffers negatively—pain, disadvantage, fear, disempowerment. In this rendering, colonialism is a form of violence, as is state-induced structural violence, which results in disadvantage, poverty and other forms of harm for people (Galtung 1990; see also Farmer 2004, 2005). My definition of violence also includes spiritual violence (Stewart and Strathern 2002: 89) such as acts or threats of witchcraft (see Gibbs, Ch. 3), sorcery and spirit beings, as well as spiritual violence as a consequence of contemporary Christian beliefs and practices (see Hermkens 2007, 2008 and Ch. 4). Invoking gender violence typically draws the mind to concentrate on domestic violence, usually violence against women perpetrated by men who are usually the women's spouses but sometimes their fathers, brothers, or sons (e.g. see Chowning 1985; Counts 1992; Counts, Brown and Campbell 1992; Hammar 1996; Wardlow 2006). Violence also occurs outside the spousal relationship, perpetrated by women against other women, men against other men, adults against children, and even children against adults, and, as Wardlow (2006: 75) shows so effectively, even forms of negative agency, violence against oneself that usually results in self-harm (see also Counts 1993). However, violence against women by men is the most prevalent form of gendered violence today (Heise 1997: 414). In this paper I focus primarily on spousal violence, grounded in the hegemonies of patriarchal masculinity, and men's physical and emotional violence against women's overburdened bodies, their spirit, self-esteem and quality of life. Women grow up and enter marriage knowing that their words, behaviours and, indeed, their agency could ignite their husbands' anger and result in abuse. Masculine violence finds its outlet on female bodies which are hit, kicked, cut, violently bruised, battered and broken; they are made black and blue.

Taking these shades of violence as given, I want especially to consider how cultural concepts of gender and power imbalance (woman/man; adult/child; young/old) *permit* and *legitimise* violent masculine behaviour toward girls and women, and how these cultural concepts prevent women (and men) from seeing any alternatives to the abuse and disempowerment they live with on a day-to-day basis. Questions arise about how girls and women come not only to expect masculine aggression directed towards them, but also to accept that they must endure that violence; in other words, how does the structure and meaning of gender violence persist and become normalised (see Heise 1997: 424; McCaughey 2008). To help think about these issues, I am adapting Johan Galtung's concept of 'cultural violence' defined as 'those aspects of culture, the symbolic sphere of our existence—exemplified by religion and ideology, language and art, empirical science and formal science … that can be used to justify or legitimize direct or structural violence' (1990: 291). Here I am particularly concerned to take up what Galtung argues are the two problems dealt with in violence research: 'the use of violence and the legitimation of that use' especially, 'those aspects of a culture that serve to justify and legitimize' violence (1990: 291). Clearly, rather than assume an innate or essentialist theory of masculine violence we need to explore the ideological, socio-economic and spiritual ethos that permits and perpetuates violence. Gender relations are relations of 'power over', more specifically, gender asymmetry is a structure of violence, reflected in masculine domination/feminine subordination. My primary goal is to explore those aspects of culture that make structures of 'violence look, even feel *right*—or at least *not wrong*' (Galtung 1990: 291, my emphasis).

My discussion is framed within my ethnographic work over several years with the Bariai, who live in the province of West New Britain, Papua New Guinea. The Bariai are subsistence horticulturalist and fisher folk whose ten villages are spread along the northwest coast of the province. They are sufficiently removed from the centres of urban and peri-urban development that no road finds its way to them, sea transport is sporadic, unreliable, and expensive, and there are no amenities such as power or piped water. Access to the 'bright lights' of modernity only exist in the provincial capital at Kimbe, over two hundred kilometres by sea away and most women and many men don't get there. Over the six occasions from 1981 to my visit in 2009, I have witnessed an entire generation of young people grow up, raise their families and take the place of their elders. All the elders with whom I began my research in 1981 were deceased by 2009. Other changes included a doubling of the population and almost a tripling of population in the village where I normally reside, the demise of the men's secret-sacred ritual house (*lum*) and the presence of a strong charismatic Catholic movement whose leaders are predominantly represented as current village leaders. While I discuss shades of violence within this ethnographic context, it needs to be clearly understood that the Bariai are no more violent than any other social group in PNG; indeed, there is far less violence in Bariai culture and society than in many other cultures in Papua New Guinea.[2] Over the course of working with the Bariai during this time period, I have accumulated a number of examples and explanations of violent events—gendered violence in particular—that, when articulated in one breath, so to speak, may give the impression that the Bariai are a violent people. Nothing could be further from the truth. This discussion is thus situated in a historical and cultural context, and people's understanding of, and participation in, social, cultural and economic change in the globalising world they inhabit.

In terms of a world view that legitimises violence, I begin with a brief excursion into Bariai mythology to explore a primal charter for masculine violence against women. The myth not only locates masculine empowerment and feminine disempowerment in a primal past, thus normalising masculine acts and experiences of violence as a kind of ascending anachronism, but also sets a mythic precedent for a type of spiritual violence against women. I then discuss how mythic charters play out on a day-to-day level in considerations of violence experienced by women because they are female—wives, daughters, schoolgirls—and how violence is taught by adults and learned by children in the guise of creating strong persons who stand up for themselves. Finally, I explore a kind of spiritual violence experienced by women as members of their faith, especially of Catholicism as understood and practised here, that reinvests and reinforces masculine hegemonies: the authority of men, the father as head of household, and masculine sexual privilege. My overarching point is to expand our understanding of engendered violence as a non-reductive, highly complex, structurally situated cultural concept that creates, informs, and condones violent acts against others.

Primal violence in Bariai mythology

Creation myths which set precedents for gender relations are common throughout Melanesian cultures (e.g. Gewertz 1988) and, equally commonly, these myths often depict what Eric Silverman (2001: 104) calls the 'primal theft of sacra' from women by men. This Bariai origin story was immediately offered to me as an 'answer' in response to my question, why women and uninitiated youth and children of both sexes, had to 'run away' from the village in anticipation of the entrance of *Tivuda,* a spirit being. As Bariai understood it,[3] the universe, and

---

2   The Bariai do not practise any physical ritual violence against children beyond ear-piercing (girls) and superincision (boys).

3   I use the past tense purposely as this and other origin narratives are heavily overlaid now by Christian origin narratives, such as Genesis. Which of these creation stories (or a syncretic version of them) were offered as a means to understanding Bariai cosmology depended on to whom I was speaking and the context of that discussion.

all it contains, including humans, was created by Upuda (B: *pu,* origin; *da,* our). Upuda created human beings, one female and one male, carved from a single piece of wood divided into equal halves. The two humans prospered, bearing fifty children and they all lived in a primal men's house (B: *lum*) together with autochthonous spirit beings. And so time and events passed....

> One day, women were chopping firewood from a mangrove tree called *Taltalnga* when a piece of wood flew off making a whirring noise. The surprised women exclaimed, 'Oh, how wonderful!' and made it sing again. Later, they took it back to the village and hid it from the men. One day the women prepared a huge feast of taro pudding. They designated one person, called *Ola* [B: messenger], to send the men from the village so they wouldn't see the Bullroarer [B: *Tibuda*]. When the women were ready to 'pull' the Bullroarer, Ola put on ceremonial finery and sent the men away. While they were gone, Bullroarer entered the village plaza to sing and eat pork and roasted taro with the women. When Bullroarer went back inside the woman's house [B: *luma*], Ola called the men back. And so it was for some time.

> After a while, the women constructed a ceremonial food platform [B: *kabokabo*] and prepared a large feast for the Bullroarer. As before, Ola sent the men away, and during the exodus, an old man tripped, spilled his lime powder and broke his lime spatula. 'What's going on?' he exclaimed angrily. 'These women have us running in all directions while they stay here and do things with their Bullroarer.' The old man conspired against the women. He sent lengths of shell-money attached to pieces of women's grass skirts [a call to battle] to every men's house [B: *lum*]. On the prescribed day, all the men's house groups joined against the women. From the oldest grandmother to the littlest girls, they were all killed. The only females spared were infant girls who still suckled. The men captured the Bullroarer and now no woman knows how to make it sing because the memory was killed. Since that time, the Bullroarer has belonged to men and women flee its fearsome presence.

That women once interacted with powerful autochthonous spirit beings and were displaced by men who stole from the women those artifacts symbolic of that spirit being (the 'primal theft of sacra') is, as we have seen, a common theme in Melanesian creation stories. In this story, all is fine until a senior male falls and breaks the gourd holding his lime powder and spatula for preparing betel nut. The lime powder gourd and spatula are metaphors for female and male genitalia respectively and to tell a man that 'your lime powder has spilled' is to point out that his genitalia are exposed. When an old man falls, spills his lime powder and breaks his spatula (a metaphor for a detumescent penis), his anger at his emasculation knows no bounds as he seeks to avenge his masculine pride by punishing the women. But men do not simply take over; they violently dispossess the women by calling for a true gender war. They send messages to men in other villages who attend a battle whose sole purpose is to murder all females who had any knowledge of the origins of the Bullroarer and its emasculating relationship with men. Female infants at the breast are spared only because they have no capacity for speech, and hence, no way of knowing. These infants grew up to become wives with no memory of the origin of Bullroarer or the gender war; consequently, they were no threat to men's control of the spirit being and its autochthonous primal powers. Now, when the Bullroarer comes to the village, women are excluded on pain of death from seeing or interacting with the Bullroarer. Although all those females who might have remembered this incident were killed, the memory of the women's loss of their primal sacra and interaction with the powers of the cosmos is invoked through this mythic narrative that all women and girls have heard many times during their lives, not least when it was told to this anthropologist. To this day, the Bullroarer is a terrifying and destructive spirit being for all, and is summoned to avenge a wrong committed against a firstborn child.

Interestingly, men are not condemned for their femicide in this myth; indeed, men often exclaim at the barbarism of their ancestors, which they, as the contemporary generation have transcended. The story is a 'social charter' in the Malinowskian sense, which explains why things are the way they are—women must not interact with spirit beings—and should they transgress, they will be killed, thus things should remain the way they are. An ascending anachronism pushes events back into the dim recesses of time thus normalising and naturalising those events which we now call upon to explain why things are the way they are, in this instance, why women run away from the Bullroarer. Ascending anachronisms become a circular logic or tautologies in explaining why things have to be the way they are, because of that normalising process (see Conkey and Williams 1991). Women's exclusion from male sacred powers is upheld until today through threat of death at the hands of that spirit being. When I asked what would happen if women ventured into the men's house and its environs when a spirit being was in residence, both men and women responded that she would be taken into the men's house, gang raped, murdered, unceremoniously buried in the men's house, and her jaw bone would be thrown into the village plaza as a lesson to all other women. No one would be permitted to grieve or bury her, and she would never be spoken of again. This legitimised cultural violence creates fear in women and they learn not to impinge on masculine spaces and activities. Should they transgress, the myth legitimates masculine violence in the form of institutionalised rape, murder, and dismemberment as punishment, a 'teaching moment' to deter other women from similar transgressions. Rather than seeing injustice, women take the men's murderous behaviour as a cautionary tale that they should not involve themselves with spirit beings (and male sacra) since, to do so, is to risk death and/or gang rape for their transgression. This overarching threat of rape and murder in order to keep women in their place—that is out of men's places—fits with Jane Caputi's (1989: 439) definition of rape and sexualised murder as being 'direct expression[s] of sexual politics … ritual enactment[s] of male domination, a form of terror that functions to maintain the status quo.'

This fraught relationship between women and feminine things and spirit beings runs through a number of Bariai stories (McPherson 2008a; 1994). Myths also explain how the distribution of peoples and languages is founded on sexuality and gender violence: long ago, when fifty men's houses still existed, an Aulu spirit being seduced a married woman. Her cuckolded husband was furious and instigated a brutal war between humans and spirit beings. Terrified, people fled and resettled throughout northwest New Britain. This war resulted in severing the relationship between human beings and spirit beings who now inhabit separate domains which intersect only on ritual and ceremonial occasions. In another myth, women laugh and 'play' (a euphemism for sexual intercourse) with spirit beings who are processing sago for the women. Men spied on the women and due to their sexual jealousy, declared that henceforth men would process sago and interact with the spirit beings. But the spirit beings were so offended by the men's jealousy that they removed themselves from the human domain, leaving the hard work of processing sago to the men. Access to the power of the spirit beings and the domain of the sacred—once the privilege of females—is now the prerogative of males. Their possession of the primal sacra and these stories offer precedents and thus justifications for why this is so. The consequence for women is spiritual disempowerment reinforced by fears of masculine violence justified by mythic social charters.

While we might dismiss these stories, these rationalisations of masculine violence against women as mere myth, in reality all women fear for their persons and their lives during the presence of spirit beings. Let me offer some examples. In 1981, a young woman visitor went looking for the women's bush toilet, unintentionally walking into the place where men were preparing for a spirit being. She was grabbed, trussed like a pig, and carried back to the village where men debated for a very tense few hours about what to do (gang rape was favoured over murder). In the end, cooler heads prevailed and her father was made to pay compensation for her transgression, including a tusked pig, to the spirit being resident in the men's house. On another occasion in 1983, when we women, uninitiated youths, and children were called back to the village after the Bullroarer spirit had rampaged through, we discovered that an elderly woman had fallen asleep while peeling sweet potato and stayed behind in her house. The men held a long and stressful discussion among themselves (causing fears and tears among the women) to determine the old woman's fate; all of us, including the old woman herself, feared for her life. In the end, the men decided that she was old, thus on the cusp of the spirit domain herself (death), and no harm should befall her provided she pledged (and she did) not to reveal anything to the excluded group about what she may have seen or heard while the Bullroarer was manifest in the village. In another instance, in 1985, a new men's house was being constructed and the central posts (B: *kadanga aranga*; 'male posts') erected. Women who normally left the village due to the nearness of spirit beings were permitted to remain by senior men of that men's house. While I couldn't believe my ethnographic good fortune, the women were exceptionally uncomfortable: they stayed away from the construction site, refused to look at the work going on there, and found other paths to get to their destinations rather than walk by the site. When construction difficulties plagued the erection of the 'male house posts' (B: *aranga kadanga*), the men concluded that the spirit beings were angry because women had not left the village. Women's fears are thus deeply enculturated and do not go away simply because men lift a restriction that previously, if breached, would have cost women their lives. Moreover, having lifted the restriction, men still blamed women's essential femaleness for failures in the process of their construction.

Violence in the name of the father: Domestic violence

Bariai mythology relates the wresting away from women of their spiritual powers, with a simultaneous minimising of their earthly powers. In a patriarchal, male-dominated society, Bariai women are not only systematically excluded from the spiritual sources of male power (access to spirit beings), but they experience everyday secular gender inequalities in myriad forms. Cultural constructions of gender define the essential 'nature' of woman/the feminine ambiguously. Negatively, women are dangerous, weak-willed, weak-minded, and their bodies are soft and leaky. Women's bodily fluids and their physical presence can negatively affect male enterprises and virility, hence the necessity to keep women away from male places and spaces. On the positive side, women have powers for creation. It is those soft, damp and creative female bodies that bring forth children who are indicative of a man's virile masculinity, exemplars of parental renown, and a source of paternal wealth through their labour and marriages. As a wife, an adult woman's productive labour supplies men with food, pigs and other forms of wealth that men publicly transact to gain socio-economic prestige and political renown (in a system of prestige akin to what has been designated the Bigman system).

Although the female is defined as weak minded, men fear women's knowledge and are suspicious of women's abilities to use contraceptives or abortifacients and condemn these practices. All men are considered fertile by nature and capable of fathering children; no male is thought sterile. Women, too, are considered fertile as part of their inherent nature; thus, a woman who does not become pregnant in a reasonable time after marriage (or does not conceive often enough) faces spousal violence because female sterility is not natural, but rather a consequence of her actions: she must have engaged in adultery or she has utilised contraceptives.[4] Women are deemed by men to be lustful and overly jealous and not in control of their sexuality; thus men need to control it for them. When a wife invariably quarrels with her husband's other wives or mistresses, she is likely to be beaten by her husband *and* her father for not being stoical and accepting of her co-wives, and for disobeying her husband's demands that she accept his decision on polygyny. Women, like children, must be constantly socialised (see Eves 2006: 24), a process that is beaten onto their bodies in order that, among other things, they learn a lesson, do their work, behave properly, and show the proper degree of obedience to their fathers and husbands. Given that much adult violence is perpetrated by men on their wives and daughters, the question arises: Are men monsters? Of course they are not. From birth women and men have learned these cultural constructions of gender and sexuality, gendered role expectations, values and behavioural norms as part of their world view. All children are enculturated to be aggressive towards others; this is not seen as a 'bad' thing, but as a positively acquired trait for developing a strong personality. Small children and infants are encouraged to '*pait em, pait em*' a Tok Pisin (TP) phrase meaning 'hit her' or 'hit him'. Even in infancy, the person holding the child will take the child's arm and make hitting motions towards the other person while laughing, 'hit him, hit her'. Small children, even before they learn to walk or talk, learn to hit other children (and animals), and children of all ages will hit their parents and other adults all of whom think this is 'cute', childish behaviour. During play when children disagree, feel wronged, slighted, or teased, with no encouragement at all, they will aggress the other child(ren) and fight with hands, feet, rocks, sticks or other handy objects (fishing spears, knives). Children of all ages, are struck and/or beaten by their mothers, fathers or elder siblings of either sex for disobeying, skipping school, perceived laziness, eating food they shouldn't have, and other transgressions. Children, male and female, grow up surrounded by aggression and violence and become aggressive adults and, in the case of women, 'learn' how to be the recipient of the violence of others, particularly from their husbands.

---

4   I have written about this in more detail in Scaletta 1986.

Many incidents of abuse came to my attention over the years as women (but only one man) came to me for first-aid for their wounds, some of which are related below.

Some scenarios of spousal violence

Case 1. (1982) A young man arrived at my house with a long, deep gash on the back of his calf muscle. As I cleaned and dressed the wound, I asked what happened. He told me it was an accident; he had slipped off his house ladder and gashed his leg on a piece of corrugated metal roofing. After he left, the women sitting with me burst out laughing and told me that, in reality, he and his wife had quarrelled and his angry wife, tired of him accusing her of infidelity, attacked him with her bush knife.

Case 2. (1983) A young couple was having ongoing marital arguments and physical fights. The husband was often away for weeks at a time in the provincial capital and when he returned to the village they argued and each accused the other of infidelity. The wife came to me with a deep gash on her head where her husband had hit her with a heavy metal spoon. Not long after this incident, the wife attempted suicide by drinking bleach; in great pain and near death she was taken to the local clinic some fifty kilometres away. She did recover, but eventually left the marriage.

Case 3. (1983) A newly married woman from another village asked me to dress a very nasty cut on her shoulder delivered by her husband as he whipped her with his bush knife. The issue was her seeming inability to become pregnant, despite being married for several months. This marriage broke beyond repair, as eventually the woman went back to her family to escape ongoing beatings.

In these three examples, sexual jealousy plays a large role in spousal relations and abusive behaviour, as does male sexual privilege and any challenges to it. But it is not just women who are jealous. The man above lied to me to cover his shame and embarrassment that his wife had attacked him in response to his constant harangue charging her with infidelity while he was away. The women who witnessed this interaction told me that when provoked by men, women grab a stick, piece of firewood, canoe paddle as a weapon for hitting their husbands. Using a 'weapon' is culturally unacceptable for men when beating their wives; it is acceptable for women because they are perceived to be at a disadvantage in size and strength. Women don't always succeed in hitting their spouses, but when they do, the reaction is laughter from others rather than condemnation. Men's jealousy, even insecurity about their wives' feelings for them, is expressed in physical lashing out, both to defend their masculinity—they won't be cuckolded—and, presumably, with the intention of instilling in their wives proper spousal behaviour, such as ignoring his adultery, having sex on demand, or not accessing contraceptives since limiting numbers of children limits masculine virility. Women can leave their marriage, especially if there are no children or her bride wealth has not been received, and a man may throw out a lazy or adulterous wife. For some abused women, the only recourse seems to be a form of 'negative agency' (Wardlow 2006) manifested as self-destructive violence in the form of suicide (see Counts 1993; Scaletta 1986). The most dangerous 'ghost' for a man is that of his wife who committed suicide or died in childbirth as a consequence of spousal abuse.

Case 4. (1985) After a visit to another village, I returned to find a close kinswoman with a black eye, swollen face and bandaged forehead. I was told that her husband was annoyed with her constant 'nagging' at him to do some work to repair garden fences and to fix the roof of the house before the monsoon rains came. He silenced her complaints by hitting her several times with his fists. This was very unusual behaviour for these two people; retrospectively, this was the beginning of the end of their thirty plus years of marriage.

Case 5. (2003) A young mother who had been severely beaten the night before came to me for first-aid and told me her story. While she was napping in the afternoon, her husband took her string bag (TP: *bilum*) to bring back pumpkins from their garden. When he returned, she flew into a rage at him for taking her only and thus her best string bag. He responded to her angry tirade by giving her a black eye as well as several cuts on her back where he hit her with his machete. Most of the cuts were minor, but one was long and quite deep and should have been stitched had medical care other than my first-aid been available.

Case 6. (2003) Next day, while changing the bandages for the woman in case 5 above, another injured woman arrived. Her husband had beaten her the evening before with an axe handle. Her scalp was swollen in two spots around a deep gash and she was bruised and swollen on her back and on her forearm, which she had raised to fend off the blows. She told me what led up to the event. She was returning from the garden with a fully loaded string bag hanging down her back from the strap on her forehead, a basket with a load of tubers balanced on her head, and a child too young to walk on her hip. She slipped and fell, spilling everything; inadvertently, the child was hit by spilled sweet potatoes. Shaken and tired, she arrived home and began to prepare the evening meal. The baby cried and woke its father who ordered his wife to quiet the child. Her husband demanded a fork, and the wife told him to get it himself. But their firstborn daughter handed her father the fork. The mother then hit the girl, knocking her down, for indulging the father. The husband then attacked his wife for not bringing him his fork, for not quieting the infant who was crying due to being hurt by falling sweet potatoes (i.e. it was the wife's fault), and for hitting the daughter.

In these examples women were beaten because they were verbally aggressive, nagged or disobeyed their husbands. I had witnessed the wifely scolding in case 4 many times before, but they had never resorted to violence. After this event, the wife simply stopped being a wife. She stopped speaking to him. She served his food last, often flinging it in the direction where he was sitting or setting it where he had to get up and fetch it. Eventually she stopped feeding him at all, so the husband turned to his daughters-in-law and to me for food and when his wife refused to share a house with him, he moved into his son's house. From the moment of their fight and over several years, I watched this marriage of thirty years or more with six adult children fall apart. She did not attend his funeral some years later and in 2009, when we looked at pictures where he was included, she showed no emotion at all or simply walked away.

Everyone remarked on the young woman in case 5 who had had her second child within eleven months of her first, necessitating the weaning of the firstborn. With two infants on her hands, and not much sympathy from other women, she did not go to her gardens very often. The village in general was fed up with her firstborn who flew into temper tantrums, was in constant distress, and cried day and night. The mother was blamed for the child's behaviour because *she* was too lustful and 'worried' (i.e. concerned) about sex; thus, she breached the postpartum taboo on sexual intercourse while breast feeding. She became pregnant too soon thus necessitating early weaning of the firstborn, whose behaviour was later attributed to the affect of breast milk contaminated by sperm. This is an interesting illustration of how married women are responsible for policing their own *and* their husband's sexual desires during postpartum, since men are considered incapable of controlling their own sexual urges. Both the blame for the child's behaviour and the fault for the woman's problematic second pregnancy were acknowledged to be *her* inability to control her sexuality, and no one said that he shouldn't have had sex with her. While people said the husband should not have beaten her so badly, they did say that she 'deserved it' for being so unreasonable about a string bag. After all, pumpkins are not dirty like sweet potatoes.

The woman in example 6 is tired, carrying a very heavy load, bruised from a fall, harassed by a crying child, stressed by her late return as she rushed to collect water and prepare a meal in the dark. Her husband had apparently been in the village all day. In this example, the husband struck out at his wife when she challenged his lazy behaviour with an aggressive raised voice, nagging, and refusal to comply. Husbands are deemed justified in beating their wives for such angry outbursts of disrespect. As I tried to patch her up, she pointed out to me (rather gleefully, actually) that because of her badly injured arm and head, she was unable to carry food and water or prepare meals. But her husband was not inconvenienced as their ten-year-old daughter, who had witnessed the entire altercation, took on her mother's daily chores—laundry, minding the baby, collecting water and food, cooking—and obeying her father. In this way, gender roles and rules, gendered inequalities and inequities are transmitted to the next generation of women as the enculturation process engenders both girl and boy children.

Case 7. (2005) During my usual census taking, I met a girl of seventeen who was the unmarried mother of a six-month-old daughter. She was living with her mother and I discovered the girl's pregnancy was a consequence of rape. The girl had been living with her 'uncle' (a patrilineal kinsman) in another village so she would be closer to her school. The uncle pressured her for sex and forced her into an affair with him. When she became pregnant and informed her family, her furious elder brother set upon the 'uncle' and beat him very badly and then he beat his pregnant sister so severely, her mother said, that she was unable to walk for days. The 'uncle' was summoned to local court where on arrival he was again set upon and given a severe beating. He managed to get away; the court case was dropped because the local magistrate felt the man had been punished enough. The uncle moved to the mainland to avoid any further attacks. On my next visit to the village, the girl and her child had been sent to a relative in town where she would be nanny and housekeeper while her 'aunt' worked.

Case 8. (2009) I followed up on a story I had heard about on my previous trip. A youth with a reputation for causing trouble locally forced his patrilateral cross-cousin (a taboo, incestuous relationship) into having sexual intercourse; he raped her. He threatened that if she told anyone he would 'cut' her. Initially formed under duress and threat the relationship developed to the point where the girl began to enjoy her sexual relationship with her cousin. A kinswoman had seen the youth sneaking into and out of the girl's sleeping area and reported to the girl's father who decided to keep quiet to avoid gossip and trouble from kinspeople. They tried to keep the two apart; but, despite this, the youth continued to stalk the girl who under duress again gave in to his demands. She became pregnant and when she told her family, they decided on a bush-medicine abortion. But nothing stays quiet in a village; indeed, the girl herself told other girls the 'secret' of her affair and abortion. Her father's agnates heard and turned up to beat the girl severely. During another altercation on this issue, a man lost a finger to an attacker's bush knife, and the girl was again beaten very badly. During my fieldwork in 2009, the youth was in and around the village and walked by my house each day en route to school; the girl and her child were living far away to protect her from her kin (and presumably from her cousin). She was not in school.

In these two instances, young girls were forced into sexual intercourse by older men or by their peers with threats to their personal safety. While men may be beaten by the women's kinsmen when they find out, the ultimate blame and punishment is worn by the girls. Females are perceived to be lustful and unless women are controlled, their sexuality can wreak havoc and seduce men causing their downfall. Men on the other hand are perceived as always susceptible to the power of female sexuality, indeed they are powerless before it and, once excited are deemed unable to control their arousal which must be consummated even if that means rape, that is, *ikado arala* ('sexual intercourse') without the woman's consent. This was made clear to me in a discussion of the famed 'pocket trousers' which almost all village women now wear (usually under a sarong, see also Gibbs, Ch. 3).[5] Because these knee-length pants have wide legs, if women sit improperly men might see up the trouser legs to the genital area; or, when toileting, women remove the trousers entirely, thus exposing themselves. Glimpses of forbidden bodies, a senior woman told me, inflames a man's desire to see more and to have sex. His desire will be ignited each time he sees the woman in passing and he might stalk her and rape her when he gets an opportunity. My female friend argued that these trousers were a main *cause* of rape and young women should not wear them. She bluntly noted that without question, men are unable (or are not expected) to control their sexual arousal which, once excited, must be consummated, if not at the moment, then whenever the opportunity arises.

The above examples all suggest a kind of impunity that surrounds men's recourse to physical or sexual violence against women that is inscribed in mythologies, taught from early life lessons, and lived routinely in women's experiences. In the Bullroarer myth, the slaughter of women for behaviour men perceived as emasculating continues to be 'not wrong' because a woman who transgresses masculine prerogative 'deserves' her punishment. This shows up time and again in situations where women who express their thoughts, nag, disobey or otherwise offend their husbands or fathers are 'deserving' of masculine abuses because their behaviour drove him to it; thus, it is his duty to 'teach her a lesson.' Similarly, when women are sexually attacked, it is her sexuality that caused her to be raped, not the rapist's inability to regulate his own sexuality (see also Zorn Ch. 5 and Hukula Ch. 6).

Violence in the name of our father

Missionisation is a form of structural violence built on an ethnocentric perception of the inferiority of the missionised peoples' culture, society and

---

5   Apparently, the number of pockets on the pocket pants is not the issue with this garment at all.

indigenous spirituality. Missionisation has had dramatic effects on women (Jolly 2000: 307), and Catholic or Protestant, the Christian message and Biblical teaching 'legitimized forms of domestic violence, the corporal discipline of husbands over wives and of parents over children, performed not in the name of indigenous hierarchy but Christian love' (2000: 308). Catholicism has reinforced Bariai gender constructs and their indigenous patriarchal ideology of masculine authority and privilege, women's inferior status in society and the household, and women's primary role as wife, child bearer and labourer. While women do not endure exclusion from participating in Christian beliefs and rituals, they are constantly being asked to sacrifice themselves in the name of the Father, in the name of marital and familial peace, and for the sake of their souls (see Hermkens 2007, 2008 and Ch. 4). Bariai men (and some women) have taken Catholic teachings against birth control as further evidence that women interfere with the reproductive process at their peril; not only will their husbands beat them, but now they will also spend eternity in Hell. Catholicism has reinforced Bariai patriarchal authority and obedience, the concept of female lust and original sin, and masculine pro-natalism.

During 1982, when the local health nurse came to discuss family planning with the women, the local catechist, whom I will refer to as Geri, warned all women, in a public moot, that they need not attend the nurse's discussion because contraception was against the laws of the Pope. Only three women and I attended the meeting. Geri later stopped by to chat with me about the church's position on family planning. He explained to me, that the church forbade birth control, which he interpreted as murder, on the premise that Papa God gave women the ability to create life and thus interference with this process through contraception and/or abortion is murder. He lectured me that the purpose of marriage is to beget children and to increase the population (i.e. be fertile and multiply).

This seemed to coincide with other discussions I was having with Bariai men who expressed concern about their lack of 'development,' which they saw as a consequence of not receiving government attention and assistance for development projects because their population (about 1000 at the time) was too small to warrant government support. A burgeoning population, they believed, would hasten government assistance with economic development. Family planning was thus a way to 'keep the people down' by encouraging them to break the law of God (and be punished for their sins) and by diminishing the population (and be punished by a lack of development projects and access to modernity). According to Geri, the church position on birth control[6] might be reconsidered only if (1) a woman is sick and unable to have children without

6   This has also carried over into the non-use of condoms as protection against STIs or HIV (see McPherson 2008b).

risking her own life; (2) a couple already has more than ten children and are worried about being able to provide for them; or (3) one or the other parent does not provide well for the family. In these instances, the couple must first present their case to the lay catechist (Geri) who might/might not agree that they have a case to take to the parish priest. If the request for family planning is approved by the parish priest, wife and husband must both attend the clinic to receive contraceptives. Since the 'husband is head of family', a woman cannot access birth control without his consent and thus without his presence there. A woman who secretly practised birth control was disobeying her husband, committing a sin against the church, and impeding government development projects for everyone. She was also accused of 'shutting herself down' so she could indulge her sexuality with any number of men and not suffer the telltale consequences of unwanted pregnancy. A woman who might secretly access birth control, or even if she has not will—after a reasonable time of non-conception—be beaten for her efforts (see above and Scaletta 1986).

During fieldwork over the past ten years, married women have told me that if they refuse sex or practise birth control, their husbands will abandon them or take a second wife. If a husband leaves for another woman, it is perceived to be the wife's fault for somehow driving him away. To be left a single parent with even one child, let alone five or six, condemns the woman to a life of exceptionally hard work, dependence on others, and an overriding sense of shame and failure. Thus, some women fret with jealousy when their husbands are away in the bush or visiting another village or town, fearing that they may find another woman/wife. Men for their part complain about their wives' jealousies, and some tend to stay close to home and their wife in order to avoid quarrels about their fidelity. This combination of masculine sexual privilege, a wife's 'duty' to have sex with her husband on demand, sexual jealousy, threats of violence and abandonment and no contraception make for frequent marital sex, many babies, and may account for the burgeoning practice (condemned by the church) of polygyny among young men in the village.

Sexual jealousies: The perils of polygyny and many babies

Case 9. (2009) A young couple with a three-month-old child were constantly fighting because of their sexual jealousies. The woman left her husband (went home to her mother) and the husband left the village for several weeks. He returned with a new wife from a neighbouring culture/linguistic group who did not know that he already had a wife and child. His first wife attacked and thrashed the second wife, kicking and screaming and accusing her of seducing her husband away. The second wife had been living with the man as her husband for weeks and would be ashamed to return home having been 'used' in this way. So she stayed. There were two more altercations between the two women and quarrels between the woman and her husband. The first wife left to stay with her mother at the far end of the village. But her father exerted his authority and berated her for her unruly behaviour, told her to go back to her husband and live with him and his new wife. If she didn't he, that is her father, would beat her into wifely submission. The first wife fled to another village, frightened of her father and his threat to beat her, but was too stubborn to accept a polygamous marriage. She stayed away for some weeks and when she came back, she tried to live with her husband and his second wife in the same house and the same bed.

The dual pressures on women to provide sex on demand from husbands (or lovers) and admonishments from the church that sex is only for the purpose of having babies have increased the number of births per woman. Up to about 1985, women observed a postpartum taboo on sexual intercourse for the period the child is breast fed (up to three years or more, see example 5 above). Bariai conceptualise the female body to include a 'tube' that connects breasts with womb. Thus semen entering her vagina would travel along the 'tube' to contaminate her breast milk and the nursing child would become ill and possibly die from respiratory problems. My censuses and genealogies, now going back ten generations, show that to 1985, this postpartum taboo contributed to an average birth spacing per woman of one child every four years.

Sometime in the 1990s, Catholicism really took hold and, encouraged by their husbands, women stopped observing the postpartum taboo on the basis that western medicines, such as antibiotics and rehydration kits, could cure any childhood illness (especially respiratory problems, diarrhoea) caused by semen in mother's milk. My censuses in 2003, 2005 and 2009 showed an astonishing increase in births and decrease in birth spacing as women averaged two births in three years, or even, as in the case cited above, two children in eleven months. This did not go unnoticed by senior women who were grandmothers who remarked to me that in their mother's day, nobody had such large families of children; rather they had two or three children per family.[7] These older women pointed to how young women's daily work had increased to breaking point. As women are now averaging larger families of six to ten children and often have both toddlers and an infant to care for at the same time, they need to create more and larger gardens to cultivate more food. They also needed to go to the gardens more frequently to harvest because they couldn't carry much more than one day's food. They also used more water and thus had to haul

---

7   It should be noted that there is a difference between the number of pregnancies a woman has and the number of living children she has. From what I can tell from colonial reports, the infant mortality rate in Bariai was not very high at all, nor was the maternal mortality rate. Senior women in the 1980s explained that when women had two or three living children, they accessed bush medicine for contraceptive purposes.

more water from the stream on a daily basis, and they did far more laundry. Women also worked harder to make larger gardens to have produce to sell as a source of cash income to pay for processed foods (rice, sugar, tin meat and fish, treats), clothes, and school fees for their children. They also spent their nights fishing for *bêche de mer* (sea cucumber) to sell to the buyers who came regularly. This extra work has an effect on women's health, but also on girl children who are increasingly depended upon by their mothers for carrying water, cooking, laundering, gardening and caring for younger children. Consequently, girls are regularly pulled out of school to do this work.

Such contemporary fecundity results from a network of intersecting factors. Both men and women allowed that the postpartum taboo isn't necessary anymore due to the availability of western medicines which would cure childhood illnesses believed to be caused by semen-contaminated breast milk. The Catholic Church encourages wives to defer to and obey their husbands as patriarchs and authoritative heads of family and to fulfil their wifely duties to provide sex for reproduction, though not recreational purposes (see Hermkens 2007, 2008 and Ch. 4) and punishes any form of birth control as a sin. Transgressors are spiritually threatened to an afterlife in Hell and husbands physically punish real or imagined efforts by their wives to practise birth control. Thus, women are having too many babies too close together. Two infants in three years means that the nursing infant is weaned too soon, and the mother is not having sufficient recovery time between pregnancies. Frequent pregnancies, inadequate birth spacing, and increased manual labour, have a detrimental effect on women's overall health. If sex is by spousal demand and only for reproduction, fathering many children validates the constant indulgence of men's sexual demands, their virile masculine identity, and reinforces their adamant refusal to practise 'family planning'. Both forms of patriarchal authority—husbands in the family and priests in the church—are aligned in meting out punishment to women who want to use birth control methods to space or curtail their pregnancies.

Married women also pointed out to me it is very difficult to deny a husband sexual access since any lack of interest in marital sex a wife exhibits is taken to mean she is having sex with someone else. She is likely to be beaten for adultery and/or raped by her husband to teach her a lesson about male authority and wifely duty and obedience. Men use a kind of emotional blackmail wrapped in threats of abandonment and immoral behaviour on her part and wives acquiesce to avoid being beaten, to forestall false accusations about their fidelity, and to keep their husbands. The ban on birth control also prevents women from using or requesting the use of condoms as protection against HIV infection (see McPherson 2008b).

Another key factor in this mix is that the last men's ceremonial house (B: *lum*) built in 1985 has long since been razed with no replacement built (or, as of 2009, even planned). With the demise of the men's ceremonial house (B: *lum*), which housed spirit beings, sacra and Bariai cosmology in the late 1980s, the Catholic Church has assumed a central role in defining the Bariai world view, their ethos and daily life. For the past twenty years men's lives are no longer homosocial, framed by the men's house as the icon of gendered exclusivity and enforcing the sexual division of space and place. As of 2000, residential sexual segregation is no longer practised; men do not retire to the men's house to share masculine company, to teach and learn, to plan ceremonies, eat, and sleep away from the seduction and dangers of the female sex. Indeed, the family has become the Christian nuclear family consisting of husband, wife, and dependent children living under the same roof. In contrast to the traditional matrifocal household, when males lived separately in the ceremonial men's house, married men now live in the 'woman's house' (B: *luma*), with their wife/wives and children. The husbands, under the aegis of church teaching that he is the patriarchal head of household and indigenous concepts of masculine power and privilege, has assumed the role of overseer of the household and of women's domestic labour. The domestic domain is no longer a female domain; husbands have taken control of the household, bossing and finding fault with women's work in the home, village, and gardens, an intrusion that often ends up in arguments and physical violence. Two examples will help illustrate some of these factors.

Contested domestic power

Case 10. (2009) Everyone liked to have their photograph taken, so villagers and I decided that I would systematically go from house to house and photograph each nuclear family—father, mother, children. As I got to the last house in one hamlet, the husband called out to me to meet them underneath the house, which I assumed they wanted as their background in the snapshot. When I arrived, I saw the wife from behind, hunched over tightly holding her infant. Another woman looked on, visibly upset. I enquired if the baby was unwell, but the husband loudly proclaimed that he had just beaten his wife severely with a branch. Couldn't I see the gash on her head, her swollen face and arm, the blood on the sitting platform and on the ground? He said there was no point taking their photo today as the younger children were frightened and had run away into the bush and not come back. Furious and anxious for my woman friend, I demanded to know why he had beaten his wife. His answer: she had disobeyed him. He had specifically told her not to sell her *bêche-de-mer* to buyer A because he didn't pay as well as another buyer, B. Buyer A had come in that morning and she had sold to him against her husband's express orders to wait for buyer B. Surely that's no reason to beat her, I said. No, he laughed, he beat her to teach her a lesson, to teach her to do as she was told and not to go against his instruction. He was after all 'head of the family' and 'boss' of his wife and children.

We had a bit of a discussion about his behaviour specifically and men's behaviour generally in beating their wives before I left to take the next household's picture. When I arrived at this next house, everyone there immediately told me that the man I had just left had been beating his wife and how they could hear the poor woman shrieking and crying in pain. It was awful what he was doing, they said, he should never use a stick. But, they didn't intercede, because this was a private matter between husband and wife. Indeed, the whole village buzzed with this event, yet no one (except a very few women) condemned or censured the husband as his wife had disobeyed his authority and women know they will attract a beating for this; and, besides, it was a 'private', family affair. This is a big departure from past understandings when kinspeople would interfere in a situation of spousal abuse to ensure it didn't get out of control. There was no such presumption of a household's privacy. Often the woman's clan brothers would turn up to chastise their brother-in-law about how he was abusing their sister, and that perhaps he should rethink his behaviour.

The scenario of the failed family photograph took place a few days before my departure from the village. When the wife in example 10 didn't turn up to my going away feast three days later, I enquired after her to a group of women. One woman replied that she was still swollen and bruised, but it had been three days and she should be over it by now. In general, women's pragmatism in the face of abuse that they, as I know from experience, also suffer, reinforces my contention that violence is engendered and embodied within a framework of 'cultural violence' that both men and women come to accept as a way of life. My final example occurred the day before I left the village to return home.

Case 11. (2009) I was sitting plaiting pandanus textiles with some women, when a senior woman approached and called me aside. She handed me something carefully wrapped in a plastic rice bag. It turned out to be a photograph, so blotched with mildew that only a small face at the bottom of the photo was visible. This was her deceased daughter and she wanted me to send her a new copy of the photo. Her daughter had married into a neighbouring village and her husband had killed her during an argument. He was hitting her and she fell down whereupon he kicked her very hard, many times in the ribs. A rib broke and punctured her heart. This ruined photograph was her only remembrance of her daughter. I had not taken this particular photograph. However, I offered to bring her only precious copy home with me to get her daughter's image photo-shopped. My local camera store did a great job and my friend now has a plasticised photo of her dead daughter.

Why had they been arguing? Who knows, newly married people argue a great deal as they settle into married life, usually about sex, fidelity, and jealousy. Was the husband arrested and charged with his wife's murder? No, the husband was made to pay a large compensation in money (K10,000 or approximately $4200 CAD), plus a few pigs and traditional shell valuables. The deceased woman's family didn't want to put themselves in danger (of sorcery) by demanding police, homicide charges, and courts. It is doubtful that her death was even registered officially. So, a young woman's life is valued at about $4200 together with a few pigs and shell valuables. All that remained was a tattered photograph lovingly protected in a plastic rice bag by her mother.

Some final thoughts

I began this look at spousal abuse and men's violence against women by agreeing with the Seville Statement on Violence which proclaims that masculine violence is not an essential feature of human biology or human evolution. Instead, I suggested that violence in general and masculine violence against women in particular is culturally embedded in concepts of gendered relations and therefore, violence is a learned trait. Employing Galtung's concept of 'cultural violence' or the ways in which violence is culturally legitimised and justified, I considered examples of Bariai myths as primal charters for masculine violence against women and male social, sexual and sacred privilege. I then observed how violence informs child rearing and domestic life. The enculturation process, in this instance the transmission of a culturally legitimised violence, is obvious in how Bariai children, both boys and girls, are taught from infancy to be aggressive and to hit out at others. The several examples of specific incidents of violence I have described and analysed illustrate how 'cultural violence' finds expression in the lives of women and men. Men have 'power over' women in terms of patriarchal authority underwritten both by indigenous masculine world views and by the Catholic Church. All these cases illustrate a masculine 'power over' wives and daughters. Women are enculturated as much as men, and most (not all) accept cultural concepts of their gender and sexuality, their subordinate position in the social structure, and the physical abuse they all suffer because they are female, woman, wife and daughter. Men feel they have a right, indeed, an obligation to beat their wives given that women are culturally defined as weak-minded, weak-willed, and need to be taught lessons and controlled. The notion that 'lessons' are best learned when beaten onto the body is not totally expunged from the culture and history of corporal punishment in child-rearing practices, patriarchal violence, and spousal abuse in Euro American societies. In the past, spousal abuse was seen as a private behaviour within the family, behind closed doors. Excessive violence was culturally determined by a 'rule of thumb' whereby a wife couldn't be hit with anything bigger than a circumference of a man's thumb. There was a notion that children ought not to be spared the rod, and wives needed to be beaten into submission.

The examples presented here show how gender relations cannot be understood through essentialist sociobiological or evolutionary explanations such as 'man-the-hunter' scenarios of masculine sexual aggression and violence. Rather, a cultural ethos of engendered violence justifies and legitimates beliefs and behaviours, becomes part of a cultural narrative that creates a consensus shared by women and men alike. Gender relations are thus relations grounded in masculine 'power over' the feminine. With very few exceptions, all Bariai men and women hold that physical violence against women is permissible in certain circumstances. A wife will be beaten (and she expects to be) when she fails to fulfil her obligations to produce food (productive labour); fails to produce children (reproductive labour); fails to care for her husband's pigs (produce wealth); or when she refuses or is reluctant to have sexual intercourse with her husband. Further, all females were refused access to the secret-sacred aspects of the men's house culture where spirit beings and important ceremonials were carried out under threat of institutionalised rape and murder. Most women believe in (although some question) their gendered inadequacies as much as men do. It is this enculturation process in all its complexity that makes gendered 'violence look, even feel right—or at least, not wrong' (Galtung 1990: 291).

References

Banks, Cyndi, 2000. Contextualising sexual violence: rape and carnal knowledge in Papua New Guinea. In *Reflections on Violence in Melanesia*, ed. Sinclair Dinnen and Allison Ley, 83–104. Sydney: Hawkins Press and Asia Pacific Press.

Caputi, Jane, 1989. The sexual politics of murder. *Gender & Society* 3(4): 437–56.

Chowning, Ann, 1985. Kove women and violence: the context of wife-beating in a West New Britain Society. In *Domestic Violence in Papua New Guinea*, ed. Susan Toft, 72–91. Monograph No. 3. Law Reform Commission, Port Moresby: Papua New Guinea.

Conkey, Margaret with Sarah Williams, 1991. Original narratives: the political economy of gender in archaeology. In *Gender at the Crossroads of Knowledge: Feminist Anthropology in the Postmodern Era*, ed. Micaela di Leonardo, 102–39. Berkeley CA: University of California Press.

Counts, Dorothy A., Judith K. Brown and Jacquelyn C. Campbell, 1992. *Sanctions and Sanctuary: Cultural Perspectives on the Beating of Wives*. Boulder, CO: Westview Press.

Counts, Dorothy A., 1992. 'All men do it': wife-beating in Kaliai, Papua New Guinea. In *Sanctions and Sanctuary:Cultural Perspectives on the Beating of Wives*, ed. Dorothy Ayers Counts, Judith K. Brown and Jacquelyn C. Campbell, 63–76. Boulder, CO: Westview Press.

-------- 1993. The fist, the stick and the bottle of bleach: wife bashing and female suicide in a Papua New Guinea Society. In *Contemporary Pacific Societies: Studies in Development and Change*, ed. Victoria S. Lockwood, Tom G. Harding and Ben J. Wallace, 249–59. New Jersey: Prentice Hall.

Dinnen, Sinclair and Allison Ley, eds, 2000. *Reflections on Violence in Melanesia*. Sydney: Hawkins Press and Asia Pacific Press.

Eves, Richard, 2006. *Exploring the Role of Men and Masculinities in Papua New Guinea in the 21st Century: How to address violence in ways that generate empowerment for both men and women*. Report for Caritas Australia. Online: http://www.baha.com.pg/downloads/Masculinity%20and%20 Violence%20in%20PNG.pdf. Accessed 28 November 2010.

Farmer, Paul, 2004. An anthropology of structural violence. *Current Anthropology* 45(3): 305–25.

-------- 2005. *Pathologies of Power: Health, Human Rights and the New War on the Poor*. Berkeley, CA: University of California Press.

Galtung, Johan, 1990. Cultural violence. *Journal of Peace Research* 27(3): 291–305.

Gewertz, Deborah, 1988. *Myths of Matriarchy Reconsidered*. Sydney: Oceania Monographs.

Gewertz, Deborah B. and Frederick K. Errington, 1991. *Twisted Histories, Altered Contexts: Representing the Chambri in a World System*. Cambridge: Cambridge University Press.

Hammar, Lawrence, 1996. Bad canoes and *bafalo*: the political economy of sex on Daru Island, Western Province, Papua New Guinea. *Genders* 23: 212–43.

Hays, Terence and Patricia H. Hays, 1982. Opposition and complementarity of the sexes in Ndumba initiation. In *Rituals of Manhood: Male Initiation in Papua New Guinea*, ed. Gilbert H. Herdt, 201–38. Berkeley: University of California Press.

Heise, Lori L., 1997. Violence, sexuality, and women's lives. In *The Gender/ Sexuality Reader: Culture, History, Political Economy*, ed. Roger N. Lancaster and Micaela di Leonardo, 411–32. New York: Routledge.

Herdt, Gilbert H., ed., 1982. *Rituals of Manhood: Male Initiation in Papua New Guinea*. Berkeley: University of California Press.

Hermkens, Anna-Karina, 2007. The power of Mary in Papua New Guinea. *Anthropology Today* 23(2): 4–8.

-------- 2008. Josephine's journey: gender-based violence and Marian devotion in urban Papua New Guinea. *Oceania* 78(2): 151–67.

Hussey, Mark, ed., 2003. *Masculinities: Interdisciplinary Readings*. Upper Saddle River, NJ: Prentice Hall.

Jolly, Margaret, 2000. Epilogue: further reflections on violence in Melanesia. In *Reflections on Violence in Melanesia*, ed. Sinclair Dinnen and Alison Ley, 305–24. Sydney: Hawkins Press and Asia Pacific Press.

Keesing, Roger, 1982. Introduction. In *Rituals of Manhood: Male Initiation in Papua New Guinea*, ed. Gilbert H. Herdt, 1–43. Berkeley: University of California Press.

Krohn-Hansen, Christian, 1994. The anthropology of violent interaction. *Journal of Anthropological Research* 50: 367–81.

McCaughey, Martha, 2008. *The Caveman Mystique: Pop-Darwinism and the Debates over Sex, Violence and Science*. New York: Routledge.

McPherson, Naomi M., 1994. The legacy of Moro the Snake-Man in Bariai. In *Children of Kilibob: Creation, Cosmos and Culture in Northwest New Guinea*, ed. Alice Pomponio, David R. Counts and Thomas G. Hardy. Special issue. *Pacific Studies* 17(4): 153–81.

-------- 2008a. Galiki the firstborn: mythic female and feminine ideal in Bariai, West New Britain, Papua New Guinea. In *Sexual Snakes, Winged Maidens and Sky Gods: Myth in the Pacific, An Essay in Cultural Transparency*, ed. Serge Dunis, 181–201. Nouméa and Pape'ete: La Rocher-à-la-Voile and Éditions Haere Po Tahiti.

-------- 2008b. *SikAIDS*: deconstructing the awareness campaign in rural West New Britain, Papua New Guinea. In *Making Sense of AIDS: Culture Sexuality, and Power in Melanesia*, ed. Leslie Butt and Richard Eves, 328–54. Honolulu: University of Hawai'i Press.

Poole, John Fitz Porter, 1982. The ritual forging of identity: aspects of person and self in Bimin-Kuskusmin male initiation. In *Rituals of Manhood: Male Initiation in Papua New Guinea*, ed. Gilbert H. Herdt, 99–154. Berkeley: University of California Press.

Riches, David, 1986. The phenomenon of violence. In *The Anthropology of Violence*, ed. David Riches, 1–27. Oxford, Basil Blackwell.

Scaletta, Naomi (McPherson), 1986. Childbirth: a case history from West New Britain, Papua New Guinea. *Oceania* 57: 33–52.

Silverman, Eric Kline, 2001. *Masculinity, Motherhood, and Mockery: Psychoanalyzing Culture and the Iatmul Naven Rite in New Guinea*. Ann Arbor: University of Michigan Press.

Stewart, Pamela and Andrew Strathern, 2002. *Violence: Theory and Ethnography*. London: Continuum.

Tracy, Karen K. and Charles B. Crawford, 1992. Wife abuse: does it have an evolutionary origin? In *Sanctions and Sanctuary: Cultural Perspectives on the Beating of Wives*, ed. Dorothy A. Counts, Judith K. Brown and Jacquelyn C. Campbell, 19–32. Boulder, CO: Westview Press.

Tuzin, Donald, 1997. *The Cassowary's Revenge: The Life and Death of Masculinity in a New Guinea Society*. Chicago: University of Chicago Press.

Wardlow, Holly, 2006. *Wayward Women: Sexuality and Agency in a New Guinea Society*. Berkeley: University of California Press.

Zimmer-Tamakoshi, Laura, 2001. 'Wild pigs and dog men:' rape and domestic violence as women's issues in Papua New Guinea. In *Gender in Cross Cultural Perspective*, ed. Caroline B. Brettell and Carolyn F. Sargent, 565–80. Upper Saddle River, NJ: Prentice Hall, 3rd ed.

2. Troubled Masculinities and Gender Violence in Melanesia

Laura Zimmer-Tamakoshi

Abstract

The subject of this chapter is how young men's marital and economic prospects, their conflicts with older men, and their engagement with modernity and *kastam* are related to gender violence in Melanesia.[1] I also examine what young women think and how women of different ages make the most of increasingly unequal economic and marital circumstances and I argue for a shift from the use of the term 'gender violence' to 'engendered violence', a more encompassing term allowing for complex explanations and findings. Drawing on the accounts of early missionaries, oral and written histories and thirty years of my own research and writing about the Gende of southern Madang Province and elsewhere in Papua New Guinea, I build a profound case against any simple understanding of gender violence. The Gende case demands that researchers focus on both men's uneasy confrontation with modernity and *kastam* and women's efforts at achieving a semblance of agency and personal security in the midst of deeply challenging economic, cultural and social changes.

Introduction

Violence against females (often referred to as 'gender violence') is the most common form of interpersonal violence in Melanesia. In Papua New Guinea (PNG), such violence is prevalent in urban and rural households and reported rates of rape and sexual assault against women and girls exceed those in many industrial and developing countries. Equating 'gender violence' with violence against females, however, excludes from discussion male victims of domestic or sexual violence. It also underplays the complexities of Melanesian gender relations and ignores men's uneasy confrontations with modernity and *kastam* (resulting in 'embattled masculinities' Jolly 2000), men's status insecurities amidst some women's new agency, and the changing structures and contexts (e.g. kinship, age and gender) that promote violence against females *and* males.

---

1 We are using the Tok Pisin orthography for *kastam*. *Kastom* is more common in Solomon Islands pidgin and the Bislama of Vanuatu.

While Melanesia is renowned for its diverse concepts of masculine social, bodily and sexual development (Knauft 1999), there are few studies on how changing masculinities play into gender violence.

Troubled masculinity is a recurring theme in my research. In a 1984 paper I explored the economic and cultural bases of male identity crises among the Gende in PNG (Zimmer 1984). Then as now, uncertain development and inequality spurred by migration and urban remittances put pressure on Gende exchange relations, resulting in the bachelorisation of Gende society (Zimmer-Tamakoshi 1993a), domestic and intergenerational violence as older persons favour wealthier men as exchange partners and sons-in-law (Zimmer 1990a; Zimmer-Tamakoshi 1993a), and often deadly conflicts over land and the interpretation of *kastam* (Zimmer-Tamakoshi 1997a, 2001). While unemployed wives of migrants may suffer an imbalance of power in their affinal and other exchange relationships, many Gende women enhance their influence and personal security as the 'owners' of large pig herds, as the thrifty (and indispensable) wives of less prosperous migrants or as successful businesswomen (Zimmer-Tamakoshi 1993a, 1996, 1997a). A few earn enough to delay marriage or forego bride price, asserting an independence that does not sit well with men or women's families (Rosi and Zimmer-Tamakoshi 1993).

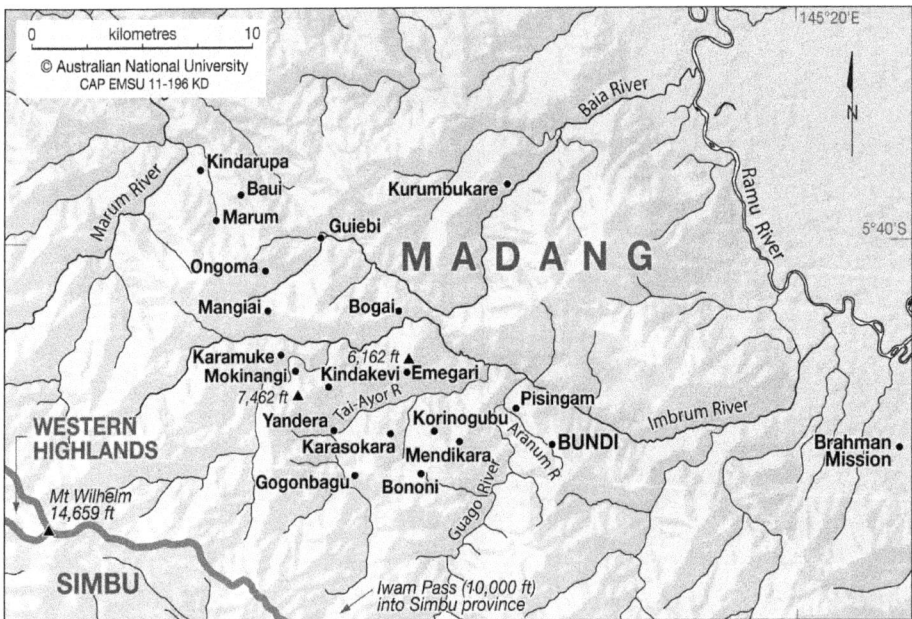

Map 2. Gende villages are located in a mountainous region of the Madang Province which borders Simbu Province. Map production by Education and Multimedia Services, College of Asia and the Pacific, The Australian National University.

In recent years, two large mining ventures within the bounds of Gende territory promise to usher in prosperity and bolster threatened masculinities. The Ramu Nickel Project, however, is already generating a wave of second marriages (and domestic violence) as older men bank on future compensation, and a storm of ancestral gerrymandering as men *and* women negotiate over who are legitimate landowners, often leaving younger (and unmarried) men out of the negotiations (Zimmer-Tamakoshi 2001, 2006). In Spring 2007, I returned to PNG to investigate further how the Gende are responding to expected reversals of fortune, focusing on (1) emergent and competing masculinities as older and younger men enact their manhood in the supercharged atmosphere of large-scale mining operations and (2) the impacts of changing masculinities on women's strategies and well-being.

I begin this chapter with several recent dramatic twists in Gende men and women's situations and prospects—brought on by the rapid intrusion of two international mining operations. I then present an overview of theoretical works on gender violence in Melanesia followed by an account of troubled masculinities among the Gende over the course of eighty years and an analysis of young men's violence and contradictory experiences of power. Throughout, it is apparent that Gende gender relations have always been fluid and complex. A lengthy period of bachelorisation and poor local prospects during the Gende's post-contact period was followed by an explosion of opportunity for young men, especially for those living in Yandera village and other areas of interest to Marengo Mining, and in Gende villages closer to the Ramu Nickel prospect at Kurumbukare (in Gende territory). During the same time period Gende women have experienced their own ups and downs, often in contrast to men's experience, with balanced gender relations becoming more a rarity than a norm in some Gende locales.

Throughout the chapter, I demonstrate how the agency of both males and females is encompassed in matrices of social relations and obligation. I show how failures of young men and women to live up to their elders' expectations and demands negatively affect their relations with one another. And I argue that the use of the term 'engendered violence' makes more sense than 'gender violence' when explaining a young husband's violence against a wife for whom his family paid a large bride price and from whom they have not received the expected redemption of the bride price known as *tupoi*; or when a younger man attacks an older man who interferes with the younger man's marital prospects by hoarding the benefits of land 'ownership' and compensation for his own ends and failing to pay bride price for a wife for the younger man in a society in which marriage is still the only road to social adulthood.

None of what I argue is intended to excuse violence of any kind. In my conclusion I elaborate on how looking at gender violence in broader ways may make it possible to find solutions to male violence. By putting gender back into its larger socio-cultural contexts, I avoid separating issues involving women and children—too often relegated to the domestic sphere (e.g. 'domestic violence')—from ones involving the entire community such as tribal violence, inter-generational and class conflicts over *kastam* and modernity, and globalisation. Only by unravelling the matrices of engendered relations that men and women live and act in—such as relations between older and younger men and how these impact both older and younger men's access to and relations with women and power—can we truly understand male violence (or for that matter, women's acts of violence and rebellion).

Twists and turns in the road to development: The new polygynists and 'merry' widows of Yandera

In 2007 I returned twice to PNG after a hiatus of nearly seven years. My objectives were threefold: to update my ongoing research on troubled masculinities among Gende males; to investigate a Gende woman's run for the Usino-Bundi Open in the National elections; and to design and carry out a census in Yandera village in southern Madang Province, the centre of a new mining prospect run by Marengo Mining of Australia. Collecting 227 eleven-page household interviews with the help of four graduates of Madang's Divine Word University and spending four and a half months with Gende men and women in Yandera, Madang and in between, I left 'the field' with a mountain of data and some startling observations on what appeared to be a seismic shift in young men's marital prospects (at least in Yandera) and some surprising developments in women's situations and attitudes.

After a long history of bachelorisation and its attendant social frustrations for many males in Yandera and other Gende settlements, suddenly there was plentiful and well-paid work with the arrival of Marengo in 2005 and the start-up of exploratory drilling and other operations. Those working for Marengo could now afford the larger bride prices that had kept many out of the marriage market in decades past. There were virtually no bachelors over the age of twenty-four in Yandera. What startled me most, however, was not that men in Yandera had apparently gained an edge in the marriage market, but rather the upsurge in polygyny, not among older men but among very young men. The 'new polygyny' along with the disturbing fact that there were few older men over the age of fifty still alive in Yandera were linked with an abundance of strong and seemingly merry widows. I say 'merry' because the widows were happily building up and securing their own high social standing in the community by raising pigs for their deceased husbands' (and other male relatives') funeral and death payments (*kwiagi*) and their sons' marriage payments.

Figure 4. Laura Zimmer-Tamakoshi instructing her field assistants on how to do the Yandera household survey, 2007.

Photo courtesy of Laura Zimmer-Tamakoshi.

Clearly, the money earned by working at Marengo was being turned into matrimonial capital and it appeared that young polygynists were replicating the practice of Big Men of yore by marrying two or three wives: one from Yandera or some other Gende village along with one or more from nearby Simbu and Ramu peoples. In such a manner past Big Men developed large networks of exchange partners along an ancient trade route connecting the north coast with the central highlands. What the new polygynists were up to, however, required several more seasons of fieldwork and reflection to figure out, as did the question of why pigs continue to be a critical part of exchanges when their cash equivalents are known down to the last *toea* (about half a cent) and pigs are less readily accessible to men who work in town or whose wives have not accompanied them back to the village.

Figure 5. Yandera men working at Marengo's core shed, 2009.

Photograph by Hugh Brown, courtesy of Marengo Mining Ltd.

The situation I confronted in Yandera in 2007 seemed to bear little resemblance to what I had observed at Ramu Nickel in 1995 and 2000. In 1995, there were many young bachelors at Ramu Nickel's prospect at Kurumbukare and they and their mothers were in constant and sometimes deadly conflict with the older men who were using land compensation payments (and the likelihood of larger payments once Ramu Nickel took off) to acquire second and third wives (wisely keeping them in town away from angry first wives). Based on data collected in 2007 and subsequently, however, some of the younger workers at Ramu Nickel are now also acquiring wives (although not two or three as in Yandera) as a number of older men have since died of malaria in the mosquito-infected lower hills and swampy plains around the expanding Ramu Nickel projects and in Madang, or succumbed to more suspicious causes associated with accusations of sorcery. In this context, the absence of so many older men in Yandera's population was all the more disturbing as it raised the question of whether or not they too had been killed or driven into an early demise. While my household surveys showed that many of the deceased men had died of natural causes, some had indeed been murdered because they were alleged sorcerers and still others reportedly died of stress related to conflict with wives and children. That the new polygynists and merry widows in Yandera seemed immune to similar accusations of sorcery begged explanation.

Expanding their area of interest and exploratory drilling in 2008, Marengo requested that I extend my survey/census to include two sets of Gende settlements often referred to by the old Gende clan names 'Gegeru' and 'Karizoko'. Both of these old clans long ago segmented into inter-marrying clans that continue to inhabit the same general locations as formerly: Gegeru villages strung out along steep ridges between Yandera and Kurumbukare (the centre of the Ramu Nickel prospect); Karizoko villages and hamlets across from Yandera on the side of the mountains closer to Madang's border with Simbu Province. What I learned in the months I spent in the field in 2008 strengthened my longstanding argument against any simple understanding of gender violence.[2]

A significant outcome of my analysis of data collected in 2008 is the finding that—at least in the Gende villages surrounding the Ramu Nickel prospect— sociability has constricted such that fewer marriages are being made with partners who are not members of one or the other Gegeru clans (the Gende clans with the strongest claims on the land at the Ramu Nickel prospect at Kurumbukare). In the past Gegeru clansmen helped their in-laws in Yandera to fight off attacks by Karizoko and Emegari warriors, providing safe haven for years when the defence failed. This relatively recent constricted sociability is in part explained by Gegeru attempts to keep the benefits of land ownership and work at Kurumbukare and Ramu Nickel to themselves. It is also related to the higher bride prices now being asked by Yandera parents for their daughters' hands in marriage. It turned out that the Gegeru clan villages I surveyed had higher rates of divorce than either Yandera or Karizoko settlements. Many of the

---

2   Papua New Guinea requires that mining companies and other large resource extraction operations carry out environmental and social impact studies during the feasibility stages of operation. Accordingly, I was hired on several occasions by two different mining companies to do social assessment and census work among the Gende with whom I have carried out anthropological research since 1982. The first was Highlands Gold Limited which hired me to do a genealogical survey of the settlements around the Ramu Nickel prospect at Kurumbukare in 1995. Kurumbukare is located in the forested foothills to the north of the Gende's main villages but within Gende territory. In 2000 I revisited the Ramu Nickel prospect at the behest of the renamed Highlands Pacific Company to assess social changes going on among those living in the vicinity of the mine. The local population had continued to grow exponentially as many Gende left their home villages to move closer to the Ramu Nickel prospect, hoping to find work and gain compensation for the use of their land.

In 2007, 2008, 2009, 2010 and 2011 a second mining company—Marengo Mining—hired me to carry out social assessment and census studies in the higher altitude Gende villages that lie within their area of exploration and in areas where the company proposes to build hydro dams, airstrips and other mining infrastructure, should their prospect be approved by the government. Because the studies include every household (including absentees) within the project areas and the interview I devised is eleven pages long, I have assistants to work alongside me in interviewing household heads and family members, mapping settlements and taking photo censuses. Because the company pays for all of this the data base is essentially theirs (although I retain my own copies and rights to write about my findings as well as other research I carry out in tandem with the surveys). After each period of fieldwork I input the data and do an analysis of the quantitative data, writing large reports in which I contextualise the data and which go to the company and, at my request, to the National Research Institute in Port Moresby. The data bases and my reports cover many areas of the Gende's life (e.g. kinship, identity, marriage and residence patterns, house construction, education, use of local resources, work, income sources, nutrition and health) and form an important baseline for future comparative studies assessing various impacts of the mine on local populations.

divorced men and women had shed non-Gegeru partners and almost all then married a Gegeru partner. This appeared surprisingly parsimonious given that the Gende in general are very worldly, having migrated to all parts of PNG in the years when local development was sparse. But then, as several newly remarried Gegeru husbands told me: 'the people in Yandera have Marengo now so we don't have to share Ramu [Nickel] with them' and 'They are greedy. If we marry them, they move in and want money from the company [at Ramu Nickel]. I won't let my sister marry a Yandera man' and 'They are trying to steal our land'.

A second interesting finding of the 2008 census is that the Karizoko clans associated with Karasokara village and its nearby hamlets—all bordering on Yandera's territory—are even more heavily intermarried with Simbu peoples than in the past. It turns out that many Karizokos—who like every other Gende clan also suffered a glut of bachelors in years past—eventually acquired wives as a result of their sisters' marriages to Simbu men and, accepting invitations to move to Simbu settlements, married Simbu wives, and helped sisters and sisters' husbands' families raise coffee and other cash crops. On the Simbu side of the mountains, the Simbu are better connected to the Highlands Highway and greater economic opportunities than was the case—until very recently—for the Gende.

This tactic of the Karizokos has had some 'alarming' results as Marengo's drilling on Karasokara territory has generated a tidal wave of returning Karizoko men and women anxious to impress their claims to land on both the company and those villagers who remained 'at home'. Never before had a mining company shown interest beyond the immediate vicinity of Yandera's territory and Karizoko peoples have even fewer claims to land at the Ramu Nickel prospect than most Gende, so it was natural for them to try their luck in town or with Simbu neighbours and in-laws. Although Karasokara village has always been deemed to be similar in population to Yandera, the 400-plus household interviews I collected from Karizoko households in 2008 significantly outnumbered the 227 I collected for Yandera and its garden settlements in 2007. The Yandera clans have had decades of mining interest in their lands and time to slough off migrants who failed to maintain their rural option; while people living in Karasokara and other Karizoko clan settlements have not. During the 2008 census, non-residents crowded into Karasokara and its nearby settlements and other absentees sent emissaries to warn residents not to leave out anyone. Nervous old men visited us late into the night with lists of absent sons and daughters and their many Simbu in-laws. More so it would seem than in Yandera or the Gegeru villages, Karizoko men are beholden to sisters and Simbu in-laws for helping them marry and have families.

After finishing the 2008 survey and while I was still in Madang preparing to return to the United States, there was a shocking incident in one of the Gegeru villages that reflects just how deadly tensions over land can be. With Gegeru territory near Yandera also suddenly of interest to Marengo, the Madang-based nephews of one Gegeru landowner we had interviewed only weeks before, returned to the village and axed him to death in an argument over their rights to land once owned by their deceased father. They alleged that their uncle was a sorcerer who had caused his brother's death so he could claim his land as well as his own, but it was widely agreed in the village that the young men had never done much for anyone, that their uncle had paid *kwiagi* (death payment) for their father, and that the young men were greedy and hoping to profit from future land compensation from Marengo. When the youths escaped to Madang, villagers took three women into custody and threatened to bury them alive if the young men did not turn themselves in and pay compensation to bereaved kin. The nervous old Karizoko men undoubtedly feared similar retribution if they failed to include daughters and sisters in the survey/census as being stakeholders who had earned the right to be included (and they did, certainly more than the young Gegeru migrants).

In 2009, I returned twice to Madang to extend my survey/census even further to include yet another ten Gende settlements, some along a proposed easement route that is near the Ramu Nickel prospect and mostly populated by Gegeru clans, and others closer to Karasokara and populated by Gende belonging to Mendi and Nombri clans. While the analysis of the data for the Mendi/Nombri is not yet completed—and I have done yet more research in 2010 and 2011 in Gende and non-Gende locations (along the Ramu and North Coast)—the situations and words of Gende migrants and villagers I interviewed in 2009 and 2010 have contributed many insights to my understanding of the current situation and so shall be included where relevant in my description and analysis of troubled masculinities and engendered violence among the Gende.

Theorising gender violence

Violence against females—often referred to as gender violence—is the most common form of interpersonal violence in Melanesia (Dinnen 2000). In PNG, violence is prevalent in urban *and* rural households (Toft 1985, 1986; Toft and Bonnell 1985) and reported rates of sexual assault and rape exceed those in many industrial and developing countries (Zimmer-Tamakoshi 1997e). Most theories about gender violence focus on distorted traditions (Garap 2000), women's weaker political presence (Counts, Brown and Campbell 1992), psychological and economic pressures of development and inequality (Josephides 1993; Bradley 1994), the effects of urban lifestyles (alcohol abuse, reduced social support networks), increased eroticism and sexual conflicts (Rosi and Zimmer-Tamakoshi 1993; Jenkins 1994), and a renewal of tribal fighting and rapes of enemy women (Garap 2000). Also cited are the intersection of urban/elite sexual politics with nationalist and class interests and rhetoric (Hogan 1985; Zimmer-Tamakoshi 1993b, 1995, 1997e, 2004) and the difficulties experienced by weak states in preventing lawlessness and rampant police violence (Strathern 1993; Dinnen 1996; see also Ch. 7).

Melanesian women activists and scholars agree with most of the above arguments, decrying increasing violence and women's lack of freedom to make their own choices (Molisa 1987, 1989; Billy, Lulei and Sipolo 1983; Billy 2000; Garap 2000; see Zimmer-Tamakoshi 1995). A few western critics, however, caution that adopting western perspectives on what is 'normal' overlooks the fact that 'domestic' and 'sexual violence' are cultural concepts (Borrey 2000) and that some violence is accepted in many Melanesian societies (O'Collins 2000). A perhaps more compelling criticism is that equating 'gender violence' with violence against females excludes from discussion male victims of domestic and sexual violence (Coursen-Neff 2005). Also ignored are men's uneasy confrontations with modernity and *kastam* resulting in 'embattled masculinities' (Jolly 2000: 312), men's status insecurities amidst some women's new agency, and the changing structures and contexts (such as kinship, age and gender) that may promote violence against females *and* males. Both Margaret Jolly (1994, 1997, 2000) and Martha Macintyre (2000 and Ch. 8) have argued against simplistic models of changing gender relations and identities, citing the diversity and fluidity of women's situations and the multiple trajectories women take in efforts to achieve a desirable status within changing contexts.

In this chapter, I explore in more depth Jolly's notion of 'embattled' or—as befits the Gende case, 'troubled masculinities'—in Melanesia and how changing masculinities play into various forms of engendered violence. I am especially interested in exploring a particular aspect of men's violence, that sociologist Michael Kaufman calls the 'fourth P' or *paradox* of men's privilege and power (1994, 1999). In 'The 7 P's of Men's Violence' (1999), Kaufman wrote that among the paradoxes of patriarchal power are what he has called 'men's contradictory experiences of power' (1994). In the context of troubled masculinities in Melanesia, I argue that such contradictory experiences include most young men's abject lack of control over the resources they need to achieve both local and global ideals of masculine social and individual power. Today, some of these necessary resources include higher education, being recognised as legitimate landowners in places where land ownership is lucrative (such as near mine sites), and having access to large sums of cash to be used for bride-price payments and other key exchange transactions. Unable to achieve community (much less global) expectations, many of today's young men feel unfairly placed in social-psychic pressure cookers of impossible expectations, feelings that may contribute to acts of compensatory violence as well as violent efforts to force others (such as parents, more prosperous siblings and other relatives) to help them achieve social manhood. The introduction and wide-spread use of guns in parts of PNG has exacerbated the situation (Dinnen and Thompson 2004: 2), with guns being one more thing that ambitious or frustrated young men need—along with gang membership and crime (Goddard 2005)—to succeed in today's gift economy and to achieve or hold onto a measure of prestige and manhood.

In an overview of men and masculinities in PNG, Richard Eves notes that while violence is not everywhere condoned there does seem to be an emergence of an almost global masculine ethos which sees violence as a legitimate means to an end (2006: 15). He further notes that men's violence against women should be situated within a larger context of power relations (2006: 37), and that keeping women in their place is a prevailing characteristic of gender relations in PNG. Again I would argue—along with Macintyre and most of the authors in this volume—against any simplistic notion that 'keeping women in their place' is a prevailing characteristic of gender relations in PNG. Rather, I would argue that it is more fruitful to see the encompassment of young men's ambitions and struggles within changing cultural-economic matrices and global-local realities such as the one I describe below; one in which young Gende women may well be encompassed within a bride-price system and male authority but also one in which there are both traditional and new ways for women to succeed in having their way (and sometimes thwarting men's ambitions) without resorting to the dangers of prostitution and rebellion of Holly Wardlow's *Wayward Women* (2006). Among the Gende—as with people everywhere—males and females live (and often are caught) in webs of relationships that change over time. Understanding what those webs are composed of and how they change goes far in explaining not only men's violence against women but also men's violence against other men and women's violence against both men and other women (an often overlooked component of gender violence).

Finally, in attempting to understand the complexities of engendered violence, it is worthwhile touching on issues of 'morality' and 'desire'. In *The Making of Global and Local Modernities in Melanesia* (Robbins and Wardlow 2005), the authors examine Marshall Sahlins' assertions on continuity and discontinuity in culture change. Drawing on a wealth of ethnographic data and individual situations, the authors expand on Sahlins' useful but simplistic premises that indigenous categories shape people's understanding of novel experiences—hence his concept of *develop-man*—and that radical cultural change—and 'development'—only occurs in the face of cultural humiliation (see Sahlins 2005, 1992). As with the Chambri middle-class (Errington and Gewertz 2005), some Gende are masters in both *develop-man* and 'development', managing their affairs with others in keeping with Gende *kastam* at the same time as they build and sustain successful commercial enterprises. In the Gende case, questions arise as to just how well such 'mastery' is tolerated by other Gende and whether or not 'humiliation' is a necessary factor in change and if so what kinds of change. Many Gende have suffered grave humiliation in the decades since first contact with Europeans in 1932, but degrees of, reactions to and choices arising from past humiliation differ according to many factors, not the least of which are age and gender. Unfortunately, what appears to be not in question (see Filer and Macintyre 2006; Jorgensen 2006) is that past and present choices made with the best intentions of *develop-man* (or *develop-woman*) will *not* save the Gende from the inequalities and violence commonly associated with large mining operations (see also Banks 1999).

Troubled masculinities

When I first did fieldwork with the Gende, some fifty years after they began leaving home to work in other parts of New Guinea, many Gende men were asking themselves whether they were 'pigs' or 'men', and if they were 'men', why was it that 'money' bossed their every move rather than it being they who bossed money as their ancestors had bossed pigs? Ever since western goods and cash were accepted into the Gende exchange system, their uneven distribution has been a factor in migration. In 1982 and 1983, disparities in wealth and the ability to participate in the exchange system had become so vast that it was no longer possible for either the Gende or me to describe most migration as voluntary. While it can be interpreted as a problem of inequality, the Gende— and especially Gende males—saw it as a question of masculine identity (Zimmer 1984).

Like most Melanesians, the Gende are organised on the basis of a complex system of reciprocity and competitive exchange, which mediates kinship, marriage, land, and personal and gendered identities. Within this system, individuals reveal themselves to be more or less 'good' and 'human' on the strength of their exchange performances relative to competitors both within and outside their clan. Men who are active in promoting the affairs of their clan are known as Big Men (G: *wana nambaio*). Big Men often have two or more wives to assist them in buying brides for younger men, giving obligatory presentations to children's matrilateral kiŋ, redeeming land which is lost to non-clan members, and ensuring the physical and spiritual well-being of clan members by sponsoring pig feasts and giving away huge amounts of pork and now cash to other clans.

Lesser men do the same things as Big Men, but on a smaller scale. The lowest form of men are 'rubbish men'. Lazy or too weak to attract wives, they have little wealth to invest in their clan, and must work like 'women' in the service of men. While women may achieve a full and powerful humanity and even a certain independence in Gende society, calling a man a 'woman' is an insult. Traditionally, women, like pigs, move between clans. Men who cannot compete or fulfil their exchange obligations are in danger of making 'women' or 'pigs' of themselves, losing their children (if they are married and have them) to their wives' clans or to other men (like so many pigs) and in some cases being cast out of village society.

Over the years, migration and economic inequality have had a considerable impact on the marriage chances and conjugal relations of over three generations of Gende men and women (Rosi and Zimmer-Tamakoshi 1993; Zimmer-Tamakoshi 1993a and b, 1996, 1997c, 1998, 2001). While women have had their share of suffering and challenge, one of the most dramatic impacts was the bachelorisation of Gende society (Zimmer-Tamakoshi 1993a), a process that until very recently showed no sign of easing (Zimmer-Tamakoshi 2001). As late as the 1990s there was a preponderance of unmarried males in their late twenties and thirties in both villages and town and a large number of young Gende women who had married non-Gende husbands who were able to pay the higher bride prices being asked for them as a means of helping their brothers attract wives.

Traditionally, older men and women arranged marriages for their sons and daughters and—with the help of relatives and ambitious Big Men (and women)— gathered the pigs and other valuables given as bride price to a girl's family. Young men and women proved themselves worthy of support in the context of male and female initiation and puberty rituals and in their willingness to work hard so as to one day repay their elders for their efforts on their behalf. The size of the bride price reflected on both the young husband and wife as they were expected to eventually redeem the bride price—a practice known as *tupoi* (G: returning the pigs)—as well as repay whatever support they received in paying obligatory payments to the wife's clan. As bride prices began to include cash and other non-traditional valuables, young men were under pressure to earn money to assist their parents in accumulating bride prices for them. As local developments were patchy and unreliable sources of income, many young Gende were forced to migrate and take their chances finding a job. Differences in education and success in finding well-paid employment began to translate into some young men receiving all the attention (i.e. bride-price support and land rights) while others remained unmarried, in some cases labouring on their wealthier clan brothers' lands, in others living precariously in town. From the 1970s into the 1990s, as many as one half of Gende men between the ages of eighteen and forty-five were living in towns far distant from their home villages.

Women constituted a smaller proportion of the absentees as many young and middle-aged couples split their residence between town and village. While the wives of prosperous migrants contended with their husband's economic independence and sometimes their infidelities and violence, village women and women living in peri-urban settlements were still able to achieve some ideals of womanhood by raising pigs and tending well the incomes of less-prosperous husbands (Zimmer-Tamakoshi 1998). For young (and not-so young) bachelors, however, the situation was dire.

Within the past fifteen years, two foreign mining companies have begun what look to become highly profitable mining operations on Gende lands. One—best known as Ramu Nickel and run by the Chinese Metallurgical Construction Corporation (MCC) since 2005—is located in the forested hills and low mountains south of the Ramu plains in southern Madang Province. In the past this area was used by the Gende primarily for hunting and male initiation. In 1962, lateritic nickel was discovered at Kurumbukare and throughout the sixties and seventies a succession of companies held exploration titles to the Kurumbukare prospect. During the 1980s, exploration moved to the alluvial chromite deposits just north of Kurumbukare (near Daunangare village) but with improving nickel prices exploration resumed at Kurumbukare in 1989 and continued through the early 1990s.

In 1995, Highlands Gold (later known as Highlands Pacific) hired me to do a genealogical survey of Gende and Ramu peoples living in the area as part of a pre-feasibility study. Most of the people included in the survey had only recently moved in to the area to take advantage of potential developments. As the intermittent exploration at Kurumbukare throughout three decades had mirrored the same on and off again exploration and work at the Yandera copper prospect, many Gende 'landowners' had a hard time deciding where they should be investing their greatest efforts—at either Yandera or Kurumbukare. As I wrote in 2001 (and earlier in 1997b and 1997d), I was as first caught off guard by the wholesale 'ancestral gerrymandering' I witnessed at Kurumbukare and Daunangare village in 1995 and again in 2000 on a revisit. By participating in traditional *kwiagi* and other exchanges, alleged landowners at Ramu Nickel were negotiating new and old clan identities. Some of the alleged landowners were claiming membership (or rights on behalf of their children) in more than one clan in order to retain ties in Yandera as well as Kurumbukare—a legitimate but expensive process involving investing pigs and cash in both one's own and a second clan (most often one's wife's clan). Others, less able or unwilling to spread resources so far, denied membership in Yandera clans claiming I had got it all wrong during my earlier fieldwork there and that I was confusing their wives' clan membership with theirs (interestingly, most of these same individuals came rushing back to Yandera in 2007 to reassert land claims there with the arrival of Marengo Mining).

By the year 2000, initial cash payments had been distributed by Ramu Nickel to leading landowners and male heads of family at Kurumbukare. While the foreign concepts of 'landowner' and 'family head' do not fit Gende social reality in which hard-working women of renown can invest in land and speak for their family, Gende men and women see themselves as forced to accept western concepts if they are to receive compensation for their land. The results of this masculine-marked 'development', however, generated a wave of second marriages and domestic violence as older men spent their money and were banking on future compensation payments to fulfil bride prices for new wives. Older wives were angry not only because their husbands left them in the bush to tend gardens while the husbands were in Madang with their new wives, but also because the men were not helping their unmarried sons get wives of their own. All of this was generating inter-generational violence as well as sorcery accusations and physical violence against the older men and in some cases their younger brides. After my 2000 visit, email from Gende who were closer to the situation than I suggested that lethal violence and sorcery accusations were increasing as young men physically attacked their fathers and uncles or accused them (and sometimes their new brides) of sorcery. As one of the cases of young men's violence described below demonstrates, accusing someone of sorcery may be a convenient excuse for killing them and then demanding compensation (or land rights) for 'ridding the village' of the threat of further sorcery. Surprisingly little of the violence described here has ever made it into court, but the Gende's situation begs comparison with Philip Gibb's recent analysis of Simbu sorcery accusations (Gibbs 2010 and Ch. 3).

The other, most recent mining venture in Gende territory is run by the small Australian company Marengo Mining Limited. Marengo's base camp is located adjacent to Yandera village, the location of much of my early fieldwork with the Gende. In 2005, the same year that the Chinese Metallurgical Construction Corporation took over the development of the Ramu Nickel Project, Marengo Mining became involved with the Yandera project. In 2006, Marengo moved from 50 to 100 per cent ownership of the project and in May commenced drilling. The Yandera porphyry system contains one of the largest undeveloped porphyry copper-molybdenum deposits in the southwest Pacific region. For many people living in and around the project, the hope is that decades of frustration over the absence of any significant development are at an end.

In 2007, as part of the required feasibility studies begun by Marengo in July 2007, I and a team of four assistants carried out a social assessment and census of the entire Yandera community including both residents and absentees. We collected 227 household interviews, mapped Yandera village and its garden settlements, and took family photos of the entire village as part of the census data. As I discussed earlier, my analysis of this data showed that—at least for the moment—Yandera was virtually bachelor-free as men were either earning money by working for Marengo or winning it in card games with Marengo employees (and their families). It was also virtually lacking in older men, there were many confident older women raising pigs for sons' bride prices and *kwiagi* for their deceased husbands, and there were many subdued younger women pondering their husbands' polygyny and assumption of superiority over them in the context of mining's inevitable gender-biased plenitude (Zimmer-Tamakoshi 2008a).

In 2008, the team and I extended our census to include a number of Gende villages populated by Gegeru clans (former lineages of the old Gegeru clan) and a number of closely-related clans that I refer to here as 'Karizoko' (Karasokara is the place name of the largest of the Karizoko villages). The Gegeru villages we surveyed—Mangiai, Karamuke, Mokinangi, Kindakevi and Mondomo—are populated by families who constitute many of the major landowners at the Ramu Nickel prospect (as well as in the vicinity of their home villages) and most households have relatives working at Ramu Nickel. Now that Marengo is drilling in their territory and there is speculation that Mangiai may become the 'company town' (as opposed to Yandera or Bundi), many Gegeru families who have been away at Ramu or Madang are now returning to stake their claims. Tensions are high as families and individual family members argue over who retains land rights in the village after many family members have been away for years and some have not maintained active exchange relations relevant to the land in question (a reprise of the situation at Kurumbukare in the 1990s when claimants there argued over who had or had not maintained land rights during decades of disinterest in the then largely uninhabited rainforest). The outcomes of my research also show that at least since the early 1990s and even before, Gegeru peoples have been inter-marrying with members of other Gegeru clans as opposed to making marital alliances with their old allies in Yandera and elsewhere. This redirected sociability has been one way of limiting ownership of Kurumbukare lands (and related compensation payments) to Gegeru clansmen and clanswomen. Enabling this trend, divorce has been a more frequent occurrence among the Gegeru population in recent years as Gegeru men and women have shed non-Gegeru spouses in preference for second marriages with closely related Gegeru clan members. A second factor underlying this turning inwards seems to be a desire of many to forego the overlarge bride prices other Gende clans have been asking from the fairly prosperous Gegeru clans. With two mining companies interested in their lands, the Gegerus are in the arguably enviable position of being able to bargain over how and where they will work and sell their resources. An article in the *National*, 'Mine Shuts Down' (28 August 2008: 1) reported that workers at Kurumbukare were on strike demanding pay raises and demanding the Madang government and the China Metallurgical Construction Company pay heed to their grievances over 'poor working conditions'. How all of these new developments are affecting gender and inter-generational relations will be addressed in the next section. Suffice to say that lower bride prices give Gegeru women more opportunity to pay back their bride price through *tupoi* and to achieve a more equitable position in their marriages. This gender equity is also supported by brothers and sisters marrying nearby landowners and thus consolidating rights to large tracts of land (newly valuable because of the minerals it contains).

After completing the Gegeru census, the team and I moved on to a set of settlements—Karasokara, Ruvutara, Gogobagu, Imuri, Waganogoi, and Duatai—that are frequently lumped under the village name 'Karasokara'. The Karizoko and related clans in this area have for generations been enemies of Yandikari peoples (people living in Yandera) as well as Yandera's primary competitors in the large pig kills that were a focal point in the lives of Big Men and Women (see Zimmer-Tamakoshi 1997c).[3] Since Marengo started up work in 2006, Yandera men have dominated the workforce, demanding that they—and only they—should be hired. Conflicts between Karasokara people and Yandikaris have increased as a result of the mine with fights between Karasokara and Yandikari youths a frequent occurrence and Karasokara parents afraid to send their children to the local school in Yandera. In 2010 the situation worsened with parents from Karasokara and several other villages complaining that drunken Marengo workers were sexually assaulting young school girls.

Karasokara's social situation was rapidly changing in many ways, and like the Gegeru situation, the changes were resulting in increasing divisions in Gende society. My 2008 census of the Karasokara villages revealed that while some Karasokara men had waited for decades—along with other Gende—for the Yandera and Kurumbukare prospects to fulfil promises to usher in prosperity for all, bolster threatened masculinities and end the loss of so many marriageable women to non-Gende men, many had not. Over the years, not only had many Karasokara women married Simbu husbands but their brothers were marrying Simbus as well, most moving to the other side of the mountains to live with their Simbu in-laws. Few of these transplanted Gende men had more than one wife but with the help of their sisters and Simbu brothers-in-law they had carved out prosperous livings raising coffee and vegetables and selling them to markets more easily accessible because of the better network of roads on the Simbu side of the mountains.

In 2008, Marengo Mining surprised everyone by expanding their drilling operations into Karasokara clan territory. Every time the core samples showed evidence of copper and molybdenum near Waganogo village, Karasokara clansmen celebrated with dancing and singing. On Sunday 8 June 2008, the people at Waganogoi hosted a pig kill at which they killed over thirty pigs

---

3   Although rare, Gende have referred to some women as *ana nambaio* or Big Women. Women who are actively engaged in the Gende exchange system and generous to others are more commonly referred to as *ana mogeri* or good women. In exceptional cases they are referred to as *ana mogeri yonua* (very good women) or *ana nambaio*.

and gave one very large pig—subsequently named Napoleon—to the Marengo project manager. Most of the cooked pork and pigs were given to allies and in-laws, thereby excluding much of Yandera's population. Now that they too have the possibility of mining in their territory, the Karasokara people are demanding that only they—and certainly no Yandakaris—work at drill sites and camps in their territory.

Unfortunately for those Karasokara people living in the village—as opposed to those who have migrated out—their Simbu in-laws and local absentees are now showing up in the villages and demanding to be part of the expected bonanza. Many absentees have been hard put to pay their Simbu in-laws the higher bride prices demanded for Simbu brides and so are under pressure themselves to make sure that they too are considered fully-invested landowners back in their home villages. Conflicts between parents and brothers of absentees broke out on several occasions as my team and I carried out our interviews or I took my photos for the census record. While I was interested in getting full coverage of potential landowners, local citizens were beginning their battles with one another over who should or should not be included. Eventually this will be the focus of landowner associations but at that moment there was a panic about being included (or not). Older informants worked late into the night to include the names and families of daughters married to Simbu husbands as they fully expected that the daughters would return home to be compensated for land.

While Karasokara women married to Simbu husbands may be experiencing a new importance within their families and marriages, women in Yandera were beginning to voice their dissatisfaction over the general lack of employment for women within the mining operation. Washer women were already divided into several shifts who alternated work weeks. When the daughter of an out-married Yandera woman—who makes a hefty profit selling vegetables raised by Simbu women to the company—started working for Marengo as one of the laundry girls, all hell broke loose and she was driven off by young wives in Yandera village who themselves desired to earn some cash to help balance things between themselves and their employed husbands. Similarly, early on the morning of 24 June 2008, a group of women and children stormed the camp, throwing stones at the security gate and shouting their grievances and obscenities at the men. Several young women in particular were angry that there was no work for them at the camp, wanting the management to fire the camp secretary—who is Gende but whose father is the head of one of the Kurumbukare landowners' associations and who the young women said didn't need the work as much as they. They were especially angry with the daughter of an absentee who had arrived at the camp to do a practicum. The angry group drove her away and, on another day, physically attacked and bit the camp secretary. These angry demonstrations were in sharp contrast to young women's apparent biding their time in 2007. In 2010 I heard stories that women were being further oppressed by some Community Affairs officers (all male) demanding—and getting—sizeable kick-backs from women in order that the women be included in the list of laundry workers.

The above conflicts over work opportunities do not by any means exhaust women's conflicts with one another. Some of the most heated and long-lasting are, ostensibly, over men. For the remainder of this paper, I will examine some of the cultural and economic underpinnings of the escalating violence within the Gende community, focusing primarily on violence and men's contradictory experiences of power but also looking at the impact of changing masculinities on Gende women's strategies and well-being. I end the paper with some initial reflections on engendering solutions to male violence.

Violence and men's contradictory experiences of power

Melanesia has long been an important region for gender studies with its diverse concepts of masculine social, bodily and sexual development over the life cycle (Knauft 1999; Strathern 1988) and yet there are few comprehensive efforts—such as Jolly (2000), Richard Eves (2006) and John Taylor's collection (2008)—on how changing masculinities play into gender violence. In 1990, I published two papers that together investigate both traditional and contemporary attitudes and circumstances associated with young men's violent behaviour towards women and their elders (Zimmer 1990a and b). Both articles demonstrate the pivotal role of young men's access to crucial resources for attaining social manhood and the contradictory messages and experiences surrounding young men's coming of age. In 'Sexual Exploitation and Male Dominance in PNG' (1990b), I argued that 'rape, prostitution, and pornography are by no means new phenomena in Papua New Guinea' (p. 225). Citing ethnographic accounts as well as more recent cases reported in the *Post-Courier*, I argued further that 'while poverty or a sense of political injustice may motivate individuals to strike out at the society that has failed them, the form rebellion takes is culturally patterned' (p. 258). In many PNG societies, the basis for the subordination of women and the exploitation and manipulation of their sexuality was older men's control of most economic resources and male ideologies which portrayed women as dangerous, inferior, and untrustworthy creatures who were to be feared, kept under control, and avoided whenever possible. Such ideologies were directed primarily at young men as a means of keeping them away from women until the young men's elders felt it was time for them to marry. At the same time, the use of rape and physical violence to control 'unruly' women was commonplace and young men were sometimes encouraged to participate in the rapes and sexual abuse of women. While older men no longer control all economic resources and having a wife who raises pigs is no longer an absolute necessity for men of ambition, many young men are still dependent on their elders for bride-price support and access to land rights (which are especially key in areas of new development). For young men who opt (or are forced) to stay in town, unmarried and unrespectable by their parents' standards, joining gangs of other young men who make their own rules and standards is an attractive, albeit ultimately dead-end, proposition. In town, new ideas of women's inferiority and men's right to dominate them have been grafted onto the old, and definitions of masculinity are more free-floating and no longer under the control of the larger society young men act in.

A chilling example of how some young men justify their actions is the young urban gang-member I quoted in 'Wild Pigs and Dog Men' (1997e: 569) who back in 1982 bragged to me about kidnapping and raping young women. In response to my obvious shock he said, 'They liked it! It was like it is in a James Bond movie – sexy! The woman fights with James Bond and tries to kill him and then he forces her to have sex with him and she is his woman from then on. Sometimes he kills her if she is a really bad woman.' In reply to my question as to whether or not he had killed anyone, he said he had killed the one married woman because he feared she would tell her husband that he raped her (which he denied, insisting that it wasn't rape and that 'She liked it! I'm sexy!') In the past such a woman may have been safe—or at least avenged by husband or brother. Today such rapists must first be caught and then tried in a court system that is often too lenient or indifferent (see Hukula, Ch. 6; Zorn, Ch. 5). At the time, this young man had returned home to Yandera village to take advantage of a big pig feast and all the associated wealth (including cash) circulating among participants and in local card games. He and several other youths went on a month-long robbery spree as well as assaulting girls and women and mocking older men's frustrated threats of bodily harm to the offenders—frustrated because older men are no longer free to axe or bludgeon someone they desire to be rid of.

In another article published in 1990, on 'Conflict and Violence in Gende Society' (1990a), I focused on older persons as victims, trouble-makers and perpetrators of violence. Several key points in that article were (1) in efforts to balance their own exchange obligations, older persons favoured more prosperous migrants as exchange partners, often at the expense of their own sons; (2) delaying sons' marriages and/or withholding clear access to garden lands was a constant sore point between the generations; and (3) often—but not always—tensions were taken out on sisters or daughters with brothers and parents pressuring the girls to marry for larger bride prices regardless of a girl's personal choice of mate. Not every young man was violent, of course. Some who helped their mothers raise bride-price pigs also participated in high-stakes card games which enabled them to 'play at being men' (Zimmer 1987). A few swallowed their pride and worked on land belonging to wealthier clan brothers, sharing some of the pigs they raised with the absentee landowner (along with the help of their mothers and sisters or in a very few cases their young wives). This form of rent to the landlord practically guaranteed that such young men would not become renowned Big Men (since it made prosperous migrants even wealthier and more influential than they already were). But for some young men, this was preferable to living in town and becoming part of a gang of thugs or living off the kindness of others indefinitely.

Figure 6. Young men playing cards in Yandera in 1982.

Photograph by Laura Zimmer and courtesy of Laura Zimmer-Tamakoshi.

While violence against their elders was not common during the first twenty years I observed the Gende, there were incidents and even deaths (Zimmer 1990a). The relationship with the most conflict was that between father and sons. Sons expect fathers to help with land and bride-price support and to side with them in disputes involving other persons. While such support also comes from other persons, there can be quite a lot of bitterness when a significant amount of help is not forthcoming from a man's biological father. The same holds true for fathers who expect to be taken care of by their sons in later years.

A son's divided loyalties may become a source of irritation and recrimination and trigger violence, usually a few blows and the destruction of property and often the diversion of tensions onto a third party.

Relations between a father-in-law and his daughter's husband are also sources of conflict and violence and can pull in all sorts of aggrieved parties, including disappointed sons who pressure their fathers and sisters to end marriages that have failed to bring in bride prices large enough for them to acquire brides of their own. Acts of violence involving mothers and their children are rare, as women find many ways of helping children, be it in town or village, tending grandchildren while adult children work or themselves working indefatigably raising pigs. Relations between women and their daughters-in-law are less amicable, at least until the younger women have made *tupoi* (that is redeemed the bride price that was paid for them).

That the Gende have been and are a people under enormous stress became painfully clear in early 1991 when a leading Big Man was killed by a younger clan member in a fight over land (Zimmer-Tamakoshi 1997c). The argument began in 1982 when the younger man returned from town with his wife. He discovered that land that he had assumed was his, on which to plant gardens and coffee, was being used by one of the Big Man's three wives. The Big Man, Ruge Angiva, argued that he had been a large contributor to the deceased owner's death payments (*kwiagi*) in contrast to the returned migrant who had been away for years and contributed little to village exchanges. He graciously offered to allow the younger couple to use some of the land in question in return for a pig or two. This infuriated the younger man whose anger simmered and erupted periodically over the next nine years until he and another man got into an argument with the older man, hitting Ruge until he fell to the ground and then kicking him to death. That other men, including the Big Man's sons, watched without intervening suggests a great deal of resentment on the part of young men. During a visit in 1994, there was the sense that there were no longer any leaders who could command the respect of younger men and manage capitalist development and all its attendant inequalities for the good of the people.

In this case and others, it became clear that one of the biggest contradictions, or paradoxes, young Gende men struggle with is that despite patriarchal assertions of male superiority, traditionally Gende women can achieve great influence and even power through their participation in the Gende exchange system and young men and women were (and in many cases still are) as dependent on women's help as they are on men's. In 'Empowered Women' (Zimmer-Tamakoshi 1997a), I showed how Gende women, by redeeming their bride prices (*tupoi*) and helping husbands fulfil child wealth (TP: *bun pe*; G: *wana yamindikai inime*, a Gende figure of speech meaning paying 'those who gave bones' to the child, i.e. mother's clan) obligations to the women's families, achieved a measure of independence and respect within their own and their husbands' clans. At this point in their lives, usually middle-aged and no longer bearing children, ambitious women were free to invest the pigs they raised pretty much as they wished and even to leave unruly husbands (a disaster for most men). Such women never had a lack of male helpers as there were always young men or ambitious brothers or Big Men who would help them clear gardens so the women could raise many pigs.

In recent times, with cash part of every bride price and every other form of exchange, it is more difficult for most women to redeem their bride prices much less catch up in the exchange cycle. Even so, most women contribute significantly to their *tupoi* obligations, giving pigs as well as cash they have earned from selling pigs to others. Ordinary women still manage to wield a certain amount of influence over others as I have shown in past writing. Older women were crucial in bringing about the closing of a large cardamom plantation that threatened their control over young women and did little to help them keep up with inflationary exchange payments (Zimmer-Tamakoshi 1996). Women living in a small settlement of Gende on the outskirts of Goroka managed their husbands' fairly low incomes in ways that allowed such couples to raise their children in urban environments (with better education and health care), while at the same time they held on to land rights in their home villages by raising pigs and nurturing cash through good financial management of their less-prosperous husbands' incomes (Zimmer-Tamakoshi 1998). Without their wives, these men would be nothing, which the wives were quick to remind their husbands should they come home drunk or try to fool around.

While young men sometimes chafe at all this feminine control, perhaps most annoying is the unusual success of some women, particularly the extremely successful entrepreneurial daughter of the aforementioned Big Man, Ruge Angiva. Towards the end of his life, as local development seemed more and more of an impossibility, Ruge's daughter pulled her business ventures out of Yandera village, and he urged his followers to follow her to her new business location. Then the Big Man began calling himself her *boi*. In using a negative colonial term to describe himself, the Big Man was both attempting to manipulate his daughter into giving him a more respectable position in her business enterprises and expressing his own despair over his lack of control of the bigger process. Not wanting to be anyone's *boi*, much less that of a fairly young woman, the Big Man's killers were quite clear in their deadly intentions.

With cash now pouring into the Gende exchange system in decidedly unequal ways, there are unfortunately plentiful opportunities to examine violence of all kinds among the Gende. Based on what I have witnessed during my most recent field seasons (2007, 2008, 2009, 2010 and 2011), older men no longer have the upper hand at Yandera, but they do in the Gegeru home villages we surveyed.

How long that will last, however, remains to be seen as the following incident demonstrates. Towards the end of my 2008 fieldwork I was in Madang working on an interim report for Marengo Mining and interviewing Ramu Nickel landowners when I heard news of a vicious killing in Kindakevi village. The unmarried nephews of one Gegeru landowner we had interviewed had axed their uncle to death, claiming he was a sorcerer. According to my informants, few people believed in the accusation, stating that the nephews had been angry with their uncle for claiming ownership of both his own and their deceased father's land. To prove they were acting on a sincere belief that their uncle was a sorcerer, the youths chopped up his body and burnt it along with his house. Angry villagers threatened the young men, calling them good-for-nothing murderers. The youths fled to Madang to avoid arrest. In response, close kin of the murdered man then bound up several women (including the young men's mother), threatening to bury them alive if the killers did not return to face their accusers and pay compensation for the murder. More than a month after this event, the youths had not returned to Kindakevi, there was no serious police action taken (there are virtually no police at Bundi station since most had moved down to Brahman to be closer to Ramu Nickel) and the women were shaken but unharmed. The murder is not forgotten, but many Gegeru 'landowners' are now nervous about the possibility of more violence and wondering if old customs surrounding land ownership will prevail in an extremely tense, virtually lawless and greed-inducing situation.

The above violence shows how young men's frustrations and need to acquire (or control) wealth in order to be 'real men' can lead to violence when older men and women seemingly, or in actuality, disregard their needs. It also demonstrates how the violence can spread to include the taking of hostages and threats of reprisals against female relatives of the accused. I would claim that all of this violence and threats of violence—young men against older men, men against women—is best described as 'engendered' violence because the root causes are gender-related: a desire to achieve manhood through marriage, the threat of losing one's mother and best bride price supporter. The new lawlessness suggests an individual man or woman can take things into their own hands and wrongly deprive another of their life in order to gain something of newly-heightened value.

After a season of quiet among the young wives at Yandera in 2007, their outbursts in 2008 suggested that Gende women were not going down without a fight. I was also not surprised when one very angry Gegeru wife and mother of several children arrived at my field home in Mangiai village one evening demanding an interview. Abandoned by her Kindakevi husband for another woman, the old wife had taken her family to her home village where she was planting gardens and raising pigs to complete her *tupoi* obligations to her Kindakevi in-laws.

Her husband was living in another Gegeru village along with his new wife, a Mondomo woman who had recently left her Yandera husband—who has a well-paying job at Marengo—because he was too *bik het* (TP: big-headed). The cast-off wife was angry that her Kindakevi in-laws had not included her and her children in the interview for the house she and her husband had shared. Given that she had repaid much of her bride price to them and that she had always supported her husband's clan's exchange events, she and her children—including her teenage son—had every right to be angry at their attempt to erase them from the record. That her Kindakevi in-laws favoured the new wife, however, was not surprising for the land surrounding her home village of Mondomo is also under consideration by Marengo whereas the first wife's is not.

Conclusion: Engendering solutions to male violence

In addition to documenting violence and its probable causes, it is essential to explore solutions. The violence I have described is engendered. It rises out of tensions within the gendered matrix of Gende social relations, as well as the larger, equally—albeit differently—gendered systems within which the Gende are citizens and workers. I expect the most useful solutions will also be structurally gendered. In her work exploring Kup women's efforts to address issues of tribal fighting and violence against women and children in the Kup Sub-District of Simbu Province, Sarah Garap (2004) makes a distinction between two forms of violence, calling the one 'tribal' and the other 'gendered'. By separating tribe/community and 'women and children', however, Garap misses the point that the Kup community is pervasively gendered. What are the tribes fighting about if not the impact social inequalities have on the have-nots? And what is it they have-not? Women, land (without which one does not get or keep a wife) and cash. The artificial separation of tribal fighting from 'gendered' violence is also evident in Garap's statement that women and young girls are prime targets for vengeance to shame and provoke the enemy (2004: 5). Without unravelling the complete matrix of engendered 'tribal' relations—such as relations between older and younger men and how these affect both older and younger men's access to (or better yet, relations with) women and power— one misses out on fuller explanations for violence against Kup women and children. Just as relatives of the murdered Kindakevi man threatened vengeance against female relatives of the killers in order to cut them off from the valuable resources the women represent for the young men, so too is it logical that 'tribal' enemies would strike against the enemy's wives and children considering their culturally and economically high value to male relatives. Other attempts to connect 'domestic' and 'public' violence include Jolly's Epilogue to *Reflections on Violence in Melanesia* (2000) (see also Jolly's Introduction, this volume).

While it is important that women are taking a visible stance against violence and destruction, Kup women's objectives and strategies are not focused on how to better deal with young men's violent behaviour other than to get them to surrender their weapons and receive amnesty from the government, to publicly apologise and to promise not to involve themselves in any 'bad habits and criminal behaviour' again (2004: 8). Garap describes some of the short-term euphoria over temporary halts in tribal fighting but goes on to conclude that 'there are no quick fix solutions to the many socio-economic and political problems of Papua New Guinea' (2004: 12). Indeed! Until young men (and young women) are included within our models of 'community' as being something other than merely trouble-makers, and until we take their social needs seriously, there will be no peace. Community-based initiatives require the input and support of all segments of society along with more fine-grained analyses of local social relations. In an article on women in PNG's village courts, Michael Goddard argues that women use village courts more than is commonly recognised and are less put-upon because of it (2004). That this may not be as effective as Goddard supposes is evident in the extreme measures taken by Wardlow's 'wayward women' to assert their value and independence from 'the system', however negatively expressed (2006). In this chapter I have explored the notion that we need to pay greater attention to young men's social needs than we have in the past and be wary of conflating 'gender' with 'woman' and perpetuating stereotypes regarding who is or who is not affected negatively by changes brought about by development and globalisation (Zimmer-Tamakoshi 2008b).

Paying attention to the voices of different segments of Gende society over the years—including those of both bachelors and young women—I have documented in some detail how marriage and the bride-price system have proven to be minefields in one way or another for most Gende (e.g. Zimmer 1984, 1987 and Zimmer-Tamakoshi 1993a, 1996). Some societies, such as the PNG fringe-highlanders studied by James G. Flanagan (1997) and Susan M. Pflanz-Cook (1993) have, at least in the past, reined in their bride-price systems preferring balance in inter-group relations and exchange, resisting the outright sale of sisters and other women documented by myself (Zimmer-Tamakoshi 1993a) and Dan Jorgensen for the Telefolmin (1993).

Any community-based solutions to gender violence and other gender-related violence such as that occurring between the generations must address the possibility that the bride-price system ought to be curtailed and cut off from local and global market forces (as was reported for the Tolai decades ago, see

Epstein 1968: 93, 150). As I have shown here and elsewhere, the Gende's bride-price system includes the possibility for women to acquire prestige and influence through *tupoi*. I would not therefore suggest the eradication of the Gende's exchange system (Gende women still use *tupoi* as an expression of their involvement and importance in Gende society). It would be better if it were reined in and some thought given to a more equitable distribution of household compensation monies by both the government and those in charge of the distribution of wealth from such gender-biased industries as the mining industry. In such an ideal scenario, the wealth of the community would be directed towards males and females of all ages. Nor am I suggesting that the young killers in Kindakevi be given what they have not worked for. Rather, landowner associations and all legitimate claimants, with the support and oversight by the government, should be joint recipients of any compensation, thereby allowing a greater range of actors to participate in locally desired social relations. While it seems unlikely that the flush former bachelors of Yandera are going to change their competitive exchange system any time soon, at least some Gende, the Gegerus, for example, have managed their marriages in a way that reduces bride price and ensures that land rights and compensation stay closer to home. How much compensation actually will end up in the hands of Gegeru women remains to be seen. With lower bride prices, they have more of a chance to fulfil their *tupoi* obligations to in-laws and therefore more of a voice in their communities. But unless women as well as men serve on local landowner associations, it is unlikely that men will pay as much attention to women as they should. 'Troubled masculinities' are not a thing of the past for Gende males and even men who are now out of the woods are not likely to forget the sting of past humiliations. Holding fast to their newfound gains, Gende men may bring about a form of 'development' that is no development at all: unbalanced, full of new conflicts, and humiliating for both women and men who do not benefit from the current development 'opportunities'.

References

Banks, Glenn, 1999. The economic impact of the mine. In *Dilemmas of Development: The Social and Economic Impact of the Porgera Gold Mine 1989–1994*, ed. Colin Filer, 88–127. Canberra: Asia Pacific Press.

Billy, Afu, 2000. Breaking the silence, speaking out truths: domestic violence in Solomon Islands. In *Reflections on Violence in Melanesia*, ed. Sinclair Dinnen and Allison Ley, 172–77. Sydney: Hawkins Press and Asia Pacific Press.

Billy, Afu, Hazel Lulei and Jully Sipolo, eds, 1983. *'Mi Mere': Poetry and Prose by Solomon Islands Women Writers*. Honiara: University of the South Pacific, Solomon Islands Centre.

Borrey, Anou, 2000. Sexual violence in perspective: the case of Papua New Guinea. In *Reflections on Violence in Melanesia*, ed. Sinclair Dinnen and Allison Ley, 105–18. Sydney: Hawkins Press and Asia Pacific Press.

Bradley, Christine, 1994. Why male violence against women is a development issue: reflections from Papua New Guinea. In *Women and Violence*, ed. Miranda Davies, 10–26. London: Zed Books Ltd.

Counts, Dorothy Ayres, Judith K. Brown and Jacquelyn C. Campbell, eds, 1992. *Sanctions and Sanctuary: Cultural Perspectives on the Beating of Wives*. Boulder: Westview Press.

Coursen-Neff, Zama, 2005. 'Making their own rules': police beatings, rape, and torture of children in Papua New Guinea. *Human Rights Watch*, 30 August. Online: http://www.hrw.org/en/node/11626/section/1. Accessed 6 April 2011.

Dinnen, Sinclair, 1996. Law, order, and state. In *Modern PNG Society*, ed. Laura Zimmer-Tamakoshi, 333–50. Kirksville, MO: Thomas Jefferson University Press.

‒‒‒‒‒‒‒‒ 2000. Violence and governance in Melanesia: an introduction. In *Reflections on Violence in Melanesia*, ed. Sinclair Dinnen and Allison Ley, 1–16. Sydney: Hawkins Press and Asia Pacific Press.

Dinnen, Sinclair and Alison Ley, 2000. *Reflections on Violence in Melanesia*, Sydney: Hawkins Press and Asia Pacific Press.

Dinnen, Sinclair and Edwina Thompson, 2004. Gender and small arms violence in Papua New Guinea. Discussion Paper 2004/8. State, Society and Governance in Melanesia Project, Research School of Pacific and Asian Studies. Canberra: The Australian National University.

Epstein, T.S., 1968. *Capitalism, Primitive and Modern: Some Aspects of Tolai Economic Growth*. Canberra: Australian National University Press.

Errington, Frederick and Deborah Gewertz, 2005. On humiliation and class in contemporary Papua New Guinea. In *The Making of Global and Local Modernities in Melanesia*, ed. Joel Robbins and Holly Wardlow, 163–170. Hampshire: Ashgate Publishing.

Eves, Richard, 2006. *Exploring the Role of Men and Masculinities in Papua New Guinea in the 21st Century: How to address violence in ways that generate empowerment for both men and women.* Report for Caritas Australia. Online: http://www.baha.com.pg/downloads/Masculinity%20and%20 Violence%20in%20PNG.pdf. Accessed 28 November 2010.

Filer, Colin and Martha Macintyre, 2006. Grass roots and deep holes: community responses to mining in Melanesia. In *Melanesian Mining, Modernities: Past, Present, and Future*, ed. Paige West and Martha Macintyre. Special issue of *The Contemporary Pacific* 18(2): 215–32. Honolulu: University of Hawai'i Press.

Flanagan, James G., 1997. Exchanging sisters is not a game. In *Social Organization and Cultural Aesthetics: Essays in Honor of William H. Davenport*, ed. William W. Donner and James G. Flanagan, 61–72. Lanham, MD: University Press of America, Inc.

Garap, Sarah, 2000. Struggles of women and girls – Simbu Province, Papua New Guinea. In *Reflections on Violence in Melanesia,* ed. Sinclair Dinnen and Allison Ley, 159–71. Sydney: Hawkins Press and Asia Pacific Press.

-------- 2004. Kup women for peace: women taking action to build peace and influence community decision-making. Discussion Paper 2004/4. State, Society and Governance in Melanesia Project, Research School of Pacific and Asian Studies. Canberra: The Australian National University.

Gibbs, Philip, 2010. Witchkilling and engendered violence in Simbu. *Catalyst* 40(1): 24–64.

Goddard, Michael, 2004. Women in Papua New Guinea's village courts. Discussion Paper 2004/3. State, Society and Governance in Melanesia Project, Research School of Pacific and Asian Studies. Canberra: The Australian National University.

-------- 2005. *The Unseen City: Anthropological Perspectives on Port Moresby, Papua New Guinea.* Canberra: Pandanus Books.

Hogan, Evelyn, 1985. Controlling the bodies of women: reading gender ideologies in Papua New Guinea. In *Women and Politics in Papua New Guinea*, ed. Maev O'Collins *et al.*, 54–71. Working Paper No. 6, Canberra: Department of Political and Social Change, The Australian National University.

Jenkins, Carol (and The National Sex and Reproduction Research Team), 1994. *National Study of Sexual and Reproductive Knowledge and Behaviour in Papua New Guinea.* Monograph 10. Papua New Guinea Institute of Medical Research.

Jolly, Margaret, 1994. *Women of the Place:* Kastom, *Colonialism and Gender in Vanuatu*. Chur and Reading: Harwood Academic Press.

-------- 1997. Woman-nation-state in Vanuatu: women as signs and subjects in the discourses of *kastom*, modernity and Christianity. In *Narratives of Nation in the South Pacific*, ed. Ton Otto and Nicholas Thomas, 133–62. Amsterdam: Harwood Academic Publishers.

-------- 2000. Further reflections on violence in Melanesia. In *Reflections on Violence in Melanesia*, ed. Sinclair Dinnen and Allison Ley, 305–24. Sydney: Hawkins Press and Asia Pacific Press.

Jorgensen, Dan, 1993. Money and marriage in Telefolmin: from sister exchange to daughter as trade store. In *The Business of Marriage: Transformations in Oceanic Matrimony*, ed. Richard A. Marksbury, 57–82. ASAO Monograph No. 14. Pittsburgh: University of Pittsburgh Press.

-------- 2006. Hinterland history: the Ok Tedi Mine and its cultural consequences in Telefolmin. In *Melanesian Mining, Modernities: Past, Present, and Future*, ed. Paige West and Martha Macintyre. Special issue of *The Contemporary Pacific* 18(2): 233–63. Honolulu: University of Hawai'i Press.

Josephides, Lisette, 1993. Gendered violence in a changing society: the case of urban Papua New Guinea. *Journal de la Société des Océanistes* 99: 187–96.

Kaufman, Michael, 1994. Men, feminism, and men's contradictory experiences of power. In *Theorizing Masculinities*, ed. Harry Brod and Michael Kaufman, 59–85. Thousand Oaks, CA: Sage Publications.

-------- 1999. *The 7 P's of Men's Violence, 1998 Workshop Organised by Save the Children (UK), Kathmandu, Nepal*. Printed online in Toronto, Canada, October. Online: http://www.michaelkaufman.com/1999/10/04/the-7-ps-of-mens-violence. Accessed 11 April 2011.

Knauft, Bruce, 1999. *From Primitive to Postcolonial in Melanesia and Anthropology*. Ann Arbor: The University of Michigan Press.

Macintyre, Martha, 2000. Major issues in law and order affecting women and children. Discussion Paper (1–25 September). Port Moresby: Royal Papua New Guinea Constabulary Development Project Phase III.

Molisa, Grace Mera, 1987. *Colonised People*. Port Vila, Vanuatu: Blackstone Publications.

-------- 1989. *Black Stone II*. Port Vila, Vanuatu: University of the South Pacific, Vanuatu Centre.

O'Collins, Maev, 2000. Images of violence in Papua New Guinea. Whose images? Whose reality? In *Reflections on Violence in Melanesia*, ed. Sinclair Dinnen and Allison Ley, 19–34. Sydney: Hawkins Press and Asia Pacific Press.

Pflanz-Cook, Susan M., 1993. Manga marriage in transition, from 1961 to 1981. In *The Business of Marriage: Transformations in Oceanic Matrimony*, ed. Richard A. Marksbury, 105–26. ASAO Monograph No. 14. Pittsburgh: University of Pittsburgh Press.

Robbins, Joel and Holly Wardlow, eds, 2005. *The Making of Global and Local Modernities in Melanesia: Humiliation, Transformation and the Nature of Cultural Change*. Hampshire: Ashgate Publishing.

Rosi, Pamela and Laura Zimmer-Tamakoshi, 1993. Love and marriage among the educated elite in Port Moresby. In *The Business of Marriage: Transformations in Oceanic Matrimony*, ed. Richard A. Marksbury, 175–204. ASAO Monograph No. 14. Pittsburgh: University of Pittsburgh Press.

Sahlins, Marshall, 2005 [1992]. The economics of develop-man in the Pacific. Reprinted in *The Making of Global and Local Modernities in Melanesia*, ed. Joel Robbins and Holly Wardlow, 23–42. Hampshire: Ashgate Publishing.

Strathern, Andrew, 1993. Violence and political change in Papua New Guinea. *Pacific Studies* 16(4): 41–60.

Strathern, Marilyn, 1988. *The Gender of the Gift: Problems with Women and Problems with Society in Melanesia*. Berkeley: University of California Press.

Taylor, John P., ed., 2008. *Changing Pacific Masculinities*. Special issue of *The Australian Journal of Anthropology* 19(2).

Toft, Susan, ed., 1985. *Domestic Violence in Papua New Guinea*. Monograph No. 3. Law Reform Commission, Papua New Guinea.

-------- 1986. *Domestic Violence in Urban Papua New Guinea*. Occasional Paper No. 19. Law Reform Commission, Papua New Guinea.

Toft, Susan and Susanne Bonnell, eds, 1985. *Marriage and Domestic Violence in Rural Papua New Guinea: Results of a Research Project Conducted by the Law Reform Commission and Administrative College of Papua New Guinea*. Port Moresby: Papua New Guinea Law Reform Commission.

Wardlow, Holly, 2006. *Wayward Women: Sexuality and Agency in a New Guinea Society*. Berkeley: University of California Press.

Zimmer, Laura J., 1984. Pigs, money, migrants, or men? Identity crisis in the Highlands of Papua New Guinea. Paper read at the session on 'Migration' at the 83rd Annual Meeting of the American Anthropological Association in Denver, Colorado, November.

-------- 1987. Playing at being men. In *Gambling with Cards in Melanesia and Australia*, ed. Laura J. Zimmer. Special issue of *Oceania* 58(1): 22–37.

-------- 1990a. Conflict and violence in Gende society: older persons as victims, trouble-makers, and perpetrators. In *Domestic Violence in Oceania*, ed. Dorothy Counts. Special issue of *Pacific Studies* 13(3): 205–24.

-------- 1990b. Sexual exploitation and male dominance in PNG. In *Human Sexuality in Melanesian Cultures*. Special issue of *Point* Series 14: 250–67.

Zimmer-Tamakoshi, Laura, 1993a. Bachelors, spinsters, and *'pamuk meris'*. In *The Business of Marriage: Transformations in Oceanic Matrimony*, ed. Richard A. Marksbury, 83–104. ASAO Monograph No. 14. Pittsburgh: University of Pittsburgh Press.

-------- 1993b. Nationalism and sexuality in Papua New Guinea. *Pacific Studies* 16(4): 20–48.

-------- 1995. Passion, poetry, and cultural politics in the South Pacific. In *The Politics of Culture in the Pacific*, ed. Richard Feinberg and Laura Zimmer-Tamakoshi. Special issue of *Ethnology* (Spring & Summer): 113–27.

-------- 1996. The women at Kobum Spice Company: tensions in a local age stratification system and the undermining of development. In *Women, Age, and Power: The Politics of Age Difference Among Women in Papua New Guinea and Australia*, ed. Jeanette Dickerson-Putman. Special issue of *Pacific Studies* 19(4): 71–98.

-------- 1997a. Empowered women. In *Social Organization and Cultural Aesthetics: Essays in Honor of William H. Davenport*, ed. William W. Donner and James G. Flanagan, 45–60. Lanham: University Press of America, Inc.

-------- 1997b. Everyone (or no one) a winner: Gende compensation ethics and practices. In *Compensation for Resource Development in Papua New Guinea*, ed. Susan Toft, 66–83. Papua New Guinea Law Reform Commission Monograph No. 6. Port Moresby.

-------- 1997c. The last big man: development and men's discontents in the Papua New Guinea Highlands. *Oceania* 68(2): 107–22.

-------- 1997d. When land has a price: ancestral gerrymandering and the resolution of land conflicts at Kurumbukare. In *Rights to Land and Resources in Papua New Guinea: Changing and Conflicting Views*, ed. Paula Brown and Anton Ploeg. Special issue of *Anthropological Forum* 7(4): 649–66.

-------- 1997e. Wild pigs and dog men: rape and domestic violence as women's issues in Papua New Guinea. In *Gender in Cross-Cultural Perspective*, ed. Caroline B. Brettell and Carolyn F. Sargent, 538–53. Upper Saddle River: NJ: Prentice-Hall.

-------- 1998. Women in town: housewives, homemakers and household managers. In *Modern Papua New Guinea*, ed. Laura Zimmer-Tamakoshi, 195–210. Kirksville, MO: Thomas Jefferson University Press.

-------- 2001. Development and ancestral gerrymandering: David Schneider in Papua New Guinea. In *The Cultural Analysis of Kinship: The Legacy of David Schneider and Its Implications for Anthropological Relativism*, ed. Richard Feinberg and Martyn Ottenheimer, 187–203. Champaign, IL: University of Illinois Press.

-------- 2004. Rape and other sexual aggression. In *The Encyclopedia of Sex and Gender*, ed. Carol R. Ember and Melvin Ember, 230–43. New York: Kluwer.

-------- 2006. Uncertain futures, uncertain pasts. Paper presented in working session on Mine Closure in the Pacific: Past Experiences and Anticipated Futures, co-organised by Dan Jorgensen and Glenn Banks. ASAO annual meeting, February, San Diego CA.

-------- 2008a. *Final Report: 2007 Yandera Survey/Census*. Prepared for Marengo Mining Ltd. Perth, Australia.

-------- 2008b. It's not about women only. In *Pulling the Right Threads: The Ethnographic Life and Legacy of Jane C. Goodale*, ed. Laura Zimmer-Tamakoshi and Jeanette Dickerson-Putman, 56–76. Champaign, IL: University of Illinois Press.

3. Engendered Violence and Witch-killing in Simbu

Philip Gibbs

Abstract

Belief in *kumo* witchcraft has led and continues to lead to the gruesome deaths of many people in Simbu and elsewhere. This belief, whether real or imaginary, has consequences in thought and behaviour. Whether the victims are those killed by 'witches' or those accused of being 'witches', the suffering, death and social disruption are real. With reference to twenty cases, the paper seeks to shed light on the engendered nature of *kumo* witchcraft in Simbu. How true is it that women are much more likely than men to suffer this form of violence? Aside from direct violence, to what extent is the *kumo* phenomenon 'engendered'? Are traditional or contemporary gender relations a significant feature and, if so, how are such gender relations influenced by modernisation and other socio-economic factors? It seems that Simbu people believe that males are more likely than women to die as a result of witchcraft. However, from the cases presented and the police and hospital records there is every indication that women are more likely to suffer violence as a result of being *accused* of witchcraft.

Introduction

Newspapers in Papua New Guinea (PNG) frequently carry headlines such as 'Sorcerers burnt alive' (*National* 2–4 May 2008: 1), 'Duo tortured, butchered and burnt' (*National* 5 February 2008: 3), 'Callous murder' (*Post-Courier* 10 January 2008: 1) or 'Woman "hanged" for sorcery delivers baby' (*National* 26 February 2008: 5). Most of these cases involve the brutal torture or killing of women accused of sorcery or witchcraft.[1]

An Amnesty International Report on Violence Against Women in PNG, which received considerable international publicity, reports the PNG Minister for Social Welfare Dame Carol Kidu as saying that although both men and women

---

1 I wish to thank the many people who contributed to this paper in sharing their ideas and experiences. For obvious reasons it is better that they remain anonymous. An earlier version of this paper appeared as: Witchkilling and engendered violence in Simbu, in *Catalyst* 40 (2010): 24–64.

are targeted, women are reportedly six times more likely than men to suffer violence (Amnesty International 2006: 24). These forms of violence are described in the Amnesty International report as follows:

> Often when a person within a community falls ill or dies unexpectedly, the community suspects that a curse or spell has been cast. The alleged sorcerer is identified, interrogated, tortured and often murdered in 'pay back' for the harm they are thought to have inflicted. The methods of torture used include beating (often with barbed wire), breaking bones, burning with red hot metal, raping, hanging over fire, cutting body parts slowly, amputating and pulling behind vehicles. If treatments of this kind do not result in death, often the victim is then killed by being thrown over a cliff, into a river or cave; burned alive in a house fire; buried alive; beheaded; hanged; choked to death, starved; axed or electrocuted; suffocated with smoke; forced to drink petrol or hot liquid, stoned or shot (Amnesty International 2006: 24).

The horrific list of torture and methods of murder is indeed correct, according to my enquiries. But is it correct to say that women are six times more likely to be subject to this violence? Dame Carol Kidu, when asked about the reference in the Amnesty International Report, replied that she does not recall making any statement about a six to one ratio of women to men, to Amnesty International or anyone else (Personal Communication, 27 Nov 2006).[2] Yet Michael Unage and Patrick Kaiku have also suggested that five out of six victims of witchcraft execution are women (*National* 5 March 2008: 15; 6 May 2008: 18).[3]

Reports on these brutal killings focus mainly on the PNG Highlands or communities of Highlanders in coastal towns. Behind such violence, the principal motive is belief in *kumo* witchcraft in the Simbu Province, PNG.[4] There are related beliefs in parts of the Western Highlands (Reay 1959: 138) and the Eastern Highlands (Newman, 1965). This paper seeks to shed light on the engendered nature of *kumo* witchcraft in Simbu. How true is it that women are much more likely than men to suffer this form of violence? Apart from the violence experienced, to what extent is the *kumo* phenomenon 'engendered'?

---

2 'I can't think why figures were attributed to me. I keep trying to remember the conversations I had with Amnesty International and the context and if I had heard anything at the time that I would have referred to in passing. However I cannot recall the details' (personal communication with Dame Carol Kidu, 27 November 2006).

3 Michael Unage also replies that he cannot now recall where he got that statistic from for the statement that five out of six victims of witchcraft execution are women (personal communication, 30 March 2009).

4 This is a peculiarity of parts of the Wahgi Valley, Simbu and the Eastern Highlands, because in other parts of the PNG Highlands, such as Enga and most of the Southern Highlands, people generally attribute death to the malevolent work of the spirits of the dead, not to spirit beings inhabiting the living. At Independence the Province was known as the Chimbu province; however, the Provincial Government now uses the term Simbu, which is becoming the accepted form.

Are traditional or contemporary gender relations a significant feature and, if so, how are such gender relations influenced by modernisation and other socio-economic factors?

Witchcraft or sorcery?

A search for the term 'sorcery' in the *Post-Courier* and the *National* daily newspapers between January and December 2008 shows eighty reports in which twenty-five refer to women sorcerers and seventeen to men as sorcerers. In thirty-nine reports the gender of the sorcerer is not specified (one report referred to both male and female sorcerers). Of the eighty reports, seven locate the sorcery in the Simbu Province and of those in Simbu all refer to women accused of sorcery, although one of these reports also included a male along with two women.

A search for the term 'witchcraft' in the same two papers from January to December 2008 revealed twenty-six reports. It is of note that all but five of these referred to witchcraft along with sorcery—usually in the expression 'sorcery and witchcraft'. The gender of the witch is mentioned in only two cases. In twenty-four out of twenty-six cases the gender of the witch is not specified. Simbu is mentioned in one report and in that case the reference is to a male. In nineteen out of twenty-six reports the place was not specified.

Table 1. Use of three terms in the *Post-Courier* and the *National* Daily Newspapers, Jan. to Dec. 2008.

	Male	Female	Unspecified	From Simbu Province
'Sorcery'	25	17	39	7 (all women)
'Witchcraft'	2	-	24	1 (male)
'Sanguma'	1	-	5	2 (1 male, 1 unspecified)

A search for the term *sanguma* in the same papers revealed six reports. In all but one, the gender is not specified and in the one case where it is specified it refers to a male, in Simbu. Simbu is mentioned in two cases and the other four leave the place unspecified. Such varied use of terms in the media calls for clarification on the use of terms in this paper.

Writing on witchcraft among the Azande in West Africa, Edward Evans-Pritchard (1937: 387) distinguished sorcery and witchcraft in terms of the former using techniques of magic, while the later uses hereditary psycho-physical powers. Leonard Glick, writing on Papua and New Guinea, offers a similar distinction, 'A sorcerer's capacity to harm … depends on his ability to control extrinsic powers; whereas a witch, who can inflict sickness or death on others simply by staring at them or willing evil on them, possesses powers inherited or acquired as an intrinsic part of his or her person' (1973: 182). Aside from the extrinsic/intrinsic distinction it is notable that Glick allows for both men and women as witches. This is in contrast to western imagery where the term 'witch' is strongly gendered as female. Garry Trompf (1991: 92–93) uses gender to distinguish witches (female) and sorcerers (male).

Heinrich Aufenanger, writing on the Central Highlands in the 1960s, considered witchcraft and sorcery together as 'an evil, supernatural power, which a man or a woman acquires from a bad, personal spirit or spirit-like being, and which he or she uses for asocial purposes, for doing harm to people and animals' (1965: 104). I will use Aufenanger's description of witchcraft in Simbu in this chapter.

The translation of indigenous terms into English can be complex. The Simbu themselves use the term *sanguma*, normally used in a wider context for assault sorcery, to refer to *kumo* witchcraft.[5] Caspar Damien writes how 'In Simbu, *sanguma* is used to mean *kumo* and its evil activity .... *Sanguma* is used widely for *kumo* and has the same meaning in this context' (2005: 116). Damien is correct when referring to Simbu, however, because of the ambiguity of the term in other parts of PNG, this chapter will not utilise the term *sanguma* but rather the local Simbu term *kumo* or the English terms 'witch/witchcraft'.

Joachim Sterly notes how the Simbu do not hold *kumo* responsible for all unexpected deaths. He distinguishes malevolent spirits, sorcery and witchcraft in Simbu (1987: 87). The Simbu fear a multiplicity of super-powerful beings, which can bring sickness and death. For example spirits of the dead may punish people with insanity, constipation and body pains. There are also *dingan* 'demons' that appear in the form of earthworms *dengreme amban* and strike people with emaciation, kidney pains, blood in the urine and swelling of the private parts. Paula Brown notes the existence of potentially dangerous spirits in the mountains and bush, some able to be controlled and some not (1995: 29–30).

There are also practices of harmful magic—to be used against stealing from gardens, to punish a tardy debtor or to weaken an enemy before a fight. The Simbu know about lethal sorcery as it is manifest elsewhere in New Guinea, including their neighbours on the Madang side of the Bismarck Range, but it is not part of their own traditions. Sterly notes how people feared a Simbu sorcerer who obtained his magical spells and accessories from the Ramu as gifts in the bride-price process, and brought them into the upper Simbu, yet they did not equate such sorcery with their own *kumo* (Sterly 1987: 96).[6] When a witch gives

5   For a discussion of the various meanings and derivation of the term *sanguma*, see McCallum 2006.
6   Sterly notes that it is not possible to completely demarcate the two realms from each other, because both magic and witchcraft go on in a context of magical powerfulness (Sterly 1987: 87).

someone something to eat with evil intent, what kills that person is the *kumo*, not the food. The source of harm in *kumo* is a creature residing within the witch while magical forms of harming and killing are practical procedures, sometimes involving occult power.

Kumo witchcraft

Kumo refers to a malevolent power said to take the form of a creature such as a rat, bat, frog, snake, or flying-fox (usually a nocturnal creature), with the power to kill or harm people. The *kumo* creature lives within the body of its host, the so-called *kumo*-person *kumo yomba*. Individuals who have *kumo* are variously called *kumo yagl* (*kumo* man), *kumo ambu* (*kumo* woman) and *kumo gage* (*kumo* child). *Kumo* is said to be passed from parent to child or grand-parent to child and runs in families. However, it can also be passed to an unsuspecting or curious person who touches a *kumo*-person on the head or hands.[7] The recipient starts to feel different and soon realises that he or she is controlled by a being within them—a being that calls them their new 'father' or 'mother'. *Kumo* are said to be able to fly and to pass through walls or doors. While the *kumo* person sleeps at night, the *kumo* creature can take human or other form and roam at night, eating human waste and searching for human flesh, particularly vital organs like the heart or liver (Damien 2005: 128).[8] The movement of *kumo* at night may be traced by moving lights (said to be similar to fireworks)—'witches torches' (*kumo ken*).

Traditionally it was believed maladies caused by *kumo* included infections of the liver (*munduo nongwa*), inflammation of the lungs (*munduo mongungwa*), bloody diarrhoea (*dem boromai sungwa*), or unusual swelling of the body (*nangie yakungwa*) (Sterly 1987: 90). However, Aufenanger notes that 'nearly always when there occurred a death, people thought, *kumo* was the reason for it' (1965: 104). Even today any form of death may lead to *kumo* accusations. Moreover, *kumo* may be linked to accidents such as when a person is injured falling from a tree or in a traffic accident. The victims of witches are regularly those of their own clan, and mostly relations inside the same *hauslain* (sub-clan). Sterly notes the case of a woman accused of killing her own son. Other close relatives threatened with, or thought to be killed by *kumo* include husbands, in-laws, nephews, grandchildren and brothers and sisters (1987: 85).

---

7 Women accused of *kumo* witchcraft are seldom if ever raped, perhaps because to do so would expose a man to the *kumo* creature which some say can reside in a woman's genitals.
8 If the *kumo* roaming at night (usually in the form of an animal) would be killed, then the *kumo* person sleeping at home would die also. Also, the *kumo* dies when its 'mother/father'—the *kumo* person—dies; hence the practice of killing accused *kumo* persons.

No one knows for sure who is a *kumo* person, as they live in the community just like anyone else in the village. Suspects are accused during funerals, perhaps with reference to some form of 'strange' behaviour such as staring at people or having been seen wandering aimlessly at night. Another significant factor is suspicion that the accused may have had a grudge against the deceased. A confession may be forced through threats and torture, but whether they confess or not, the accused are often killed or banished from the community.

Sometimes communities enlist the help of a *kumo* 'doctor' or 'witch doctor' to identify the culprit. A *kumo* 'doctor' is a 'retired' *kumo* person who has declared that he or she will not practise *kumo* for malevolent purposes. I have spoken with retired *kumo* persons about their understanding of the *kumo* creature and they seem to be reluctant carriers.[9] One elderly woman told me how her *kumo* creature (taking the form of a rat) entered her body when she was a young woman.[10] She claims that she didn't like having the *kumo* creature, which would go around doing 'bad' things, but, although the creature was not totally independent, there was often little she could do about it. She observed that her *kumo* creature was becoming thin and weak, just like her. A young man who acts as a *kumo* doctor referred to his *kumo* creature as 'nature.' He had learned to control it as he was not happy with the 'bad' things that his *kumo* creature would do. He said that at times he sent the creature away but it would return to him. Being a *kumo* 'doctor' is a recognised occupation and the practitioner is paid, sometimes handsomely, for the exercise of his or her profession.

The reader can learn more about *kumo* from publications on the topic including those by Heinrich Aufenanger (1965), John Nilles (1950), Paula Brown (1964), Joachim Sterly (1987) and Casper Damien (2005). The principal issue to be addressed here is whether gender relations are a significant factor in *kumo* witchcraft.

Traditional gender relations in Simbu

In the Kuman language the term *ambu* means 'woman'. The word carries with it connotations of weakness and inferiority. There is a common conception that women are physically weak, powerless, helpless and dependent on men for

---

9   Sterly gives an account—originally from Heinrich Aufenanger—of a woman who tricked her own *kumo* creature (a bat) so that it would emerge and she could kill it by stabbing it with a knife and then throwing the head into the fire (Sterly 1987: 67).

10   In order to prove that she was a *kumo* person and to be recognised as a *kumo* 'doctor' she had brought what she claimed was human flesh to the Kundiawa hospital for the hospital authorities to confirm as human flesh, but she did not receive a response. She is not yet officially recognised as a *kumo* 'doctor.' This was the only case I heard about where someone asked the hospital to confirm that flesh was human. It is certainly not a normal requirement.

security and support. One hears expressions from men such as '*Ambu yombugln ta pai kurma yoko moglo*' ('You, woman, have no strength so be quiet') or '*Ambu yomba we digua motna yoko moglo*' ('You are just a woman so keep quiet and do not talk'). Girls hear such denigrating expressions from an early age and are encouraged to behave accordingly.

The Kuman term *yagl* means 'man', but also signifies strength, power, superiority and independence. One hears expressions such as '*Yagl makan sugl yomba meglkua*' ('Men are the inheritors of their fathers' land'), '*Yagl ka kaugo yomba meglkua*' ('Men are the public speakers'), or '*Yagl kunda yomba meglkua*' ('Men have the power to enter into war and solve disputes'). Both young men and women hear such expressions as part of the socialisation process.

Traditionally, women's lives were associated with looking after pigs, raising children, gardening and household duties. Men were rather more focused on constructing houses and defending the interests of the clan. Men distanced themselves by living separately in the men's house, usually public and located on high ground. In public events men did the talking while women took the back stage and remained spectators. In the domestic context women ensured that the fire kept burning and that their husband, children, pigs and dogs were fed every day. Wife beating was defended as an appropriate way of disciplining women since the woman had been procured through 'bride price'. A woman was expected to attend and mourn at funerals lest she be suspected of being implicated in the cause of the person's death.[11] Most of these gendered roles and expectations continue in people's lives today, despite modernisation and social change. Women often have a say in the domestic sphere since they are the ones who tend the gardens, raise the pigs and children. It is in the public arena where the well-being of the clan is at stake that men typically assert power over women.

Yet, the traditional configuration of gender relations was an ideal that was not always strictly adhered to. There were cases where physically powerful women took on men's roles in fighting, and daughters of prominent village leaders or war heroes were sometimes allowed to live in the men's house and play the sacred flutes (*kua*) normally reserved for men. An old woman recalls, 'When I was a young girl, my father used to bring me to the men's house and I lived with my father and my tribesmen in the men's house. In the men's house my grandfather used to teach me how to play the flute.'[12] There are also cases in Simbu where men took on what were considered women's roles: remaining silent in public forums, tending to sweet potato gardens and looking after pigs.

---

11 Women play a more prominent role in grieving at funerals, but men are also expected to participate (carrying large pieces of firewood and the like).

12 She adds, 'They just said, "*Ogoyagle orko Andeyagle orko orma kondo*"' (K: She is a woman but she is gifted by the great grand-father spirit in the sky so let her alone) (personal communication 10 April 2009).

Changing relationships

Traditional notions still influence ideals of gender relations in Simbu today. However, Simbu society has experienced major changes, at first with colonial and mission influence, and in recent decades since PNG independence with modernisation and ongoing global influences. Traditional initiation rites and courting ceremonies have disappeared. Husband and wife share the same house; boys and girls attend school together and in the weekends take part in sporting events followed by social evenings and movies.

Most old men who went through initiation or who married after traditional courting and bride-price ceremonies claim to have found a balance in gender relations within marriage.[13] Older women too generally accept the roles and responsibilities expected of them, including child rearing, gardening, cooking, cleaning, looking after animals, welcoming guests and attending funerals. Amongst older people, gendered differences are accepted and there is little competition.

However, many younger people are unsettled. Money plays an ever-increasing role in relationships, and there has been a commoditisation of bride-price payments. Young unmarried women feel pressure to bring income for their family either through bride price, finding employment, or marrying a man with money. Education is seen as a way out of village life and if they are forced to leave school because of lack of school fees, many women will go from one relationship to the next. Unemployed, unmarried young men spend much of their time looking for cash necessary to attend socials, picture shows, or to obtain homebrew and marijuana. They feel that they have to compete with women and many are angry with their female counterparts, who prefer men with money. They claim that girls look down on them as mere *drakbodis* or *stimbodis* (derogatory Tok Pisin terms referring to them being drug addicts and useless). Unemployed young men say that marriage is a 'mistake'—in the sense that unintentionally getting a girl pregnant obliges him to take her as his wife whether or not he feels capable of supporting her and the child.

Today men reluctantly concede that women can do almost everything that their mothers had never even thought of doing. Some women now contest for elections, deliver public speeches, take an active role in public gatherings, drive cars and run businesses. There is a gap between commonly held beliefs about gender and actual practice. Men are said to be the head of their family, yet a substantial number of men let their wives handle family finances because the women are often better at budgeting. It is said that women do not wear trousers and if they do—particularly the 'pocket' variety—they risk being raped, yet

---

13   Writer's interviews with men at Goglme, Genai and Gaglmambuno 20 September–3 October 2008.

today the majority of younger women do wear trousers. These developments pose a threat to men's social dominance. Men have to compete with women in ways that were unheard of before. Some men admit to feeling frustrated and envious as a result. Unemployed young men who say they have left school due to the lack of school fees feel angry and let down, many seeking solace in home-made liquor and marijuana. 'They don't smoke marijuana or drink home brew for nothing—they do it out of frustration.'[14]

A number of people have admitted that negative feelings, especially when combined with intoxicating substances, can lead to aggressive and violent reactions towards others, especially towards women and girls. Village leaders admit that they can do little to control the behaviour of youth today. 'Many don't listen to us. They just do what they want. Then when they feel hungry they steal from someone else. This is what is happening and it is destroying the community.'[15]

Witch killing in pre-colonial and colonial times

Who were the witches and how were they treated in pre-colonial and colonial times? The first contact of Simbu people with the outside world occurred with the arrival of the Leahy brothers and the first Catholic and Lutheran missionaries in 1933. Heinrich Aufenanger, a Catholic priest and an ethnologist from the Anthropos school, researched Simbu witchcraft in the period between 1934 and 1961. He tells how he saw a would-be *kumo* woman killed with a broad double-edged arrow in her chest. In another case a young man had shot at his own mother. On yet another occasion a mother of several small children just escaped death after an arrow had lifted up the skin of her chest (Aufenanger 1965: 114). In the first part of his paper Aufenanger provides five examples and it is notable that in all cases the suspected *kumo* persons were elderly women and all the 'victims' of *kumo* were male. Writing during Australian rule prior to PNG Independence he notes how in former days such women would be killed, but 'now they are merely dismissed because the government does not allow this kind of punishment any longer' (1965: 109–10). Murder, whether of accused witches or anyone was discouraged by the harsh rule of the colonial *kiap* (TP: government officer), however the writer has only anecdotal evidence and no reliable data to determine whether witchcraft accusations actually decreased during the colonial period.

---

14 'Em ol i gat wari o i gat as tingting na ol smok. Ol i no smok na dring stim nating, ol i gat wari ya' (TP) (middle-aged man, 21 September 2008, Goglme).
15 'Planti tru em ol i no harim tok bilong mipela. Ol i stap long laik bilong ol. I go go na ol hangre nau em ol i go stilim kaikai bilong narapela man. Mipela tok liklik long ol, em ol i no harim. Ol mekim dispela pasin i stap olsem na long komyuniti bilong mipela i bagarap na bagarap olgeta' (TP) (older man, 22 November 2008, Waingar).

However, the following nine examples from elderly people in Simbu recalling events from their younger days in colonial or pre-colonial times offer suggestive evidence of past patterns.[16]

Case 1. A middle-aged widow was accused of killing one of her in-law's sons through *kumo*. She was dragged from her house, tortured and thrown into a cave where she died. No one came to her aid because it happened in the night and this woman had no brothers to support or defend her. Her deceased husband too had no brothers who could come to her aid. It seems that the men who accused her were angry because they had wanted to marry her after the death of her husband, but she had refused.

Case 2. Two blood relatives quarrelled over a plot of vacant land. Two weeks later one man's daughter became ill and died. Some men accused the wife of the other relative of *kumo* and killed her. When the husband tried to support her they killed him as well. People suspected that the quarrel was a motive for killing the girl. The couple that died had no children to support them. Even the husband had no blood brothers to support them. They were tortured and killed and their bodies thrown into a cave.

Case 3. There was an ugly bachelor whose parents died when he was small. He tended to isolate himself, not coming to the men's house. Despite his ugliness he was known for his skill in hunting. He would return from hunting trips laden with possums that he would share with those living nearby. Other men became envious of his hunting skill. One time after a feast an old man died. People accused the bachelor of killing him with *kumo* and the men shot him with an arrow. They dragged him back inside his house and set fire to the house so that he burnt to death. His parents were dead and he had no other family members to support him.

Case 4. There was a tribal fight and one of the young warriors was shot in the abdomen and died. During the funeral some of the men went out to relieve themselves and noticed an unusual light on the other side of the river. The men mobilised themselves and secretly went to that place with their bows and arrows to find out who was lighting a fire on such a night. On arrival they did not find a fire, but rather an old married couple in a house. Because of the light they had seen, the men immediately suspected the old couple of *kumo*. They set fire to the house and burnt the couple alive. The couple had no sons, only three daughters who had already married out to other places.

Case 5. During a pig-killing festival a woman argued bitterly with a male relative saying that she was not receiving enough pork. A month later the man with

---

16   These cases were recorded in the Kerowagi District with the help of a Kuman-speaking researcher during the month of June 2008.

whom the woman had quarrelled fell ill. The son of the sick man tried to heal the broken relationship by giving a large pig in the hope that she would remove whatever was making his father ill. However, the sick man's condition got worse and he died. The son ordered the relatives not to cry. He got his spear and went to the woman's house and speared her to death. He also tried to kill her husband but missed and the husband escaped to his uncle's place. The couple had one son who also ran away and joined his father in their uncle's place. They never returned for fear that the angry son would kill them.

Case 6. During a food festival the two wives of one man argued over the amount of food they had received. The community was in favour of the first wife because she was customarily seen as the legitimate wife of the husband. After two months the only son of the first wife became ill and died. Because of the quarrel that the two wives had had some time before, the people thought the second wife, who was dissatisfied over the food during the food festival, had killed the boy with *kumo*. However they did not harm her because she had four sons who were strong and very aggressive. The people were afraid to attack the woman lest the four sons would retaliate and fight back.

Case 7. A woman who was a relative of the deceased came to mourn at a funeral. When she entered her crying sounded strange—more like shouting than crying. This unusual behaviour raised suspicion in people's minds that she was not really sorry and that she might be a *kumo* person who had caused the man's death. After the burial the villagers, especially the men, accused the woman, tied ropes round her neck and threw her over a cliff and she died. The woman was married and had a son and a daughter, but they could do nothing to defend her. Her husband took his son and daughter, left the village and went to live elsewhere.

Case 8. A very old man told how when he was young he had a girlfriend in another village. One time he visited her place for a courting ceremony but he found the place deserted. He remained quietly in a corner of the house. All of a sudden his girlfriend and her mother entered the house carrying meat, which to the young man looked like human flesh. He ran for his life to the nearest men's house to report what he had seen. The men promised they would burn the women and have the father and son killed as well. A few days later he heard that his girlfriend's house had burned, and later heard that her father and brother had been shot to death. (The person giving the account felt that perhaps the girl had refused to marry this man, so he made up the story about human flesh, knowing that it would most likely result in her being suspected of being a *kumo* person.)

Case 9. An old man in his seventies told how in his early years he had adopted a young girl. The girl often stayed out—presumably sleeping at the homes of other people. After a while her unsocial behaviour upset the man and led him to believe that she might be a *kumo* person. One day he prepared a good meal and invited her to come. While she was there he told her that they would go for a feast in another village and that she should wear her best traditional attire. They set out for the next village which was on the other side of a river. When they came to the middle of the bridge over the flooded river he came up behind the girl and pushed her into the river and she drowned.

The nine cases above reveal a pattern similar to that noted by Aufenanger. Of the nine cases, eight of the suspected *kumo* persons were female. The one male accused was an ugly bachelor who did not frequent the men's house—and so did not conform to dominant models of masculinity. In six out of the seven cases where the *kumo* had killed someone, the 'victim' was male. We might also note that in a majority of cases the accused person had little or no defence and in the case where the woman had strong sons, people were afraid to attack her lest her sons retaliate. Several men died, but in all cases except one the men were not the principal *kumo* agent, but rather husbands, sons, or brothers of a female *kumo* person. In several cases tense relationships leading to suspicion of *kumo* had to do either with jealousy or with arguments over food distribution. In former times the killing was done in secret without the public humiliation and extended torture that accompanies accusations of *kumo* witchcraft today.

The victims

Discussions about *kumo* witchcraft reveal divergent opinions as to just who are the 'victims'. Some consider the victims to be those who suffered the direct effect of acts of witchcraft. Most of these victims are dead. Others consider the victims to be those who have been accused of being witches. Most of these have been tortured and many are dead. Others have suffered but survived torture and abuse. Still others have fled their homes and gone to survive in other provinces. The identification of 'victims' in this situation thus depends on how one considers violence and the reality of witchcraft.

When the term 'violence' is used, it is necessary to consider who is labelling a given act as such. In Simbu, the people apprehending, torturing and killing a 'witch' often consider themselves to have done something meritorious, ridding their community of yet another threat.[17] The apparent moral propriety of the act would lead many to consider it acceptable and legitimate. The core purpose is to protect the community from the perceived threat of witchcraft. It is the actions

---

17   Laura Zimmer-Tamakoshi (Ch. 2) describes how Gende sorcerers demand compensation for ridding the village of a person who is seen as a threat to the community.

of the witch which are rather seen as unacceptable and illegitimate, thus calling for radical measures amounting to self-defensive homicide. All of this depends on how people understand the reality of witchcraft.

Belief in and fear of witchcraft are obvious in Simbu. However, one must distinguish the empirical (verifiable) from non-empirically real (believed) and the real from the imaginary. Some things may be considered real though not verifiable (e.g. a quality such as love). Many aspects of Simbu witchcraft appear incapable of empirical verification which is imputed from its effects. For example, it is said that the *kumo* comes in the form of an animal residing in the body of the witch, that the *kumo* kills by eating internal organs of the victim, that there is a 'parliament' of witches located within Mt Elimbari in Simbu, and that witches now resort to modern means such as the use of a '*kumo* gun' or '*kumo* helicopters'. It is difficult to subject such beliefs to empirical analysis. Simbu people themselves sometimes look for verification by having the 'witch' kill a chicken from a distance. It seems that witchcraft is real to those who believe in it.

Both the perception of violence and the belief in a phenomenon like witchcraft need to be taken seriously. *Kumo* is certainly 'real' in its consequences and to insist on asking whether it is verifiably real is to risk dismissing its social reality in favour of a presumption of the real as empirically verifiable. Whether the victims are those killed by witches or those accused of being witches, the suffering, death and social disruption are real. This belief has real consequences in thought and behaviour. Belief in *kumo* has led and continues to lead to the gruesome deaths of many people in Simbu and elsewhere. The wider society in PNG is starting to confront the reality of such suffering. A recent newspaper editorial quoted Judge George Manuhu as saying, 'Such deaths are a very long way indeed from traditional and customary methods of punishment of those who break traditional and customary laws. ... It may be that the time has come to regard murder as murder, without the subtleties of sub-definitions common in other societies' (*National* 24 July 2008). In April 2009 the Constitutional and Law Reform Commission established a working committee to review the law on sorcery and sorcery-related killings in Papua New Guinea.

The *National* newspaper, in an editorial, has raised the issue of how there can be so many cases of witchcraft-related violence in a so-called Christian country (*National* 29 February 2008: 24). Some churches interpret *kumo* as a form of spirit possession or demonic deception (Bartle 2005: 247–55; Johns 2003). Sometimes, however, recognising evil power as real may only confirm accusers in their belief and practice. The Catholic Diocese of Kundiawa takes a different approach with an eight point pastoral plan, emphasising pastoral presence in communities where people have died, and also care for the accused. The diocese has a policy that those who accuse others of being witches and who are involved in abusing, torturing or killing are excluded from the sacraments and the active life of the church until they give compensation, are reconciled and restore the good name of the accused.

Victims of witches

One needs to distinguish two different scenarios for becoming a victim. The first is the death of a person through some form of illness or accident. In Simbu these are often thought to be the victims of witchcraft. The victims in this case are predominantly male. The second scenario is the torture and/or death of a person accused of being a witch. The victims accused of witchcraft are predominantly female.

Cases 1–9 above were from pre-colonial and colonial times. The seven cases below are from incidents in recent years.

Case 10. An elderly widowed woman was accused of witchcraft after a boy died and people remembered that she had been looking for lice in the boy's hair shortly before he became ill.[18] Under torture she admitted to participating in killing the boy, but also accused another woman of joining her in the act. In doing so, she was claiming not only to be a witch but also to be a witch 'doctor', who could detect other witches. People did not believe her, so to prove that she was a witch she produced some flesh which she claimed was human flesh taken from a grave. She says that the flesh was sent to Kundiawa hospital for examination, the hospital did not release the results. Since that time she has left her community and lives in Kundiawa town, spending time at the hospital with her disabled son and with relatives.

Case 11. A brother and sister, both in their late fifties, were accused of *kumo* witchcraft after the death of a local boy. The brother had found that the boy had killed his chicken and discovered him eating it. Naturally he was unhappy about this. Shortly afterwards the boy got sick and died. (The boy had been visiting his brother in the coastal town of Lae and the medical report says that he died from malaria.) The dead boy's relatives accused the elderly brother and sister of being responsible for this boy's death. Both were tortured and killed. People claimed that the sister was surely a witch because she had been seen doing strange things, such as removing her intestines to clean them in the river. The brother's two sons were away at the time. Those responsible for killing the

---

18   In an interview at Kerowagi a local leader referred to her case and independently confirmed the details of her story.

couple say they were not aware that the boy had died of malaria until the report was read out to them later. Upon hearing this they paid compensation of money and pigs to the two sons of the deceased couple.

Case 12. A popular, thirty-nine-year-old married woman, with three children and excellent gardens, got very upset about her husband going around with other women. Finally she committed suicide by drinking Gramoxone herbicide. After her death some young men, close relatives of her husband, claimed that she died of *kumo* witchcraft. These young men then accused and tortured people from several families. Some of the families fled to other places. Three of those accused and tortured badly were an elderly man and his wife and their only daughter. The man was not originally from the village, but came there as a school teacher who taught Tok Pisin. Eventually he and his family were chased out of the village and their land and property were taken over by their accusers. Afterwards the father of the woman who had committed suicide came and forcefully demanded compensation for her death. There was no compensation for the man and his wife and daughter, or for any of the others who were threatened and fled, losing their land and possessions.

Case 13. A widow in her forties had two children, one living in Port Moresby and one, a young man, staying with her. Two of her brothers had died. After her husband died her brother-in-law wanted to marry her but she declined, preferring to live alone with her son. Later a young man died, after returning from schooling on the coast. It is likely that he died from malaria. However relatives of the young man accused her of causing the death of the student through *kumo* witchcraft. When interviewed in Kundiawa hospital she felt that some people might have been jealous of her for having good, productive gardens. When interviewed two years later she told how she had found out that men had initially accused another woman, but her brother-in-law had told the other woman that she would be released if she would accuse the widow instead.[19] She has now left her husband's village and lives with her mother in her home village. Her son uses part of her land in her husband's village, but part has gone to those who assaulted her.

Case 14. A young man with a university degree and a good job died in a coastal town. His body was brought back to Simbu and during the funeral, a group of young men, led by a brother of the deceased, came accusing a forty-five-year-old woman of having worked *sanguma* on the deceased when she gave him a sweet potato to eat. They dragged her out of the house and tortured her by thrusting heated iron rods into her vagina and into her abdomen. The grieving family were in the mourning house. Other women were afraid and ran

---

19 After partially recovering from her horrific injuries there was a court case in which she was awarded compensation of K20,000 and fifteen pigs, which, after two years, has not been paid.

away. Some of the village leaders tried to intervene but they were powerless. The woman was a church leader. She would not admit to being a witch and told them that she was prepared to be crucified as Jesus had died. She was a widow—her husband having died in a tribal fight. She had no children of her own but had two adopted sons who were too young to defend her. The woman was also a 'mother' to the young men who did the killing, as they were her husband's brothers' sons. She died and they buried her in a shallow grave in a place used as a toilet.

Case 15. A young man who had been a seminary student died in Kundiawa hospital—most probably from cancer. After his death, some relatives of the dead young man's mother accused the two older brothers of the young man's father and their wives of causing his death through *kumo* witchcraft. Neither of these families had any children of their own but had adopted children. One of the wives was killed and her body thrown into a pit toilet. The two brothers and the remaining wife fled. People claimed that it was not a coincidence that one of the brothers and his wife hosted a celebration for bride-price exchange in the village on the very day that the young man died in Kundiawa hospital, and that this was a sign that they were to blame for the young man's death.

Case 16. A high profile male public servant died in Simbu and relatives were accused of 'Sorcery' (*Post-Courier* 23 September 2008: 6). One night during the funeral a woman was hit over the head with a piece of firewood and dragged unconscious towards the village cemetery. She was never seen again. A witness notes, 'Although the house was filled to capacity with people, nobody dared to stand or do something. It happened all of a sudden like lightning. I presume everyone was dumbfounded' (Witness report – Police files). That same night the woman's husband and his other wife were also accused and attacked. 'They started chopping, cutting, kicking, punching, hitting us with sticks and stones. My wife and I were helpless. They set fire to my house and screamed, "*Sanguma*! (TP) Cut their throats and throw them into the toilet!"' (Report – Police files). The two were interrogated and taken to the Wahgi River, where, however, a magistrate intervened; pointing out that the accused man was a village leader. So they were not thrown into the river. I spoke with the two later when they were recovering from their serious injuries in Kundiawa hospital.

Cases 10 to 16 show characteristics similar to those observed in the earlier cases. All 'victims' of witchcraft were male. In all six cases women were accused of causing the deaths through witchcraft. All were widows or elderly and none had children capable of defending them. In cases 11, 12, 15 and 16, men were also accused. However, the men were accused along with a woman and in the case of the brother and sister (case 11) it seems that people had more 'evidence' of his sister having been seen participating in witch-like behaviour (cleaning her intestines in the river). The two men in cases 11 and 12 were not prominent men but marginalised, with no one to defend them. The brother and his sister in case 11 were both old and living together on their own. The other man was an immigrant from another village. In case 12, the man and his wife and daughter were not killed but permanently ostracised. The two brothers in case 15 had no children of their own. The land of those killed or banished in case 13 was taken over by the accused. In case 16 a woman was killed, but her husband's life was spared because he was a village leader. Unlike in former times when killing would be done quickly and in secret during the night, and by authoritative figures, the torturing or killing in cases 10 to 16 was a lengthy process, occurring during the day, and was carried out mostly by groups of young men.

Joachim Sterly, observing *kumo* cases during the 1970s and 80s, appears to have witnessed a similar pattern with regards to the victims of witchcraft.

> From what I have seen the victims of *kumo* are more often children and men than they are grown women. It is often said that the *kumo* people who want to take revenge on other adults 'strike' the children of these people. But it is hard to say why more men than women fall victim to the *kumo*. Is it that *kumo* women deliberately avoid harming those of their own sex? (1987: 85).

It is hard to know whether Sterly is correct in speculating that *kumo* women avoid harming those of their own sex, however, based on my own much more recent enquiries, it appears that it is indeed women who provoke harm to other women by accusing them of being witches. A number of informants, both male and female, agree with Aufenanger (1965: 112) that it is women, usually older women, who first start talking about *kumo*. 'The women are behind the accusations with their gossip, so women first talk about witchcraft and the men listen and take the lead in assaulting the accused.'[20] Why would a woman want to start talking about another woman and witchcraft knowing that it might lead to the death of that woman? A suggested reason given is that knowing that there is a very good chance that it will be a woman who will end up being accused, getting in first to focus suspicion on someone else is a form of self-defence. 'The woman will raise the topic of witchcraft and will influence her husband. She will accuse another person of witchcraft and her husband will talk with others and then go and do violence to the person who they think is the witch.'[21]

---

20 *'Ol meri em as bilong sutim tok na tok baksait so ol meri save go pas tok sanguma na ol man bilong ol save harim na take lead na paitim ol manmeri long sanguma'* (TP) (young married woman, 6 June 2007, Goglme).

21 *'Meri em bai olsem tokim man bilong em long pasin sanguma na samting olsem kamap long haus, na em bai sutim bel bilong man bilong em na em bai tok olsem em dispela manmeri save wokim sanguma na man bilong em bai go na tokim ol narapela na ol bai paitim dispela man or meri husait ol i ting olsem em sanguma'* (TP) (interview with young adult male, 8 July 2007, Kerowagi).

Victims as accused witches

As well as this collection of cases that I have assembled, quantitative data is available from an investigation of police and hospital records in Kundiawa, the provincial capital of the Simbu Province.

Police records

Police records (2000–2007) with the Homicide Office in Kundiawa, record 121 persons accused of being witches and killed or badly abused, and complaints being laid with the police. Of these people, seventy-three were killed and forty-eight escaped death, though often with terrible injuries. The police report that they were beaten, burned, shot or chopped with axes or knives. Of these accused, sixty-one (50.4%) were women and sixty (49.6%) men. Of those who died, thirty-seven were women and thirty-six men. Most were older or elderly people in the forty to sixty-five age bracket.[22]

Hospital records

Hospital records (1996–2005) with the Kundiawa hospital, presented to a Melanesian Institute Symposium in 1996 by Dr Joe Aina, revealed that forty-nine cases admitted were a result of the injuries suffered after having been accused of witchcraft. Of these people admitted to hospital three died. The rest somehow recovered from their terrible injuries. Many were suffering from burns over much of their body and some had deep cuts, to the extent they had to have limbs surgically amputated. Sixteen (33%) were male and thirty-three (67%) female. Again, most were older or elderly people in the forty to sixty-five age bracket.

Another study of entries in the Admissions books for the Surgical ward at Kundiawa hospital (1992–2006) revealed forty patients identified as 'Sanguma Cases'. (It was a practice that the nurse would enter a note as a comment in the

---

22   Police action could be traced in 87 of the 121 cases. Action on these 87 cases is as follows:

Convictions: 28 cases
Pending investigation: 19 cases (some go back as far as 2001)
No lead: 19 cases
Solved out of court: 11 cases
Pending: 4 cases
Withdrawn: 2 cases
Suspects in Moresby: 3 cases
Suspect escaped: 1 case

admissions book at the time.) Of these twenty-five (63.5%) were female and fifteen (37.5%) male. Again, most were mature or elderly people in the forty to sixty age bracket, with some simply marked as 'advanced age'.

Table 2. Data from the Kundiawa Police, Hospital and Surgical Ward Records.

	Female	Male
Kundiawa Police Records	61 (50.4%)	60 (49.6%)
Kundiawa Hospital Records	33 (67.0%)	16 (33.0%)
Kundiawa Surgical Ward	25 (63.0%)	15 (37.0%)

Male witches

From the data above it appears that a substantial number of men are victims of being accused of witchcraft. Almost half the victims reported to the police are male. More than half these males (37) had died, their mean age being forty-one years. Also at least one third of those appearing in hospital records are male. Sterly notes, 'It is true that in the nearby Asaro and down at Bundi that *kumo* is classed as woman's sorcery but in Simbu it is exercised by men as well and can be directed against women' (Sterly 1987: 85).[23] In the cases discussed so far most of the accused men have either been elderly or marginalised or both. However, four cases (17–20) below are examples where strong men in high-profile positions have been accused of witchcraft.

Case 17. The accused was a village councillor in Simbu. As councillor he was a prominent leader in his village. In 2006 the wife of his younger brother—who had a job with a good salary—died from an unidentified illness. Some people suspected that the councillor's wife might be behind the death. They apprehended her and tortured her. The councillor was accused of having got *kumo* from his wife and he too was accused. His house was burned and property destroyed and he was sent out from the village. The councillor had a brother and a son, but both were afraid to support him lest they too be accused.

Case 18. The case of a village magistrate is related to case 17 above. As a magistrate he occupied an important position in the community. After the death of the young woman, some people went around looking for possible culprits. They apprehended the magistrate's daughter. Under duress she told them that she, her mother and the wife of the councillor had planned to kill the young woman because she had not given them money. Angry young men hung the women from trees and tortured them, but did not kill them. The magistrate and

---

23 Patterson notes how among the Gururumba of the Eastern Highlands both men and women may be witches, but only women are ever accused (Patterson 1974: 145).

his wife and daughter fled from the village, abandoning their land and leaving their possessions behind. The magistrate has three brothers but they were afraid to intervene lest they suffer the same fate.

Case 19. A young man died and the wife of a policeman was accused of causing the death through *kumo*. His wife was tortured by a group of angry young men. The policeman tried to intervene to support his wife, but was accused also and forced to flee with his wife and daughters. They now live elsewhere, but he maintains that they were falsely accused and that one day he will return to his village to reclaim his land and coffee gardens.

Case 20. This refers to case 16 above. One of the accused was a prominent village leader. Most of his sons were not present at the time he was attacked by the mob and the one son staying with him escaped during the night to seek help, through the back window of the house. One of the leader's wives has disappeared and is presumed dead. The other wife was so badly injured that she had to spend several months in hospital. The leader is pursuing the matter through the court system.

In the four cases above, one of those who died was a young man, another a high profile male public servant and the other a young woman with a good job. By earning a salary she was not an average woman but had a high status in the community due to her education and more importantly, because of her wages and the money she brought into the community. In all cases it was initially women who were accused of being witches and the men accused were husbands or fathers of the women. The women were tortured but the men—all with high status or with the capacity to bring money into the community—were not killed. Some were ostracised and had to leave their land and possessions and go to live elsewhere.

Engendered violence?

The data given above from the police and hospital records appear to raise doubts about assertions noted at the start that women accused of sorcery or witchcraft are six times more likely than men to suffer violence. However, they are suggestive of certain engendered patterns of violence around *kumo* witchcraft.

It does appear that women are more likely to be targeted than men. The term for '*kumo* person' in the Kuman language used around Kundiawa is *kumo ambu—*

which is feminine.[24] The masculine form *kumo yagl* can be used but it is not so common. The ratio of men and women in police records could be biased because, as one woman noted, 'Women are unimportant, so don't merit the trouble of bringing the police in on the case.'[25] Others have voiced similar views about the status of women and their having less chance of their cases being reported to the police. Hospital records show that women are twice as likely to end up in hospital after such violence. This ratio could also reflect a bias if men would generally have more means by which to reach a hospital.

On the other hand, one sees in cases 12 and 17 to 20 that some men were not tortured or killed. Their lives were spared, although some were sent away from the village. Such cases would most likely not appear in police or hospital records, thus suggesting bias in a different direction.

Nevertheless the larger question remains as to the engendered nature of *kumo* witchcraft. Two factors linked to gender relations will be considered here: women marrying in from outside and contestations about status.

Women marrying in

Mervyn Meggitt (1964), accepting Kenneth Read's view of antagonism pervading inter-sexual encounters throughout the Highlands, correlated variations of sexual antagonism with the degree of hostility existing between affinally related groups, the presence or absence of men's purificatory cults and the social status of women. His main point was that where hostile groups inter-marry there is a likelihood of antagonism between the sexes. Such a situation may well have influenced the exogamous and predominantly virilocal marriage arrangements in Simbu. Paula Brown has refined this argument for Simbu, suggesting there were hostile clans yet friendly affines (Brown 1964). John Nilles (1950: 49), describing the separation of the sexes amongst the Kuman of Simbu, tells how men keep secrets from women in order to keep them in subordination and that for a woman to dare learning these secrets would be to risk being killed.

In Simbu the majority of women move to join their husbands when they marry. Thus the married woman, particularly with bride-price exchange, is indeed accepted into the clan, but never achieves the same identity with the clan as her husband. Sterly notes how 'the *kumo* men live on their own land among their blood relatives, while witches, once married, are strangers to where they live. … Their only blood relationship is with their own children' (Sterly 1987: 141–

---

24 People find it difficult to answer the question as to whether *kumo* is male or female. One person suggested that all *kumo* must be female because they can reproduce themselves to be passed onto another person.
25 *'Ol meri ol i no important so ol ken i dai nating na ol no inap long reportim kain case long police'* (TP) (interview with young married woman, 6 June 2007, Goglme).

42). During tribal warfare men suspected that women might bring information to support the woman's brothers in the opposing clan. A similar dynamic could apply to women when the clan is perceived as being threatened by witchcraft. Despite friendly affines, suspicion could fall on women who marry into the clan rather than on the clan's own men, who trace their clan identity back through ancestral links. People would be particularly suspicious if the woman comes from a family with a history of *kumo* witchcraft. When women accuse other women of witchcraft at funerals, they will have come from different in-marrying clans. One cannot expect women's solidarity in such a precarious situation.

Status

One must be careful not to presume that women are merely of lower status. Sterly comments that 'no woman in Simbu society will be despised precisely for being a woman, even if she is a witch' (Sterly 1987: 141). Sterly associates the lower status of women with their coming into the community from outside as affines. Whatever the reason, males tend to claim exclusive right to leadership—a factor which influences witchcraft accusations. In all but two cases, those said to be killed by witches were male—the death of a male being thought, according to tradition, to be a greater loss. In the two cases above in which witchcraft accusations came after the death of women, both were women of high status in the sense of providing leadership and bringing resources into the community—one a successful thirty-nine-year-old woman with excellent gardens (case 12) and the other an educated young woman earning a wage (cases 17 and 18).

Status associated with gender also appears as a factor in who will be accused. In the cases given above it is women, particularly widows or the elderly, who are targeted. We do not have sufficient information from the police and hospital data to be able to assess from those sources the status of those who were presumed to have died of witchcraft or those who were accused of witchcraft. However, in a recent example from Simbu, people said they did not even bother to accuse anyone over the death of a young woman (who died of cancer) because she was 'useless', having been involved with several men but without marrying and consequently not bringing bride price to the family. As I have noted in another publication, people often feel ashamed when it is thought that a family member dies from AIDS, so they are buried quickly without time for discussion about *kumo* witchcraft (Gibbs 2009). Stigma and discrimination associated with AIDS locates an infected person very low on the social hierarchy.

Socio-economic factors

Socio-economic factors and modernisation are also at work. Often people use the Tok Pisin term *jelas* to describe a motive for witchcraft accusations. The meaning of *jelas* goes beyond the English term 'jealous'. To be *jelas* is to be in a state of desiring something held by another. Wardlow glosses the term as 'uncontrollable, angry desire' (2002: 8). Unlike Wardlow's Huli 'wayward women', who embody the modern woman taking control of her economic power, even with hazardous results, the Simbu witch represents traditional culture rather than modernity and an accusation renders one powerless. Where the Huli woman goes through a form of social death to become modern, the Simbu witch faces physical death as a consequence of the angry desire (*jelas*) of others in the clan. Inevitably when a person is accused of witchcraft and they are killed or flee, their house and possessions are stolen or burned and their food gardens and coffee plots taken over by their accusers. There is a shortage of good agricultural land in Simbu, and with the breakdown of postpartum sex taboos, and better health facilities, there are more surviving children to provide for than before. When in a *jelas* state one could fight over land and possessions but perhaps to accuse another of witchcraft and take over their land is a more socially acceptable alternative.

Moreover, witch 'doctors' and diviners are paid well for their work of identifying those responsible for sickness and death. Divination is a lucrative job, and there is also the temptation to accuse others falsely just to get one's hands on the money.

Power and the powerless

Witchcraft is the mystical powers in the possession of those usually found at the bottom of the social hierarchy' (Unage 2008: 29).[26]

Engendering in Simbu witchcraft is not just an issue of gender relations, but also power relations. Women are outsiders marrying into the clan. There are clear differences of status and power deriving from both traditional and modern sources. A common scenario is becoming the victim of *jelas* sentiments. This all points to powerlessness as a significant factor in witch killing in Simbu.

Torturing and killing accused witches is an act of power, not of status seeking. Women are unanimous that those executing the accused (mostly young men—often under the influence of alcohol or marijuana) are not considered heroes in a way that tribal fighters are heroic. Tribal fighting requires bravery, whereas the people we interviewed recognised that in killing witches a whole group gangs

---

26   Michael Unage, *National* 12 March 2008: 29. For discussion on power, sorcery and witchcraft, see Zelenietz 1981: 3–6.

up against one person, which is not heroic at all. Some young women said that seeing men act so violently makes them less attractive as potential marriage partners.

Women are more likely to be accused of witchcraft because of their weaker social and political presence. They are disadvantaged physically, socially and ideologically. Women, particularly older women can hardly defend themselves from physical attack by an angry mob. A woman generally does not have the same social status in the clan as her husband or her sons. Ideologically women were and are regarded as weaker, inferior and dependent on men. Despite modernisation and social change, ideals and expectations derived from tradition continue to influence gender relations today. So, when a family, believing that death comes through human agency, looks for a scapegoat to accuse, fingers will very often point at a woman without influential brothers or strong sons.

Women tell of their feelings of total powerlessness when they are accused of being witches. Recently I conducted surveys in several clans in Simbu asking about who had died in the past year and the perceived cause of these people's deaths.[27] In some cases, elderly women were accused of being witches and tortured even before a person had died. In several cases men were seriously ill in hospital and women were waiting back in the village with a death sentence hanging over their heads. People had told them that if the man in hospital died, their funeral would be at the same time as his. It could be that they were being threatened with the intention that they would somehow reverse the power of witchcraft, thus allowing the patient to recover, but I am more inclined to think that such threats fit in with a pattern of scapegoating and accusing people of occult powers, and only those people who at the same time had no physical power to defend themselves. One woman put it this way, 'I couldn't speak. I felt totally powerless when they called me a witch. All fingers pointed at me and everyone stared at me.'[28] Another woman said, 'I live here and people think I am a witch. My immediate reaction was to feel ashamed and I felt like drowning or hanging myself. They beat me and it hurt me deep inside and I just cried.'[29] The

---

27   In the survey of clans asking about the perceived cause of death, the underlying cause in most cases was witchcraft, even though a person may have died in an accident, a tribal fight or from a recognised medical ailment such as cancer or malaria. For example, a young boy died of an intestinal complaint and parents and relatives of the boy accused an old woman of witchcraft because the day before his death the boy had said 'thank you' to the woman as she passed even though they had not seen her give him anything. It was presumed that her *kumo* spirit must have given him something which caused his death.

28   '*Mi nogat pawa bilong toktok. Olgeta strong na powa ol kisim pinis taim ol i kolim mi sanguma. Olgeta pinga na olgeta man i lukluk long mi*' (TP) (interview with middle aged woman, June 2008, Kerowagi).

29   '*Mi bai slip kirap long dispela ples ol man bai glasim mi olsem sanguma. Na mi skelim kwiktaim insait long mi i stap laip yet na kisim sem na i laik kalap long wara o hangamap long rop. Na ol paitim mi long en em mi pilim dispela insait tru long lewa bilong mi na mi krai tasol na mi stap*' (TP) (interview with elderly woman, April 2009, Papnigl).

same woman continued, saying that as they tied her and tortured her she felt powerless and thought of her daughters who were married in other parts of the province and of her young son who was too small to defend her.

Young men today in Simbu view it as almost an obligation to avenge the death of a family member through accusing and torturing or killing some person thought to have been the cause of the death. One young man put it this way, 'The boys were very angry because of our father's death. It is bad to lose a father and my mates felt sorry for me. They were not concerned about doing right or wrong. We thought we were doing the right thing because a witch had killed our father. We would be happy if we killed the witch.'[30] For these young men violence is a justifiable response to an act that threatens the well-being of the clan.

How is it that some of the accused were able to live to tell of their experience? My survey of recent deaths reveals that the accused survived or were released when police (who were not family members) were called to the scene or where a strong church leader was present to remind people that for Christians in the modern world there are alternatives to witchcraft. In effect it means that if sufficiently motivated to act, the power of the police and civil authorities or the power of the church can be enough to defend a person who is otherwise powerless.

A Simbu Catholic theological student tells how he attended a funeral of a family friend. The Mingende hospital staff had said that the cause of death was heart failure. Nevertheless as part of the mourning process the sons of the deceased saw it as their role to ask 'who' was behind the death of their father, and to accuse women of witchcraft. However they noticed that the theological student was among the mourners and thought that it would offend him if they would assault a woman among the mourners. So they declared, 'X is here and we don't want to upset him, so you *sangumas* are safe.' They then made some general statements and warned the '*sangumas*' not to kill again.[31] This is not an isolated case, as a number of church workers have related similar stories.

The sons of the deceased believed that there were powers of witchcraft active within the community responsible for death and misfortune and that they had a responsibility to take an aggressive and violent stand against that power. The irony of witch killing in Simbu is that the one accused of occult power is most often physically or socially powerless. Sometimes village leaders give their direct

---

30   '*Ol bois i belhat nogut tru bikos em i kilim wanpela papa bilong mipela. Lusim papa bilong mi em i samting nogut tru na ol wan-skwad bilong mi ol i sori long mi. Ol i no wari ol i mekim rong o nogat. Mipela i ting olsem samting mipela i mekim em i rait bikos em bin sangumaim na kilim wanpela papa bilong mipela. Mipela bai amamas sapos mipela i kilim em i dai*' (TP) (son of deceased, April 2009).

31   Gabriel Kuman, 'Sorcery, Witchcraft and Development in Papua New Guinea.' Unpublished manuscript, 2009.

or tacit approval to killing and torturing those accused of witchcraft. However even if they would want to stop the violence they have little power today in the face of a village mob—particularly when many young men within the mob are affected by alcohol or drugs.

Conclusion

Richard Eves (2006) writes about violence against women and how many men see their manhood as dependent on their power over women and use violence to achieve this. Could it be that young men thus seek to validate themselves in the eyes of the community and their peers? Other scholars perceive male violence against women to be fuelled by male resentment over women's gains in economic and social independence (Zimmer-Tamakoshi 1997) or humiliation over women's refusal to abide by personal obligations (Wardlow 2005). Surely feelings of dependence, resentment and humiliation figure in the violence directed against those accused of witchcraft in Simbu. However, I am of the opinion that an equally significant motive comes from a sense of loathing and fear, thinking that a person who harbours a *kumo* creature has killed a family member and may kill again. Thus violence against accused witches differs from that of rape and domestic violence. Suspects will be people identified as marginalised, appearing to act strangely, as harbouring a grudge against the person who has died or is dying and as someone who cannot retaliate. Most often the person fulfilling those criteria is a woman. Those doing the accusing, who may be men or women, are looking for a scapegoat—someone to blame.

It should be noted that while young men play a leading role in hitting, torturing or killing the accused, women too might participate in the violence. 'It wasn't just the men who beat the three witches. The women too took up stones and sticks to hit them. Old and young women together were involved in accusing and hitting the three.'[32] Other women express different sentiments. They would like to help but feel powerless. 'They were just killing helpless people.'[33]

How true is it that women are much more likely than men to suffer this form of violence? From the cases presented it appears that Simbu people believe that males are more likely than women to die *of* witchcraft. However, from the cases given and the police and hospital records there is every indication that women are more likely to suffer violence as a result of being *accused* of witchcraft. But, apart from the incidences of the death and injury to both victims, to what

---

32 '... i no ol man tasol involve long paitim ol dispela tripela sanguma manmeri, ol meri tu involve na kisim ston na stik na paitim ol dispela tripela lain. Ol lapun na yangpela meri olgeta ol involve long paitim na krosim ol dispela tripela lain'(TP) (interview with middle-aged woman, 1 July 2007, Goglme).
33 From interview with middle-aged woman, 1 July 2007, Goglme.

extent is the *kumo* phenomenon 'engendered'? Traditionally women were regarded as weaker, inferior and dependent on men. Despite modernisation and social change, the ideals and expectations deriving from tradition continue to influence gender relations today. Women are still vulnerable as outsiders who marry into the clan, particularly if they have 'only' daughters or if they do not have mature strong sons. If a woman has large flourishing gardens that others might envy or if she stirs up bad feelings by refusing to marry she may well generate bad feelings that lead to her being a candidate for blame at the death of a relative. Moreover, women have to cope with other women pointing a finger at them in self-defence. Most men do not wish to see their wives, daughters or sisters treated so violently, but in Simbu they realise that they too might be accused of being partners in witchcraft and suffer the same fate. So often such men remain as powerless witnesses or they absent themselves when mob rule takes over.

The tragedy of *kumo* witchcraft today is exacerbated by the deterioration of law and order at the community level. Who has power and authority these days to bring justice, order and stability to communities? The 'bottom' of the social hierarchy becomes even more insecure as social norms and practices break down or become dysfunctional. Changing ingrained cultural attitudes and practices associated with witchcraft will require far more than teaching people scientific, verifiable explanations for sickness, death (Zocca 2008: 58). It also requires a multidimensional approach to developing a cultural coherence where antisocial behaviour associated with alcohol and drugs is an exception; where there is trust rather than mistrust within families; where there is a collective response to protect the powerless, so that society can be a safe place, rather than a place where fear and powerlessness persist in the face of the terror of witchcraft.

References

Amnesty International, 2006. *Papua New Guinea: Violence Against Women: Not Inevitable, Never Acceptable*. AI Index: ASA 34/002/2006. Online: http://www.amnesty.org/en/library/info/ASA34/002/2006/en. Accessed 20 January 2011.

Aufenanger, Heinrich, 1965. Kumo, the deadly witchcraft in the Central Highlands of New Guinea. *Asian Folklore Studies* 24(1): 103–15.

Bartle, Neville, 2005. *Death, Witchcraft and the Spirit World in the Highlands of Papua New Guinea: Developing a Contextual Theology in Melanesia*. Goroka: Melanesian Institute for Pastoral and Socio-Economic Service Inc.

Brown, Paula, 1964. Enemies and affines. *Ethnology* 3(4): 335–56.

-------- 1972. *The Chimbu: A Study of Change in the New Guinea Highlands.* Cambridge: Schenkman.

-------- 1977. Kumo witchcraft at Mintima, Chimbu Province, PNG. *Oceania* 48: 26–29.

-------- 1995. *Beyond a Mountain Valley: The Simbu of Papua New Guinea.* Honolulu: University of Hawai'i Press.

Damien, Casper, 2005. The myth of Kumo: knowing the truth about Sanguma in Simbu Province. *Catalyst* 35(2): 114–34.

Evans-Pritchard, E., 1937. *Witchcraft, Oracles and Magic among the Azande.* Oxford: Oxford University Press.

Eves, Richard, 2006. *Exploring the Role of Men and Masculinities in Papua New Guinea in the 21st Century: How to address violence in ways that generate empowerment for both men and women.* Report for Caritas Australia. Online: http://www.baha.com.pg/downloads/Masculinity%20and%20 Violence%20in%20PNG.pdf. Accessed 28 November 2010.

Gibbs, Philip, 2009. Sorcery and AIDS in Simbu, East Sepik and Enga. Occasional Paper no. 2, Port Moresby: National Research Institute.

-------- 2010. Witchkilling and engendered violence in Simbu. *Catalyst* 40(1): 24–64.

Glick, Leonard, 1973. Sorcery and witchcraft. In *Anthropology in Papua New Guinea: Readings from the Encyclopaedia of Papua and New Guinea*, ed. Ian Hogbin, 182–86. Melbourne, Carlton: Melbourne University Press.

Johns, Vic, 2003. Sanguma and the power of the Gospel in reference to the Gumine People (Simbu People). *Melanesian Journal of Theology* 19(1): 46–76.

Kuman, Gabriel, 2009. Sorcery, witchcraft and development in Papua New Guinea. Unpublished Manuscript, viewed at the Melanesian Institute, Goroka, PNG.

McCallum, P. Maurice, 2006. 'Sanguma' – tracking down a word. *Catalyst* 36(2): 183–207.

Meggitt, Mervyn, J., 1964. Male-female relationships in the Highlands of Australian New Guinea. *American Anthropologist*, New Series 66(4) Part 2: 204–24, New Guinea: The Central Highlands.

Newman, Philip, 1965. *Knowing the Gururumba.* New York: Holt, Rinehart and Winston.

Nilles, John, 1950. The Kuman of the Chimbu Region. *Oceania* 21: 25–40.

-------- 1953. The Kuman people: a study of cultural change in a primitive society in the Central Highlands of New Guinea. *Oceania* 24: 199–220.

Patterson, Mary, 1974–5. Sorcery and witchcraft in Melanesia. *Oceania* 45: 132–60, 212–34.

Read, Kenneth, 1965. *The High Valley*. New York: Colombia University Press.

Reay, Marie, 1959. *The Kuma*. Melbourne: Melbourne University Press.

Sterly, Joachim, 1987. *Hexer und Hexen in Neu-Guinea*. München: Kindler Verlag.

Trompf, Garry, 1991. *Melanesian Religion*. Cambridge: Cambridge University Press.

Unage Michael, 2008. *National*. 12 March, 29.

Wardlow, Holly, 2002. Headless ghosts and roaming women: specters of modernity in Papua New Guinea. *American Ethnologist* 29(1): 5–32.

-------- 2005. Transformations of desire: envy and resentment among the Huli of Papua New Guinea. In *The Making of Global and Local Modernities in Melanesia: Humiliation, Transformation and the Nature of Cultural Change*, ed. Joel Robbins and Holly Wardlow, 57–72. Aldershot, Hampshire: Ashgate Press.

Zelenietz, Marty, 1981. Sorcery and social change: an introduction. *Social Analysis* 8: 3–14.

Zimmer-Tamakoshi, Laura, 1997. 'Wild pigs and dog men': rape and domestic violence as 'women's issues' in Papua New Guinea. In *Gender in Cross-Cultural Perspective*, ed. Caroline B. Bettell and Carolyn F. Sargent, 538–53. New Jersey: Prentice Hall.

Zocca, Franco, 2008. Sorcery, witchcraft and Christianity worldwide and in Melanesia. In *Sorcery, Witchcraft and Christianity in Melanesia*, ed. Franco Zocca and Jack Urame, 10–20. Melanesian Mission Studies no. 5. Goroka: Melanesian Institute.

4. Becoming Mary: Marian Devotion as a Solution to Gender-based Violence in Urban PNG

Anna-Karina Hermkens

Abstract

This chapter deals with how, in the urban setting of Madang in Papua New Guinea, Marian devotion is deployed in response to gender-based violence, including in the context of HIV.[1] While providing insight into the lived religious experiences of Catholic women and, in particular, female members of the Legion of Mary, this chapter shows how women seek help from Mary and God in order to find a solution to the everyday violence they face. The experiences and perceptions described here reveal women's engagement in painful processes of self-analysis and self-transformation to hopefully adapt to and change their situation. In such processes, Mary is used as a role model.

Introduction

The association between Mary, the mother of Jesus, and violence may seem unlikely, but in Papua New Guinea (PNG), as elsewhere in the world, people turn to Mary in order to seek a solution for the problems they face (Hermkens 2007; Hermkens *et al*. 2009).[2] This chapter deals with how, in the urban setting of Madang, Marian devotion is deployed in response to gender-based violence and HIV. In analysing the experiences and perceptions of female members of

---

1 I am indebted to all who have accommodated and assisted me with my research in PNG. Special thanks to Father Joe Forstner, the members of the Legion of Mary, and the Catholic Women's Association for assisting me with my research in Madang and Port Moresby. Thanks also to Father Jürgen Ommerborn, Philip Gibbs, Richard Eves, John Barker and Lawrence Hammar. Special thanks to all participants of the ASAO session 'Engendering Violence', and to Margaret Jolly, Christine Stewart and Carolyn Brewer for their insightful comments and suggestions on various drafts of this chapter. I thank the 'Netherlands Organization for Scientific Research' (NWO) for funding and the research programme 'The Power of Pilgrimage' at the Radboud University Nijmegen, Netherlands and The Australian National University and the Australian Research Council Laureate Fellowship, *Engendering Persons Transforming Things* for institutional support. This chapter is a shortened and revised version of an article which was published in the journal *Oceania* 78(2) (July 2008):151–67. I thank the editorial board of *Oceania* for permission to republish it in a revised form.
2 While in this paper it is shown how Marian devotion helps women to cope with violent environments, other cases show that Marian devotion can be used as a powerful and subversive tool to challenge existing economic, social and church hierarchies (see for instance Ram 1991; Margry 2009; Hermkens *et al*. 2009).

the Legion of Mary we must relate this to the current debate on Christianity in PNG (e.g. Robbins 2004; Jebens 2005), and to earlier calls for a more intensive anthropological investigation of the experience of Christianity by Melanesians (e.g. Barker 1990: 9; 1992).

The influence of Christianity in PNG is profound. Christian values are part of the country's constitution, which states that 'We, The People Of Papua New Guinea … pledge ourselves to guard and pass on to those who come after us our noble traditions and the Christian principles that are ours now.' Moreover, almost all Papua New Guineans say they are Christian and political discourse is saturated with Christian rhetoric and references (Gibbs 2005). In urban areas, the abundance of churches, evangelical rallies and the popularity of gospel music testify to the popularity of Christianity and its pervasiveness in daily life.

The majority of people living in the urban areas of Madang Province are Catholic (35%), followed by Evangelical Lutheran, Pentecostals and Seventh Day Adventists (NSO 2002).[3] The predominance of Catholicism in Madang Province is also visible in Madang town, which is the Papua New Guinean cradle of 'The Legion of Mary', a lay Catholic organisation founded in Dublin, Ireland in 1921. Spread throughout the world, its members give Glory to God 'through the holiness of its members developed by prayer and active co-operation in Mary's and the Church's work.'[4]

All over the world, the basic unit of the Legion of Mary is called a *praesidium*. The secretary and president of each *praesidium* report to their council, their *curia*, who in turn report to their *regia*, which falls under a *consilium*. In PNG there are two *regiae*, one on the mainland of PNG and one in the islands of PNG. These *regiae* work with the *consilium* in Ireland. The *regia* on the mainland of PNG has its headquarters in Madang and looks after fifty-four *curiae*, making Madang the centre of all legion activities in the country.

Each week, both male and female members of the Legion of Mary in Madang gather for a *praesidium* meeting, intermingling prayer with reports and discussion. In addition, each member is assigned work to be performed during the week, which is done in co-operation with another member. Mostly, this implies visiting sick people in Madang hospital, but sometimes legionaries also visit people in prison or others in need of spiritual help. For the women I interviewed, the weekly legionary meetings and assigned works constitute only part of a Catholic schedule. In addition to the legionary meetings and

---

3   According to the Catholic Church in Papua New Guinea, the number of Catholics in Madang Province is larger. In 2004, reportedly 142,000 people (49.8%) were Catholic (Archdiocese Madang, Statistics http://www.catholic-hierarchy.org/diocese/dmada.html, accessed 2 November 2011).

4   Concilius Legonis Mariae, *The Legion of Mary*, 2010, online: http://www.legion-of-mary.ie/, accessed June 2009.

related duties, there are other activities: Sunday mass and subsequent meetings with legionary members and other Catholics, weekly evening prayer groups, visiting evening masses in the Madang area, and occasional Church work, such as fundraising, cooking and cleaning.

From the late 1970s, Father Ernest Golly was the Legion's national director. In addition to translating the Legion's handbook, he published several dozen pamphlets on Marian devotion. Besides being the national director, he was also the spiritual director of the mainland *regia* and parish priest of Jomba parish in Madang.[5] In exercising these functions, he also largely controlled the practices of the Legion of Mary in Madang and the PNG mainland, and how Catholicism, and in particular Marian devotion, was practised in Jomba parish and beyond.[6] In Fr Golly's view, devotion to Mary was an essential part of Catholicism and Christianity. Moreover, when dealing with issues such as HIV and domestic violence, faith in God and devotion to Mary are both crucial considerations.

This chapter focuses on the experiences of Catholic women and, in particular, of female members of the Legion of Mary. It offers insights into how Marian devotion is practised and used by individual women in seeking a solution for the violence they face. In what follows, I offer an overview of the various forms of violence Papua New Guinean women confront, and how these simultaneous personal acts of violence and structural 'states of violence' shape their individual everyday experiences.[7]

Acts and states of violence

My daughter was working as a teacher in a remote area. On their way back their truck was looted and all the female teachers, including my daughter, were dragged out of the truck. The male teachers were trying to help them but there were too many *raskols* [TP: roving band of criminals]. They pulled my daughter aside and she was raped. When she told me, I cried. At that time, my husband came home and found us

---

5   Father Golly passed away in May 2010.

6   Although Fr Golly had a huge influence among Catholics (both legionaries and non-legionary members) in Madang, he was certainly not representative of all Catholic priests in PNG. In Madang alone, there are several Church officials who do not concur with Fr Golly's point of view and the way that he used his fire and brimstone theology to counsel his legionary and Parish members. However, he faced little or no interference from the Catholic community and his superiors.

7   Women (and men) turn to Mary and God to seek guidance, help and empowerment in addressing and redressing violence. Although I also interviewed male members of the Legion of Mary, and Catholic men in general, focus in this chapter is on how Legionary women live their devotion to Mary and cope with gender-based violence in particular. The men I interviewed did not approve of domestic violence. Some used devotion to Mary to reduce and control their own feelings of anger. All were of the opinion that the husband is the head of the family.

crying. He started hitting me, beating me, saying it was my fault that my daughter was crying. My daughter then started crying because of me. I asked him to stop so I could take care of our daughter. He stopped and I took her to the hospital; we were so afraid of AIDS. She had a boyfriend and we did not know how he would react upon my daughter having been raped. Fortunately, the test was negative; no AIDS. Her father did not know what had happened to her. He just left us for three years. So, this is what we as women are facing! (Interview with Alice: Madang 2005).[8]

This story was told to me by Alice, a woman of forty-nine years—mother of seven children, grandmother of five and member of the Legion of Mary. The story recounts not just Alice's experiences, but her reflection on the different forms of violence that women in PNG might face. The violence addressed in the previous narrative is pervasive (Kleinman 1997), comprising both 'acts of violence' and 'states of violence' (Mounier in Brown 1987: 34). Acts of violence are violent practices such as beating or robbing someone, while, according to Robert Brown (1987: 34–5), 'states of violence' refer to violence that is so part of the given social order as to be institutional or structural.

The several acts of violence that are addressed in Alice's narrative are criminal violence (including being held up and robbed), sexual violence (rape by strangers), domestic violence (physical beating and emotional abuse by the husband) and violation of health (risk of being infected with HIV). In Alice's and other women's experiences, such acts may occur on public streets, in the community, in domestic settings, at work and even in institutions such as the Church.

Alice's experiences with different forms of violence are not unique. As argued by Christine Bradley (2001: 2), 'the majority of adult women of Papua New Guinea have been physically assaulted by their husbands, forced to have sex with them, or have been raped or sexually assaulted by other men.' Statistics also reveal that domestic violence is the most dominant form of sexual violence. Surveys conducted in the mid-1980s showed that 67 per cent of rural women and 56 per cent of urban women have been hit by their husbands (Toft 1985: 14).[9] In my own research among Catholic women in Port Moresby and Madang from August 2005 till February 2006, I found that twenty-two of the forty-two female members of the Catholic Women's Association and the Legion of Mary that I interviewed reported having experienced domestic violence.[10]

---

8   Although the key informants of this article emphasised they wanted to be mentioned by their full names, I have instead decided on protecting their identities by using pseudonyms.

9   The PNG Law Reform Commission conducted research on domestic violence between 1982 and 1992. The final report (1992) showed that 70 per cent of all women in PNG had been beaten by their husbands.

10   From August 2005 until February 2006 I did fieldwork in, amongst other places, Port Moresby and Madang concerning Marian devotion and domestic violence. In addition to five interviews with Christian

A census conducted in the 1980s revealed that marital fights are mainly the result of alcohol, money and jealousy, followed by problems with the children and violence perpetrated by the husband (Conway and Mantovani 1990: 121–22). Domestic violence was attributed to men's drinking, gambling and bad temper, and to women's behaviour, such as 'gossiping', going out alone, not performing their 'duties' and talking to strangers of the opposite sex (Conway and Mantovani 1990: 127). In more recent studies, alcohol is frequently mentioned as a precipitating factor in family problems (see for example Banks 2000: 89). The perceived 'misbehaviour' of women, however, suggests that there is an underlying cause for domestic violence, namely male domination and men's fear of losing control over women. Alice's case, as well as others, shows that in general violence against women occurs when 'men perceive they have lost control over women; when women are perceived by men to have breached certain expectations of conduct; and when there are underlying prior injuries within the family' (Banks 2000: 95). In particular, continuing presumptions of male dominance (Kidu 2000: 30; see also Macintyre, Ch. 8) and gender-based hierarchies seem to fuel violence towards girls and women (Eves 2006: 26).[11] This suggests that violence experienced by Alice and other women is actually part of what Emmanual Mounier referred to as 'states of violence' (Mounier cited in Brown 1987: 34), violence which is institutional and structural. Other scholars of PNG suggest that gender violence is a form of structural violence. Martha Macintyre (Ch. 8) argues that in PNG violence against women is an expression of deeply-entrenched political discrimination against women at personal, local and national levels.

Moreover, gender-based violence can lead to another form of structural violence: the endangering of women's health. One of the major problems PNG is facing today is an HIV epidemic (Butt and Eves 2008). Some of the reasons for this crisis and the increasing rate of infection among women involve both gender-based violence and growing impoverishment which ensure increased vulnerability to the virus (Jenkins 1995: vii). This risk is exacerbated by the fact that women have hardly any means of protecting themselves against HIV. While the government advocates the use of condoms, most women are unable to negotiate

women who are not affiliated with particular religious groups, interviews were conducted with women belonging to the Catholic Women's Organisation (CWA) in Madang (19 women), and with people belonging to the Legion of Mary in Madang (10 women and three men) and Port Moresby (13 women). Of the nineteen CWA women, sixteen reported that they had been beaten by their husbands, while among the Legion of Mary members in Madang and Moresby six women (three in Madang and three in Port Moresby) had faced domestic violence. The women I interviewed belong to different tribal backgrounds. Moreover, they belong to different socio-economic strata, although none of them lives in the so-called squatter settlements. The majority could be labelled as middle-class with a few women belonging to the lower-class and one woman to the upper-class.

11　Various studies have attempted to analyse the 'culture of violence' in PNG (Bradley 1994, 2001; Dinnen 1997; Dinnen and Ley 2000; Jenkins 1995; Kidu 2000; Toft 1985; Zimmer-Tamakoshi 1990, 1997, 2004). In addition to existing gender hierarchies and male dominance, factors that have been identified in relation to sexual violence are: economic impoverishment and increasing criminality, changing gender relations, as well as a decline of morality, especially in urban settings.

for safe sex, and so many are unable to use them or 'Just say "No"' (Hammar 1999: 151; 2007: 79). In addition, especially among Catholics, there is a strong belief that condoms interfere with God's divine will through contraception, and in HIV awareness condoms are actually spreading HIV as they encourage sexual promiscuity (see also Wardlow 2008).[12] Julie, who works at the Archdiocesan HIV/AIDS office, is of a similar opinion, urging her clientele to instead practise the calendar or rhythm method or abstinence and faithfulness. Yet her own experiences show that this might be difficult to achieve. Julie's husband had unprotected sex with others and she could not refuse him. So, it seems that women, and especially Catholic women, are unable to protect themselves against being infected with HIV and other sexually transmitted diseases (STDs, see also Hammar 2007: 79). Moreover, once infected, women can find it difficult to obtain help because husbands and families may prevent women from seeking medical attention as they do not want their wives, sisters and daughters to be seen as 'sexual beings or to admit that they have been affected by male relatives' (Hammer 1999: 50–51).

The different forms of violence endured by Alice, Julie and other PNG women result in, and are the result of, acts and states of violence that effectively structure their everyday lives (Schmidt and Schröder 2001: 1). In Alice's experience, the domestic violence she endured for twenty-seven years was not only physical. The fact that she and her husband were always arguing is as much a part of her perception of the violence of her everyday life as the physical abuse. In a similar way, her husband's regular adultery and his disrespect towards her amplified Alice's sense of having to endure a lifetime of violence. The effects of this violence on her children contributed to Alice's own sense of suffering. Alice is convinced that the violence that was part of her married life resulted in her first daughter's sudden death. But, she feels that she is responsible for her daughter's death. This guilt results in an all-pervasive sense of suffering, which is in itself a form of everyday violence (Kleinman 1997). Women thus not only have to cope with violent acts which are both physical and emotional assertions of power by

---

12 This negative perception towards condoms is, however, not characteristic of the whole of PNG. Lepani (2008), for instance, shows the positive attitude that the Trobriand people have towards condom use and how they conceptualise HIV in terms of their socially-constructed realities, as enabling the transformation of high-risk sexual practices (Lepani 2008: 266).

On 21 November 2010, Pope Benedict XVI, in Peter Seeward's book, *Light of the World: The Pope, the Church and the Signs of the Times*, appeared to endorse condom use by male prostitutes when he said: 'There may be a basis in the case of some individuals, as perhaps when a male prostitute uses a condom, where this can be a first step in the direction of a moralization, a first assumption of responsibility, on the way toward recovering an awareness that not everything is allowed and that one cannot do whatever one wants. But it is not really the way to deal with the evil of HIV infection.' Church commentators were quick to explain that while Pope Benedict XVI was talking of male prostitutes and homosexual acts, he was not discussing sex between married heterosexual people or sex between a man and a woman. Indeed, as Scott P. Richert (2011) explained, 'Pope Benedict did not change one iota of Catholic teaching on the immorality of artificial contraception.'

men (Schmidt and Schröder 2001: 1), but also with their own embodied state of violence suffused by their suffering. Such everyday violence is both confirmed and enhanced by media coverage.

Almost every day, newspaper reports inform Papua New Guineans, as well as the world, that PNG is a violent society. In addition to violent burglaries and hold ups, sexual violence against women and girls appears to be endemic, and, according to some reports, even increasing. For example, Papua New Guinea's daily newspaper, the *Post-Courier*, stressed its role in representing domestic violence stating that 'family violence is PNG's national shame'. In its 4 June 2009 editorial, the editor stated:

> Family violence in Papua New Guinea is a story that needs to be told, over and over. For the consequences of this crime against people are huge. That is why we make no apologies for telling you of the tragic event which unfolded in Port Moresby this week as the police family and sexual violence office continued its probes into complaints by victimised women and children (Editorial 2009).

The regular front-page news coverage and the activities of both government and non-government organisations concerning the occurrence of sexual violence seem to have created a concern which Anou Borrey (2000: 105) termed a 'social panic'. While Borrey puts sexual violence in PNG in perspective, the fact is that especially in Papua New Guinean towns, women do live in a state of 'low level terror' (Macintyre in Bradley 2001: 2). This state of terror is exemplified by Elaine, a forty-three-year-old teacher and mother of four children living and working in Madang:

When my husband is away for travel I protect myself by hanging the rosary at the doorway so Mary will protect me and the children. I am very scared when my husband is away, but we are always all right as the rosary makes sure *Mama Maria* is with me during such times.

Seeking solutions

To address this 'state of terror' occasioned by gender-based violence, the PNG government conducted large-scale research through the Law Reform Commission in the 1980s (Toft 1985a, 1985, 1986; Toft and Bonnell 1985). Despite these reports and more recent studies (AusAID 2007 preliminary; AusAID 2009) however, the government has been slow to respond and take adequate measures (Bradley 2001). Only recently has the government supported public campaigns in which gender-based violence and the relationship between violence and HIV have been addressed. These campaigns are mainly the initiative of foreign AID donors or NGOs. Deploying huge billboards, advertisements and posters, the official message is clear: Real men do not harm women and girls; and if men and women want to have sex they should use condoms. Likewise, organisations such as the Country Women's Organisation in Madang and the Madang Family and Sexual Violence Committee have launched poster campaigns against domestic and sexual violence by addressing men's lack of respect towards women. However, the success of these campaigns is debatable, especially as posters are frequently 'misread' (Eves 2006: 55, 88–89; Hammar 2008; McPherson 2008).

In contrast to poster and action drama campaigns (see McPherson 2008) that often seem to fail, the impact of religious movements in addressing morally threatening issues such as violence and HIV seems to be enormous (see for example Eves 2003, 2008; Hammar 2008). With regard to HIV, the Catholic Church strongly objects to the government's express policy of advocating condom use as the solution for HIV. The Church, its clergy and many of its members strongly oppose the use of condoms, first, because it allegedly encourages promiscuity and thereby seems responsible for spreading HIV, and second, because condoms interfere with the divine plan of God. Fr Golly, who, as we have seen, was both the national and spiritual director of the Legion of Mary in mainland PNG and priest of Jomba Parish in Madang, was, until his recent death, very outspoken against condom use. As reported in the *National* newspaper:

> During a Jesus March in Madang in May 2006, Parish priest Fr Golly spoke against fornication and sex before marriage. He told the large group that 'the only sure way of avoiding HIV/AIDS was to use Abba, a Hebrew term meaning 'father'. ABBA is the acronym and stands for 'abstinence, be faithful, be faithful and abstinence.' In his concluding remarks, Fr Golly said condoms were not of any help in preventing this deadly disease and should not be used as an alternative (*National* 29 May 2006).

In an interview I had with Fr Golly (Jomba Parish 2005), he explained his attitude towards condoms as follows:

> God does not allow us to use condoms. We are not animals! People should use the calendar method. This is the way of God. Condoms are the Devil's work! The only country where AIDS is decreasing is Uganda. They took the way of the Lord![13]

Julie, who works at the Archdiocesan HIV/AIDS office, has a similar view to that of her spiritual director, Fr Golly, but at the same time is pressured to follow, to a certain extent, the point of view of the government which advocates condom

---

13   The 'calendar method', referred to by Father Golly, is similar to the rhythm method of contraception.

use. Caught between religious norms and values and government policy, she promotes the ABCD (abstinence, be faithful, condoms, delay).[14] However, when asked to explain her standpoint she states:

> When a woman comes for advice regarding adultery committed by her husband, I talk: 'You are in danger. You must take good care of your body and talk with your husband.' I tell her where to get a blood test. I do not tell her to use condoms, because maybe they do not use it well, get AIDS and blame me. The Catholic Church does not approve of condoms. This is to encourage moral understanding of sex. One must practice delay, abstinence, get married and stick together. '*Condoms i stap, sapos yu animal, yu usim!*' [TP: Condoms exist: if you are an animal you use condoms!] (Julie, Madang 2006).

People working in healthcare and hospitals often juggle their religious attitudes and official government rhetoric (see Wardlow 2008). For example, Anna, a Catholic nurse working in Madang hospital, is strongly against the use of condoms and told me that despite the hospital's policy of promoting condoms, she advises her patients not to use them.

> I object to the use of condoms, it is my faith. Because my faith in the mother. I tell my nieces, keep yourself Holy for Him. Do not use medicines or injections to intercept the baby. I work in the hospital and I do not want to go against the government but I speak from my faith. It is our body, It is God's way for us to have a baby or not. Condoms interrupt the plan of God (Anna, Madang 2005).

Such attitudes of hospital workers in privileging Church policy over government policy are also reported by Holly Wardlow in her study of HIV among the Huli. The hospital workers that Wardlow interviewed depicted condoms as encouraging illicit sex and as being useless in preventing HIV infections (Wardlow 2008). According to Naomi McPherson in her study of HIV awareness campaigns in the Bariai district in West New Britain, the church is also responsible for exacerbating the HIV problem in stressing the sinful nature of promiscuous sex, making condom use even more out of the question (Dundon 2010; Wardlow 2008: 196–97; McPherson 2008: 244; McPherson, Ch. 1).

Importantly, the link between 'immoral' behaviour and HIV implies that those who are infected have somehow called down misfortune on themselves through immoral behaviour. McPherson notes that most of her informants believe that 'it [HIV] is God's punishment for immoral behavior' (2008: 244). In fact, in some areas of PNG, HIV is not only seen as an aspect of moral decay, but as

---

14   The abstinence here links directly to the 'Abstinence', Be Faithful' and 'No Condoms' policies associated with USAID during the Bush era (Butt and Eves 2008).

actually marking the approach of the end of the world within the framework of apocalyptic Christianity (Eves 2003). Among members of the Legion of Mary, I did not encounter such apocalyptic views of the 'end-times', but the general perception was that HIV was still a sign of a general moral decay that is believed especially to affect urban areas like Madang.

To confront and change 'immoral' behaviour which allegedly results in illnesses such as HIV, many people look for spiritual help. Certain Catholic healing ministries and individual healers make use of statues of Mary and other Saints, holy water, prayer and the rosary to free people from demonic possessions and illness. Pamphlets with personal accounts of having been healed from AIDS, of having overcome alcohol abuse and of having resolved family problems through faith in God are distributed widely. One such pamphlet reads:

> Are you happy? Sick? Suffering? Searching for God? Come and hear God's salvation message about miraculous healing testimonies of: HIV/ AIDS, other diseases, broken marriages, old habits (Revival Centres of Papua New Guinea 2005).

This faith in divine healing is grounded in both Christian doctrine and locally established concepts about the nature and purpose of healing as well as of sickness in general. The two streams of knowledge reinforce the belief that illnesses like HIV are not just medical but are also social and moral phenomena.

The question is: how do Catholics and in particular Catholic women prevent themselves from getting infected? Faced with a high probability of being a victim of rape and/or domestic violence (as are all other Papua New Guinean women), since the use of condoms is not an option for them, they seem to be especially vulnerable to HIV infection. As Julie said,

> The time I was married, I did not know about AIDS. I was teaching at the Family Life Office, so I should have realised. But I thought I was safe because I was married. Only after my husband left us I realised this danger. Just recently, when we did this program about voluntary testing, I had my blood tested. I got worried ... but fortunately, God has been protecting me.

> My husband did not use condoms when having sex with me. I did not either. I do not think he used condoms when sleeping with other women. So I say: 'Thanks Lord! You protected me!' (Julie, Madang 2005).

Julie's narrative indicates that Catholic women feel protected because they are married, even if they know that their husbands have extramarital relationships.

Moreover, as indicated by Julie, these women are convinced that God will protect them, as long as they have a strong faith and lead a good Christian life (Hammar 2010).

Among Catholics in Madang, not only belief in God, but also devotion to Mary is believed to prevent one from getting infected. In order to stay on the right path, Mary is promulgated as a role model, thereby on one hand preventing infection and, on the other, enabling salvation. For example, in the *Post-Courier* (December 29, 2004) medical doctor Thomas Vinit (Madang Hospital) argues: 'Let us use good models that portray chastity and purity, such as the devotion of the Virgin Mary' in order to address the root of the HIV problem in PNG, which are 'moral and socio-economical problems'.[15] This emphasis on using Mary as a role model in order to solve moral and social problems is also instrumental in how Catholic women deal and cope with various forms of domestic violence. Confronted with domestic violence and divorce in an environment where this is seen as sinful, many Catholic women like Alice and Julie seek spiritual guidance; finding solace in prayers directed to Mary and gaining strength by using Mary as their example.

Mimicking Mary and the power of self-transformation

> Sometimes I wonder: how did I survive all this? I thank God and our Lady, she is my role model: a simple, humble woman (Alice, Madang 2006).

All over the world, Mary's celebrated virtues of humility, obedience and faith are appropriated by women and inscribed on women's bodies. Especially among members of the Legion of Mary, this use of Mary as an example, as a 'role model' whose virtues must be aspired to, is propagated. *The Official Handbook of the Legion of Mary* (Concilium Legionis Mariae 1993: 12) describes Mary's virtues, which constitute its members' aspirations, as follows:

> The Legion of Mary in particular aspires to Mary's profound humility, Her perfect obedience, Her angelical sweetness, Her continual prayer, Her universal mortification, Her altogether spotless purity, Her heroic patience, Her heavenly wisdom, Her self-sacrificing courageous love of God, and above all Her faith.

---

15   Dr. Vinit, while strongly opposing condoms, is now head of the Lifestyle Diseases Division of the National Department of Health (Hammar 2007: 75).

Mary the 'Immaculate Conception' is the Legion's worldwide leader. The image of Mary crushing the serpent's head symbolises that Mary is the Immaculate Conception: the Divine Maternity born without sin, 'the crushing of the serpent's head in redemption, and Mary's motherhood of men' (Concilium Legionis Mariae 1993: 20). As a legionary, members are expected to submit to Mary completely: 'the legionary distrusts the promptings of his [sic] own inclinations and in all things listens intently for the whisperings of grace' (Concilium Legionis Mariae 1993: 30). In fact, 'the giver places himself [sic] in a condition equivalent to that of a slave possessing nothing of his own, and wholly dependent on, and utterly at the disposal of Mary' (Concilium Legionis Mariae 1993: 37). In addition, the members of the Legion are also perceived as Her 'warriors'. Based upon Genesis 3:15, the Legion perceives itself as Mary's warriors against sin that turns to Mary's enmity with the devil as a 'source of confidence and strength in its warfare with sin' (Concilium Legionis Mariae 1993: 20). The legion is thus perceived as an army, which 'throws itself in the warfare of Christ' in which its members submit themselves 'to His glorious commands'. Being both slave and warrior is actually seen to empower the legionaries. As the handbook states: 'The imitation of Mary's humility is both the root and the instrument of legionary action' (Concilium Legionis Mariae 1993: 27).

Figure 7. Legionaries in Madang preparing for a meeting, placing their leader the 'Immaculate Conception' on a make-shift altar, 2006.

Photograph by Anna-Karina Hermkens.

As an example, Mary teaches legionaries to aspire to qualities such as humility, patience, faith and obedience—characteristics that are ascribed to Mary in particular by the Legion of Mary and the Catholic Church in general (Ruether 1993; McLauglin 1974). As Alice observed:

> Mary is a model to me: *Pasin bilong en, em daun passin* [Her style/fashion is humility]. Understanding and following Mary, brought understanding about my own self. Now, I believe in humility and the truth. I find peace in not making others angry, but helping them instead.

When asking other female members of the Legion of Mary in both Madang and Port Moresby what role Mary plays in their lives and in their families, I encountered similar expressions. For many, Mary is their spiritual mother who guides and protects them and whose virtues of peace, humility and caring, are loved and admired. Theresa, a sixty-three-year-old auxiliary member of the Legion of Mary, suggested:

> Mary is an example to all women. She is the mother of the Holy Family and as a woman and a mother she understands the problems and hardships that we [women] go through. She is the comforter (Theresa, Port Moresby 2005).

But Mary is not just an example to women in the sense that they admire Her and seek Her out as their spiritual mother. The women I interviewed actually aspire to be as Mary. By 'becoming' Mary they try to come closer to her, and consequently, to God. This mimesis is achieved by praying the Rosary. Furthermore, members of the Legion of Mary aspire to achieve Mary's virtues by dressing in blue. In this context, mimesis is not simply 'imitation'. Mimicking Mary implies not only that a spiritual connection is achieved, but that 'a palpable, sensuous connection between the very body of the perceiver and the perceived' is created (Taussig 1993: 21). This bodily connection is an important dimension of any form of belief (Ram 2005) and crucial in women's sense of self-transformation and spiritual passage. According to many of the women I interviewed, becoming like Mary meant internalising Mary's virtues, transforming their bodily behaviour and, consequently, changing their lives. As explained by teacher Elaine:

> Mary is a very good example. I follow her footsteps, as she understands everything. She changed my life. To me, I am very impatient. I get cross easily because I am so impatient. I often get cross with my husband, who is a quiet man. Then we started to pray [the Rosary] and I realised I could not be impatient to my children and husband anymore. Also in my work, I have to be patient. My husband realises I have changed. I am trying to be a good mother, instead of screaming and beating them.

Now I do not do it that way. Thank God I realise this now. Maria is my example. I admire her motherly care for her children, her humility and humbleness, and her love for Jesus. She is a woman of prayer. I ask her what to do and follow her.

What is striking in such narratives by women in their aspirations to be like Mary is the emphasis on self-transformation. As articulated by Elaine and others, Mary provided insights into their bad habits, which they subsequently tried to change. According to Alice and Julie, Mary's qualities as a humble woman showed them how they had failed in their own marriages. By changing themselves, by changing their own anger into humility, they did, alas, not change their husbands, but they received peace and acceptance of their situation as it was at the time. For many of the other abused women I spoke to, this emphasis on self-transformation was not just the only way to change their situation, but also the way to change their husbands.

Faced with domestic violence or other problems, the most effective way to achieve results is to focus on what can be changed: oneself. To scrutinise oneself and to work and turn oneself into a good Christian wife is, for most women, the most accessible way to change their situation. In this, women attribute power and agency to themselves. As argued by Griffith (1997: 166) in describing published narratives of Aglow women in the US, 'women centre their narratives on their own capacity to initiate personal healing and cultivate domestic harmony.' This personal power is, according to Griffith, encoded in a 'doctrine of submission'. In women's narratives described by Griffith (1997: 166), 'good results will follow a wife's willing acquiescence: once women's attitudes are transformed and they accept their submissive roles, their husbands also become happier and more benevolent.'

Such a doctrine of submission is also visible in Catholic women's narratives, wherein submission is not only to Mary and to God, but also to one's husband. As Mary, president of the Legion of Mary in Madang, expressed: 'Mary is our role model. She is obedient to God. So we submit to our men. They are the head of the family.' Others equally stressed Mary's role in providing them with a good example of being a good Christian woman who submitted to both God and her husband. As one of the Legion's members stated: 'I imitate Mary's humility, Her faith, praying, sacrifices, obedience. Obedience to my husband and towards religious duties.' Importantly, this religious doctrine of submission resonates strongly with gender hierarchies in PNG where, in general, male domination is the status quo and women are expected to submit and be obedient to men (see also Macintyre, Ch. 8). As such, religious doctrine, just like *kastam*, emphasises male domination, empowering women to submit, rather than resist, and thus promoting domestic harmony. This union of Christian and cultural values results in a powerful doctrine of submission which is, despite growing opportunities for women to divorce and circumvent cultural values of female submission, difficult to resist. Women's social and religious environment keeps re-inscribing woman's responsibility in attaining domestic harmony and being obedient to both husband and God. Failing to do so means failing socially, religiously and personally and can lead to social isolation and even depression, as Alice and Julie discovered. Mary provides women with a shining example of how to fashion themselves into good Catholic wives in PNG.

Importantly, mimicking Mary not only involves changing women's attitudes. It involves the transformation of one's self. The emphasis on self-transformation into the image of Mary actually calls for the submission and suppression of the self. As stated in the *Handbook of the Legion of Mary*: 'The legionary, in turning towards Mary, must necessarily turn away from self' (Concilium Legionis Mariae 1993: 30). The 'humble Virgin's heel' not only crushes Satan, but it also crushes 'the serpent of self with its many heads'. These are the heads of self-exaltation, of self-seeking, of self-sufficiency, of self-conceit, of self-love, of self-satisfaction, of self-advancement and of self-will (Concilium Legionis Mariae 1993: 30). Yet paradoxically, this Christian rhetoric which calls for the denial of the self also emphasises the self.

Negation or suppression of the self?

As argued by Joel Robbins (2005), Christianity focuses on the subject, on the self. More precisely, 'Christianity forces oneself to identify with one's own inferiority, one's sinful nature.' It teaches people to look inward and to alter their notions of subjectivity as something to be regulated (pp. 46–47). Focus is thus on the subject, on the formation of self. Richard Eves makes similar observations in his study on modernity, morality and illness among the Lelet people in New Ireland. By converting to Evangelical Christianity, Lelet converts 'create a new self, a self-refashioning' in which they seek to cultivate a new Christian way of being (Eves 2005: 28).

In contrast to Robbin's (2002: 311) claim that Christianity increases individualism, Mark Mosko (2010) stresses the personal partibility in Melanesian Christianity. Relying heavily on Marilyn Strathern's insights on Melanesian 'dividual' personhood, which is the product of relations with other persons, Mosko argues that the sociality of (Melanesian) Christianity is not individualistic in the sense of bounded personhood but consists instead 'in elicitive transactions between dividual persons, human and spiritual' (p. 222). My experience with Catholic women in Madang is that both representations of personhood, individual and relational (or dividual) coexist, albeit sometimes in conflictual tension (see also Wardlow 2006: 19–20). The Catholic Church, and in particular the rhetoric of the late Fr Golly, continually confront the legionaries and parish members with their sinful nature, which calls for self-reflection and, importantly, self-transformation. In addition to this emphasis on the individual self, this rhetoric also impacts on women's relational and dividual personhoods as it promises women that they can change their husbands by giving up their sinful selves and giving themselves to Mary and God—thereby receiving divine help and blessings.

The women I spoke to in Madang and Port Moresby engage in similar processes of self-refashioning. Women are encouraged to monitor their behaviour, to stop cursing and arguing with their husbands, to be patient and obedient. By internalising and re-enacting Christian values through the image of Mary, their focus is thus on self-discipline (see also Robbins 2005: 51). In Michel Foucault's terms, these women engage in 'self-surveillance' (Foucault 1997). Self-surveillance is usually understood as 'the attention one pays to one's behaviour when facing the actuality or virtuality of an immediate or mediated observation by others whose opinion he or she deems as relevant' (Vaz and Bruno 2003: 273). In this case, one of the main observers of women's behaviour is Mary—an inescapable omnipresence.

So Mary becomes a powerful icon around which women rework (part of) their identities and transform themselves into ideal Christian women through self-surveillance. In Madang, the doctrine of religious and domestic submission that is adhered to is empowered by Christian rhetoric which demands obedience and, especially, submission from the wife, both in her relationship towards God and towards her husband. These values are propagated through books concerning Mary (for example Hahn 2001) which are extremely popular among Marian devotees, and Christian booklets that are published and distributed in PNG (for example Fountain 1984; Malins 1987; Sala 1999). Moreover, these values are part of the rhetoric and advice given by legion members as well as by its erstwhile spiritual director, Fr Golly:

> I was told to pray, pray. My spiritual director [Fr Golly] told me to find my weakness and perform. He told me: 'You go back to your husband!' I cried. I cried and I prayed. I was so scared to go back. But I went back, and … I was again abused. I went back to Father Golly and I told him that I valued my life. Who is going to take care of my children? But he was looking at my marriage, not at my own safety.

> In 1991, for six months, I did not give myself to my husband. Father Golly told me to break my heart of stone. And I prayed to do this and I did it, but without love, to satisfy my husband (Alice, Madang 2006).

Marie Griffith (1997) argues that personal power is intrinsic to women's submission as this enables them to change their situation by changing themselves. However, Griffith fails to offer insights into how women's reworking of their identities is actually a very difficult and painful process, and may not elicit a parallel self-fashioning in the husband, who may continue to act in aggressive or other difficult ways or even, like Alice's husband, desert the family. For women like Alice, the effort of becoming an ideal Christian woman was painful and the price paid was high.

The power of Mary: Re-enacting normative violence?

This chapter has addressed the place of Mary in the negotiations of a particular group of urban Catholic women with various forms of violence. As shown, women like Alice and Julie not only have to cope with violent acts such as rape, but also with 'states of violence'. These states of violence are linked to the dynamics of the urban context in which morally troubling issues such as gang violence, criminality, gender and sexual violence, and the threat of HIV affect people's lives. As argued, acts of sexual violence are not only a form of violence against women's bodies and their mental health. Women's medical health is also threatened as sexual violence is linked to impoverishment and vulnerability to HIV and other sexually transmitted diseases.

While seeking solutions for the morally troubling issues that affect their lives, the women I interviewed turn to Mary, the mother of Jesus. Mary not only offers women solace and help, She also appears to empower women to endure their suffering. Following Mary's example, they gain confidence in the process of self-transformation into good and strong Christian wives. The women I interviewed see this transformation as empowerment—of being able to change themselves, their situations and, eventually, their husbands.

This form of empowerment refers to the process whereby women become aware of their capacity to change their lives. However, as argued by Macintyre (Ch. 8), this power has to come from somewhere. In the cases described by Macintyre, 'empowering women' often means wresting power from men so that women might represent their own interests (Ch. 8). The Catholic women I interviewed draw power from Mary. And since the effects of her power—obedience, patience, humility—are not considered problematic by men, this process does not generate conflict with them. Instead, it is often welcomed and supported, both by the male clergy and by women's husbands.

The question is: to what extent can we view the process of becoming Mary as empowerment? When seen in the light of Foucault's notion of self-surveillance, such a form of empowerment looks very feeble. As shown, women's self-surveillance is constituted by dominant gender relations, by the religious community—such as the members of the Legion of Mary and Church clergy like Fr Golly—and, perhaps even more importantly, by the Virgin Mary. Mary exemplifies, to use Antonio Gramsci's (1971) term 'hegemony', the quintessential 'hegemonic femininity'—a femininity that is accepted as dominant (cf. Connell 2005 [1995] on hegemonic masculinities). Mary's submissive image coincides with pre-existing gender relations and gender hierarchies, in which women's roles are constituted as being submissive to their husbands with an emphasis on their roles as caretakers of the family and as mothers. As already noted, the Church's teachings on Mary 'reflect and express the ideology of the patriarchal feminine' (Ruether 1993: 149). The virtues ascribed to Mary in the teachings of the Church and the Legion of Mary, such as silence, obedience and modesty, constitute the very essence of passive, female submission (McLauglin 1974). The advice given by clergy such as Fr Golly to abused women, urging them to stay in abusive relationships, to be patient and show forgiveness towards those who abuse them, is equally part of the hegemony and disciplinary power. In fact, it can be argued that Marian devotion and its focus on self-surveillance is actually a form of normative violence—a 'state of violence' that submits women to a violent doctrine of submission. In Foucault's terms, this doctrine of submission reduces women to docile and subjected bodies and thus seems to deny the possibility of resistance and agency.

However, as we listen to women's stories and experiences, Mary also seems to offer an escape. Mary is held up to women as a model and is appropriated by women as a model. But this model is appropriated and internalised in ways which do not always coincide with the Church's teachings or notions of the patriarchal and hegemonic female. Women like Alice and Julie not only admire Mary's virtues of patience and modesty, they also see Mary as a strong woman, as a leader. Julie, who has ambitions of being and becoming a leader herself, explains: 'Mary is a big female leader. When we women look at her, we can see our responsibilities in our family and in our communities' (Julie, Madang 2006).

Considering women's agency, we can speak in Margaret Jolly's (1992) and Holly Wardlow's terms of 'encompassed agency' (Wardlow 2006: 13). In the case of Catholic women legionaries of Mary, women's agency is not only constrained by male and social domination as described by Wardlow, but also, and perhaps more strongly, by Catholic doctrine, its clergy and Mary. In fact, one could describe women's agency in terms of 'ecclesial encompassment', as the women I interviewed exercise their agency and their creation of new subjectivities within the policed boundaries of the ecclesia.

So Mary's role is even more ambiguous than is evident in her paradoxical role of helping women to stop violence and of facilitating a hegemonic patriarchal power which constrains women. In fact the figure of Mary as a submissive image can transform into that of a strong and powerful woman, reflected in the portrait of the worldwide leader of the Legion of Mary, the Immaculate Conception (see Figure 7). This particular image of Mary encapsulates Mary's virtues of goodness, sweetness, humility and obedience, but at the same time evinces her power to crush evil and lead an army against sin. Mary thus provides women not only with an example of how to be a good Christian mother and wife, but also how to be a strong woman leader. Mary's role as a strong woman also enables her followers, like Julie, to assume leadership positions and endure the struggle that goes with such positions and aspirations in the context of contemporary Papua New Guinean society.

This powerful dual role of Mary reflects how religious women's groups are in the foreground of changing things in PNG—including gender relations (Dickson-Waiko 1999, 2003; Lee 1985; Sepoe 2000). Religious women may actively resist male domination and violation against women, urging men instead of women to change. Unlike the female members of the Legion of Mary described in this paper, who seek empowerment through individuated agency while being supported in this quest by their Legion members, women in certain other Christian groups successfully exert agency in collectives. Perhaps it is the identification with a highly individualised Mary and her personal virtues and experiences of suffering that prevents legionaries in Madang from collectively taking up arms against domestic violence. Or perhaps it was the power exerted by the Legion's spiritual director, the late Fr Golly, who confined women to their roles of docile and forgiving mothers and wives, and prevented them from acting, both collectively and individually, as warriors against the sins of men.

References

Banks, Cyndi, 2000. Contextualising sexual violence: rape and carnal knowledge in Papua New Guinea. In *Reflections of Violence in Melanesia*, ed. Sinclair Dinnen and Allison Ley, 83–104. Sydney: Hawkins Press and Asia Pacific Press.

Barker, John, 1990. Introduction: ethnographic perspectives on Christianity in Oceanic societies. In *Christianity in Oceania: Ethnographic perspectives*, ed. John Barker, 1–12. ASAO Monograph 12, Lanham,

-------- 1992. Christianity in western Melanesian ethnography. In *History and Tradition in Melanesian Anthropology*, ed. James Carrier, 144–73. Berkeley: Studies in Melanesian Anthropology 10.

Borrey, Anou, 2000. Sexual violence in perspective: the case of Papua New Guinea. In *Reflections of Violence in Melanesia*, ed. Sinclair Dinnen and Allison Ley, 105–18. Sydney: Hawkins Press and Asia Pacific Press.

Bradley, Christine, 1994. *Why Male Violence against Women. Methodological and Personal Perspectives*. London: Sage Publications.

-------- 2001. *Family and Sexual Violence in Papua New Guinea: An Integrated Long-term Strategy*. Report to the family action committee of the consultative implementation and monitoring council. Waigani: Institute of National Affairs.

Brown, Robert Mcafee, 1987. *Religion and Violence*. Philadelphia: Westminster Press.

Butt, Leslie and Richard Eves, eds, 2008. *Making Sense of AIDS. Culture, Sexuality, and Power in Melanesia*. Honolulu: University of Hawai'i Press.

Concilium Legionis Mariae, 1993. *The Official Handbook of the Legion of Mary*. Dublin: Concilium Legionis Mariae. De Montforte House.

Connell, R.W., 2005 [1995]. *Masculinities*. Berkeley and Los Angeles: University of California Press.

Conway, Jeannette and Ennio Mantovani, 1990. *Marriage in Melanesia: A Sociological Perspective. Point* Series 15. Goroka: The Melanesian Institute.

Dickson-Waiko, Anne, 1999. Civil society and development, non-government organisations and churches. *Development Bulletin* 50 (October): 44–46.

-------- 2003. The missing rib: mobilizing church women for change in Papua New Guinea. *Oceania* 74(2): 98–110.

Dinnen, Sinclair, 1997. Law, order and state in Papua New Guinea. Discussion paper 1. State, Society and Governance in Melanesia Project, Research School of Pacific and Asian Studies. Canberra: The Australian National University.

Dinnen, Sinclair and Allison Ley, eds, 2000. *Reflections on Violence in Melanesia*. Sydney: Hawkins Press and Asia Pacific Press.

Dundon, Alison, 2010. AIDS and 'building a wall' around Christian country in rural Papua New Guinea. The *Australian Journal of Anthropology* 21(2): 171–78.

Editorial, 2009. Family violence is PNG's national shame. In *PNG Post-Courier*, 4 June. Reprinted in *Pacific Islands Report*. Online: http://archives.pireport. org/archive/2009/june/06-05-ed2.htm. Accessed 20 February 2012.

Eves, Richard, 2003. AIDS and apocalypticism: interpretations of the epidemic from Papua New Guinea. In *Culture, Health & Sexuality* 5(3): 249–64.

-------- 2005. 'In God's hands': modernity, morality and illness in a Melanesian Society, paper prepared for 'Old and New Religions, Hybridisation, and the Challenge of Modernity' at the Australian Anthropological Society (AAS) Annual Conference, Adelaide, September.

-------- 2006. *Exploring the Role of Men and Masculinities in Papua New Guinea in the 21st Century: How to address violence in ways that generate empowerment for both men and women.* Report for Caritas Australia. Online: http://www. baha.com.pg/downloads/Masculinity%20and%20Violence%20in%20 PNG.pdf. Accessed 28 November 2010.

-------- 2008. Moral reform and miraculous cures: Christian healing and AIDS in New Ireland, Papua New Guinea. In *Making sense of AIDS: Culture, Sexuality and Power in Melanesia*, ed. Leslie Butt and Richard Eves, 303–25. Honolulu: University of Hawai'i Press.

Foucault, Michel, 1997. The subject and power. In *M. Foucault The Essential Works 1954–1984, Vol. III. Power*, ed. J. Faubion, 326–48. New York: The New Press.

Fountain, Ossie C., 1984. *Marriage the Melanesian Way*. Wewak: Christian Books Melanesia Inc.

Gibbs, Philip, 2005. Political discourse and religious narratives of church and state in Papua New Guinea. *SSGM Working Papers* 1: 1–30.

Gramsci, Antonio, 1971. *Selections from the Prison Notebooks*. London: Lawrence & Wishart.

Griffith, R. Marie, 1997. Submissive wives, wounded daughters and female soldiers: prayer and Christian womanhood in Women's Aglow Fellowship. In *Lived Religion in America. Toward a History of Practice*, ed. David Hall, 160–95. New Jersey: Princeton University Press.

Hahn, Scott, 2001. *Hail Holy Queen*. New York: Doubleday.

Hammar, Lawrence, 1999. To be young, female, and 'normal': the health risks of absent sexual citizenship. *Journal of Medical Humanities* 20(2): 135–54.

-------- 2007. Epilogue: homegrown in PNG – rural responses to HIV and AIDS. *Oceania* 77(1): 72–94.

-------- 2008. Fear and loathing in Papua New Guinea: sexual health in a nation under siege. In *Making Sense of AIDS. Culture, Sexuality and Power in Melanesia*, ed. Leslie Butt and Richard Eves, 60–79. Honolulu: University of Hawai'i Press.

-------- 2010. *Sin, Sex and Stigma: A Pacific Response to HIV and AIDS*. Wantage: Sean Kingston Publishing.

Hermkens, Anna-Karina, 2007. The power of Mary in Papua New Guinea. *Anthropology Today* 23(2): 4–8.

Hermkens, Anna-Karina, Willy Jansen and Catrien Notermans, eds, 2009. *Moved by Mary. The Power of Pilgrimage in the Modern World*. Farnham: Ashgate.

Jebens, Holger, 2005. *Pathways to Heaven: Contesting Mainline and Fundamentalist Christianity in Papua New Guinea*. Oxford and New York: Berghahn.

Jenkins, Carol, 1995. Women and the risk of AIDS: A study of sexual and reproductive knowledge and behaviour in Papua New Guinea. Women and AIDS Research Program. Research Report Series 10. Washington: USAID.

Jolly, Margaret, 1992. Partible persons and multiple authors (contribution to Book Review Forum on Marilyn Strathern's *The Gender of the Gift*). In *Pacific Studies* 15(1): 137–49.

Kidu, Carol, 2000. Reflections on change, ethnicity and conflict: family and ethnic violence in Papua New Guinea. *Development Bulletin* 59 (November): 29–33.

Kleinman, Arthur, 1997. The violences of everyday life. The multiple forms and dynamics of social violence. In *Violence and Subjectivity*, ed. Veena Das, Arthur Kleinman, Mamphela Ramphele and Pamela Reynolds, 226–41. Berkeley: University of California Press.

Lee, Wendy, 1985. Women's groups in Papua New Guinea: shedding the legacy of drop scones and embroidered pillowcases. *Community Development Journal* 20(3): 222–35.

Lepani, Kathy, 2008. Fitting condoms on culture: rethinking approaches to HIV prevention in the Trobriand Islands, Papua New Guinea. In *Making Sense of AIDS. Culture, Sexuality and Power in Melanesia*, ed. Leslie Butt and Richard Eves, 246–66. Honolulu: University of Hawai'i Press.

Malins, Ian, 1987. *Christian Marriage and Family Life*. Wewak: Christian books Melanesia Inc.

Margry, Peter, 2009. Paradoxes of Marian apparitional contestation: networks, ideology, gender, and the Lady of All Nations. In *Moved by Mary. The Power of Pilgrimage in the Modern World*, ed. Anna-Karina Hermkens, Willy Jansen and Catrien Notermans, 183–99. Farnham: Ashgate.

McPherson, Naomi M., 2008. *Sik AIDS*: deconstructing the awareness campaign in rural West New Britain, Papua New Guinea. In *Making Sense of AIDS. Culture, Sexuality and Power in Melanesia*, ed. Leslie Butt and Richard Eves, 224–45. Honolulu: University of Hawai'i Press.

McLauglin K. Eleanor, 1974. Equality of souls, inequality of sexes: woman in medieval theology. In *Religion and Sexism. Images of Woman in the Jewish and Christian Traditions*, ed. Rosemary Radford Ruether, 213–66. New York: Simon and Schuster.

Mosko, Mark, 2010. Partible penitents: dividual personhood and Christian practice in Melanesia and the West. *Journal of the Royal Anthropological Institute* 16(2): 215–40.

National Statistical Office (NSO), 2002. *Papua New Guinea Census 2000 Provincial Report – Madang*. Port Moresby. The National Statistical Office.

Ram, Kalpana, 1991. *Mukkuvar Women: Gender, Hegemony and Capitalist Transformation in a South Indian Fishing Community*. London and New Jersey: Zed Press.

-------- 2005. Religion, gender, and the postcolonial crisis of the present: reflections on and from India. *Australian Religion Studies Review* 17(2): 20–31.

Revival Centres of Papua New Guinea, 2005. Pamphlet for an international rally organised by the Revival Centres of Papua New Guinea in 2005.

Richert, Scott P., 2010. Pope Benedict and condoms: what he did and did not say, in *Catholicism About.com*, 23 November 2010. Online: http://catholicism.about.com/b/2010/11/23/pope-benedict-and-condoms-what-he-did-and-did-not-say.htm. Accessed 17 March 2011.

Robbins, Joel, 2004. *Becoming Sinners: Christianity and Moral Torment in a Papua New Guinea Society*. Berkeley: University of California Press.

-------- 2005. The humiliation of sin: Christianity and the modernization of the subject among the Urapmin. In *The Making of Global and Local Modernities in Melanesia. Humiliation, Transformation and the Nature of Cultural Change*, ed. Joel Robbins and Holly Wardlow, 43–56. Hampshire, Burlington: Ashgate Publishing.

Ruether, Rosemary Radford, 1993. *Sexism and God-Talk: Toward a Feminist Theology*. Boston: Beacon Press.

Sala, H., 1999. *10-pela lo bilong marit*. Wewak PNG: Christian Books Melanesia Inc.

Schmidt, Bettina E. and Ingo W. Schröder, 2001. Introduction: violent imaginaries and violent practices. In *Anthropology of Violence and Conflict*, ed. Bettina E. Schmidt and Ingo W. Schröder, 1–24. London: Routledge.

Seeward, Peter and Pope Benedict XVI, 2010. *Light of the World: The Pope, the Church and the Signs of the Times*. San Francisco: Ignatius Press.

Sepoe, Orovu, 2000. *Changing Gender Relations in Papua New Guinea: The Role of Women's Organisations*. India, New Delhi: UBS Publishers.

Taussig, Michael, 1993. *Mimesis and Alterity: A Particular History of the Senses*. New York: Routledge.

Toft, Susan, ed., 1985. *Domestic Violence in Papua New Guinea*. Monograph No. 3. Law Reform Commission, Papua New Guinea.

-------- 1986. *Domestic Violence in Urban Papua New Guinea*. Occasional Paper, No. 19. Law Reform Commission, Papua New Guinea.

Toft, Susan, 1985a. Marital violence in Port Moresby: two urban case studies. In *Domestic Violence in Papua New Guinea*, ed. Susan Toft, 14–31. Monograph No. 3. Law Reform Commission, Papua New Guinea.

Toft, Susan and Susanne Bonnell, 1985. *Marriage and Domestic Violence in Rural Papua New Guinea: Results of a Research Project Conducted by the Law Reform Commission and Administrative College of Papua New Guinea*. Port Moresby: Papua New Guinea Law Reform Commission.

Vaz, Paulo and Fernanda Bruno, 2003. Types of self-surveillance: From abnormality to individuals 'at risk'. *Surveillance & Society* 1(3): 272–91.

Wardlow, Holly, 2006. *Wayward Women. Sexuality and Agency in a New Guinea Society*. Berkeley: University of California Press.

-------- 2008. 'You have to understand. Some of us are glad AIDS has arrived': Christianity and condoms among the Huli, Papua New Guinea. In *Making Sense of Aids. Culture, Sexuality, and Power in Melanesia*, ed. Lesley Butt and Richard Eves, pp. 187–205. Honolulu: University of Hawai'i Press.

Zimmer-Tamakoshi, Laura, 1990. Sexual exploitation and male dominance in Papua New Guinea. In *Human Sexuality in Melanesian Cultures*, ed. J. Ingebrittson, 250–67. *Point* 14. Melanesian Institute, Papua New Guinea.

-------- 1997. 'Wild pigs and dog men': rape and domestic violence as women's issues in Papua New Guinea. In *Gender in Cross-Cultural Perspective*, ed. Caroline B. Brettell and Carolyn F. Sargent, 538–53. Englewood Cliffs, New Jersey: Prentice-Hall.

-------- 2004. Rape and other sexual aggression. In *The Encyclopedia of Sex and Gender*, ed. Carol Ember and Melvyn Ember, 230–43. Kluwer: Academic Press.

5. Engendering Violence in the Papua New Guinea Courts: Sentencing in Rape Trials[1]

Jean G. Zorn

Abstract

Rape is endemic in Papua New Guinea, and the courts in Papua New Guinea have not been effective at decreasing its incidence. This may be in part because the very courts that are supposed to be a bulwark against the culture of engendered violence are themselves part of it. Some judges today are beginning to adopt a more empathetic view towards the women who are victims of sexual attacks, but most judges in Papua New Guinea, both expatriate and indigenous, from the colonial period onward, have found it impossible to take women's pain (especially emotional pain) seriously, and therefore have not taken rape seriously. Many judges view it as prurient, but not violent. Many of them continue to believe, despite evidence to the contrary, that most women who are raped probably 'asked for it'. As a result, although new sentencing guidelines introduced by Parliament allow for much longer gaol sentences for rape than were possible in the past too many judges find ways to give shorter sentences than the guidelines would permit.

Introduction

Crimes of sexual violence such as rapes and sexual assaults of women and children, are disturbingly prevalent in Papua New Guinea (PNG), and are all too often carried out in a particularly sadistic and gruesome fashion. Parliament and the Papua New Guinean courts all recognise the gravity of the problem and have attempted to use the law to decrease the incidence of these crimes. Over the last thirty years, the courts have gradually increased the length of prison sentences for persons convicted of rape. Prior to the amendment of the PNG *Criminal Code* by the *Criminal Code (Sexual Offences and Crimes Against Children) Act*

---

1   I wish to thank all of the members of the ASAO panel on 'Engendering Violence' for their suggestions and support, especially Christine Stewart, Dorothy Counts and Margaret Jolly. My special thanks to Stephen Zorn and Carolyn Brewer without whose excellent editing this piece would have been neither as concise nor as cogent.

2002 (*Sexual Offences Act*), the applicable provision of the Code, then Section 347, gave the courts broad latitude in determining sentences for rape. Among other changes to the Code, the *Sexual Offences Act* divided the crime of rape into two categories: ordinary and aggravated. The Act set the penalty for ordinary rape at fifteen years and made offenders convicted of aggravated rape liable for penalties up to life imprisonment. I am not in a position to assess the extent, if any, to which passage of the *Sexual Offences Act* has contributed to a decrease in crimes of sexual violence. What I do in this chapter is to analyse the ways in which the courts have responded—first to crimes of gender violence (the chapter focuses on rape of women) and then to the new Act. The PNG courts are very ambivalent about rape. On one hand, the judges say, over and over, that rape is widespread, that the 'community' is deeply upset by it, and that something needs to be done to decrease the incidence of rape. At the same time, however, the courts initially set prison terms for rape at very low levels and have increased them only very gradually.

The source for this ambivalence on the part of the judges can be traced to women's subordinated status in PNG. Most of the judges are men and they have been since colonial times. To the end of the colonial era, almost all the judges came from Australia, a very few from other Commonwealth countries. None were Papua New Guinean or even from other Pacific nations until after Independence. The judges, therefore, are most accurately reflecting the beliefs and values of PNG's male-dominated communities (both indigenous and expatriate) when they say that, in and of itself, rape is neither violent nor even particularly painful, either physically or emotionally. This stems from their ingrained notion that women act more emotionally than men so that, somehow, women's emotions are not as strong or real as men's, and psychological trauma is not as real as a wound from a bush knife or gun. It is an interesting albeit distressing paradox that many judges perceive women to be stereotypically more emotional than men, whilst at the same time, or perhaps as a result of this, they fail to register either the physical or the emotional pain that rape inflicts on women.

The judges in PNG operate in a society that has inherited its views of women from three sources. First, sexual distance and—in some areas of the country—sexual aggression were (and still are) integral parts of many pre-colonial cultures. Second, sexism was also characteristic of PNG's German and British colonisers.[2] And third, sexism is a by-product of the rapid and uneven development, or lack of development, that has characterised PNG's post-colonial history. So it is no surprise that sexism is prevalent, though not universal, amongst the members of

---

2   For lack of a more precise term, I am using the word 'sexism' to describe the approach that too many PNG judges take to the crime of rape. Sexism is a term frequently heard, but seldom defined. While the term is too broad to capture the complex and often contradictory emotions, values and beliefs of Papua New Guinea's lawyers and judges, sometimes a mutually understood shorthand is needed. By 'sexism', I mean simply a mode of thought that positions women as subordinate to men.

PNG's legal profession, including its judges. Systemic sexism is a cause both of the pervasiveness of rape in PNG and of the courts' tepid response to it. In her chapter in this volume, Laura Zimmer-Tamakoshi explains some of the reasons for the relationship between sexism and rape:

> In many PNG societies, the basis for the subordination of women and the exploitation and manipulation of their sexuality was older men's control of most economic resources and male ideologies which portrayed women as dangerous, inferior, and untrustworthy creatures who were to be feared, kept under control, and avoided whenever possible. Such ideologies were directed primarily at young men as a means of keeping them away from women until the young men's elders felt it was time for them to marry. At the same time, the use of rape and physical violence to control 'unruly' women was commonplace and young men were sometimes encouraged to participate in the rapes and sexual abuse of women.... For young men who opt (or are forced) to stay in town, unmarried and unrespectable by their parents' standards, joining gangs of other young men who make their own rules and standards is an attractive, albeit ultimately dead-end, proposition (Ch. 2).

Not all judges are equally impervious to the pain caused to women by rape. As early as the mid-1980s, a few judges were urging their colleagues to adopt the more victim-centred policies that have long since been adopted by Australian, British and American courts (Zorn 2010: 14). And, more recently, whilst Australian male judges on the Papua New Guinean bench have continued to insist that, in and of itself, unaccompanied by a knifing, beating or other physical injury, rape does not involve much pain or violence, some indigenous judges appear more empathetic, although this appears to be primarily where village women (rather than urbanised women) are the victims.

Still, almost every case in PNG determining the fate of a man who has raped or otherwise sexually abused a woman is decided by a man; the length and nature of the sentence is determined by a man; and it is a man who writes up the case, in a document called a 'judicial decision', in which he lays out his reasons for the sentence. Today, it is impossible to read these decisions without reference to feminist legal scholarship, which first posited the notion that the law itself is inherently male, not only in its overt attitudes towards women and women's bodies, but also in its glorifying of masculine values, such as reason and autonomy (Thornton 1998; Grbich 1991: 75). An analysis of the decisions would suggest that Marilyn Strathern (1988) is incorrect in her insistence that Papua New Guinean cultures do not hold to the same gender bifurcations that dominate the perceptions of women by men in other (primarily western) cultures. But, given the heavy influence of western legal categories on PNG's legal system and on its judges, one would hesitate to draw that conclusion.

Limits on the sanctions available to the courts

It must be said that the continuing epidemic of gender violence in PNG, including the high incidence of rape, cannot be laid entirely at the judges' door. Even the most sexist of PNG judges have responded to the high incidence of rape by gradually increasing prison sentences so that, overall, sentences for rape have increased, from an average of nine to twelve years in the mid-1980s to an average of fourteen to nineteen years today. The primary reason for the increase, ironically enough, is that the ever-more-severe sentences are not succeeding in decreasing the number of rapes. Quite the contrary, the number and gruesomeness of rapes have increased markedly in PNG, particularly in urban areas, in the last twenty-five years. Rapes are increasingly a side-effect of robbery involving gangs of men or youths repeatedly raping a victim over a period of several hours or days. But, despite the trend toward longer sentences, the effects of the inherent sexism of Papua New Guinean cultures and of its legal system are still evident.

If longer sentences have little effect on rape, then we must look to other remedies, but the courts are unable to come up with any means, other than making sentences longer and longer, to deter future rapists. There are at least three reasons for this. First, the narrow Anglo-Australian judicial tradition limits the kinds of sanctions that a judge may employ. Second, there are forces beyond the control of judges, principally the unwillingness or inability of other governmental and non-governmental agencies to do what the courts themselves are neither funded nor authorised to do. Finally, the various male sub-cultures within PNG, sub-cultures of which its male judges are a part, seem unanimous in their dislike or fear of, or distance from, women.

There are only a few tools that legal traditions (and statutes) authorise judges to employ: sentencing defendants to a term in prison, with or without the possibility of an early release on parole; ordering a defendant to pay a fine; or sentencing the defendant to a suspended sentence for a term, which means the defendant will be free unless the terms of the suspension are violated.[3] In tandem with any of these sentencing options, judges can order the defendant to do community service. In PNG, there is an additional sanction available: judges can order defendants to pay compensation.

Judges are supposed to utilise these sanctions, singly or in combination, to attain the four goals that are constantly cited as the main aims of the criminal law: (1) rehabilitating the defendant; (2) deterring the defendant from committing further crimes; (3) protecting the community against further bad acts by this defendant; and (4) deterring others from committing similar crimes. The

---

3   PNG *Criminal Code*, Section 19.

limited range of sanctions available to the courts is not always best suited to the attainment of these goals. Prison, for example, is more likely to teach young offenders how to commit more serious crimes than it is to rehabilitate them, and much research has proven that the spectacle of offenders going to prison does not necessarily deter others from committing the same crimes.

Moreover, judges are dependent on other governmental and non-governmental agencies for assistance. For example, a judge can sentence a defendant to a prison where, the judge hopes, rehabilitative services such as educational facilities and counselling will be available, but if the state has not seen fit to provide such services there is little the judge can do. PNG prisons offer little in the way of education, counselling or any other kinds of assistance that might improve prisoners' lives and deter them from committing more crimes. Moreover, judges may presume that there is community oversight of defendants who are on probation or serving a suspended sentence. In PNG, that is almost never the case.

Different goals have assumed precedence in different cultural milieux and at different moments in history. The eighteenth-century emphasis in England and the European continent on protecting the community from the criminal had led to the creation of fortress-like prisons, many of which were located on islands far from European settlement, as well as to the use of Australia and parts of the United States as penal colonies. This was followed in the nineteenth century by an emphasis on rehabilitation, exemplified by the adoption of new names for prisons, like penitentiary and correctional institution (Foucault 1975). In PNG today, at least where rape is concerned, deterrence—both the specific deterrence of the defendant from committing further crimes and the more general deterrence involved in persuading others to abstain from committing similar acts—has become the primary goal of the judiciary.

There are at least two ways in which the courts could play a more effective role in reducing the incidence of rape in PNG. One way would be to take rape more seriously, consciously recognising the pain it inflicts, and to impose sentences that reflect such pain. A second would be to persuade other governmental and non-governmental agencies to devote more resources to solving the problem. Neither is likely, in large part because of the bias against women. This bias is characteristic both of Papua New Guinean culture generally and of the specific sub-culture in which the judges have been educated and in which they lead their professional lives. Despite the judges' sincere hatred for the crime of rape, they too are prisoners of the sexism of their society and of their own sub-culture.

The judges' own written decisions demonstrate the insidious impact that the combined sexism of PNG generally and of legal institutions in particular has had on the courts' ability to devise sentences that contribute in any meaningful way to decreasing the incidence of rape in PNG. In two landmark cases, both decided in 1987, *State v Kaudik* and *Aubuku v State*,[4] the courts adopted 'starting points' (ranging from five to eight years) for determining how long a convicted rapist should be incarcerated. These 'starting points' were to be added to, or occasionally subtracted from, depending upon the existence, in the rape itself and in the defendant's background, of aggravating factors or mitigating circumstances. Aggravating factors might include the degree of violence associated with the crime, or the relationship between the rapist and his victim: was he, for example, abusing a relationship of trust? Mitigating factors include the age of the defendant (ordinarily, youthful offenders receive lighter sentences) or his criminal record (the lighter the record, the lighter the sentence). The judges adopted these guidelines intending to create a set of rules that would be fair and neutral in application. As I will demonstrate, however, the guidelines are infused with sexism, both in substance and in application.

Deconstructing sentencing decisions

There are multiple ambiguities at the centre of the judges' masculinist views of rape. Feminist theorists have long posited that rape is, primarily, an act not of sexual longing, but of violence which the rapist perpetrates on a woman primarily in order to cause her pain and suffering (Brownmiller 1975; Bourke 2007). But feminist scholarship also confronts the conundrum that in cultures like most of those in PNG, including those of the urban centres, men's views of women's ability to feel pain and suffering are paradoxical and contradictory. Men believe that women feel too much, that they follow their emotions when they ought to be guided by reason. At the same time, men believe that women are not fully human, that although women are over-emotional creatures, they do not have feelings in the same deep way that men do. So rape is also an exercise in frustration for the rapist, who is trying to cause pain and fear in a person who, he believes, is not capable of experiencing true pain or fear. Thus, women are, at the same time, too human and not human enough, too emotional and not emotional enough (Lloyd 1984; Lutz 1998).

Judges are products of their gender, class and conditioning. Neither Papua New Guinean nor expatriate judges can escape the cultures in which their ideas were formed. The legal profession, which was for a long time a male-only bastion, still has a culture of masculinity. There are, as R.W. Connell (1987, 2005) has made us realise, many masculinities. That of the courtroom is a masculinity derived not

---

4   Only the names and dates of the cases are given in the text. Generally, the full decisions can be found by searching, under the appropriate name and year, either in the printed *Papua New Guinea Law Reports*, published annually, or at Papua New Guinea Laws, *PacLII database*, online: http://www.paclii.org/databases. html#PG, accessed 5 November 2011.

from violence and physical strength, but from privilege, reason and logic (Collier 2010, 431; Dowd 2010). It is, therefore, an axiom of the (western, including colonial) legal system that judges decide cases and hand down sentences based upon law and logic. Everyone connected with the legal system—including the judges themselves—believes this to be true. Emotions are supposed to play no part in judicial decision making; instead, reason and logic are supposed to be transcendent. So, to the members of the legal profession, it is a display not of feeling for the victim, nor even of anger at the accused, but of logical, rule-based argument that gives judicial decisions their legitimacy. It is presumed that judges decide fairly and honestly, by a logical application of the law to the facts of the case, and not by the subjectivity or bias of feeling, culture or kin. This same conceit is also another aspect of the sexism of the western legal system: reason and logic are associated with maleness; emotions like envy, bias or greed that would colour decision-making are associated with femaleness—a dichotomy in masculinist thinking that has been central to feminist analysis at least since Sherry Ortner and Harriet Whitehead (1981). To the extent that the law is praised (by judges and lawyers) for eschewing emotion in favour of reason, it is being praised for being male (Thornton 1998; Dowd 2010).

However, a close reading of judges' decisions—not only in PNG, but in any common law jurisdiction—uncovers depths of emotion, and the clear suggestion that the judges' choices are as impelled by these emotions as they are by reason. Although it is true that the vast majority of articles in law reviews treat legal argument and judicial decision making as if they were based solely on reason, there is also a significant body of work pointing out that legal decisions are equally influenced by emotions, values, biases and experience. Scholars writing from this perspective include critical legal scholars, feminists, critical race theorists and others, loosely grouped under the rubric 'Outsider Scholarship', a term which in itself suggests how far from the mainstream this view continues to be (Coombs 1992; Valdes 1999; Foley 2010: 26). This approach to the texts reveals that judges share the same ambiguous and mutually contradictory views of women held by other men (and, because they too were raised in that society, by most women). That is, the male judges are excited (and repelled) by the facts of rape, by the terror and pain of it, at the same time that, different and distanced from women, they cannot believe in the reality of women's feelings. Many of the decisions dwell, with what almost amounts to salacious interest, on the clinical and lurid specifics of the rape, featuring detailed descriptions of the degrading sexual acts that the rapists forced upon their victims At the same time, in the same decisions, judges write that the rape they have just described is not particularly painful, thus making a longer sentence for the crime unnecessary. And, though the judges write stock paragraphs about the psychological wounds caused to women by rape, they do so in such a rote fashion as to suggest they truly do not feel what they are saying.

Unfortunately for the women, who feel pain, anguish, defilement and depression, the men who hear about their ordeal (including, I believe, judges) feel none of those. Although rape itself is not sex but violence, hearing about rape is all about the ways in which gender violence breeds sexual excitement.

'Moira's' story

We'll call her Moira.[5] The written decision does not tell us her name, though it tells us a little about her. Moira and her family were expatriates. In 1986, when she was just seventeen and still in high school, her father took a position with a Papua New Guinean university. The University provided on-campus housing, and that is where Moira and her parents were living when she was the victim of a particularly brutal pack rape. She had spent the evening babysitting for the children of another couple who also lived on campus, and was about to get into her employer's car to go home, when a gang of eight men approached the vehicle, shotguns drawn, surrounding her employer and dragging her into the garden where her ordeal began. It would last for the entire night, and involve multiple rapes and other forms of sexual abuse by a number of gang members.

Like Moira's, many rapes in PNG are particularly violent, because, like this one, a very high number of rapes in PNG are pack rapes. Pack rapes have developed their own norms: they all seem to begin with a house or vehicle robbery and to include the subjugation of the victim's male companion, the abduction of the victim, hours of repeated sexual attack and what seem to be contests amongst the participants as to which of them can subject the victim to the most indignity. Of the cases that I randomly sampled (a substantial but still incomplete sampling of all those that have been preserved, either in PNG Law Reports or in PacLII), a very high number involved pack rapes—groups of men (usually young from their teens to twenties) abduct women (usually teenage girls or young women), typically as a sequel to a brutal armed robbery or house invasion. The victim is subjected to the horror of repeated group rapes, often throughout the night, sometimes for several days, with multiple defendants serially forcing sex upon the victim, often several times each.

The facts of the case: the law as pornography

It is possible to write a judicial decision in a fashion that omits the pornographic details, that does not strive for novelistic specificity, that does not dabble in graphic excess and that, nonetheless, conveys enough of the particulars to show that the elements of the crime were indeed proven. Yes, it is necessary to a rape

---

5   *State v Kaudik* (1986).

conviction to prove that sexual penetration occurred.[6] But a judge does not have to describe it over and over—as happened in this case. Certainly, if a sentence longer than one of those at the 'starting points' is to be imposed, it is necessary to show aggravating factors, but, again, a judge can do this without dwelling on each and every penis being forced into the girl's mouth—as the judge did in this case.

Feminist legal theorists were among the first to note that unnecessarily detailed and repetitious descriptions, like those in the decision in Moira's case, are examples of legal description becoming pornography (see MacKinnon 1985: 1). There are many key resemblances between the decision and the kinds of writing found in pornographic magazines. For example, the decision never gives a name to the victim. We are told the name of the defendant (the rapist), we are even told the (completely irrelevant) name of the family for whom the victim was babysitting when she was abducted, but we are not told her name. The law's reason for refusing to name the victim is to protect her and perhaps, while it succeeds in protecting one young woman, it does so at the expense of women generally. Because namelessness reduces women to objects, and objectification and anonymity allow readers to revel in the arousal that the sexually explicit descriptions elicit, without having to feel the guilt or shame that would occur if the victim were somebody real, somebody with a name. At the same time as the decision permits distance, by depriving the victim of the personhood that comes with having a name, it also invites a certain voyeuristic intimacy, by obliging the victim to recapitulate every horrifying and sordid moment in the first-person narrative of her affidavit. She is violated twice, first by the rape itself, and then by this legal process.

First-person narratives invite the reader into the sensual experience, give it texture and immediacy; the first-person narrative allows, even invites, the reader to join in the sexual acts, which may be why most best-selling pornography is written in the first person, often in the person of the woman/victim (e.g. Réage 1954). The first-person narrative has another purpose as well: it allows the judge to avoid responsibility for its pornographic aspects. By ostensibly quoting from the victim's affidavit rather than recasting it in his own words, the judge can pose as uninvolved in the sexual details; even though he is the one behind the scenes, orchestrating the words and choosing what will go into the decision and what will not.

---

6   At the time this case was decided, the Code did not refer to 'sexual penetration' but to 'carnal knowledge'. This Victorian attempt to avoid saying what was meant caused difficulties for the courts when sexual assault consisted of anything other than the straightforward penetration; in those cases, under that prudish statute, was it or was it not rape? The more explicit and therefore much more helpful term 'sexual penetration' has now been substituted.

When a decision dwells on the specifics of the rape, it could be to demonstrate the judge's own horror at those details, to make sure he has shown that the prosecution has proven every element of the crime, or to convince readers of the pressing need for a longer sentence. However, the evidence is against any of these being the major reason. In general, and barring a few exceptions, the longer the sentence, the less the picturesque detail. Catharine MacKinnon (1985; MacKinnon and Dworkin, 1997) and other feminist scholars of pornography have suggested that there are generally two reasons, both related to distaste for, distance from, or distrust of women, that propel quasi-pornographic descriptions like these. First, the writer is often himself aroused by the recitation; he finds pleasure in describing forced sex (Binder 1995: 298). Second, and related to the first, these descriptions themselves do what the act of rape also does; they put women into a subordinate position (Banks 2000: 100). The judges are writing from a perspective in a socially hierarchical society in which men are actors and women are the ones acted upon. Rape, depending upon one's perspective and the circumstances, is either an example of taking to extremes the norms of a society based upon gender hierarchy (MacKinnon 1989: generally, but especially at 171; Zimmer-Tamakoshi Ch. 2), or it is what happens when some men who believe they should be dominant react with anger to the realisation that they are not (Banks 2000).

The courts' view of rape as a source of emotional injury

One of the many ways in which feminist studies changed our understanding of rape is by demonstrating that its purpose is seldom about desire (Brownmiller 1975; Groth 1979; Bourne 2007). Contrary to accepted wisdom, the primary purpose of rape is not sexual; the purpose is equally, if not entirely, to subjugate a woman, to wreak violence upon her, to hurt and degrade her. Rape is, for a man, an opportunity to take the thing he most fears about women—their ability to use his own sexual urges to entrap him, encircle him, make him feel weak and needy—and turn that upon a woman; to use his own weakness as a weapon against her.[7] If men choose to take out their anger at and fear of women through rape, it is because sex is, to men, the most frightening act of all. Because, in sex, the man feels himself succumbing to the woman, becoming weak, needing her, he, at the same time, loves it and abhors it, wants it and fears it, adores it and is disgusted by it.

---

7   Wardlow (2006) points out that encirclement is very much the fate of Papua New Guinean women, who are beset by boundaries. Yet another paradox of sex in patriarchal cultures is that, while it is women who are, for most important (and unimportant) purposes the encircled, bounded ones, it is men who feel it and fear it.

The link between rape and masculine anger is made patent in PNG where so many rapes are done by gangs of criminals as a postscript to the act of armed robbery. The circumstances of these rapes as well as the way that they are carried out demonstrate that there is very little about sexual desire, and a great deal about the assertion of male power, involved in rape. A pack of men break into a house or a car, threaten the inhabitants with knives or guns, rob them of everything available, and then, almost as if it were an after-thought, abduct the young women to rape them. In addition women are subjected to rape not just by one gang member but by many. They are threatened and cursed at and subjected not just to sex but to various perversions, as well as being dragged far away and, when all the raping is over, forced to walk home naked or half-clothed. These circumstances and acts of violence against women demonstrate that one motivation for rape is an attempt by young men who feel powerless in the face of social change to assert the only power that they do have, and to do so in the crudest of ways (Borrey 2000: 107).

However, although feminist and masculinist scholars both have uncovered these motives in rape, it is not the way judges traditionally view it. Many Papua New Guinean men—even members of PNG's legal profession—continue to believe that men need constant access to sex. They believe that this need is in the nature of men, and that they cannot be blamed if now and then they go a little overboard. In Chapter Six of this volume, Fiona Hukula quotes men who are serving prison terms for rape explaining that they raped women because their wives or girlfriends wouldn't give them enough sex, or their families stopped them from getting married so they just had to find it elsewhere. The offenders may even believe this. More to our point, judicial decisions suggest that even judges may believe this. At least, this view is implicit in many of the rape cases; in a few, it is even stated explicitly. In *State v Yali* (2006, *'Yali's Case'*), for example, the prosecutor is quoted as saying, 'The offender was at the time a married man who also had a second, de facto, wife. There was no need for him' to rape yet another woman. And if the offender had been single, without even a girlfriend, then would this prosecutor have said, 'Oh, okay, I understand what made you do it. Guess we won't charge you today.'

To some degree, however, lawyers and judges seem to have understood that the major purpose of rape is not to gratify innocuous sexual desires, but to hurt and degrade women, and judges say so in many of their sentencing decisions. However, few judges are able to say this persuasively or movingly, in large part because an odd thing happens in the minds of the judges who hear rape cases, and in the minds, too, of the lawyers who try these cases. Even though they know, in theory, that rape is degrading and painful to women, and that many of the victims will carry lifelong scars from the experience, very few of the male judges or lawyers seem able to empathise with the women. Although the judges say that they understand that rape is extremely painful physically; and equally painful emotionally, the tone of their writing suggests that this may be what they think, but not what they feel. The judges do write about the horror of rape for women, but, for the most part, the writing lacks credibility, urgency, and emotional force. It is as if the writer believes he ought to say this, but he isn't feeling it (see Zorn 2010 for detailed evidence).

Two contrasting cases of empathy in gang rape

Two contrasting cases demonstrate the judges' reluctance to believe in women's emotional pain: the first by atypically recognising the emotional pain and the second by downplaying the pain that the woman surely suffered. The victims in both cases were expatriates. In PNG, the largest number of rape victims is, by far, indigenous women, and I am not focusing in this section on expatriates because I think their cases any more important; quite the opposite. But the choice of these cases helps to illustrate the vagaries of empathy among the judges.

In *State v Koupa* (1987), a young Australian woman, Christine (whose name we can use because it is given in the decision—a public document), was living with her husband in Hohola when she was the victim of a gang rape. The judge in that case, an Australian himself, believed fully that Christine's physical and psychological injuries were severe enough to warrant making the defendant's sentence even longer than the court otherwise would have made it. Contrast that case with *State v Kaudik* in the same year. In that case, the young woman who was not named in the judge's decision, and whom we have called Moira, was also the victim of gang rape. The judge in that case, a Papua New Guinean, hardly even discusses the possibility of emotional injury, and certainly does not hold the defendants responsible for having caused the victim much in the way of psychological distress.

One key reason for the differences in the judges' reactions in the two cases lies in what kind of information the prosecuting lawyers in each case provided to the court. In *Koupa's Case*, one key reason that the judge believed in the emotional pain that Christine experienced was that lawyers for the prosecution gave the court a specific, graphic account, not of how the rapists behaved, but of how she acted during the rape, which demonstrated the depth of her fear and emotional pain in tangible, provable ways. The prosecution reported to the court: that Christine cried during the rape; that her rapists threatened to kill her because she was screaming; and that when the police found her she was shivering from shock. These graphic manifestations of her emotional pain made it real for the court—made it credible. Moreover, the prosecution stated that a year after the event Christine was still undergoing psychiatric treatment for the emotional trauma she had sustained. Psychiatrists are experts; courts believe them; the report that the victim was under a psychiatrist's care made her emotional injuries real, almost tangible.

The material supplied by the prosecution in *Kaudik's Case* was starkly different. It is clear from her affidavit that Moira wished to appear plucky; she wanted to be brave; she did not want to discuss how frightening it all was. Indeed, she was plucky. She had the presence of mind to count her attackers and to try to remember what they looked like. Instead of screaming and crying, she 'lay there and pretended it was not happening'. The prosecution would have done better if Moira had been frailer. Brave young women do not excite the judges' sympathy enough for them to order long prison sentences for their attackers. While Christine's primary rapist was sentenced to eighteen years, Moira's was sentenced to only twelve years.[8]

Koupa's Case is one of the very few in which prosecutors are quoted as having introduced evidence of the victim's emotional condition. More prosecuting lawyers should learn from this case. Or perhaps they cannot. The way in which people demonstrate their emotions is a product of their socialisation, even when those emotions are being experienced under extreme distress (Lutz 1998). Christine cried, screamed and shivered uncontrollably. Moira lay there and pretended she was somewhere else. Not every woman from every culture would react in the same way. In some cultures, the most likely manifestation of fear would be absolute stillness, a sinking into oneself. It would take a great deal of laying of groundwork for a prosecutor to use that behaviour as proof that the victim suffered extensive emotional or psychological injury.

Perhaps the judge in Christine's case was more likely to believe that her emotional injuries were real and severe, because she was an Australian, and so was he. In PNG, for a long while, the bias against women was exacerbated, because there was also a bias, at least amongst some Australian judges, against Papua New Guinean women (Crenshaw 1991: 1270–71). White judges could write with real feeling about the terrible effects that rape must have on a white woman, and find none of that emotion accessible when the victim was Papua New Guinean.

The attitude of judges towards women who are victims of rape depends very much on stereotypes of different kinds of women. Kimberlé Crenshaw coined the term 'intersectionality' to point out that black women are subjected to a double bind; they are prejudiced against both because of their race and because of their

---

8   Although both women were raped by gangs of men, in each of the reported cases only one defendant was being tried. This is a common practice in the PNG courts. We do not have information on what happened to the other members of the gangs, but it is likely that some escaped the police's notice, and that others pleaded guilty, on the assumption that if the court found one of the gang guilty, it would most probably find others guilty as well.

gender, and this double prejudice does not lead merely to more discrimination but to discrimination of different kinds. Writing about judges' responses to rape cases in the United States, Crenshaw (1991) noted that judges were more likely to believe that, because of the historical position of black women, they had consented to sex and therefore had suffered no real pain. As slaves, they had been at the mercy of the sexual urges of white masters. Since society did not care to blame slave owners for these sexual assaults, the blame was shifted to the hapless women, who were deemed sexually promiscuous. Papua New Guinean women suffered similar treatment during the colonial period, when they endured the sexual advances of *kiaps* and planters. Unwilling to blame themselves for this, white Australians deemed Papua New Guinean women 'soiled goods', immoral and promiscuous. Thus the double bind: because Papua New Guinean women were presumed to be immoral and promiscuous, men continued to take advantage of them.

Sentencing guidelines

Judges' fearful, emotional and, at times, pornographic perceptions of women and rape have infiltrated the sentencing aspect of rape cases in a number of respects. These perceptions are evident not only in the ways in which the judges explicitly talk about the victims and the crime, but in the very guidelines that the judges have devised to shape sentencing decisions. These guidelines, whose purpose is supposed to be to ensure that judges determine sentences rationally and fairly, are imbued with non-rational attitudes towards women and rape. The overall principles for sentencing in rape cases are laid out in the PNG *Criminal Code*, but these statutory mandates are quite general, and could lead to great disparities in sentencing, so the courts have tried to make them more predictable by establishing more specific guidelines. The guidelines seem to emanate from the judges' masculinised beliefs about women, as do the ways in which the judges apply the guidelines.

Prior to the amendment of the *Criminal Code* in 2002, the applicable provision of the Code, then Section 347, stated that the penalty for rape was, 'subject to Section 19, imprisonment for life'. That hurried reference to Section 19 was all important, because Section 19 provided that any offender liable for a life-time prison term could be sentenced to imprisonment for any shorter term, or ordered to pay a fine, or even given a suspended sentence. Courts thus had almost complete leeway in determining the sentence for rape, all the more so because they interpreted the statute to require a life sentence only for the 'worst types of the crime of rape'. However, the latitude is not quite as wide as might appear, because courts do some policing of themselves. Judges do not like to be unduly dissonant in sentencing. Common law notions of fairness, coupled with the desire not to have their sentences overturned by an appellate court, propel most judges to believe that the sentence for one offender should, all else being equal, roughly approximate the sentence handed down to a similar offender for a similar crime. A large part of judicial thinking about sentences, then, takes the form of a search for ways to achieve that equivalence between offenders, while also achieving the four goals of criminal sanction, mentioned above.

Creation of the rape-sentencing guidelines

In 1987, in the two otherwise unrelated rape cases, *State v Kaudik* (Moira's case) and *State v Aubuku*, the Papua New Guinean courts, as part of their search for fairness and efficacy, established guidelines that they could follow in rape sentencing. The judges in both these cases adopted, as 'starting points' for rape sentences, the same terms that had been adopted a year earlier in England, even quoting from *R v Billiam*, the English case.[9]

Although a total of four judges, two of them Papua New Guineans, opined that this formulation was appropriate to PNG, these starting points fail to take into account important differences between the circumstances in England and PNG— differences that have caused judges in subsequent cases great difficulties when they attempted to apply the guidelines. For example, the per capita incidence of rape in PNG is much higher than in England. Second, pack rapes, which have become endemic in PNG, are rare in England. Given these disparities, it might have occurred to the judges that longer sentences and other more stringent measures not contemplated by the English courts would be needed in PNG.

It may be, however, that the pervasive nature of rape in PNG was not yet apparent to the judges in 1987. Pack rape was just beginning to rise to the consciousness of the courts as a widespread problem that had to be addressed. The starting sentence of eight years for pack rapes must have seemed at the time a considerable leap from past sentencing practices. Prior to 1987, sentences for rape tended to be a lot less than ten years, many were under five years. A striking example of the very short sentences then usually handed down is *Acting Public Prosecutor v Konis Haha* (1981). The trial court sentenced the two defendants to

---

9   'For rape committed by an adult without any aggravating or mitigating features, a figure of five years should be taken as the starting point in a contested case. Where a rape is committed by two or more men acting together, or by a man who has broken into or otherwise gained access to a place where the victim is living, or by a person who is in a position of responsibility towards the victim, or by a person who abducts the victim and holds her captive, the starting point should be eight years.

'At the top of the scale comes the defendant who has carried out what might be described as a campaign of rape, committing the crime upon a number of different women or girls. He represents a more than ordinary danger and a sentence of 15 years or more may be appropriate.

'Where the defendant's behaviour has manifested perverted or psychopathic tendencies or gross personality disorder, and where he is likely, if at large, to remain a danger to women for an indefinite time, a life sentence will not be inappropriate' (see *State v Kaudik* and *State v Aubuku* from *R v Billiam*).

only three years each for rape, with five months each added on for robbery. The men had attacked a soldier and his girlfriend who were walking home from a party, robbing both at knife point and raping the woman. And perhaps the PNG judges did recognise that crime in PNG needed different treatment from that in England. In both *Kaudik's* and *Aubuku's Cases*, the judges sentenced defendants to longer terms than had been the norm up to that time. In *Kaudik*, for example, the first case of pack rape in which the new guidelines were applied, Justice Amet sentenced the defendant to a term of twelve years. Even in the *Aubuku* case, which did not involve pack rape, the trial court sentenced the defendant to ten years.

Applying the guidelines: Aggravating factors

The sentencing guidelines adopted in *Kaudik's* and *Aubuku's Cases* provided for sentences to be longer if there were aggravating circumstances, and perhaps shorter if there were mitigating circumstances. Quoting from the English case, the judges in *Kaudik* and *Aubuku* listed the aggravating factors:

(i) violence over and above the force necessary to commit rape;

(ii) use of a weapon to frighten or wound the victim;

(iii) the rape is repeated;

(iv) the rape has been carefully planned;

(v) the accused has previous convictions for rape or other serious offences of a sexual or violent kind;

(vi) the victim is subjected to further sexual indignities or perversions;

(vii) the victim is either very old or very young; and

(viii) the effect upon the victim, whether physical or mental (*State v Kaudik* 1987).

'Where any one or more of the following aggravating factors are present the sentence should be substantially higher than the suggested starting point [of 8 years]' (*State v Kaudik*). Most of these factors are present in most of the PNG cases—especially those relating to violence, the use of weapons, and the subjection of the victim to further indignities.

Violence as an aggravating factor

As I noted above, PNG's male judges, whether Australian or Papua New Guinean, do not view rape itself as particularly painful. Their definition of aggravated rape—which includes a situation in which 'violence is used over and above the force necessary to commit the rape'—suggests that they do understand that the act of rape itself usually involves some degree of force and violence. But they differentiate between the fear produced in a victim by the threat of violence and actual violence. In *Waim v State* (1997), for example, two university students, the victim and her boyfriend, were walking towards the campus. Accosted at the campus gates by the appellant and five or six other men, the boyfriend was chased into the campus, and the girl was carried away:

> Seven of them took turns in raping the victim. She was also forced to engage in oral sex and was further subjected to sexual perversions and indignities. The gang with the victim then headed back towards … the Waterboard Station at which they stopped the vehicle. The victim was then raped in turn by the appellant and his six accomplices. This forced sex was indulged in vaginally, orally and anally. Then proceeding further into the bush, the victim was once again subjected to forced sexual intercourse by the appellant and the other members (*Waim v State*).

The trial court sentenced the appellant, who was characterised as the person who first accosted the couple and as the ringleader of the group, to a total of twenty-five years on four counts of rape. On appeal, a three-judge panel (two Papua New Guineans and one Australian) was supposed to weigh these facts against the sentencing guidelines to determine whether that sentence was proper. The panel's decision that the sentence was excessive and its substitution of an eighteen-year sentence were based upon a number of considerations. Most important for our investigation at this moment is the court's finding that, though the victim had been made to suffer 'a harrowing and terrible experience at the hands of the appellant and his accomplices', nonetheless:

> There were no weapons used, and no violence other than that associated with forced sexual intercourse was involved here. No life was lost here. And there is no evidence of any long-term injuries sustained by the victim, although it was a terrible experience (*Waim v State*).

Even the fact that the young woman was raped—not just by one person but by an entire gang—did not shake the court's assurance that no aggravating violence had occurred. The old English and Australian rule was that a woman could prove she had been raped—that she had not been consenting to mutually agreeable sex—only if she had the cuts and bruises that would show she had fought off her attacker. Although that rule has been discredited when it comes to proving whether a rape occurred, it seems that a similar notion is still pervading the sentencing part of rape decisions in PNG. Rapists will serve a minimal sentence unless their victim can show that, in addition to raping her, they performed other acts of violence. In fact, the way the rule is worded, rapists will serve a minimal sentence, even if they have acted violently, so long as they can show that they used only as much force as was necessary to enable them to commit rape.

Rape by a person in a position of trust and responsibility

James Yali was a married man, forty-one years old, Governor of Madang Province and a Member of Parliament from Madang, when he raped the seventeen-year-old sister of the woman he was living with. The rape-sentencing guidelines provided for a higher 'starting point' (eight years, rather than five) if the rapist was in 'a position of responsibility' towards his victim and, since the adoption of the guidelines, the PNG courts have tended to add even more than three years to the sentence of any rapist who has breached a position of trust.

There is no definition of 'position of responsibility' either in the *Criminal Code* or the cases that originally set out the guidelines, so it is left up to the courts to fill in the substance. A 'position of responsibility' is a role or status and, as such, can be defined in two different ways—either formally or functionally. A formal definition would create a list of relevant positions and the rule would then apply automatically to anyone in such a position, and not to anyone else. A functional definition, however, would describe the purposes or properties of the role, and the rule could then apply to anyone fulfilling these purposes or having these properties, regardless of the formal name of their position. The Supreme Court had ventured to rule on the topic in *Meaoa's Case* (1996), decided ten years before *Yali*. But that decision left both arguments open to the participants in *Yali's Case*, because, in *Meaoa*, the court had, in essence, subscribed to both. The *Meaoa* court held that certain relationships (such as parent/child or teacher/pupil) are, by their nature, positions of trust, a formalist definition. And, in addition, the way in which a person 'conducts himself can give rise to a relationship of trust; and … if such a relationship is violated, it is an aggravating factor'—a functionalist definition.

In *Yali's Case*, not surprisingly, the defence and the prosecution each argued that the court should adopt the definition that would work best for their side. Counsel for the defendant argued that the phrase should be interpreted formalistically. It connoted, he said, persons who were in certain positions in relation to the victim, such as 'her counselor, basketball coach, physiotherapist, doctor, schoolteacher or someone similar.' Not only was the defendant not in any of these positions, but 'he was her big sister's boyfriend. He was just the sort of person who should *not* have been trusted [emphasis added].' Counsel for the prosecution, on the other hand, argued that the phrase should be interpreted functionally: 'The offender was living in a de facto relationship with the victim's sister. He was providing shelter to the victim and her family. Therefore, she was entitled to trust him.'

Counsel for the prosecution did not base his argument solely on functionalism, however. He also pointed out that, under some neo-customary conceptualisations, Yali, who was formally married to another woman but living with the victim's older sister, could be said to be the de facto husband of the victim's sister and, thus, could be shoehorned into the formalist definition as a kind of brother-in-law to the victim. Having done that, the court was able to use this as an aggravating factor in assessing a sentence of imprisonment for twelve years. Like the prosecutor, however, the court did not base this conclusion on custom; in fact, the judge does not give any provenance for this finding, other than the facts of Yali's living arrangements. In rape cases, the 'position of responsibility' is almost always viewed as a relationship of the rapist to his victim. Yali's case added another dimension because, as a Member of Parliament and Provincial Governor, Yali could be said to have a position of responsibility not only to his young victim, but to the country as a whole. This is not an interpretation of the term that had arisen in earlier PNG cases, but the judge in this case asked counsel to comment on the relevance of Yali's governmental position to the sentencing decision.

Yali's counsel argued, of course, that it was utterly irrelevant. He argued that, for purposes of rape cases, 'position of responsibility' is to be defined solely in relation to the victim. Therefore, Yali's governmental position would be relevant only if they aided his access to or control over the victim, or if his governmental power caused the victim to fear him. Counsel for the State disagreed, suggesting that the definition has to be broadened to include responsibilities beyond those that the defendant had to the victim. The court agreed with the prosecution, holding that 'the offender's status as a member of Parliament and as the Provincial Governor is something that aggravates the offence.' In an era when most people see elected office primarily as a means of self-aggrandisement, this case becomes a precedent with import beyond rape and sentencing.

Disturbing traditional village harmony and discouraging development as aggravating factors

As more Papua New Guineans became judges, and as more of them came out of a legal education dominated by Papua New Guinean lecturers, they began to add to the list of aggravating factors some that are particular to Melanesian cultural mores. For example, in an important set of decisions in 2004, Justice Kandakasi identified the rapists' disruption of the peace, security and unity of the extended family unit as an aggravating factor:[10]

> This was a gang rape, which also involved some element of breach of trust the victim placed in you.... This makes the commission of the offence by you three men in the way you did very serious. This is because ... there is already so much danger for our women, girls and children in the streets. Therefore, the village and the family unit and relations are the only place where our women, girls and children could turn to for their protection. Hence, a commission of an offence against a member of one's own community, village, family and other close relations destroys the remainder of any sense of security and hope for living. It also sends a wrong signal to outsiders that the chances of people like you attacking them are far greater. Therefore, they should not come to this province to help it to develop.... Thus, the commission of the kind of offence you committed in the particular setting of your case has the potential of contributing to a destruction of the province to a greater deal, as it has the potential of preventing other people with ability to help develop the province from coming out of fear over theirs and their families' security (*State v Sasoropa (No 2)* 2004).

What makes Justice Kandakasi's decision unusual is not just his references to traditional Papua New Guinean village life, but also his ability to combine the traditional and the modern, village unity and provincial development, customary law and the formal legal system. This blending was what the drafters of the *Constitution* had hoped would happen in the Papua New Guinean court system, but their hopes have been, until recently, little realised (Zorn 1991, 1992).

In that case, the perpetrators were members of the same extended family as their victim. In *Setep v State* (2001), another decision in which Justice Kandakasi participated, the rapists were not related to the family whose home they invaded, though they were known to their victims:

> The appellant and his accomplices ... committed the unlawful acts with full knowledge of the identity of the victims for no reason whatsoever save only to commit the acts against the victims. They also made their unlawful intentions known. This kind of conduct is the very cause of break down in community respect and trust and consequently a break down in our society. It is already worse that serious offences are

---

10   *State v Sasoropa, Aremeiko and Melton* (2004); *State v Paulus Moi & Clement Samoka* (2004); *State v Donald Angavia* (2004); *State v Sina* (2004).

committed outside the family or community units. When they creep into those units it renders no place else safe not even a dwelling house (*Setep v State* 2001).

The focus on clan and family solidarity—the suggestion that housebreaking, robbery and rape are even more reprehensible when done to people one knows, to people to whom one might have a kinship connection—seems to be an articulation of customary PNG values. In making these observations, Justice Kandakasi is making comprehensible to Papua New Guineans the notion that rape is a serious crime. He is also doing something that, from the colonial era onwards, western-educated judges found impossible to do: he is melding customary values and norms into the imported legal system (Zorn 1991, 1992). The problem, of course, is that, albeit implicitly, it characterises rapes committed against foreigners, whether westerners or Papua New Guineans from another village or region, as not quite so bad. In doing so, it demonstrates, without discussion or resolution, one of the key conflicts between the formal legal system (which positions itself as impartial, at least as between citizens) and customary law (which privileges the 'in group'). Prior to the creation of the state, the 'in group' consisted almost exclusively of kin and fellow villagers.

Changes to the sentencing guidelines: The increasing rate of rape

By the mid-1990s, it had become apparent to many of the judges that the sentences mandated by their guidelines had not succeeded in lessening the incidence of rape in PNG. Sentences had increased, but so had the prevalence and brutality of rape. Some of the judges became convinced that even higher sentences were needed and they wanted to change the guidelines. Parliament, too, grew uneasy and, as part of the *Sexual Offences Act*, enacted new sentencing rules which also seemed intended to mandate longer sentences.

Judge-made changes

The judges who are currently deciding rape cases differ from the judges of twenty years ago, and separate into two camps: those who are able to bridge, or even ignore, PNG's huge gender gap and to appreciate and understand women as human beings; and those for whom the gender gap looms larger than ever. Moreover, the willingness of judges to embrace new approaches to sentencing in rape cases—whether the new approach consists of a change to their own guidelines or to an appreciation of the statutory changes—correlates with the judges' perceptions of women.

One would think it would be easy for the courts to change the guidelines that they themselves have created. However, the common law is inherently conservative: one of its basic principles (*stare decisis*) requires that in the absence of extraordinary circumstances, judges do not change rules once they have made them. The principle of *stare decisis* guarantees consistency in legal decisions, whilst still permitting the law to change gradually to meet society's changing needs and circumstances. When it has come to changing the guidelines for rape sentencing in PNG, some judges have found it easier to argue for immediate change than have others, and the difference seems to turn on the judge's view of women. Judges like Justice Kandakasi, recognising the humanity of women and seeing their welfare as important, argue strongly for instantaneous change. Other judges agree that some increase in sentences is necessary, but find that the law's demands for stability and predictability move them more than the social problems and human pain that rape has caused, and therefore argue that any change should come slowly and by degrees.

Waim's Case (1997) was among the first in which the judges of the Supreme Court admitted that the sentences possible under the guidelines were not succeeding in decreasing either the prevalence or viciousness of rape in PNG. In *Waim*, a university student was abducted by a gang of seven men, threatened with death, raped at least four times by each of the men and subjected by them to oral and anal sex and other 'sexual perversions and indignities'. The trial court sentenced the ring leader to sentences of eight, fifteen, twenty-five and eight years respectively for each of the four rapes, and ordered that the four sentences be served concurrently, which meant that the defendant would serve a maximum of twenty-five years, significantly above the maximum sentence that had been handed down for rape at that point. The trial judge argued that the vicious nature of this particular rape, and the increasing number of gang-related rapes, made longer sentences necessary. On appeal, a three-judge panel of the Supreme Court agreed with the trial judge that longer sentences were becoming necessary in order to combat the ever-growing incidence of gang-related rapes. Nevertheless, the Supreme Court found the twenty-five-year sentence excessive, and substituted a sentence of eighteen years, arguing that the courts should start to impose longer sentences for rape, but ought not to make them too much longer too abruptly.

> We are of the respectful view that the sentence of twenty-five years was a 'quantum leap' under the circumstances. A progressive increase in sentencing for particular offences is reasonable and justified, depending on the circumstances of each case. But a sentence that constitutes a huge jump or increase from the prevailing practices ought not be imposed (*Waim v State*).

Although the purpose of a written decision is to give the court an opportunity to give the reasons behind its holdings, this court did not give any reasons for holding that sentences ought not to be raised a 'quantum leap'. Nothing beyond its own temerity stopped the court from imposing a twenty-five-year sentence. Or, if it believed it unfair to impose a large increase on defendants without warning or to risk inequality by imposing sentences much longer than those imposed on earlier defendants, it could have said so. It could also have used the opportunity provided by this case to announce an intent to impose longer sentences in every case thereafter. It did neither.

The 'quantum leap' principle is not without critics on the bench, and those foremost are judges whose empathy extends beyond the gender gap. In the important quartet of cases decided in 2004, Justice Kandakasi questioned the efficacy of the principle in the face of rapidly escalating rape statistics, noting that 'there was no expressed [*sic*] legislative prohibition against "quantum leaps"' (*State v Sina* No. 2 2004). He did not say so, but he probably intended by this to suggest two things: first, that the courts were not totally bound by the 'quantum leap' rule, as they would be if it had been imposed by statute; and, second, that the principle was part of a whole set of guidelines that the court was in the process of rethinking. In *State v Sina*, he laid out more substantive reasons for objecting to the quantum leap principle:

> [It is] inappropriate that sentencing judges should be unnecessarily limited by concepts such as no 'quantum leaps' or 'disparity in sentencing of co-accused' or such other concepts that have no reflection of the particular circumstances of a case. They should instead be left to be guided by the main purposes of sentencing, such as deterrence, rehabilitation and the rest to meet the society's expectation of stiffer penalties to deter the recurrence of such unacceptable evils in our society (*State v Sina*).

Before we leave the topic of the court's approach to changing its own guidelines, it should be said, in the court's favour, that, within five years of the *Waim* decision which had struck down a twenty-five-year sentence, the Supreme Court *did* impose a twenty-five-year sentence. The court's aim to allow sentences to drift gradually upward was fulfilled. In *Setep's Case* (2001), the trial judge had imposed a life sentence, because the defendant was a convicted prisoner, already serving thirty years for armed robbery and murder, who had escaped from prison and promptly committed a home invasion, robbery and rape. The Supreme Court refused to impose the life sentence, holding that, yes, longer sentences were needed, but this was too much of a change, too quickly (a 'quantum leap'), and the courts must increase sentences gradually. Despite its 'quantum leap' warning, the appellate panel imposed a twenty-five-year sentence. Since it also held that the twenty-five-year sentence was to be served after the defendant finished serving the thirty-year murder sentence, the court had, to all intents and purposes, subjected the defendant to a life sentence, notwithstanding the semantic difference.

Parliamentary changes: But will the courts allow them?

The *Sexual Offences Act* of 2002 made a number of significant changes to the laws governing rape, almost all of them in the direction of offering more protection to women and children. One of those changes was a new version of the sentencing rules for rape. Under the old *Criminal Code*, the PNG courts could punish defendants convicted of rape by any term of imprisonment up to, and including, life (though, as the court held in *Setep's Case*, a sentence of life was not likely). The courts, in interpreting and applying that sweeping grant of sentencing powers, created guidelines for themselves that resulted in actual sentences that were, except in a few unusual instances, and even after significant increases in sentencing, more in the range of fourteen to nineteen years than life. The two aims of the new *Sexual Offences Act* were probably, first, to codify the notion of 'starting points' which could be added to for aggravated circumstances and, second, to raise those 'starting points' to a level commensurate with the drafters' view that longer sentences were needed for all rapes, aggravated or not, in order to combat the spreading epidemic of rape.

The guidelines as originally developed by the courts in *Kaudik's* and *Aubuku's Cases* had set 'starting points' of five to eight years for non-aggravated rape, with longer sentences for aggravated rape. In recent cases such as *Waim*, the Supreme Court had indicated a willingness to raise the starting points to ten years, perhaps more. The amendments went beyond that. Section 347(1) of the *Criminal Code* as amended by the *Sexual Offences Act* provides for a sentence of 'imprisonment for fifteen years' for rape; Section 347(2), provides that 'where an offence … is committed in circumstances of aggravation, the accused is liable, subject to Section 19, to imprisonment for life.'

These oddly worded sections have provoked much disagreement in the courts. A major area of disagreement has been over how they relate to each other and, therefore, over the length of sentences that the new Act actually requires. Justice Kandakasi, for example, has interpreted the new provisions to mean that a non-aggravated rape is punishable by any term up to fifteen years and that the punishment for aggravated rape must begin at fifteen years:

> [W]here a rape case is not aggravated, it attracts a sentence of up to 15 years. However, where there are aggravating factors, the sentence should be beyond 15 years. If it was otherwise, then this amendment has

no meaning and purpose because, it makes no difference between the previous position and the new provisions (*State v Paulus Moi & Clement Samoka* 2004).

Justice Kandakasi is in all likelihood correct that the drafters of the new provisions intended to create something different from the old *Criminal Code*. Exactly what, however, is open to question. Justice Kandakasi's view is reasonable, though differing interpretations are possible. He presumes, in effect, that Section 19, which provides that any offender liable for a prison term can be sentenced to imprisonment for any shorter term, or may be ordered to pay a fine, or even given a suspended sentence, is applicable to both sub-sections, so that the fifteen-year sentence for non-aggravated rape is actually a sentence of anything up to fifteen years. Statutes are supposed to be read, however, so as to give meaning to every word in them, and Justice Kandakasi's reading overlooks the differences between the two subsections. Section 347(1) provides unequivocally for a fifteen-year term, with no conditions or qualifications; it reads very differently from Section 347(2) (the subsection dealing with aggravated rape) in two major respects: first, Section 19 is mentioned only in Section 347(2), not in Section 347(1); and, second, Section 347(2) uses the term 'liable' (as in: defendant is liable for a life term, not: the punishment is a life term), whereas Section 347(1) states baldly that the sentence 'is' fifteen years.

These differences in wording could suggest that the drafters intended that everyone found guilty of non-aggravated rape serve a fifteen-year sentence, whereas those found guilty of aggravated rape would be liable for any sentence from fifteen years up to (and including) a life term. This reading equates the new statute's provisions more closely to the court-made guidelines, which stipulated a 'starting point' sentence that would apply to all non-aggravated rapes, and then adding more years to that for each aggravating circumstance. The only notable difference, then, between the guidelines and the new statute would be the length of the 'starting point' sentence, which in the guidelines was five to eight years and in the new statute is fifteen years.

No Papua New Guinean judge has adopted my interpretation of the statute—probably because judges like to believe that sentencing is a judicial prerogative, not to be usurped by statute, and my reading would limit their discretion in non-aggravated cases. At least, Justice Kandakasi's interpretation hews fairly closely to the spirit, if not the letter, of the guidelines. Some of the judges have come up with interpretations of the new statute that actually undermine what the statute had intended to accomplish—especially if one presumes that one of the statute's aims is to ensure longer sentences. Not surprisingly, the roster of judges whose interpretations of the statute lead to shorter sentences are those whose empathy for women is severely limited. Justice Cannings, for example, in *State v Yali*, held that defendants cannot be sentenced for anything more than fifteen years, even if the rape was aggravated, unless the prosecutor's initial charge stipulated that defendants were charged under Section 347(2), and not 347(1). This interpretation has the result of making it even more difficult for courts to impose longer sentences than it was under the old guidelines, in that it requires an extra step for the prosecutors, who now must remember which section of the Code to charge defendants under, something that was not previously a requirement. Applying his arcane little rule, Justice Cannings decided there was no way he could sentence defendant James Yali, the forty-one-year-old married Governor of Madang Province, who raped his girlfriend's seventeen-year-old sister, to any more than fifteen years imprisonment. Finding that the rape was done in aggravated circumstances, Justice Cannings still sentenced the defendant to only twelve years—even less than the statute mandated for non-aggravated rape.

That is not the only way in which sexist judges have managed to undermine the new statute. In at least two cases, judges have held that although fifteen years is the highest sentence permissible for non-aggravated rape, the sentence for aggravated rape need not start at fifteen years, but can be anything from (I suppose) zero up to life imprisonment. Justice Cannings' interpretation was followed in at least two egregious cases. In *State v Aroko* (2005), the defendant came upon the victim, who was carrying her nine-month-old baby, working in the sugar cane field. In order to rape her, he struggled with her, cutting her with his knife and separating her from the baby. Although the trial judge, Justice Manuhu, found that the rape was aggravated, he presumed that Section 347(2) does not stipulate a minimum sentence, and therefore felt free to apply a sentence of only eight and a half years imprisonment—considerably below the average in recent cases that had used the guidelines.

In *State v Urika* (2006), Justice Kirriwom sentenced the defendant, who had raped an elderly woman, to only five years in prison, although prosecutors had charged the defendant under Section 347(2) with aggravated rape. Justice Kirriwom did not mention whether he could have imposed such a light sentence under Section 347(2), if he had found that the rape had been aggravated. Instead, he held that prosecutors may have charged the defendant properly, but that they had then failed to prove any circumstances of aggravation. Quite the opposite. Justice Kirrowom said it was the victim who was aggravating. She had provoked the defendant because she had not paid compensation that she owed him for malicious comments she had made about his daughter's predilection for white men.

These two judges, Justice Manuhu and Justice Kirriwom, present an interesting new (but actually very old) twist on sexism. They both approach their cases as if nothing in jurisprudence or society has changed in the past thirty years. Neither quotes from any of the key cases; both act as if the new statute was just a bunch of meaningless and unimportant words, not something they were really supposed to understand and apply. Both apply—to the men who are the defendants and the women who are the victims—standards that even the more sexist of the judges of the last generation had realised were utterly without foundation. The contrasts between their approach to the law and that of a judge like Justice Kandakasi suggests that rape law in PNG diverges between some people moving forward and others retreating into the past.

Changing patterns of empathy

Since the mid-1990s some Papua New Guinean judges have begun to write with real feeling about what rape does emotionally to its Papua New Guinean victims. In each of the cases in which a judge has displayed empathy, the victim was a blameless village woman. Among the earliest of these decisions was that of Justice Injia (now PNG's Chief Justice) in *State v Penias*. In that case, decided in 1994, the nineteen-year-old victim was on her way home from school, when the defendant, a married man in his twenties, accosted her. He wore a mask and threatened her with a bush knife. The judge's sentence of nine years was based in part on his view that the crime of rape is extremely serious:

> Rape constitutes an invasion of privacy of the most intimate part of a woman's body. Women become objects of sex and sex alone to men like the prisoner who prey upon them and rape them. But woman are after all human beings just like them. They have equal rights and opportunities as men as guaranteed to them under our Constitution. They are entitled to be respected and fairly treated. They all have the right to travel freely alone or in groups of their own, in any place they choose to be at any time of the day. At times, because of their gender, with which comes insecurity, they need the protection of men. Unfortunately, rape has become a prevalent offence in this country. Women in towns and in villages are living in fear because of the pervasive conduct of men like the prisoner. Our women in the small communities in the villages and remote islands and in small towns and centres who once enjoyed freedom and tranquillity are living under fear and feel restricted.[11]

The emotional connection evident in this paragraph includes its *cri de coeur*: 'women are human beings *just like men*'. Human beings. Just like men. In a society whose deepest structures are predicated on the oppositional difference of the genders, this is a revolutionary notion. Justice Injia writes in a way that not only demonstrates his own empathy, it also has the capacity to persuade his

---

11   In addition to the typical legal education at the University of Papua New Guinea, Justice Injia had spent a year in the US, earning a Master's degree at Harvard. Could that experience have relevance to his approach?

readers. One of the ways by which it achieves this is the veracity of its language; this paragraph is not copied from earlier decisions, as happened in many of the cases we have been looking at; it is in Justice Injia's own words. Finally, this is not just a generalised or abstract statement that rape harms women. It demonstrates that harm through specifics: because of the fear of rape, women are not free to move about; they cannot travel in groups; they cannot travel alone.[12] Not only does the judge himself experience the painful effect of rape on its victims, he succeeds in conveying the immediacy of that experience to his readers.

Two factors have come together to create the judiciary's changing view of women. First, as the years go on, the influences of colonialism wane. In particular, the racism that characterised the colonial mind and that put women in the double bind of intersectionality—subordinated not only because they were women, but also because they were Papua New Guinean—is receding. Judges now, both Australian and Papua New Guinean, come from younger generations, and are less influenced by colonial stereotypes. Second, perhaps it was easier for Justice Injia to recognise that the victim had suffered true emotional pain because she was not a 'town woman' dressed in western clothes, working in an office and otherwise acting in ways that appeared westernised and, thus, overtly sexual. In a particularly lyrical and persuasive moment, Justice Injia mentions urban women—'women in towns and villages are living in fear because of the pervasive conduct of men like the offender,' he says, and then reiterates: 'Our women in the small communities, in the villages and remote islands, and in small towns and centres, who once enjoyed freedom and tranquility, are living under fear and feel restricted.' But the victim in this case is a 'village woman' and the picture that a reader takes away from these sentences is of a particular brand of traditional Papua New Guinean woman. Perhaps it is easier for the judge—and for his readers—to empathise when they focus on the ways in which a rape would hurt a typical young Papua New Guinean village woman, rather than generalising to some imported notion of the seriousness of rape on women in general.

In *Setep v State* (2001) the correlation between the judges' empathy and the woman's identity as a traditional village woman is even clearer. The judges themselves make a point of it: The defendant in the *Setep* case escaped from prison, where he had been serving a thirty-year sentence for wilful murder; he and a fellow escapee forced their way into the victim's home, robbed and

---

12   Lawyers will notice that Justice Injia is not just describing any old thing that the fear of rape is preventing women from doing; he is taking a Constitutional provision—that all people be free to travel—and making it apparent that women are not being protected by that provision.

terrorised the family, and abducted a young girl. The two men raped her repeatedly, clubbed her with a baseball bat, broke one of her fingers, and cut her so severely that stitches were required.

The three-judge panel was made up entirely of Papua New Guineans—Justices Sawong, Gavara-Nanu, and Kandakasi—and the victim was a young, unmarried woman from a traditional Papua New Guinean village. Like Justice Injia in *Penias'* *Case*, these judges make the victim's pain real to themselves and the reader by itemising the injuries. Two things should be noted about their itemisation. First, they are focusing on her injuries; not on the pornographic details of what the rapists did. Second, the particular injuries on which they focus are those that would be of especial moment in a traditional village milieu:

> The victim in the present case, according to the medical evidence was sick, anxious and distressed as a result of the crimes perpetrated against her. No doubt, she was greatly traumatised and broken. Her esteem and pride as a young virgin girl was violated and so was her person.... We can imagine the victim's aspirations of having a good marriage and a family was shattered because of the violent and uncalled for invasion of her person. The victim is going to bear these consequences for the rest of her life. Common sense in these circumstances therefore dictates that her violators be given sentences that would make them feel the consequences of what they did for the rest of their lives as well (*Setep v State* 2001).

The judges could have focused on the victim's physical injuries—the deep knife cuts, the broken finger—as the trial judge had done, but they chose instead to focus on the emotional injuries. They do not importune their readers to empathise; instead, they elicit empathy by *imagining* in narrative cadences the consequences for this typical young woman of the village.

One of the common themes of this volume is that the social changes roiling throughout PNG have had a deleterious impact on many men, calling into question their very claims to masculinity, and that the response of many has been to amplify their already negative attitudes towards women. The *Penias* and *Setep* decisions, and others like them, suggest that for some men—in particular, for those who have benefitted, both in security and in status from the changes that their society is undergoing—a more mellow perspective may be possible. Judges are certainly in the category of people who have benefitted from the socio-economic changes that PNG is undergoing. Some of them, relatively wealthy, with high social status, their masculinity unchallenged, can afford to be generous to the subordinate gender. Whatever the reason for the change in judicial decision-writing, there seems, in recent years, to be more empathy, at least from some of the judges, and at least towards some categories of women.

Concluding comments

The judges seem to be operating at cross-purposes. In the light of the ever-escalating rape statistics, most judges have opted in recent years for longer sentences, reasoning that deterrence requires it. These cases, however, were decided prior to the enactment of the *Sexual Offences Act*, which supported the judges' wish for longer sentences, at least where rapes were aggravated. But, with the exception of Justices Injia and Kandakasi, the judges have not responded with any real understanding of the objectives of the new legislation. Instead, they have undermined their own earlier efforts, making it even harder to impose a longer sentence under the new statute than it was under their own guidelines.

Of course, longer sentences, in and of themselves, won't decrease rape—except to the extent that they are keeping people who have already committed rapes in prison, out of society and away from potential victims. There have to be other changes to the law or to culture before the rate of rape will go down. Those changes require that the sexism that is endemic to cultures in PNG be undone. Is that possible? And what would happen to the many cultures of PNG then?

References

Banks, Cyndi, 2000. Contextualising sexual violence: rape and carnal knowledge in Papua New Guinea. In *Reflections on Violence in Melanesia*, ed. Sinclair Dinnen and Allison Ley, 83–104. Sydney: Hawkins Press and Asia Pacific Press.

Binder Lisa A., 1995. 'With more than admiration he admired': images of beauty and defilement in judicial narratives of rape. *Harvard Women's Law Journal*, 18: 265–300.

Borrey, Anou, 2000. Sexual violence in perspective: the case of Papua New Guinea. In *Reflections on Violence in Melanesia*, ed. Sinclair Dinnen and Allison Ley, 105–118. Sydney: Hawkins Press and Asia Pacific Press.

Bourke, Joanna, 2007. *Rape: Sex, Violence, History*. London: Counterpoint.

Brownmiller, Susan, 1975. *Against Our Will: Men, Women and Rape*. New York: Ballantine Books.

Collier, Richard, 2010. Masculinities, law and personal life: towards a new framework for understanding men, law and gender. *Harvard Journal of Law and Gender* 33(2): 431–76.

Connell, R.W., 2005 [1987]. *Masculinities*. Berkeley: University of California Press.

Coombs, Mary I., 1992. Outsider scholarship: the law review stories. *University of Colorado Law Review* 63: 683–716

Crenshaw, Kimberlé, 1991. Mapping the margins: intersectionality, identity politics and violence against women of color. *Standford Law Review* 43: 1241–99.

Dinnen, Sinclair and Allison Ley, eds, 2000. *Reflections on Violence in Melanesia*. Sydney: Hawkins Press and Asia Pacific Press.

Dowd, Nancy E., 2010. Asking the man question: masculinities analysis and feminist scholarship, *Harvard Journal of Law and Gender* 33: 415–30.

Fineman, Martha Albertson and Nancy Sweet Thomadsen, eds, 1991. *At the Boundaries of Law: Feminism and Legal Theory*. London: Routledge.

Foley, Brian J., 2010. Applied legal storytelling, politics, and factual realism. *Journal of the Legal Writing Institute* 14: 17–52.

Foucault, Michel, 1995 [1975]. *Discipline and Punish: The Birth of the Prison*. New York: Vintage.

Grbich, Judith E., 1991. The body in legal theory. In *At the Boundaries of Law: Feminism and Legal Theory*, ed. Martha Albertson Fineman and Nancy Sweet Thamadsen, 61–76. London: Routledge.

Groth, A. Nicholas, 1979. *Men Who Rape: The Psychology of the Offender*. New York: Basic Books.

Lloyd, Genevieve, 1984. *The Man of Reason: 'Male' and 'Female' in Western Philosophy*. Minneapolis: University of Minnesota Press.

Lutz, Catherine A., 1998. *Unnatural Emotions: Everyday Sentiments on a Micronesian Atoll and their Challenge in Western Theory*. Chicago: University of Chicago Press.

MacKinnon, Catharine A., 1985. Pornography, civil rights and speech. *Harvard Civil Rights–Civil Liberties Law Review* 20: 1–70.

-------- 1989. *Towards a Feminist Theory of the State*. Cambridge, MA: Harvard University Press.

MacKinnon, Catharine A. and Andrea Dworkin, eds, 1997. *In Harm's Way*. Cambridge: Harvard University Press.

Ortner, Sherry and Harriet Whitehead, eds, 1981. *Sexual Meanings: The Cultural Construction of Gender and Sexuality*. Cambridge: Cambridge University Press.

Réage, Pauline, 1981 [1954], *Story of O*. New York: Ballantine Books.

Strathern, Marilyn, 1988. *The Gender of the Gift: Problems with Women and Problems with Society in Melanesia*. Studies in Melanesian Anthropology, No. 6. Berkeley and Los Angeles: University of California Press.

Thornton, Margaret, 1998. Authority and corporeality: the conundrum for women in law. *Feminist Legal Studies*, 6(2): 147–70.

Valdes, Francisco, 1999. Afterword, theorizing 'outcrit' theories: coalitional method and comparative jurisprudential experience. *University of Miami Law Review* 53: 1265–322.

Wardlow, Holly, 2006. *Wayward Women: Sexuality and Agency in a New Guinea Society*. Berkeley: University of California Press.

Zorn, Jean, 1991. Making law in Papua New Guinea: the influence of customary law on the common law. *Pacific Studies* 14(4): 1–34.

-------- 1992. Common law jurisprudence and customary law. In *Legal Issues in a Developing Society*, ed. R.W. James and Ian Fraser, 103–27. Port Moresby: University of Papua New Guinea Press.

-------- 2010. The paradoxes of sexism: proving rape in the Papua New Guinea Courts, *LAWASIA* 2010: 17–58.

List of Cases

Papua New Guinea

Acting Public Prosecutor v Konis Haha [1981] PNGLR 205 (Supreme Court).

Aubuku v State [1987] PNGLR 267 (Supreme Court).

Meaoa v The State [PNGLR] 280 (Supreme Court).

Setep v The State (Unreported) SC666 18 May 2001 (Supreme Court).

State v Angavia (No 2) (Unreported) N2590 29 April 2004 (National Court).

State v Aroko (Unreported) N2822 24 February 2005 (National Court).

State v Kaudik [1987] PNGLR 201 (National Court).

State v Koupa [1987] PNGLR 208 (National Court).

State v Paulus Moi & Clement Samoka (Unreported Unnumbered) CR No. 256 of 2004 29 April 2004 (National Court).

State v Penias [1994] PNGLR 48 (National Court).

State v Sasoropa (No 2) (Unreported) N2569 29 April 2004 (National Court—decision on sentence).

State v Sina (No 2) (Unreported) N2541 21 May 2004 (National Court—decision on sentence).

State v Urika (Unreported, Unnumbered) CR 434 of 2006 13 October 2006 (National Court).

State v Yali (Unreported) N2989 19 January 2006 (National Court).

Waim v The State (Unreported) SC519 2 May 1997 (Supreme Court).

United Kingdom

R v Billam [1986] 1 WLR 349.

6. Conversations with Convicted Rapists

Fiona Hukula

Abstract

Does Papua New Guinean culture influence the propensity to rape? Or is it the way in which we are socialised that influences how we treat women? Is rape more common among certain ethnic groups? These are some of the questions that have prompted this research. This chapter is based on interviews conducted with convicted rapists who have been detained at Port Moresby's Bomana Prison. It provides some preliminary insights into the type of men who rape and explores issues such as cultural and peer influence.

Introduction

When I mention that I'm from Papua New Guinea (PNG), it is not uncommon to hear negative comments regarding the law and order situation and high levels of violence against women. There has been much debate, awareness and lamenting about the situation of women and girls, especially in relation to gender violence and gender equity. A common response to issues of violence against women by Papua New Guineans is that *em pasin bilong ol* (TP: that's their way) or *em nomol ya* (TP: that's normal). Such statements insinuate that violence against women is a timeless tradition which is viewed as the norm. Many times we Papua New Guineans categorise issues of gender according to our cultural and ethnic backgrounds. For example, there is a common perception that women who come from matrilineal societies may have more positive experiences of gender equality than those who come from patrilineal societies (Sai 2007). Such stereotypical notions of cultural attitudes and practices are often used to mollify and justify reasons for gender inequality and gender violence.

This chapter attempts to capture the voices and thoughts of Papua New Guinean men who have been incarcerated for rape and sexual offences. Research into the areas of gender relations and gender violence in PNG has long been a topical issue for anthropologists, donor agencies and human rights activists alike. There is an abundance of literature which discusses aspects of violence against women and gender equality from pre-contact times through to the present. Frequently referenced are anthropological accounts of gender violence and sexual antagonism in the Highlands of PNG, documented by the likes of Langness (1967), Meggitt (1964) and Read (1981) who interpreted sexual antagonism and male domination over women as solidarity among groups of men. But violence against women is prevalent both in rural and urban Papua New Guinea (Toft 1985; Jenkins and NSRRT 1994; Hammar 1999). Discussions of social change and adaption to urban/modern life also engage with changing gender relations and gender violence, with a particular focus on marital violence (Toft and Bonnell 1985; Brown 1988; Rosi and Zimmer-Tamakoshi 1993; Zimmer-Tamakoshi 1997; Counts 1999; Dinnen and Ley 2000).

These discussions address problems associated with development, such as poverty and lack of educational opportunities. In addition, they connect these problems to the ways in which traditional notions of gender have been translated within the contemporary Papua New Guinean context. Until recently, post independence discourses on gender relations have predominantly focused on how gender inequality affects women, and especially how violence affects women and the causes of gender violence. There has been a gap in such discourses: men's thoughts and experiences of violence and masculinity have not been addressed. This gap has been recognised with ideas of changing masculinities recently discussed by various scholars (Brison 1995; Eves 2006; Sai 2007; Macintyre 2008; Haley 2008; Lepani 2008; and Bainton 2008).

Both Anou Borrey (2000) and Cyndi Banks (1997) suggest that the cultural contexts within which violence against women occur are important in isolating causes and understanding such violence in PNG. Earlier Christine Bradley (1985) argued in a similar way apropos attitudes to and practices of violence in marriage in East New Britain. This chapter follows these authors but focuses on men, through the presentation and discussion of case studies from a small study of men incarcerated as sex offenders at Port Moresby's Bomana Prison. I examine the social context within which the sexual offences were committed.

My initial research interest was centred on the factors influencing how men think and behave in relation to sexual violence. I posed several questions. Are there any differences between men who come from matrilineal societies and men who are from patrilineal societies? Or are there differences between men who were brought up in rural areas as opposed to men who grew up in urban areas? How about those whose parents are not from the same province? These were some of the initial questions which kept circulating in my mind while I tried to grapple with this serious social problem. The conversations with convicted rapists, reported and used below, are the result of my attempts to seek answers to such questions which have preoccupied me over a number of years. My research aimed to ascertain information about men who commit rape and other sexual offences, and to elicit information about the upbringing of these offenders and their perceptions about gender.

Methods

The study was conducted from October to December 2006 at the Bomana Prison, outside Port Moresby. The data was obtained through semi-structured interviews with males who were convicted for sex offences. These crimes included rape, incest and indecent assault. Initially it was envisaged that interviews would be conducted with two offenders from each province, preferably one from a rural area and the other from an urban location. The rationale behind interviewing offenders from the same province who grew up in either a village or a town was to ascertain whether a rural rather than an urban setting made any difference in terms of cultural socialisation. However this comparative approach proved impractical due to the reluctance of some prisoners. The Correctional Service officers assisted me by identifying potential interviewees and they also explained the purpose of the research to the prisoners. Those who agreed to be interviewed were then sent to the interviewer. Interviews were also carried out with Correctional Service officers who work at Bomana Prison. Prison officers have the most contact with prisoners, and through their daily interaction with prisoners they were able to offer insights based on their conversations with the prisoners. A total of fifty prisoners convicted of various sex-related offences were interviewed.

The interviews were conducted by Thomas Semo, who had previous research experience as a research assistant with the Social and Environment and Political and Legal Studies divisions at the National Research Institute. Initially I wanted to carry out the interviews myself. However, on the advice of some of my peers, I was encouraged to recruit a male research assistant. The first day of interviews proved my peers right. I carried out two interviews, one of which went quite well while the second did not. The young man that I interviewed seemed nervous and on edge as the interview was being conducted. He kept looking at his hands and giving short one word answers. I sensed that the prisoners were more comfortable with a male researcher than with me, since throughout most of PNG, men and women do not discuss sexual matters together and most times both parties can be uncomfortable in doing so. Moreover, there was an initial misconception that I was a lawyer who was seeking interviews to build a case to have their (the offenders') sentences lengthened. This, and other misunderstandings about the purpose of the research, was cleared up promptly by Thomas and the Correctional Service officers, who proved very helpful. Thomas asked the inmates a series of semi-structured questions relating to their lives and the offences that they had committed. The questions were designed to elicit information about their social and cultural backgrounds and their perceptions and experiences of gender relations.

Age, education, employment, origin and perceptions of gender

The ages of the men who were interviewed ranged from eighteen to sixty-four with nearly half of the offenders being between eighteen and twenty-five. Twelve of the offenders were over forty years of age. The educational level of the majority of interviewees was between grade six and eight (see Table 3).

Table 3. Highest educational attainment of the sexual offenders interviewed for this study.

Grade	1	2	4	5	6	7	8	9	10	Voc/College	University	Never been to school
Total	2	4	2	4	18	3	5	1	3	1	1	6

Nearly half of the men (22) said that they had had a paid job at one time or another. The types of jobs could be categorised as low-skilled, low-income jobs including a saw mill operator, fuel attendant, baker, carpenter, security guard and green-keeper. One person identified himself as a subsistence farmer and another as a fisherman while two said they were part of the informal sector; one specifically was in the business of money lending.

Twenty-eight of the fifty offenders spent most of their childhood in their place of ethnic origin while twenty-two men spent their childhood elsewhere (see Table 4). Of those twenty-two men, six stated that their parents taught them about their customs and seven said that they went to their village often. Those who were brought up in their villages said that they knew about customs relating to women. The level of knowledge of custom claimed was the same for those who grew up in their place of ethnic origin and those who grew up elsewhere. The three common responses apropos customs relating to men and women were that (1) the man owns the land; (2) the man is the head of the family; and (3) the man inherits land (except for matrilineal societies). In reality land is usually owned by groups, such as clans or lineages, and divided among members. The general consensus among those interviewed was that women are generally valued for what they bring to a man's family or clan: for her ability to bear children and for her contribution to activities such as gardening. From the perspective of her own family and clan a woman is valued because she is a potential source of bride price.

Table 4. Place of origin and where the interviewed offenders grew up.

Place of Birth	Number of interviewees	Spent most of childhood in Home Province
Eastern Highlands	6	2
Central	10	9
Gulf	1	1
Madang	1	1
Southern Highlands	2	2
East Sepik	1	1
NCD	12	
Simbu	3	3
Sandaun	2	1
Enga	1	
Milne Bay	3	3
Western	5	4
Morobe	2	1
New Ireland	1	
Totals	50	28

Over half the offenders (31) knew their victims. Eight of the victims were family members, including step daughters and adopted daughters, nieces, a sister and other distant relatives. Four offenders claimed that the victim was in a relationship with them or had consented to sex. Seventeen of the offenders stated that the victims were either girls from the communities in which they lived or were acquaintances known through friends and relatives. Previous research by the Papua New Guinea Institute of Medical Research (1994), Banks (1997) and Borrey (2000) has also indicated that most of the violence against women is carried out by men who are known to the victims.

Nine of the men who were interviewed had been in prison before; two for rape and seven for various other crimes ranging from robbery, stealing and motor vehicle-related incidents.

Retrospective rationalisations on rape

The offenders discussed their actions retrospectively and offered some insights into why they had committed the crimes. In an effort to reflect some of these insights I have included several anecdotes based on conversations with the offenders, followed by four more extended studies. The following discussion on some of the conversations gives a sense of the range of retrospective explanations for their behaviour.

Sibling or family pressure featured in the responses of several of the convicted offenders. An eighteen-year-old single man explained that, 'he was with his elder brothers and they forced him to rape the girl. He didn't want to do it but his brothers forced him and because he respected them, he did it.' In another case, a twenty-eight-year old unmarried man associated his crime with his parents who 'stopped him from getting married and he got angry and committed this crime to frustrate his parents.'

Alcohol was a contributing factor in several rape cases. A twenty-four-year-old unmarried man said, 'he was under the influence of alcohol and he took his girlfriend to his auntie's house and slept with her with her consent. The next morning the girl's relatives found out and demanded compensation from him. He refused to pay compensation so the girl's family took the matter to the police. The girl was also engaged to another man when the incident happened.' Another man who was twenty-five years old and single reported that both he and the victim were 'drunk and he raped the girl. He later realised what he had done and surrendered himself to the police.' Yet another, a thirty-seven-year-old man with two children, said that 'he was drinking with his friends along the street and it was late in the night … a woman and her husband walked past. He chased the man away and abducted his wife into the nearby block and raped her.'

Other convicted rapists blamed their actions on their wives for withholding conjugal rights. As one thirty-year-old married man with one child explained, 'his wife didn't spend enough time with him to make love.' A second man with seven children said that 'his wife often accused him of having affairs with village ladies. The incident happened when they were under the influence of alcohol, the victim gave her consent. His wife didn't allow him to have sexual relations with her.'

Some of the men blamed peer pressure and pornography for their crimes. One single twenty-four-year-old rapist explained 'he did it because his friends were doing it. He was also influenced by porn. He'd been viewing *Playboy* magazines since he was twelve.' Another single nineteen-year-old watched two pornographic CDs with his friends. 'When they finished they walked across the block where they saw the girl sleeping by herself on the verandah of her house. They dragged her down to the drain and raped her.'

For others revenge was what impelled them to rape. 'The victim accused [a 22-year-old single man] … of stealing her small brother's bicycle and selling it to one of their relatives' and so he raped her.

Some other men said that they had been set up or tricked into having what they thought was consensual intercourse with the victims. As a thirty-year-old man with two wives and three children explained, 'the girl was from an enemy tribe, her brother set him up. They got the girl to sleep with him then accused him of rape. He slept with the girl with her consent.' In another case, the fifty-seven-year-old rapist with three children 'was set up by his wife's first husband,' and a thirty-four-year-old widower with two children claimed that 'the family of the victim set him up because he had not given them any money since he began working.'

In other instances unrequited desire was a contributing factor. A twenty-two-year-old single prisoner said that 'he was attracted to the girl but didn't know how to approach her.' A twenty-four-year-old bachelor said that he had fallen 'in love with the victim a long time ago and couldn't control his desires.' In yet another case, a widower with seven children 'wanted to remarry but his late wife's relatives stopped him from getting married to another woman. He got frustrated and committed incest with his fifteen-year-old niece who was related to him through his wife.'

Finally, witchcraft is blamed for one man's actions. A forty-three-year-old man with three children raped a woman because 'it was believed that the victim's *bubu* [grandparent] killed his cousin's brother through witchcraft.'

With the exception of pornography, which presents an interesting theme for future analysis, I would now like to explore the other recurrent themes in more detail by examining five individual cases.

Taking responsibility?

Case One: She owed us!

PK is twenty-five years old, the fourth child in his family and the father of one child. He was born in Henganofi, Eastern Highlands and spent most of his childhood in Port Moresby. PK never went to school because he ran away from school when his parents tried to enrol him at the local Catholic school. His mother did not attend school while his father went up to Grade 2. In Port Moresby his mother did not work in the paid workforce and his father, who is now retrenched, was employed by a government department. PK had worked as a security guard for a local security firm in Port Moresby. He stated that according to his knowledge of his custom, men own land and women are important because their family will receive bride price for them. At the time of the interview he had served five years of his twelve-year sentence for abduction and rape. He said that his victim, a nineteen-year-old girl from another Highlands province, borrowed 100 kina each from him and his friend and didn't repay them. He and his friend approached her one evening at her house when her parents were away. She told them that she had no money to repay her debts. They then demanded that she find money somewhere to repay debts but she refused and they got mad and raped her.

Case Two: Revenging girls who slept with men from another village

UM is twenty-two years old, single and comes from the Trobriand area of Milne Bay Province. He was born and brought up in the village and completed his primary education at the local primary school. According to UM, men in his area possess yam-planting powers. He said that as he was growing up boys and girls mixed around freely and boys mixed with girls who had their breasts uncovered as this was normal and part of their matrilineal custom. He was told by his parents that this was how things had been for a long time. At the time of the interview, UM was serving a nineteen-year eight-month sentence for raping two nineteen-year-old girls. He committed the offence with three others. According to UM he and his friends committed the offence because the girls were from their village, but they had slept with men from another village. UM and his friends went to fight the men but they ran away so they belted the girls up badly. According to UM the girls then enticed them to have sex with them, so they did. Later two of the girls reported the matter to their parents and their parents reported the matter to the police and they were arrested.

Case Three: Drunken rape of a niece since wife avoiding pregnancy

ML is thirty-eight years old, married with four children. He was born and brought up in his village in Madang Province. He completed year ten at Brahman High School before moving to Port Moresby. Both his parents were subsistence farmers. He said that in his place men are told about important resources of the clan and they are also told stories from the grandparents and fathers about clan land boundaries and stories about their origin. He also said that when a woman gives birth she abstains from gardening and other household tasks for a period of time until a feast is celebrated to release her from confinement. At the time of the interview ML was serving a seven-year and one-month sentence for carnal knowledge of his twelve-year-old niece. He said he was very drunk when he committed the offence. His wife had stopped him from sleeping with her because they already had four children and she didn't want to look after any more children. He then had affairs with other women which frustrated his wife.

He said his wife always got angry at him when he returned home from work and his wife's elder sister usually supported her. These factors caused him to get drunk and do what he did.

Case Four: Unrequited love – and power!

LM is thirty years old, single and from Ihu in the Gulf Province. He was born in Ihu and spent his childhood in his village, where he completed primary education. His mother is a subsistence farmer and his father worked as a handyman in Kerema town. LM was brought up to respect girls and said that he did not take part in custom-related activities. At the time of the interview, LM had been sentenced to six years, five months and three weeks for unlawful carnal knowledge. LM said the girl was the most beautiful girl in the village and he sent word for her several times but she rejected his request. He got angry and one time when she was by herself he went and approached her to be his girlfriend but she swore at him. He tried to calm her down but he couldn't. He then stripped her and raped her.

Case Five: Overcrowding, incest and anger

HTS is forty-seven years old, and was born and raised in Port Moresby. He was educated to Grade 8. He's the second child in a family of nine. He is separated and is the father of two children. His mother is a housewife and his father worked in Port Moresby. He was raised in the Jehovah Witness religion. HTS was brought up in Port Moresby and rarely went to his village in the Gulf Province, therefore, he says, he didn't know much about custom and hadn't been through any initiation ceremonies. The first time he went to his village was when he was twenty years old and he found it difficult to stay there. He considers village life to be boring. At the time of the interview, HTS was serving a four-year two-month sentence for sexual penetration of his nine-year-old sister. HTS says he got frustrated because the house he was living in was overcrowded and he did what he did in order to scare his other family members so they would leave the house. Also his wife had left him fourteen years earlier and when he wanted to get married to other women his children and family discouraged him. This he says also made him angry.

The offender as victim

The preceding anecdotes are based on stories told by the prisoners themselves. Their stories suggest their reasons for their actions, from various points of view. Their retrospective discussion suggests that their ideas of gender are not confined merely to the description of male/female relations, but reflects a wider sociality. This insight will be used in analysis, to highlight several themes.

Avoiding pregnancy

In several interviews and especially outlined in Case Three some of the prisoners justified their actions by stating that their wives did not want to have sex with them for various reasons including not wanting to get pregnant. In this scenario the withholding of sex by the offenders' partners is perceived as a contributing factor in the committing of the offence.

Retribution

A second theme that runs through the interviews is the issue of retribution, which exemplifies, from the view of the offender, how rape is a means of eliciting a response for a prior social misdemeanour. It is therefore plausible to assume here, again from the offenders' points of view, that the action and meaning of the rapes took the form of 'restitutive actions' rather than unprovoked serious offences or crimes. The elucidation of a prior transaction or event, such as that of money being borrowed, or the death of a relative, was seen as a justification for such actions. Such findings are similar to those of Banks (1997). She offers an example of a man who was sentenced to prison for raping a thirteen-year-old girl as 'payback' because she accused him of stealing from her and she insulted him by swearing at him. Furthermore her father accused him of stealing his chickens and insulted and swore at him. These insults were further fuelled by his reasoning that the victim's brother raped his sister and, although the matter was reported to the police, no action was taken.

Frustration

Frustration is an emotion which is mentioned frequently in the conversations. Men were frustrated by their wives, by their families and by their circumstances. More specifically their frustration stemmed from issues related to sex. A husband was frustrated by his wife's refusal to have sex. A widower was frustrated by his late wife's family's refusal to allow him to remarry. A young man was angry because his parents stopped him from getting married. These prisoners constructed these prior conditions as the primary causes of their actions.

For example, in Case Three, ML's wife had stopped sleeping with him and he thus had affairs with other women to mitigate his sexual frustrations and also to frustrate his wife. As reflected in Case Five, HTS was frustrated that his house was overcrowded and he felt an additional source of anger because his wife had left him fourteen years earlier and when he wanted to remarry his children and relatives had discouraged him. Not being able to assert their masculinity by being in sexual relationships may be viewed by some men as a form of frustration which leads to sexual offences being committed. They perceive a lack of control of their emotions, such as the expression of frustration due to rejection from wives or from girls they admire. This suggests a fragile, resentful predisposition in male sexuality in contemporary PNG, similar to Wardlow's (2007) portrait of Huli men.

Set up

Three of the offenders stated that they were 'set up'. The offenders claimed that various people related to the victim arranged for the incidents to happen. The 'set ups' occurred for various reasons: the offender did not give money to the family or the offender was from an enemy tribe. Here we see the offenders deflecting attention away from their rapes through the projection of responsibility onto distant causes. A perceived pre-existing tension was being used as a social cause of their actions, such that the offenders viewed themselves as the victims of pre-determined actions. In general offenders constructed prior conditions in which their actions were more about eliciting some form of action from others. Indeed, many offenders did not consider rape to be a deviant act but rather the result of others' actions.

Consensual sex

Consensual sex is mentioned in two of the anecdotes, although, as noted by Stewart (2005: 6) the issue of consent in rape, so crucial to the introduced law's definition of the offence, is not necessarily central in customary ways of thinking (see also Borrey 2000). The Correctional Service Officers who were interviewed stated that possibly some cases involving young men could have been consensual sex, but the girls' parents did not agree with the relationship and they were then charged with rape.

Matriliny

There is not sufficient data to verify if there are any major differences between matrilineal and patrilineal societies. Case Two illustrates an example where the offender states 'as he was growing up boys and girls mixed around freely and boys mixed with girls who had their breasts uncovered as this was normal and part of their custom and they have lived and grown up with this.' In this particular case the offender is from a matrilineal society and the victims were from his own village in Milne Bay Province.

Alcohol

This research has demonstrated that alcohol is an enabling factor rather than a cause in the majority of cases. Men use their state of inebriation as a means not only to give them the confidence to act out such behaviour but also to justify their actions. According to Macintyre 'beer drinking is a form of conspicuous consumption that in PNG denotes *modern* masculinity. It is the way that many men display their economic achievement' (2008: 188). But the consumption of alcohol is both a trigger and a facilitating factor in many of the cases. In my research the men may not necessarily be displaying their economic achievements since, as low-skilled, low-income workers, their income-generating opportunities are limited.

Concluding thoughts on rape and power

In the past young men were guided through the transition from boyhood to manhood. Initiation ceremonies entailed young men gaining knowledge from their elders on subjects including women and courting and prepared them for adulthood and marriage. In many parts of PNG, both rural and urban, these rites of passage have been eroded due to Christian missionary influences and changing lifestyles. This rupture has lead to more violent contemporary forms of masculinity among groups such as the Duna of Lake Kopiago District, in Southern Highlands (Haley, 2008). Nicole Haley succinctly presents a narrative of masculine embodiment through her juxtaposition of 'traditional' and contemporary growth-enhancing spells and songs. Through the retelling of songs she shows how the ideals of masculinity have been transformed from being growth-enhancing proud songs to songs of insecurity and woe. The Palena bachelor cult which once dominated the lives of young Duna men has now been eroded with the arrival of Christianity and colonialism. Local masculinities have now emerged with young men's behaviour being moulded by guns and marijuana. Martha Macintyre (2008: 181) in her portrayal of *gutpla stail* (TP: male presentation in the forms of dress and behaviour) also addresses violence in styles of modern masculinity. She posits that contemporary styles of comportment portray a look that expresses a capacity for violence (2008: 185). The cut off jeans and the cargo pants worn by young men, and the combat trousers, bandanas and dark glasses worn by police riot squads and defence personnel embody the ideal of a modern masculinity which draws upon traditional ideas of the male body as strong and capable of violence.

One of the reasons for initiating this research was to find out more about the social background of the men who have been incarcerated for sexual offences. Various social factors have been viewed as contributing to the propensity to rape and commit such as lack of education, family breakdown, peer influence and drug and alcohol abuse (Harris 1988; Goddard 1995; Sikani 1997; Po'o 1975).

Many researchers, academics and political commentators in PNG, as in the West, have argued that rape is an act of exerting male power over women. Laura Zimmer-Tamakoshi (1990) posits that most popular explanations of contemporary sexual violence ignore sexual exploitation in traditional Papua New Guinean societies. She suggests that sexual aggression in traditional Papua New Guinean societies has been transformed into contemporary gender violence in PNG. 'New ideas about women's inferiority and men's right to dominate them have, in many instances, been grafted onto older sets of beliefs, thereby contributing to women's alienation and an increase in violence against women' (1990: 259). Similarly, Banks (1997) concurs that violence by men against women appears to arise most often when men perceive they have lost control over women; when women are perceived by men to have breached certain expectations of conduct; and when there are underlying prior injuries within the family.

I suggest that the idea of 'power' which is often used to explain such gender violence has western connotations. In saying this I am not denying that gender relations in Melanesia are grounded in relations of power. The idea of 'power' which I evince is one which is internalised as sexual violence and acted out through engagement with a wider field of social relations and not that of an isolated individual. The acting out of social relations which is at the core of Melanesian sociality provides the environment for which these explanations of sexual violence are eminent. Perceiving male power and domination over women as the sole cause does not adequately take into account the social contexts within which these acts take place—the broader realm of Melanesian sociality. Actions and consequences involve more than a man and a woman. The rhetoric of power and domination is prevalent in the explanation of rape and other offences against women in PNG. Instead of viewing the reasons offered by rapists simply as 'excuses', I seriously consider the broader context within which the offender situated the events. The power and domination of a man over a woman may not be the only or the foremost reason why these acts were carried out. However, there is still the problem of why more generalised anger and aggression is directed towards women.

In conclusion, I would advocate attempting to hear the voices of those who commit such crimes so that we are able to get a glimpse of how they are thinking. By listening to their voices we may be able to ascertain the reasons for such actions. As I have argued, the material presented reveals the pervasive themes of frustration and retribution and the need to express masculinity through sex as a justification for rape. It shows that in contemporary PNG men are negotiating their way through relationships with women in a way which is far removed from 'traditional' societies. It is important to understand the ways in which the broader relations of modernity are being transformed as it may lead us to rethink how we choose to deal with the issue of rape and sexual violence in Papua New Guinea.

References

Bainton, Nicholas A., 2008. Men of *kastom* and the customs of men: status, legitimacy and persistent values in Lihir Papua New Guinea. In *Changing Pacific Masculinities*, ed. John P. Taylor. Special issue of *The Australian Journal of Anthropology* 19(2): 194–212.

Banks, Cyndi, 1997. Contextualising sexual violence: rape and carnal knowledge in Papua New Guinea. In *Reflections on Violence in Melanesia*, ed. Sinclair Dinnen and Allison Ley, 83–100. Sydney: Hawkins Press and Asia Pacific Press.

Borrey, Anou, 2000. Sexual violence in perspective: the case of Papua New Guinea. In *Reflections on Violence in Melanesia*, ed. Sinclair Dinnen and Allison Ley, 115–18. Sydney: Hawkins Press and Asia Pacific Press.

Bradley, Christine, 1985. Attitudes and practices relating to marital violence among the Tolai of East New Britain. In *Domestic Violence in Papua New Guinea*, ed. Susan Toft, 33–71. Law Reform Commission of Papua New Guinea Monograph, 3. Port Moresby: Law Reform Commission of Papua New Guinea.

Brison, Karen, 1995. Changing constructions of masculinity in a Sepik society. *Ethnology* 34: 155–75.

Brown, Paula, 1988. Gender and social change: new forms of independence for Simbu women. *Oceania* 59(2): 123–42.

Counts, Dorothy, 1999. 'All men do it': wife beating in Kaliai, Papua New Guinea. In *To Have and To Hit: Cultural Perspectives on Wife Beating*, ed. Dorothy A. Counts, Judith K. Brown and Jacquelyn C. Campbell, 73–86. Urbana: University of Illinois Press.

Dinnen, Sinclair and Allison Ley, eds, 2000. *Reflections on Violence in Melanesia*. Sydney: Hawkins Press and Asia Pacific Press.

Eves, Richard, 2006. *Exploring the Role of Men and Masculinities in Papua New Guinea in the 21st Century: How to address violence in ways that generate empowerment for both men and women. Report for Caritas Australia.* Online: http://www.baha.com.pg/downloads/Masculinity%20and%20 Violence%20in%20PNG.pdf. Accessed 28 November 2010.

Goddard, Michael, 1995. The rascal road: crime, prestige, and development in Papua New Guinea. *The Contemporary Pacific*, 7(1): 55–80.

Haley, Nicole, 2008. Sung adornment: changing masculinities at Lake Kopiago Papua New Guinea. In *Changing Pacific Masculinities*, ed. John P. Taylor. Special issue of *The Australian Journal of Anthropology* 19(2): 213–29.

Hammar, Lawrence, 1999. Caught between structure and agency: the gender of violence and prostitution in Papua New Guinea. *Transforming Anthropology* 8(1/2): 77–96.

Harris, Bruce, 1988. The rise of rascalism: action and reaction in the evolution of rascal gangs. Discussion Paper 24. Port Moresby: Institute of Applied, Social and Economic Research.

Jenkins, Carol and the National Reproduction Research Team (NSRRT), 1994. *National Study of Sexual and Reproductive Knowledge and Behaviour in Papua New Guinea*. Monograph 14. Goroka: Papua New Guinea Institute of Medical Research.

Langness, L.L., 1967. Sexual antagonism in the New Guinea Highlands. *Oceania* 37(3) (March): 161–77.

Lepani, Katherine, 2008. Mobility, violence, and the gendering of HIV in Papua New Guinea. In *Changing Pacific Masculinities*, ed. John P. Taylor. Special issue of *The Australian Journal of Anthropology* 19(2): 150–64.

Macintyre, Martha, 2008. Police and thieves, gunmen and drunks: problems with society in Papua New Guinea. In *Changing Pacific Masculinities*, ed. John P. Taylor, Special issue of *The Australian Journal of Anthropology* 19(2): 179–93.

Meggitt, Mervyn J., 1964. Male-female relationships in the Highlands of Australian New Guinea. *American Anthropologist* 66: 257–72.

Po'o, Tau, 1975. *Gangs in Port Moresby*. Waigani: Administration for Development 2: 30–37.

Read, Kenneth E., 1981. Male-female relationships among the Gahuku-Gama: 1950 and 1981. *Social Analysis* 12: 66–78.

Rosi, Pamela and Laura Zimmer-Tamakoshi, 1993. Love and marriage among the educated elite in Port Moresby. In *The Business of Marriage: Transformations in Oceanic Matrimony*, ed. R. Marksbury, 175–204. Pittsburgh: University of Pittsburgh Press.

Sai, Anastasia, 2007. *Tamot*: Masculinities in transition in Papua New Guinea. PhD thesis, Melbourne: Victoria University.

Sikani, Richard, 1997. Live to steal and steal to live: juveniles and economic crime. Preliminary paper National Research Institute, Papua New Guinea. Political & Legal Studies Division, no. 3.

Stewart, Christine, 2005. Sex, gender and the law in Papua New Guinea. Discussion Paper No 12. Gender Relations Centre, Research School of Pacific and Asian Studies. Canberra: The Australian National University.

-------- 2008. Men behaving badly: sodomy cases in the colonial courts of Papua New Guinea. *Journal of Pacific History* 43(1) (June): 77–93.

Taylor, John P. ed., 2008. *Changing Pacific Masculinities*. Special issue of *The Australian Journal of Anthropology* 19(2).

Toft, Susan, 1985. *Domestic Violence in Papua New Guinea*. Monograph No. 3. Law Reform Commission, Port Moresby: Papua New Guinea.

Toft, Susan and Suzanne Bonnell, 1985. *Marriage and Domestic Violence in Rural Papua New Guinea*. Occasional paper 18. Law Reform Commission Papua New Guinea. Port Moresby: Papua New Guinea Law Reform Commission.

Wardlow, Holly, 2007. Men's extramarital sexuality in rural Papua New Guinea. *American Journal of Public Health* 97(6): 1006–14.

Zimmer-Tamakoshi, Laura, 1990. Sexual exploitation and male dominance in PNG. In *Human Sexuality in Melanesian Cultures*, ed. Joel Ingebrittson, 250–67. *Point* 14. Goroka: Melanesian Institute.

-------- 1997. 'Wild pigs and dog men': rape and domestic violence as 'women's issues' in Papua New Guinea. In *Gender in Cross-Cultural Perspective*, ed. Caroline Brettell and Carolyn Sargent, 2nd edition, 538–53. Upper River: Prentice Hall.

7. 'Crime to be a Woman?': Engendering Violence against Female Sex Workers in Port Moresby, Papua New Guinea

Christine Stewart

Abstract

In 2004, police raided an alleged brothel in Port Moresby, capital of Papua New Guinea, and amidst general mayhem, rounded up all present, men, women and children, and marched them to the police station where nearly forty women and girls were charged with prostitution. A newspaper report of the incident claimed that male sex workers were freed because there was no legal provision enabling their arrest. This elicited a swift response from the National AIDS Council lawyer, to the effect that this was an unfair denial of the constitutional right to equality before the law regardless of sex, and that male sex workers should have been charged as well.

This chapter asks whether, in the face of evidence that men were also abused, the violence was gendered and if so, how and why. This requires examination of the development of the gendered view of the prostitute, the continuance of the view that wayward women should be punished by violence of a sexual nature, and the transference of concepts of pollution into the sphere of social panic about the burgeoning HIV epidemic in the country.

The raid

In March 2004, early on a Friday afternoon, police raided the Three-Mile Guesthouse in the Boroko suburb of Port Moresby, the capital of Papua New Guinea (PNG).[1] The guesthouse, a converted colonial residence, is typical of the many premises which provide short- and long-term accommodation at the lower end of the socio-economic scale—rooms are also let to women who sell

---

1   This account is compiled from newspaper reports, verified statements taken from many of those caught up in the raid and other documents and reports concerning the raid, all of which I have collected as part of my PhD fieldwork from 2004 to 2007.

sex and collect their own payment. Facilities include a bar, a snooker table and gaming machines. Some women peddle cooked food, cigarettes and betel nut in the front yard or outside the gate. It is open by day as well as in the evening, which allows housewives to visit and augment their domestic finances without their families knowing.

Figure 8. Typical club, Port Moresby, 25 January 2006.

Photograph by Christine Stewart.

The police raid was accompanied by extreme violence. People were beaten with everything from pool cues to rifle butts—some women were sexually assaulted. One twenty-three-year-old reported that police forced her into a room at gunpoint, beat her with rubber hoses, told her to take off her jeans and underwear, forced an air freshener canister and then a beer bottle into her vagina and then ordered her to perform oral sex on them. Food was dumped over the vendors, beer over the drinkers. Police seized alcohol and the till takings, gaming machines, snooker tables and kitchen appliances. They snatched people from the rooms, rifled through bags and helped themselves to money and valuables. They confiscated condoms from the rooms and, by continual threats and beatings, forced the women to chew and swallow them. Then all those present—men, women and even children—were lined up and marched at gunpoint a mile or more through the streets to the police station.

The grim procession was headed by a police truck loaded with the goods looted from the premises. The women were forced to hold condoms in their mouths or wave them like balloons above their heads as they marched. A crowd gathered quickly to jeer at the unfortunates, spit on them, pelt them with stones and bottles and taunt them for selling sex and spreading disease.

At the police station, reporters from the local television station and the daily newspapers were waiting, presumably tipped off by the police.[2] More than forty men caught up in the raid were released, but the women were seated on the grass outside the station, and processed in batches. While they were waiting, the Metropolitan Police Superintendent addressed them. He told them that the raid had been conducted to prevent sex workers from contracting and spreading HIV.

Some thirty-nine women and girls were charged for 'living on the earnings of prostitution', which is the charge under the *Summary Offences Act* 1977 used in PNG for acts of prostitution. For a day and a half, they were held in hot crowded cells at the station, without food, washing facilities or medical attention for their injuries. Supporters from the National AIDS Council, NGOs and community organisations brought food and comfort. Some NGO workers managed to gain access to the station and stayed with the women in the stinking cells. That night, four young women were taken out and offered a lift home but, once in the police vehicle, were told they had to provide sex first. Two agreed, but two refused and were returned to the lockup. After two nights in the cells, the women were finally released in the early hours of Sunday morning. Legal assistance was provided by AusAID's HIV support program,[3] and some three weeks later, upon discovery that no search warrant had been issued in respect of the raid, the charges were dropped. A court claim for compensation for abuse of human rights was filed but has not been pursued, reportedly on the grounds that the individual policemen involved could not be identified (Human Rights Watch 2005: 116; see also Ombudsman Commission of Papua New Guinea 2009).

The Monday after the raid, both PNG English-language daily newspapers, the *National* and the *Post-Courier*, ran the story. The *Post-Courier's* front-page report 'Sex workers on parade' included a paragraph stating that:

> [a]mong those arrested—including both male and female prostitutes—was a 13-year-old girl (Yiprukaman 2004a: 87–88).

The *Post-Courier* also ran an editorial, which commenced by castigating the police for mounting such a

---

2   Michael Goddard mentions this tip-off process in relation to other types of raids (Goddard 2005: 20–21).
3   AusAID, the Australian government's overseas aid program, established its first HIV-specific support program in late 2000.

public humiliation ritual.... [t]hat's an interesting experiment in social reform or pre-trial processing. The defence lawyers will find it valuable in mounting a case against the prosecution. Certainly it must have been good entertainment for the street folk (Editorial 2004a).

The editor then proceeded to praise the Superintendent for his wise words of warning to the detainees:

The police commander who assembled the charged people on the lawn outside the police station and warned them of the perils of their so-called profession was doing the right thing (Editorial 2004a).

'But will they listen?' The editor went on:

The only trouble is in getting those people to take note of it after they are dealt with by the courts. Looking to the future is not a thing that prostitutes are noted for. They are often on the bottom rung of society's ladder and have few social or working skills to be able to climb higher in society.

Usually, their prime task is to find money to feed and house themselves and the knowledge that they can satisfy those needs by selling their bodies comes before the 'finer things of life'.

Will any of those charged people get off the bottom rung or will they be inevitable dregs of the hospital wards soon and among those anonymous carcasses to be bulldozed into a mass burial pit at Bomana cemetery one day soon, victims of HIV/AIDS? (Editorial 2004a).

The *National's* report included a photo and a small story, relating how the Superintendent had lamented the increase in prostitution:

It was a sad thing to see girls, as young as 14, 15 and 16 years of age sitting among the group ... some of these young girls' clients were men as old as 60 ... times were tough and prostitution among young women was increasing.... [they] were risking their lives and could easily catch AIDS ... the women are drunk in most cases and do not take safety precautions like using condoms ... prostitution was the main cause of HIV/AIDS virus spreading like bushfire (Pilimbo 2004: 5).

The following day, Tuesday 16 March, the *Post-Courier* produced another front-page headline: 'Males "freed" ... but 31 suspected female prostitutes charged!'

FORTY-FIVE men rounded up by police for alleged prostitution walked free yesterday because there are no provisions in the law to charge male sex workers.

However, 31 women were arrested and charged because Section 55 of the Summary Offences Act of the Criminal Code [*sic*] provides for female sex workers to be charged.

However, a senior government lawyer yesterday said sections 55 and 57 of the law were not designed to single out women prostitutes.

The lawyer said the charging of people was the discretion of the police depending on the kind of information at hand.

It was not right to say that the provisions did not cater for charges being filed against male prostitutes.

A prostitute is someone who earns a living from sexual favours or earns a living by providing the venue for prostitution.

National AIDS Council lawyer Bomal Gonapa ... said outside court that 35 men were released from police custody because there was no provision under the current Summary Offences Act of the Criminal Code Act that covered male prostitutes.

'The release of the male suspects was not fair to their female counterparts because they were all engaged in such an activity,' Mr Gonapa said. (Yiprukaman 2004b).

Raids such as the Three-Mile Guesthouse Raid are a common policing strategy in PNG towns, usually conducted in urban settlements in a search for stolen goods and suspected criminals (Dinnen 2001: 64; Goddard 2001: 3–4). Accompanying violence, including sexual violence, is commonplace, and derives partly from a perception on the part of the police and the community in general that the imported model of criminal justice is failing, and partly from a policing tradition based on early frontier-pacification strategies (Dinnen 1998a: 260–61; Dinnen 1998b: 360; Jenkins 2000: 22).

Raids have been conducted before at the Three-Mile Guesthouse, which is owned by a controversial former politician and diplomat (Nicholas 1996; Konia 1998; Sela 1998; Terry 1998). The brutality evidenced in these raids seems to be increasing. In a raid in 1996, reportedly the biggest to date (Nicholas 1996), the women were trucked to the police station: in 1998, when police claimed that 'the problem was worsening' (Terry 1998), the women were force-marched. Police harassment of those selling sex throughout the city appears to have increased steadily, until this 2004 raid which was clearly such an abuse of human rights that it elicited strong public comment and condemnation.

Unlike these previous raids, which rated only brief news reports, the 2004 raid provoked a number of comments and a good deal of reportage, both locally and internationally. The two PNG English-language newspaper reports of the incident and its aftermath were widely available as hard-copy and online, and included one or two letters to the editor commenting on the incident. Briefs were written shortly after the incident by the government's body the National AIDS Council Secretariat (National AIDS Council Secretariat 2004) and by the Project Manager of the Poro Sapot Project (PSP), an initiative of the international NGO Save the Children which provides awareness, condoms and clinical support for marginalised groups in various locations in PNG, including Boroko (Hershey 2004; Reid 2010). Both these briefs provided information for the narrative account above. The entire incident was documented later that year by the international NGO Human Rights Watch, which based its account on statements made by women and girls involved in the raid, and on its own interviews conducted in September 2004 (Human Rights Watch 2005: 118–21). The incident also provoked comment and discussion on two email-lists, AIDSTOK (hosted by the Secretariat of the Pacific Community for discussion on HIV and other sexually transmitted infections (STIs) in the Pacific) and ASAONET (serving anthropologists around the world working in Oceania). The coordinator of the Global Network of Sex Work Projects (NSWP), an international organisation for promoting sex workers' health and human rights, wrote to all PNG Embassies and High Commissions world-wide, protesting the violence.

A few days after the women were released the National Capital District (NCD) Provincial AIDS Committee[4] convened a meeting of government representatives, NGOs and churches. Among other things, a court claim for damages for breach of human rights was proposed, and written statements were taken by and from many of those involved. The statements taken reflected the need to emphasise the injuries, both physical and psychological, that were visited on them. The women were continually advised not to mention receiving money for sex, but one or two did.

All these accounts and ongoing discussions illustrate the interests of their makers and commentators, and exemplify the discourses operating in PNG today which surround the selling of sex, its gendering, its condemnation and the violence associated with it. The *Post-Courier* editorial of 15 March declared that:

> PROSTITUTION has been a whipping boy of politicians, social interest groups and police ever since the 'profession' was first encountered (Editorial 2004a).

Is this in fact the case? Is there a 'profession' in PNG? Has it been a 'whipping-boy' and if so why? This paper examines the Three-Mile Guesthouse Raid through the lens of several of these reports, comments and statements, all of

---

4 The National AIDS Council established these committees for each province and the National Capital District.

which exemplify the various discourses currently surrounding transactional sex in PNG today. How is the category of those who sell sex constituted through these discourses, how is it gendered, what provokes and legitimises such extreme violence?

Discourses combining and competing

Morality and the law

The formal legal system of PNG is based on English law, introduced to the two colonial territories by way of Australia. This produced a formal legal system which made a small number of piecemeal adjustments to local conditions while maintaining an overall framework of a 'sophisticated, imposed law of the white settler and administrator' (Brown 1969: 10). Practising lawyers and judges were recruited from overseas, principally Australia. Training of Papua New Guinean lawyers did not commence until shortly before Independence. After Independence, the legal system was continued largely unaltered, with its stylised procedures and reliance on written precedent derived initially from the metropole, and while it is poorly understood by non-lawyers, it impinges increasingly on daily life in PNG as society modernises.

In matters of family and sexual relationships, the introduced legal system derives its principles from medieval ecclesiastical law. Legal and Christian moralities reinforce each other, and although in the West the law has been reformed in the last half-century in the light of human rights principles, in PNG this moralistic stance is strongly maintained by Pentecostal, evangelical and charismatic preaching.

The media and the middle class

The newspaper reports provide the most immediate documentation of the raid and until very recently, with the advent of digital media such as blogging and Facebook, the principal illustration of popular opinion on national issues. The target audience has changed somewhat over the decades. Newspapers in PNG were originally produced by and for the colonists and about the colonised. But by 1985, when Colin Filer published a study of public opinion on bride price through a survey of letters to the newspaper in 1979–80, he noted a citizen readership (and letter writership) which was 'fairly distinctive', in that it was educated and concerned with national issues, but represented only a small proportion of the total population; and which self-identified variously as *elites* or *grassroots*, but usually displayed dominant themes of populism while siding with capitalism (Filer 1985: 164–65). Twenty years later, Hank Nelson noted the same demographic, of educated, urbanised middle-class Papua New Guineans, including a significant proportion of women, who took an interest in national issues (Nelson 2005: 3,10). Nevertheless, their lifestyles have a significant impact on the rural majority, not least in respect of sexuality and modernisation (Jenkins 2007: 30–31). In contrast to the arcane terminology, complex procedures, alien concepts and general air of mystique of the law, the media discourse is readily available to modern PNG society, both urban and rural, *elites* and *grassroots*. Readers both inform and are informed by populist reportage, and it is accorded a high degree of veracity. So errors in reporting, even if they are only grammatical, can be significant.

The *National's* report of the raid included a purported statement by the Superintendent that the Three-Mile Guesthouse was operating illegally because it did not have a 'proper licence to operate the brothel'—in fact there is no such thing as a brothel licence in PNG. The illegality referred to was that the establishment had no liquor licence. The *Post-Courier* reported that 'male prostitutes' involved in the raid were freed because there was no law under which to prosecute them (Yiprukaman 2004b), but this was wrong on two counts. First, as to fact: the men involved in the raid were clients, guesthouse staff, bar patrons, even band members, but they were not male sex workers (Hershey 2004: 1). Second, as to the law: as was pointed out to the reporter at the time, Section 55 of the *Summary Offences Act* does in fact allow the prosecution of any person who lives on the earnings of prostitution,[5] which would include men (Gerawa 2004). Through a unique and surprising judicial interpretation of the Law Reform Commission's attempt in 1975 to decriminalise prostitution, the gender-neutral language of the *Summary Offences Act* has been taken to mean that those earning money from selling sex are criminalised along with those originally intended to be the target of the offence, the pimps and madams (see Stewart 2011 for a detailed history). But when several prominent figures were invited to comment on the erroneous assumption of gender bias, the law itself was not questioned or their doubt was not reported.

Global HIV

Over the last quarter century, the HIV epidemic has produced a number of specialised discourses which have been promulgated, if not necessarily accepted, world-wide. In PNG, the HIV discourse has been most prominently fashioned by international organisations and their templates for the programs and solutions supported by overseas aid, whether for government or civil society: the 'ABC' (Abstinence, Be faithful, use a Condom) prevention strategy; the focus on 'high-

---

5   The reference to 'Section 55 of the Summary Offences Act of the Criminal Code' is incorrect.

risk groups' (later altered to 'high-risk settings'); the plethora of acronyms designed to avoid stigmatisation but allegedly increasingly it, such as FSW (female sex workers), MSM (males who have sex with males), VCT (voluntary counselling and testing); and human rights espoused as a basis for policy. This international discourse has been 'localised' through a range of 'cultural and moralistic lenses' (Lepani 2010: 306) and promulgated by the media to its urban readers.

In general, contributors to the Pacific AIDSTOK list, where notice of the raid was first posted on 17 March, upheld the terms of this globalised HIV discourse, though they may on occasion be wary of its wholesale adoption into the Pacific region. They were also willing to espouse elements of both the human rights discourse and the localised cultural discourse.

Human rights—hopefully

However, the international human rights discourse sits uneasily with other popular discourses in PNG. The law does support the principles of universal human rights: the *Constitution* guarantees equal treatment of the sexes (Section 55) and prohibits 'treatment or punishment that is cruel or otherwise inhuman' (Section 36). However, although the *Constitution* is theoretically the supreme law, not all laws are yet fully consistent with it, due to their having been continued from pre-Independence laws and not yet fully revised or properly tested in the courts.

The *National's* Editorial of 23 March castigated the Central and NCD Police Commander for his dismissive comment that the police 'might have got a bit out of hand' during the raid:

> No, Commander Wagambie—your men did not get a bit out of hand.
>
> They disgraced the uniform they wear, and once again brought the reputation of the RPNG Constabulary[6] tumbling down … it is impossible to avoid the impression that these policemen took a special delight in inflicting humiliation upon these women and men.
>
> This is the kind of macho image beloved of bullies the world over—the inflicting of shame and disgrace upon people who are utterly helpless…. The fact is that the law is there to protect citizens … the police are not there to make moral judgements and enforce humiliating and completely

---

6   Royal Papua New Guinea Constabulary.

illegal punishment upon a group of unfortunate women ... [who] are also citizens, with access to the full rights accorded to each and every one of us (Editorial (2004b).

The rights discourse was also adverted to in the comments of Dame Carol Kidu and the various NGOs who were present at the police station, notably the Poro Sapot Project and the Individual and Community Rights Forum (ICRAF). It prompted the Human Rights Watch investigation and reports (Human Rights Watch 2005, 2006). And, as noted above, it featured in the AIDSTOK comments on the raid.

But it does not predominate in the urban cultural setting of PNG. Those who witnessed the forced march to the police station, who jeered, pelted the marchers with stones and spat upon them, who accused them of being 'AIDS carriers', were evincing a more visceral reaction than that of an infringement of the fragile concept of human rights. Rather, they were viewing the events unfolding before them through a localised cultural lens which prompted them to condemn the selling of sex and vent their fears about the spread of HIV.

Discourse, opinion and action

Naming the profession

Transactional sex flourishes in Port Moresby as in the rest of PNG due to a combination of many factors. These include the effects of the deteriorating economy, which pushes many girls into offering, or being offered for, paid sex to support themselves and their families (Levantis 2000: 67, 69) and the commoditisation of the bride-price system which impels many women to elect to use the money they earn from their bodies for themselves rather than their kin (Jenkins 2007: 13; see also Wardlow 2006; and Kelly *et al*. 2011). It may also be provoked by resentment at kin for failure to support them over crucial issues (Wardlow 2002); and, as I learned from interviews recorded in 2007, fragile domestic situations which see many women fleeing or being ejected from intolerable and often violent marriages. The conduct of these sexual encounters takes many forms, ranging from street work out-of-doors in bushes, long grass and on the footpaths of commercial districts after hours; through the many nightclubs, guest houses and discos which serve as sexual networking venues; to the marketing of daughters, nieces, even wives, around city offices and rural economic enclaves. The relationships involved are not necessarily single encounters—some may be relatively long in duration (Wardlow 2004: 1025; and Kelly 2011).[7]

The range of situations involving monetised sexual exchanges worldwide, and the names and meanings for these transactions and those involved in them, vary enormously (Patton 2002: 89). This makes problematic the use of the terminology, categories, implications and understandings of global discourses (Wardlow 2004). The global HIV discourse has lumped all such exchanges together in the one conceptual category, which is capable of being named and then delineated and described by the names: 'prostitution', 'sex work', 'transactional sex'. The meanings of the names are fashioned by the discourses in which they are embedded, and lend themselves to interpretation in different ways by different social groups (Perkins 1991: 7; Stewart 2011).

The media reports of the raid used the terms 'prostitute' and 'sex worker' interchangeably and sometimes together in the same story, although in later weeks, in describing the various court proceedings which ensued, 'prostitute' and 'prostitution' tended to take precedence. A different set of names was used by those who gathered to witness the forced march to the police station: *pamuk meri* (TP: loose woman);[8] AIDS carriers, *sik pulap* (TP: full of disease); *spread sik AIDS* (TP: spreaders of the AIDS disease); *painim man o* (TP: man-chasers); *raunraun meri* (TP: gadabout woman). Some said *'salim samting blong yupela tumas yupela save pilim pen tu o nogat'* (TP: you sell your 'things' so much I guess it doesn't even hurt you).

The term 'prostitute' and its variants are derived from the language of the law. The Colonial Police Offences Ordinances made use of the term, referring to 'the purpose of prostitution' (both Territories) and a 'common prostitute who solicits, importunes or accosts' (New Guinea only)—this despite the fact that the terms are nowhere defined, and some of England's finest legal minds have proved incapable of providing an acceptable definition (Self 2003: 25, 30, 99, 121). Prostitution-related offences were maintained in colonial times, probably in response to concerns from the early twentieth century about dwindling populations and the spread of venereal diseases (Jenkins 2007: 27) and more recently on moralistic grounds—see, for example, the plethora of reports and Letters to the Editor in both daily newspapers of October and November 2010, following Dame Carol Kidu MP's announcement that Cabinet had approved her submission to have the laws regarding prostitution and homosexuality referred for review to the Constitutional and Law Reform Commission.

---

7 For a more exhaustive overview of the selling of sex in urban and rural PNG, see Jenkins 2006: 34–41.
8 *Pamuk* is derived from the Samoan *paumutu* (slang. *paumuku*) meaning a loose woman, and was probably introduced to PNG by returning plantation labourers (pers. comm. Penelope Schoeffel, 27 February 2005).

The recent alternative term 'sex worker' is derived from the sexual radicalism of the 1980s and the sex worker movement in the West which viewed prostitution as a form of work and sought to shift the discourse from one of morality to one emphasising economic necessity, and was officially adopted by the global HIV discourse in 1992. It was actively introduced into PNG as part of the global effort in HIV epidemic management which constructed 'high-risk groups' and then 'high-risk settings' as requiring particular attention, and thus needed to describe their members (Patton 2002: 87–89).

However, this process of naming overlooks the fact that neither 'prostitute' nor 'sex worker' is a chosen identity. This is demonstrated by the statements of the women themselves, explaining their presence at the Three-Mile Guesthouse at the time of the raid:

> I am resident ... of the premises so I was selling food stuff inside the area (woman, 33).

> I was marketing *buai* [betel nut] and smoke outside of the guesthouse gate.... I brought my son to the laundry and was showering him (woman, 34).

> I was employed as a cleaner with Guest house at 3-mile since years now.... I was inside the guest house washing floor (woman, 21).

> I was at the 3 Mile Guest house with the group that was playing cards at the back of the guest house (woman, 22).

> I went there because I heard that a band was playing (woman, 26).

> She is only there waiting for her cousin brothers (band members) to finish play and go home (woman, 38).

> I went to the guest house to check for my husband.... I am married with a small girl aged 2 years old (woman, 21).

> Whilst on my way [to visit my aunty who lives nearby] I heard life [*sic*] band was entertaining the people ... so I decided to pip [*sic*] through the gate (woman, 18).

> A band was playing in the guesthouse so myself and a girlfriend went in the premises and sat down watching the band (girl, 17).

These statements were all made for a specific purpose: as evidence in a proposed court case for damages. They were taken down by National AIDS Council officers and sub-committee members, who expressly warned them not to admit to selling sex (although one or two did so nevertheless). The stories are therefore constructed, but this does not necessarily negate the truth of the events they recount. Women and girls who sell and exchange sex in Port Moresby (as in the rest of PNG, and the rest of the world) are firstly people. They are daughters, sisters, mothers, girlfriends, wives. They are cleaners, cooks and street vendors. They lead a variety of lives, and are not fundamentally self-defined by the fact that they may sell sex (see McClintock 1993: 1). The terms publicly and 'officially' used for those who engage, however rarely or frequently, in selling or exchanging sex are not universally accepted in PNG. This is true whether it is a term sanctioned by an international aid agency, or hurled as an insult by the crowd which jeered at those in the forced march following the raid. Such terms are all construed as derogatory and based in the same kind of moralistic discourse which produced 'prostitute'.

Women themselves over the years have adopted a variety of localised alternatives. One striking example comes from the 1960s (Johnstone 1993), when an immigrant group from the Highlands termed their women who walked the streets accompanied by their husbands *bisnis-meri* (TP: businesswomen), a term which predated the western shift of emphasis to the economic nature of the activity and its discourse. Today, women continue to develop their own appellations, often based on some variation denoting 'sister' (Hammar n.d.; see also Hammar 2010). My fieldwork in 2007 revealed the popularity among homeless street-workers in Port Moresby and other towns of the term 'problem-mothers', meaning 'mothers with problems'. The fragmented nature of this self-naming indicates the shortcomings of a discourse which seeks to name and thereby categorise people by activities taking place in a range of contexts which may have little in common. This can lead to the conflicts apparent in the epithets hurled at the women as they were marched through the city streets, contrasted with the apparently sympathetic words of the *Post-Courier* editor who sympathised with those who were obliged to sell sex to 'find money to feed and house themselves' but proceeded to approve the actions of the police commander who warned them of the perils of selling sex while authorising their arrest and detention, in inhumane conditions and in defiance of normal bail procedures (Editorial 2004a, above).

The gendering process

Cindy Patton points out that the global HIV discourse enabled the conflation of AIDS and selling sex: 'sex workers were largely presumed to be women, and women at risk were assumed to be prostitutes' (Patton 2002: 92). But the gendering of the category of 'prostitute' had already been confirmed in the discourse of colonial law, simultaneously with its naming. References are made in the colonial Ordinances to prostitution by a 'female native' (*Native Regulations 1939 (Papua)* Section 85), or a 'native woman' (*Native Administration Regulations*

1924 (New Guinea) Section 87), or simply, a 'female' (*Police Offences Ordinance* of New Guinea Section 79); and to male persons living wholly or in part on the earnings of prostitution (*Police Offences Ordinance* of New Guinea Section 79). Extra emphasis is given to this female gendering by the long-standing rule in PNG's imported legal system that 'words importing the masculine gender include females'.[9]

'On the other hand,' Patton continues, 'men who sell sex to men were lumped together as men who have sex with men' (p. 92). In fact, cases from colonial times had already dealt with situations of males selling sex, mentioning monetary exchange in several. One case file specifically stated that one party to consensual male-male sex was entitled to be exonerated as 'the victim of a male prostitute' (Stewart 2008: 85). However, the criminal charges laid in all such cases are those of sexual acts between males, which carry far higher penalties than the 'prostitution' offences laid against women who sell sex. Hence no public discourse has emerged around the selling or exchanging of sex by men. Rather, in the case of sex between males, attention has focused on the conflation of consensual sex between adults with forced sex and sex with under-aged boys, all of which are lumped together in media reportage as 'sodomy' (see for example Sete 2008; Yadi 2006).

Perhaps, because of this history of avoiding reference to the selling of sex by males, it is not surprising that the comparatively novel concept of 'male prostitutes' caught up in the raid was taken up so eagerly by the media. Over the week following the raid, both newspapers solicited comments from prominent people on this topic. First was the *National* on Wednesday 17 March, reporting that officials of the NGO Individual and Community Rights Advocacy Forum (ICRAF) explained that the law

> covered both male and female prostitutes.... How can the police justify their actions by saying the law only relates to women? Where is the justice that they are supposed to be providing to the people of this land when they clearly have a prejudice against women? (Gerawa 2004).

On the same day, in a horrified letter headed 'Crime to Be a Woman?' a (male) writer complained bitterly about the discrimination evidenced by:

> this apparent male chauvinistic ideology which stigmatises the female gender as sexual entrepreneurs. After the motley gang of both male and female sex workers were detained and interrogated, males were vindicated but the females were castigated … if this case reveals an

---

9   Interpretation Act 1975 Section 6.

inherent legislative bias that privileges the male gender against moral and legal indictment, it is also a case that points to the dehumanisation of the female species. Is it a crime to be a woman? (Moutu 2004: 10).

The *Post-Courier* sought comment from the Community Development Minister, now Dame Carol Kidu, who condemned the police brutality and reportedly mentioned that 'the fact that only the women were victimised was unjust because both males and females were arrested during the raid' (Yiprukaman 2004c).

On Friday 19 March, the Minister responsible for the police Mr. Bire Kimisopa described the release of the forty-five male prostitutes as a 'joke' and a 'completely stupid' action by police because not all sex workers were females. 'I want a review on the whole incident and all male suspects to be brought in and charged appropriately,' he said, adding that he would be writing to Police Commissioner Sam Inguba to have the officer responsible charged for releasing the male prostitutes. 'The release of the male prostitutes is a terrible injustice to the female citizens of this country,' Mr. Kimisopa said (Yiprukaman 2004d).

These criticisms resorted to the argument of lack of gender equality, which should have seen 'male prostitutes' locked up as well. Even though men as well as women were treated violently, commentators assumed that the police had acted in freeing the men on the basis of gender rather than deciding whether they were or were not engaged in selling sex. But many of the defenders of gender equality failed to condemn the violence and abuse, and only Dame Carol Kidu queried the criminalisation of sex work. Others seem to have thought it more important to punish the alleged AIDS carriers than to query the justification underlying the law which criminalises all those who live on the earnings of prostitution. It seems that they preferred to ensure that all men who might behave like the outclass of women who sell sex—allegedly the vectors of disease—should be re-gendered so as to deserve equal ill-treatment.

But males who sell sex do not fit into the standard category of the mobile, financially-independent woman deserving of punishment. Violence between men is usually prompted by disputes over property, territory or status—things to which all those gendered as male are entitled. So the appeals to 'fairness' and the constitutional guarantee of equality which, it was claimed, should have seen these men locked up as well, may be seen as an attempt to render them visible— to de-masculinise them and re-gender them as feminised outcasts deserving of punishment similar to that meted out to the women.

Why the violence?

ASAONET contributors were particularly interested in the causes of the violence, and discussion centred on this aspect of the raid.[10] There have been many studies of violence against women in PNG, both in the domestic sphere and beyond. Writers such as Lisette Josephides (1994), Laura Zimmer-Tamakoshi (1997) and various contributors to Sinclair Dinnen and Allison Ley's edited volume (2000) agree that the underlying cause of the steady increase in this violence is men's fear of losing their control over women. Modernity, urbanisation, globalisation all contribute to the greater economic and social freedom of women, particularly those in urban centres. Women, albeit subordinated or downright rebellious beings, are therefore seen to invite deserved violence. It seems those who sell sex, appearing as both economically independent and powerful, and refusing to submit to the ongoing control of any one man or group of men, are particularly threatening to men.

Uncontrollable women

A frequently repeated popular view of women's status in traditional society is that they were oppressed chattels (King, Lee and Warakai 1985: 3).[11] In post-independent PNG, women's status has deteriorated even from this earlier inequality (see Macintyre 1998). Ten years after Independence, women were declaring that they had become less, not more, visible—they were discriminated against in politics, economics and education; and violence against women was increasing (Macintyre 1998: 3–4). Modernisation and development placed greater burdens on women in many ways, while men accumulated power and wealth at their expense. Tradition was manipulated and re-invented to justify the suppression of women, while men adapted to the new society with all its opportunities (Mandie 1985: 170).

Bruce Knauft (1997: 233–34, 242–43) notes how the increasing dependence on trade goods, development and wealth has altered but maintained masculine prestige and female propriety. He discusses the classic view that gendered oppositions, resentment of women and male bonding operate to sustain social cohesion in many traditional Melanesian societies, echoing and doubtless drawing upon the western double standard of femininity which constructs

---

10 Unfortunately, I have not saved this correspondence, but I do recall an initial posting by Deborah Gewertz, followed by comments from Marta Rohatynskyj, Penelope Schoeffel and Dorothy Counts, all of which inspired me to propose the ASAO meeting session from which this volume emerged.

11 However, this has been challenged by Papua New Guinean women themselves, who claim that traditional gender roles were complementary, if not always equal. See Kekedo 1985; King 1985; Mandie 1985; Dickson-Waiko 2003.

women either as virtuous mothers or wanton whores (Booth 1998: 116; Summers 1994). He contends that these oppositions have firmed in the modern PNG context, where

> masculine identities are stressed and threatened … [and] indigenous beliefs concerning sexuality abut newer practices that commoditize sex and enforce a moral divide between marriage and prostitution … rais[ing] the threat that women could use sexual favours to redirect wealth to themselves … women of traditional virtue or Christian propriety are increasingly judged not just against standards of female pollution but against those of being a loose woman or prostitute (Knauft 1997: 243).

Hence the compliant, subservient village woman becomes the virtuous urban Christian housewife; the polluting, dangerous woman-rebel translates into the geographically mobile, financially independent, beer-drinking, unmarried or no-longer-married woman who is easily labelled as loose or *pamuk* (TP) (Clark n.d.: 18; Wardlow 2006). In contemporary PNG, where sex has become commoditised and a moral divide between marriage and prostitution has firmed, it is an easy step to perceiving the latter as 'prostitutes' (Jolly 2001: 198).

HIV: Pollution and disease

The raid in 1998 was the first to be claimed publicly as having been motivated by HIV-related concerns:

> Supt. Gawi said apart from curbing suspected brothels, the police effort should be seen as an attempt to eliminate the spread of AIDS and other sexually transmitted diseases (Terry 1998: 3).

By 2004, however, HIV prevention was claimed as the prime motivation for the Three-Mile Guesthouse raid, as evidenced not only by the address of the Police Metropolitan Superintendent but also by the way in which condoms featured strongly in the abuse of the women.[12]

It is commonplace to attribute the threat of disease to women. Mary Douglas, in her classic study of pollution and taboo (1966), suggested that pollution beliefs are a way of imposing control on such chaotic phenomena as illness and desire, which threaten social boundaries. These boundaries are particularly porous in sexual relations, which transgress the body's boundaries and involve class and status struggles. In PNG, traditional beliefs relating to the potential dangers to men of sex and other contact with women, particularly with menstrual blood, are widespread (see for example Clark n.d.: 191; Langness 1999: 170; Wardlow

---

12 The advocating of condoms for HIV prevention is a highly controversial issue in PNG: it has even been suggested recently that the State should be liable in damages for their promotion (Nyan 2006).

2006: 54–56).[13] Current fears of HIV infection through sexual contact cohere with these pollution beliefs, as well as meshing with the general attribution of pollution and disease to women.

The perceived threat posed by women increases exponentially when the woman sells sex. The view of such women as vectors of disease and infection has been well-documented in the metropoles. Maggie O'Neill describes the situation in nineteenth-century France, where one of the main concerns regarding the regulation of prostitution was the fact that its practitioners were seen as diseased (1997: 5–6). In England, concerns about the spread of venereal disease in military garrisons led to the enactment of the Contagious Diseases Acts in the 1860s (Walkowitz 1982: 1; Chancer 1993: 145) and these concerns were often exported to the colonies (Howell 2004; Phillips 2002, 2005; for PNG, Reed 1997; Lepani 2008, 2012; and for Australia, see Perkins 1991: 73–74). 'Prostitutes' were condemned for carrying disease while at the same time the local sex industry was structured by regulation and policy to cater for single men,[14] a theme often repeated in the developing world, both during and after the colonial era (Phillips 2002: 343; Stoler 2003: 48; Sandy 2007: 201, 235–38).

This view of those selling sex as vectors of disease and infection was imported into PNG by way of the Anglo-Australian colonisation process, both through metropolitan laws and policy and through mission preaching. Today, the HIV discourse classifies the promiscuous purveyor of sex as one who has 'flouted the norms of monogamous heterosexuality (and mainstream public health)' (Hammar 2008: 60), and hence is considered a member of a 'high-risk group', or more recently, as conducting 'risk activities' in a 'high-risk setting'. It is a further easy step to link this woman with the dangerous polluter of traditional culture, as shown by the abusive names used to humiliate the marching women. The assault with the air freshener canister was more than rape—it was the symbolic destruction of a source of pollution.

Conclusions

Commentators on the Three-Mile Guesthouse Raid have had recourse to various social discourses in their reportage. These discourses have combined to direct opinion and ultimately action in specific, socially approved directions. Chief among them are the discourse of the media, which represents and informs urbanised opinion, both middle-class and grassroots; the discourse of the

---

13 Such beliefs are not unique to PNG. See for example Mary Douglas 1966.

14 The irony is that impartial studies which favour investigation over judgement show that the reverse is often the case: sex workers are aware that they are more endangered, and are more likely to develop strategies to safeguard their health (Chancer 1993: 149–50).

introduced legal system allied with Christian morality; the HIV discourse, founded internationally and modified locally; the discourse of traditional 'culture'; the discourse of local popular culture which saw the ready use by spectators to the forced march of abusive and insulting language; and the human rights discourse, also founded internationally but often locally in conflict with these and other discourses.

The law and the media in PNG have combined to create a female-gendered category of 'prostitute'. This category has been set apart from the 'normal' idealisation of the modern PNG woman, who is even more in need of control and containment, lest she acquire education, employment, financial independence and mobility, which are those same scarce prestigious things sought by men (Jolly 2001: 193–94). Most of all, women should observe sexual proprieties, and those who do not—who are mobile, immodest or promiscuous—are 'asking for' condemnation and punishment. This view is lent support by the HIV discourse which constructs and focuses attention on 'high-risk' groups. By persisting in criminalising the selling of sex through the charge of 'living on the earnings of prostitution', the law has facilitated an expanding culture of violence inflicted on those women classed as engaging in commercial sex. The violence may be regarded as a form of punishment for transgressing social norms and thereby allegedly threatening society.

The human rights discourse seeks such lofty ideals as equality and freedom from abuse. But it is the weakest link in the chain of combined discourses, and when it is at odds with them, it generally loses out or is qualified. Equality of the sexes is an argument employed by those wishing to prove themselves both modern and knowing. But equal treatment for all before the law and the right to state protection against gender violence—these still take second place when the groups claiming these rights feel themselves threatened from within. This is a 'borderland' which is still highly contested, where legal/moral debates still prevail (see Merry 2001, 2006). Does gender equality entail that there should be equally abusive treatment meted out to all those not observing the proprieties and threatening the social body by their becoming 'vectors of infection'? Even the gendering of the prostitute breaks down when males are believed to cast themselves as 'sex workers', as equally social outcasts.

One feature of the reportage stands out. Several commentators, in the name of the constitutional principle of gender equality, chose to criticise the police behaviour not on the grounds of violence which infringed the constitutional right to freedom from cruel or unusual treatment, but on the grounds that the men who were (erroneously) presumed to be 'sex workers' were given an unfair advantage over their female counterparts. They were freed, and this breached the right of equality. It seems that, rather than complaining about the unfair violence, or the unfair law which led to it, some preferred to ensure that all males who might behave similarly to the outclass of 'prostitutes' should be re-gendered so as to deserve equal ill-treatment.

Andrew Moutu might well ask: Is it a crime to be a woman? The answer is: yes, when the woman belongs to a category of society without rights, the sexual entrepreneur gendered female, feared and outcast. And, it seems, that in a twisted application of notions of gender equality, males who behave like female-gendered prostitutes are equally culpable.

References

Booth, Karen M., 1998. National mother, global whore, and transnational femocrats: the politics of AIDS and the construction of women at the World Health Organization. *Feminist Studies* 24: 115–39.

Brown, Bernard John, 1969. *Fashion of Law in New Guinea: Being an Account of the Past, Present and Developing System of Laws in Papua and New Guinea.* Sydney: Butterworths.

Chancer, Lynn Sharon, 1993. Prostitution, feminist theory, and ambivalence: notes from the sociological underground. *Social Text* 37: 143–71.

Clark, Jeffrey, n.d., *Huli Sexuality, the State, and STD/AIDS Prevention Programmes.* Goroka, PNG: PNG Institute of Medical Research.

Dickson-Waiko, Anne, 2003. The missing rib: mobilizing church women for change in Papua New Guinea. *Oceania* 74(1-2): 98–119.

Dinnen, Sinclair, 1998a. Criminal justice reform in Papua New Guinea. In *Governance and Reform in the South Pacific*, ed. Peter Larmour, 253–72. National Centre for Development Studies. Canberra: The Australian National University.

-------- 1998b. Law, order, and state. In *Modern Papua New Guinea*, ed. Laura Zimmer-Tamakoshi, 333–50. Kirksville, Missouri: Thomas Jefferson University Press.

-------- 2001. *Law and Order in a Weak State: Crime and Politics in Papua New Guinea,* Honolulu: University of Hawai'i Press and Adelaide: Crawford House Publishing.

Douglas, Mary, 1966. *Purity and Danger: An Analysis of the Concepts of Pollution and Taboo,* Routledge and Kegan Paul, London.

Editorial, 2004a. Give thought to rehabilitation. *Post-Courier*. Port Moresby, PNG (15 March): 10.

-------- 2004b. A sad new chapter in police arrogance. *National*. Port Moresby, PNG (23 March).

Filer, Colin, 1985. What is this thing called 'brideprice'? *Mankind* 15: 163–83.

Gerawa, Maureen, 2004. Police wrong: NGO. *Post-Courier*. Port Moresby, PNG (March 17): 4.

Global Network of Sexwork Projects, 2011. *nswp Global Network of Sexwork Projects: Promoting Health and Human Rights*. Online: http://www.nswp.org. Accessed 5 April 2011.

Goddard, Michael, 2001. From rolling thunder to reggae: imagining squatter settlements in Papua New Guinea. *Contemporary Pacific* 13: 1–32.

-------- 2005. *The Unseen City: Anthropological Perspectives on Port Moresby, Papua New Guinea*. Canberra: Pandanus Press.

Hammar, Lawrence, n.d. The 's' words: 'sex', 'sex worker', and 'stigma' in Papua New Guinea. Papua New Guinea Institute of Medical Research. Ms in author's collection.

-------- 2008. Fear and loathing in Papua New Guinea: sexual health in a nation under siege. In *Making Sense of AIDS: Culture, Sexuality, and Power in Melanesia*, ed. Leslie Butt and Richard Eves, 60–79. Honolulu: University of Hawai'i Press.

-------- 2010. *Sin, Sex and Stigma: A Pacific Response to HIV and AIDS*. Wantage, UK: Sean Kingston Publishing.

Hershey, Christopher, 2004. Statement of facts on police raid at 3-Mile Guesthouse 12 March 2004 and related incidents. Statement made on behalf of Poro Sapot Project, Save the Children in Papua New Guinea (20 March).

Howell, Philip, 2004. Sexuality, sovereignty and space: law, government and the geography of prostitution in colonial Gibraltar. *Social History* 29: 445–64.

Human Rights Watch (Coursen-Neff, Zama), 2005. Making their own rules: police beatings, rape and torture of children in Papua New Guinea. *Human Rights Watch* (30 August). Online: http://www.hrw.org/en/reports/2005/08/30/making-their-own-rules-0. Accessed 7 February 2011.

-------- 2006. 'Still making their own rules': ongoing impunity for police beatings, rape, and torture in Papua New Guinea. *Human Rights Watch.* Online: http://www.hrw.org/en/reports/2006/10/29/still-making-their-own-rules-0. Accessed 7 April 2011.

Human Rights Watch, 2011. *Human Rights Watch.* Online: http://www.hrw. org. Accessed 5 April 2011.

Jenkins, Carol, 2000. *Female Sex Worker HIV Prevention Projects: Lessons Learned from Papua New Guinea, India and Bangladesh.* Geneva: Joint United Nations Programme on AIDS (UNAIDS).

-------- 2007. HIV/AIDS, culture, and sexuality in Papua New Guinea. In *Cultures and Contexts Matter Understanding and Preventing HIV in the Pacific*, ed. Carol Jenkins and Holly Buchanan-Aruwafu. Asian Development Bank. Online: http://www.adb.org/Documents/Books/Cultures-Contexts-Matter/HIV-PNG.pdf. Accessed 7 April 2011.

Johnstone, Joan D., 1993. The Gumini *Bisnis-Meri*: a study of the development of an innovative indigenous entrepreneurial activity in Port Moresby in the early 1970s. PhD thesis. Brisbane: University of Queensland.

Jolly, Margaret, 2001. Damming the rivers of milk? Fertility, sexuality, and modernity in Melanesia and Amazonia. In *Gender in Amazonia and Melanesia: An Exploration of the Comparative Method*, ed. Thomas Gregor and Donald Tuzin, 175–206. Berkeley: University of California Press.

Josephides, Lisette, 1994. Gendered violence in a changing society: the case of urban Papua New Guinea. *Journal de la Société des Océanistes* 99: 187–96.

Kekedo, Jean, 1985. Equality and participation in Melanesia. In *From Rhetoric to Reality? Papua New Guinea's Eight Point Plan and National Goals after a Decade*, ed. Peter King, Wendy Lee and Vincent Warakai, 350–55. Waigani, Papua New Guinea: University of Papua New Guinea Press.

Kelly, Angela *et al.*, 2011. *Askim na Save (Ask and Understand): People who Sell and/or Exchange Sex in Port Moresby.* Papua New Guinea Institute of Medical Research and the University of New South Wales, Sydney, Australia.

King, Peter, Wendy Lee and Vincent Warakai, 1985. *From Rhetoric to Reality? Papua New Guinea's Eight Point Plan and National Goals after a Decade.* Waigani, Papua New Guinea: University of Papua New Guinea Press.

Knauft, Bruce M., 1997. Gender identity, political economy and modernity in Melanesia and Amazonia. *Journal of the Royal Anthropological Institute* 3: 233–59.

Konia, Ruth, 1998. 20 women held in police raid. *National*, Port Moresby, PNG (December 17): 1–2.

Langness, Lewis L., 1999. *Men and 'Woman' in New Guinea*. Novato, California: Chandler & Sharp, Publishers Inc.

Law Reform Commission of Papua New Guinea, 1975. *Report No.1: Report on Summary Offences*. Waigani, Papua New Guinea: Law Reform Commission of Papua New Guinea.

Lepani, Katherine, 2008. In the process of knowing: Making sense of HIV and AIDS in the Trobriand Islands of Papua New Guinea. PhD thesis Anthropology. Canberra: The Australian National University.

-------- 2010. 'Steady with custom': mediating HIV prevention in the Trobriand Islands, Papua New Guinea. In *Plagues and Epidemics: Infected Spaces Past and Present*, ed. D. Ann Herring and Alan C. Swedlund, 305–22. Wenner-Gren Foundation Monograph Series. Oxford: Berg Publishers.

-------- 2012. *Islands of Love, Islands of Risk: Culture and HIV in the Trobriands*. Nashville, TN. Vanderbilt University Press.

Levantis, Theodore, 2000. *Papua New Guinea: Employment, Wages and Economic Development*. Canberra: Asia Pacific Press.

Mandie, Angela, 1985. Institutional and ideological control of gender in a transitional society. In *From Rhetoric to Reality? Papua New Guinea's Eight Point Plan and National Goals after a Decade*, ed. Peter King, Wendy Lee and Vincent Warakai, 166–71. Waigani, Papua New Guinea: University of Papua New Guinea Press.

McClintock, Anne, 1993. Sex workers and sex work: introduction. *Social Text* 11: 1–10.

Merry, Sally Engle, 2001. Changing rights, changing culture. In *Culture and Rights: Anthropological Perspectives*, ed. Jane K. Cowan, Marie-Bénédicte Dembour and Richard A. Wilson, 31–55. Cambridge: Cambridge University Press.

-------- 2006. Transnational human rights and local activism: mapping the middle. *American Anthropologist* 108(1): 38–51.

More mothers, students HIV positive in Morobe, 2008. In *Post-Courier*. Port Moresby, PNG, 6 June. Online: http://www.postcourier.com.pg/20080606/frhome.htm. Accessed 21 January 2011.

Moutu, Andrew, 2004. Crime to be a woman? Letters to the Editor. *Post-Courier*, Port Moresby, PNG (March 17): 10.

National AIDS Council Secretariat, 2004. *Legal Briefing: Police Raid on Three-Mile Guest House*. Port Moresby: National AIDS Council Secretariat.

Nelson, Hank, 2003. Dear Sir...: Evidence of civil society in the media of Papua New Guinea. Paper given at USP/ANU/FDC Suva Symposium, Suva, Fiji.

Nicholas, Isaac, 1996. Forty held in capital city brothel raid. *Post-Courier*. Port Moresby, PNG, (25–27 October): 1–2.

Nyan, Avisat, 2006. Reconsider condom policy. *National*. Port Moresby (7 December).

Ombudsman Commission of Papua New Guinea, 2009. *Investigation report into the alleged unlawful and abuse of human rights by police, Three Mile Guest House, Port Moresby*. Port Moresby, PNG: National Capital District, National Parliament.

O'Neill, Maggie, 1997. Prostitute women now. In *Rethinking Prostitution: Purchasing Sex in the 1990s*, ed. Graham Scambler and Annette Scambler, 4–28. London and New York: Routledge.

Patton, Cindy, 2002. *Globalising AIDS*. Minneapolis and London: University of Minnesota Press.

Perkins, Roberta, 1991. *Working Girls: Prostitutes, their Life and Social Control*. Canberra: Australian Institute of Criminology.

Phillips, Richard, 2002. Imperialism and the regulation of sexuality: colonial legislation on contagious diseases and ages of consent. *Journal of Historical Geography* 28: 339–62.

-------- 2005. Heterogeneous imperialism and the regulation of sexuality in British West Africa. *Journal of the History of Sexuality* 14: 291–362.

Pilimbo, Peku, 2004. Police arrest 80 in brothel raid. *National*. Port Moresby (15 March): 5.

Reid, Elizabeth, 2010. Putting values into practice in PNG: the Poro Sapot Project and aid effectiveness. In *PacifiCurrents*, issues 1.2 and 2.1, (April), online: http://intersections.anu.edu.au/pacificurrents/reid.htm. Accessed 15 December 2010.

Sandy, Larissa, 2007. 'My blood, sweat and tears': female sex workers in Cambodia—victims, vectors or agents? PhD thesis. Canberra: Australian National University.

Secretariat of the Pacific Community, 2011. *SPC Secretariat of the Pacific Community*. Online: http:// www.spc.int/. Accessed 5 April 2011.

Sela, Robyn, 1998. Midday raid of house sees 25 behind bars. *Post-Courier*. Port Moresby, PNG (17 December): 3.

Self, Helen J., 2003. *Prostitution, Women and Misuse of the Law*. London and Portland OR: Frank Cass Publishers

Sete, Annette, 2008. Sodomist gets 21 year jail term. *Post-Courier*. Port Moresby, PNG (20 May): 6.

Stewart, Christine, 2008. Men behaving badly: sodomy cases in the colonial courts of Papua New Guinea. *The Journal of Pacific History* 43: 77–93.

-------- 2011. *Pamuk na Poofta*: criminalising consensual sex in Papua New Guinea. PhD thesis. Canberra: The Australian National University.

Stoler, Anne Laura, 2003. *Carnal Knowledge and Imperial Power: Race and the Intimate in Colonial Rule*. Berkeley: University of California Press.

Summers, Anne 1994. *Damned Whores and God's Police*. Ringwood, Vic.: Penguin.

Terry, David, 1998. Police parade suspects in the streets. *Post-Courier*. Port Moresby, PNG (17 December): 3.

Walkowitz, Judith R., 1982. *Prostitution and Victorian Society: Women, Class, and the State*. Cambridge England and New York, NY: Cambridge University Press.

Wardlow, Holly, 2002. Passenger-women: changing gender relations in the Tari Basin. *Papua New Guinea Medical Journal* 45(1–2): 142–46.

-------- 2004. Anger, economy and female agency: problematizing 'prostitution' and 'sex work' among the Huli of Papua New Guinea. *Signs* 29(4): 1017–39.

-------- 2006. *Wayward Women: Sexuality and Agency in a New Guinea Society*. Berkeley and Los Angeles: University of California Press.

Yadi, Abby. 2006. Sodomy Shock. *Post-Courier*, 21 January.

Yiprukaman, Michelle, 2004a. Sex workers 'on parade'. *Post-Courier*. Port Moresby, PNG (15 March): 1.

-------- 2004b. Males 'freed' ... but 31 suspected female prostitutes charged! *Post-Courier*. Port Moresby, PNG (16 March): 1.

------- 2004c. Kidu: probe raid on city brothel. *Post-Courier*. Post Moresby, PNG (18 March): 4.

------- 2004d. Police actions damned. *Post-Courier*. Port Moresby, PNG (19 March): 4.

Zimmer-Tamakoshi, Laura, 1997. 'Wild pigs and dog men': rape and domestic violence as 'women's issues' in Papua New Guinea. In *Gender in Cross-Cultural Perspective*, ed. Caroline B. Brettell and Carolyn F. Sargent, 538–53. Upper Saddle River, NJ: Prentice Hall.

8. Gender Violence in Melanesia and the Problem of Millennium Development Goal No. 3

Martha Macintyre

Abstract

This chapter explores and offers a critique of the ways that foreign aid projects engage with the problem of violence against women in Papua New Guinea. Inspired by the work of Amartya Sen and Stephen Lewis, writers who bravely defend humanist ideals and enable the exposure of much of the empty rhetoric about diversity and equality as public relations talk, I argue that aid projects directed at reducing violence have failed because they do not confront the structural inequalities between men and women. The strategies wrongly assume widespread acceptance of human rights and ignore the anthropological analyses that reveal the deeply ingrained cultural attitudes and economic relations that naturalise female disadvantage and male entitlement. As such projects also sustain the unequal power relations between donor countries and the nations who are recipients of aid. The Millennium Development Goals (MDGs) that are directed towards redressing gender inequality are strategically inappropriate. In particular, the fine research that has been done by anthropologists on gender violence in Papua New Guinea and elsewhere in the Pacific has not really been 'taken on board' by aid agencies because it documents the fact that for women to gain the control over their own lives and bodies that 'eliminating violence' entails, men are going to have to lose it. Aid agencies negotiate projects with male politicians and these deals are underpinned by masculinist politics so the real nature of the changes required is never acknowledged.

Introduction

This chapter was inspired initially by my involvement in a seminar on auditing and 'measuring' gender in aid projects in which I participated as a board member of the International Women's Development Agency, an Australian-based NGO. The brief paper[1] I wrote for that seminar set out arguments about the problems involved in dealing with the issue of violence and 'measuring' success or failure of projects. In the course of the seminar, through subsequent reading of the literature on gender and aid (see Crewe and Harrison 1998 for an excellent bibliography, but also the ACFID report 2010) and in the light of my own experience of working as a consultant on projects that had anti-violence components, I have become concerned about the ways that fundamental problems about the time, cost and nature of projects are not acknowledged. It was also inspired by reading the work of Amartya Sen (1990; 1992) and Stephen Lewis (2006), writers who I think bravely defend humanist ideals and enable the exposure of much of the empty rhetoric about diversity and equality as public relations talk—rhetoric that thinly disguises economic arguments that sustain the unequal power relations between donor countries and the nations who are recipients of aid.

Most of all, I think that the fine research that has been done by anthropologists on gender violence in Papua New Guinea (PNG)[2] and elsewhere in the Pacific (see for example Jolly 1996, 2000) has not really been 'taken on board' by aid agencies—because it documents the fact that for women to gain the control over their own lives and bodies that 'eliminating violence' entails, men are going to have to lose it. Aid agencies negotiate projects with male politicians and these deals are underpinned by masculinist politics—so the real nature of the problems is never acknowledged. I have tried to enunciate some of those problems in what follows.

In 2000 the United Nations set the Millennium Development Goals (UNDP 2010). The eight goals set out strategies for dramatically reducing world poverty and established objectives that were deemed measurable and attainable. These goals explicitly include commitment to promoting gender equality and empowering women (Item 3) and the taskforce report *Taking Action: Achieving Gender Equality and Empowering Women* (Grown, Gupta and Kes 2005), sets out seven strategic priorities as integral to the third goal:

1. Strengthen opportunities for postprimary education for girls while simultaneously meeting commitments to universal primary education.

2. Guarantee sexual and reproductive health and rights.

3. Invest in infrastructure to reduce women's and girls' time burdens.

---

1   Macintyre 2006. The paper presented a critique of the notion that measurement of incidence is necessarily useful for policy formulation and a discussion of the problems of accuracy in data collection.

2   While some of this research is hard to find because it is contextualised in broader ethnographic studies, there is a solid body of work on gender violence since at least the 1970s, for example Counts 1990, Josephides 1985, Zimmer-Tamakoshi 1990, and the sections that anthropologists contributed to the major study by the Law Reform Commission in 1985, see Toft 1985 and Toft and Bonnell 1985.

4. Guarantee women's and girls' property and inheritance rights.

5. Eliminate gender inequality in employment by decreasing women's reliance on informal employment, closing gender gaps in earnings, and reducing occupational segregation.

6. Increase women's share of seats in national parliaments and local governmental bodies.

7. Combat violence against girls and women (Grown, Gupta and Kes 2005: 3).

These seven priorities constitute an integrated approach to eliminating inequality and empowering women and draw on decades of international research and reports on aid projects that have in various ways documented discrimination against women. The final one, 'Combat violence against girls and women', requires that governments and development agencies commit to programs and policies that confront and try to eliminate violence against girls and women. The use of the term 'combat' (and the struggle it implies) resonates with the rhetoric of 'zero tolerance' and accumulated knowledge of decades that has revealed the futility of campaigns that are not supported by laws, police action and public condemnation of violence against women. It was a term deliberately chosen by the authors for two other reasons: first, to stress the seriousness of the problem and the need for confrontation in developing solutions; second, because their first choice of terminology, 'elimination', was deemed unrealistic (Geeta Rao Gupta, personal communication, May 2008). In concert with the other MDGs there is recognition that improving women's economic and political status, as well as providing better access to education and health services, will add to the armoury for this struggle. In this chapter, I concentrate on the third goal: promoting gender equality and empowering women. While acknowledging that the changes envisaged by the other six strategic priorities are critical to the elimination of female poverty, the problems posed by violence against women in PNG require an analytical approach to the cultural configurations of gender relations and the ideologies that sustain them.

The definitions of violence that are drawn upon and inform the Millennium Development Goals' objectives are extremely broad. They include physical violence, sexual violence, psychological abuse and forms of neglect and coercion, as well as such culturally and legally-sanctioned practices as genital mutilation and corporal punishments. The strategies refer to violence committed in the context of war as well as domestic, intimate partner violence and criminal violence by strangers. They also embrace ideas such as 'economic abuse/violence' which cover forms of exploitation, deprivation and exclusion. In short, the task envisaged encompasses a vast array of types of violence, only some of which are universally recognised in law. In several countries, including PNG, where mutilation and beating are viewed as customary, the characterisation undermines the capacity of states to respond to acts of violence. More importantly, as they are based on ideals of universal human rights for women, the violence that is to be combated includes acts and practices that are endorsed by state institutions in some countries.

An international problem

There is now a prolific international literature on violence against women. The number of reports, studies, projects designs and evaluations that have appeared in the last decade is quite overwhelming—as I have found in preparing this chapter. The major reports emanating from agencies such as UNIFEM, the United Nations, the World Health Organisation, the Asian Development Bank (to name but a few) draw on a vast literature from development projects as well as the academic studies based in several disciplines including psychology, sociology, anthropology, law and medicine.[3] While there are some variations in findings that can be attributed to regional and/or cultural variations, the basic conclusions are consistent. Violence against women is an expression of deeply entrenched political discrimination against women at personal, local and national levels. Women's relative lack of power in domestic relations means that they are often incapable of resisting, escaping or changing the interpersonal dynamics whereby conflict is manifest in violence against them. Women's health suffers and women who are beaten are more vulnerable to a range of illnesses, many of which compromise their reproductive health. The propensity to be a both a perpetrator and a victim are socially transmitted to successive generations. Poverty and a lack of education are both implicated in the incidence of violence against women and the perceived tolerance of violence by women. The goal of empowering women in ways that will combat violence thus requires governments and aid and development agencies to work on several fronts and to ensure that gender disparities are reduced.

Australia and aid to Melanesia

Australian aid programs have attempted to deal with gender inequality in Melanesia for at least the past two decades (OECD, CRS Aid Activity Database), most recently through policies of mainstreaming. AusAID has guidelines that aim at integrating strategies for the achievement of equality for women within all projects, albeit diverse, including those for infrastructural and economic development. It is beyond the scope of this paper to discuss the broad

---

3 See for example the study of gender equity in international health (G. Sen *et al*. 2002); or the study of the economic cost of domestic violence (Yodanis and Godenzi 1999); the psychological effects of violence (Astbury *et al*. 2000); and the international legal issues (Meyersfeld 2003; Merry 2006).

implications and effects of mainstreaming gender, but it has to be acknowledged that the desired changes in empowerment for women so that violence is significantly reduced are, so far, not apparent. Lewis' (2006) criticisms of gender mainstreaming policies as they have been applied in Africa probably holds good for Melanesia too. Too often attention to women's specific disadvantages is minimal, the commitment to women's concerns is left in the 'too hard basket' when local men refuse to cooperate and the gender components often become tokenistic in practice. While development theorists and practitioners have often been in the forefront of criticism of the alleged 'trickle-down effects' of economic improvements, frequently that is still the implicit assumption in practical engagements with recipients, especially apropos changing gender relations.

Combating violence against women has been continuously revealed as a complex and dispiriting task. The hundreds of reports and analyses on violence against women that have been generated over the past ten years are disturbing and depressing.[4] They do not suggest that much change has been made in the prevalence of violence in any country since Beijing 1995 when it was internationally recognised as a problem facing women in all countries. In PNG the dimensions of the problem have not been systematically reassessed since the Law Reform Commission studies of the 1980s, although the report prepared by Bradley (2001; see also Garap n.d.) suggests that there has been no diminution of the problem in the intervening years and that in some areas of the country the situation is now even worse.

Anti-violence campaigns and the problem of empowerment

The situations in the two Pacific countries that I am most familiar with, PNG and the Solomon Islands, present innumerable implementation problems for campaigns to combat violence, not least because so many have been tried with such limited success. Let me illustrate this problem from my own experiences. Between 1999 and 2002 I was involved in Phase Three of the AusAID project with the Royal Papua New Guinean Constabulary. This phase, like its predecessors, had a well-developed gender component that included attention to gender equity within the police force; training in human rights and gender; attention to the needs of women and children in developing and implementing community-policing policies; and specific projects on the treatment of female victims of sexual offences and violent crimes, including domestic violence. The advisors

---

4   The International Center for Research on Women (ICRW) based in Washington DC has an extensive database of studies undertaken by them for other international agencies including the United Nations. Online: http://www.icrw.org/what-we-do/violence-against-women, accessed 12 January 2011.

working on other aspects of the project were generally sensitive to the need for women's issues to be raised in other contexts—such as discriminatory practices in promotion, disciplinary procedures and responses to crime.

Working on community policing issues meant that there were meetings with people, mostly in urban centres, throughout the country. The consultations with women in villages and urban communities invariably generated heated discussions about the problems they faced—in their homes, in villages, in urban areas—from their kinsmen, strangers and police. In every meeting I was struck by the fact that women were both insightful and eloquent in their analyses of social problems and the reasons for violence and crime in their communities. The interconnections between poverty, unemployment, lack of opportunity, inadequate government services, corruption and incompetence were drawn repeatedly.

Most women I know who have worked with Papua New Guinean women leave the experience with deep respect for them. I have inevitably felt privileged to work with women whose intelligence, warmth, resilience and humour is invested in a project even when they are faced with opposition and inadequate resources. In such contexts women emerge as capable, resourceful and powerful. In terms of their 'power to' accomplish things, women regularly display their capacity to make decisions and to act upon them. I have encountered many women who have been forceful and assertive in their dealings with others and have been surprised when the projects they have been involved with have petered out once external funding or support is finished. Sometimes the reasons are simply financial. But there are numerous instances where the demise of a project is attributable to internal dissension and/or conflicts with people in the community who resent the women's power (Macintyre 2003).

In a discussion of the 'gender agenda' Emma Crewe and Elizabeth Harrison (2002: 49–68) observe that '"the power to" dimension fails to take account of what has been excluded from the observable decision-making process – that is, the way that institutional factors may succeed in excluding certain issues' (p. 53). In many instances, including ones that they note, the ways that women enact their power to act precipitate conflict with those who (quite correctly) perceive this as an infringement on their power over the women concerned. Often, but not always, these people are men.

Let me illustrate with three examples. On Lihir,[5] the descent system is matrilineal and rights over land are transmitted through the matriline. There is really no dispute about women's rights in land and in negotiations with the mining company about land agreements men would regularly refer to their

---

5 I worked on Lihir in New Ireland Province, monitoring the social impact of a gold mining project from 1995 to 2005.

'matrilineal system'. But women did not usually represent their own interests in public forums. Given that the negotiations with the mining company had no 'traditional' precedent and were carried out in accordance with the government regulations in the *Mining Act*, three prominent and highly-educated women attended a meeting and claimed their right to be involved in negotiations on the basis of their equal rights as citizens and their traditional rights as landowners. They spoke eloquently and vehemently. During this meeting the men (who outnumbered them three to one) were enraged by the women's speeches and dismissed their arguments as 'against custom'. The demeanour of the men present, especially the two most powerful leaders, was itself a display of power—they did not look at the women, some ostentatiously turned their faces away and they maintained wide-eyed, tight-lipped expressions of barely-contained fury. Shortly afterwards the landowners' association insisted that there would be attention given to the needs of women and youth, but that women did not have the right to speak in the ways that these women had done. Such rights had to be *conferred* on one representative *by the men* who were in authority. The women incurred widespread disapproval from others in the community because they were behaving in ways that affronted *kastam* (tradition/custom). Many women I spoke with about the issue agreed with the arguments that the women had made but condemned them as *bikhet* (TP: arrogant, disrespectful), insisting that they should not have confronted men in this way. The women were effectively 'put in their place' and the only avenues for presenting their opinions once again restricted to the informal and personal domains where they could be ignored.

During my involvement with the AusAID police project as an advisor, one of the community policing advisors had assisted in setting up a system of dealing with women who were victims of domestic violence and sexual assault. His counterparts were policewomen and they had worked out a sequence of attending to the needs of the women in cooperation with the medical staff of the hospital and the local women's organisation that provided aid and support for women. As part of the program, the project vehicle (funded by AusAID) was designated for community policing work, particularly for use by policewomen to take victims of violence to the hospital and the women's centre. The policewomen had gained their vehicle licences—skills that were part of the capacity-building and gender-equity components of the overall project. The improvement of services and institutional responses to female victims of violence is regularly presented as a crucial part of programs aimed at combating domestic violence and sexual crime. This small program in a provincial town was highly successful and built up cooperative links between police, medical staff and the women's group.

As soon as the male AusAID advisor left, the male senior officer at the police station commandeered the vehicle and prohibited the women's use of it. Cars, especially new ones, are symbols of male status and the man appealed to his superior rank. If the women resisted they would be guilty of insubordination. The response program fell apart—the time involved in walking to the hospital was considerable. Women who were battered did not like being seen walking through the town with police officers. In short, all the hard work of consultation, cooperative program development, capacity building and teamwork that had been part of the 'gender agenda' of this project was stymied by the senior men at the police station. These same men had attended the gender training programs, endorsed the strategies, could speak eloquently about the problems of violence against women in their region and acknowledged the need to develop a coordinated response. But they could not tolerate the affront to their status by having women drive around in a new vehicle and so were prepared to scuttle the whole program in order to retain their masculine privileges and enforce them in terms of the 'chain of command'.

My final example suggests too that at an interpersonal level 'empowerment' through gaining knowledge and awareness of rights and capacities can be hazardous when men realise the implications for their authority. At a two-day workshop on domestic violence held in Port Moresby in 2002 as part of the community policing program, a group of women in public life discussed their experiences. The majority of them were highly educated and had senior positions in government departments or private industry. Of a group of twenty, only two indicated that they had never experienced violence from an intimate partner and several told harrowing stories of abuse resulting in severe injuries. One woman, a government employee, went home on the first day and informed her husband that she was now aware of her rights and would not tolerate his violence in future. He beat her and she appeared the next day with her face and arm bruised. Her experience generated an intense discussion of the ways that being educated and employed was perceived as threatening the status and authority of husbands—especially those whose education level was lower, or whose educational achievements less illustrious, or those who were unemployed or in a lower-ranked job than their partner. Resentment and hostility towards women who were thus branded as *bikhet* were apparently often expressed in violence—in one instance when the woman was sleeping.

This sort of reaction by men towards '*elite* women' has been well documented by Laura Zimmer-Tamakoshi (1990, 1993, 1997) and Bradley (2001). It suggests strongly that in PNG education for women is not especially protective in the ways that are suggested in the MDG Taskforce volume (Grown, Rao Gupta and Kes 2005). This is not to suggest that it should not be an objective for improving women's status, but that empowering women in this way might actually in PNG be viewed as 'disempowering' men and so provoke violence. Indeed, while my own research in this area is limited, interviews with 160 educated women employed in the public sector and by mining companies reveals that a significant proportion either divorce or choose to remain single precisely because they find that men often perceive them as threatening and legitimate targets for violence (Macintyre 2011; see also Spark 2011). In the words of one woman:

> I would marry if I found someone who was happy to let me follow my career, but here I am a manager of my section and that automatically means I am gossiped about as a *bikhet*. I have big difficulties with other men in [organisation] who are in lower-paid work. Other [male] managers try to ignore me in meetings. One actually told me that if I was his wife he would never let me stay in such a job (40-year-old woman in business enterprise, Port Moresby).

Empowerment has always seemed to me to be a very problematic concept. First, because the word itself suggests that power is somehow there to be given. Or even when it is used to refer to the process whereby women become aware of their own power, or capacity to change their lives, there is a lack of content to the concept—where does this power come from? In the aid context it carries overtones of donors conferring power and authority on recipients. In PNG 'empowering women' often means wresting power from men so that women might represent their own interests. As the cases above illustrate, this process generates conflict with men who correctly interpret it as an assault on privilege and a denial of their authority over women. Although male resistance to such changes are sometimes included as 'risk factors' in project designs, consultants are considered to be failing if they suggest that antagonism from men is inevitable and that this 'risk' is not only unavoidable, but will confound the strategy of empowering women. It is as if acknowledging the possibility will miraculously produce an efficacious solution. Or, as Crewe and Harrison conclude: 'Those using "empowerment" as a development objective seldom take on board the political implication – that is, that conflict is accompanied by resistance, and the process of empowerment is not necessarily "win-win"' (1998: 53). In PNG men regularly perceive women's empowerment as a situation in which women win and men lose—and they find this intolerable.

Looking at men and change

Richard Eve's report on violence for Caritas (2006) is indubitably the most thorough analysis of the current situation in PNG, but as he notes: 'It is not easy to know whether Susan Toft's speculation [that modernity and its implications for female resistance would mean an increase in violence] has proved correct, since ... nation-wide data on domestic violence over a long period of time is simply not available' (Eves 2006: 32). However his research interviews revealed very similar views to those I have encountered. Service providers in health and welfare believed that violence was increasing in both incidence and severity (Eves 2006: 36). Women reported new forms and contexts for domestic violence. While many attribute violence to poverty, alcohol consumption and the frustrations arising from unfulfilled desires for employment, economic security and opportunities for advancement, the idea that violence against women is a 'modern' phenomenon arising from contradictions in everyday life is hotly contested. But Toft's (1995a) prediction that resistance from women who become sufficiently 'empowered' to reject male violence will actually meet with hostility and greater violence often does seem to be fulfilled. Holly Wardlow's work in the PNG Highlands (Wardlow 2006), Zimmer-Tamakoshi's in both rural and urban settings (Zimmer-Tamakoshi 1993, 1997) and the many regional case-studies that have been published (see Counts, Brown and Campbell 1999) include numerous instances where greater awareness by women of their rights does indeed lead to resistance—but often this provokes greater violence from men.

Given that the emphasis on women's empowerment as a way of reducing the prevalence of violence seems a hazardous strategy in the case of PNG, are there ways of confronting the problem head-on? Richard Eves' conclusions suggest that shifting the focus of interventionist programs from women to men is essential. But he also envisages that this is problematic not only because of the lack of resources, but because programs directed at changing men's attitudes have been most successful when they are small and enable men to be open about their experiences, attitudes and violent behaviour, making mass campaigns extremely problematic in PNG:

> The general consensus in the literature on anti-violence interventions among men suggests that addressing men's violence against women is accomplished more effectively with male facilitators in all-male groups (Berkowitz 2004a: 4). Experience from overseas has found there is a general reluctance by men and women to broach issues of gender-based violence in mixed settings. This is especially the case with sexual violence, such as rape, which men are less likely to acknowledge as a serious issue in mixed workshops (Eves 2006: 60).

Working with all-male groups of police, I found that men were often prepared to be disarmingly honest about their actions and attitudes to violence. Sometimes this openness was extremely disturbing. On several occasions men who could give excellent summaries of the human rights of women and their rights under the law (indicating that they had clearly understood the content of the training module) would conclude with comments such as:

But these laws and ways of thinking will never become popular (a term used in PNG to mean widespread or commonly accepted) because men do not believe these things are true about PNG women. They work for Australians, but not for us.

And

It will be fifty years before men in Papua New Guinea accept that women should not be hit – maybe a hundred.

Eves' report suggests that such problems in adapting 'awareness' to the local situation occur frequently (2006: 62; see also Ch. 6).

The ideal of empowering women—ensuring that they gain awareness of their rights; enabling them to take action in their own interests; supporting them to develop institutions that provide support, advocacy and assistance, all entail disempowering men. These objectives require strategies for reducing or removing their power over women's bodies; disallowing their use of force to pursue their own interests; removing customary or accepted rights to services provided by women; taking from men the rights and powers that entitle them to discipline and punish those whom they see as their social inferiors; and enabling women to participate in domains of power that men consider exclusively theirs. Moreover, men are alert to the implications for their authority if women's rights are protected by the state and as John Taylor has indicated in his work on Vanuatu (Taylor 2008), they are prepared to defend their privileges as customary rights. Even if there are people in government who support such social, economic and cultural changes, the task cannot easily be represented as inspired by the favoured 'bottom-up' approach to aid that is universally supported. It is one that divides people, especially men and women.

Violence and ideas of administering justice

All analyses of violence against women observe the multi-dimensional character of the problem. All acknowledge that the most important task is changing the values and power dynamics that are the environment for violence. This understanding underpins the AusAID gender policies that aim for the integration of gender into all aid projects. On the other hand, there is a constant call by critics of development for all projects to accommodate the cultural and social values of the recipient countries and societies. This is the sort of 'win/ win' optimism that is criticised by Crewe and Harrison (1998). In my opinion, campaigns aimed at combating violence against women will fail as long as they do not confront the fact that such programs have to challenge some of the social values and cultural norms that are currently central to power relations in PNG.[6]

One of these programs has been the AusAID Law and Justice project—which has in many respects been very successful, especially in terms of capacity building and institutional change. Within that project considerable emphasis has been placed on the need to recognise traditional, negotiated forms of justice and dispute settlement. This attention to systems—that are familiar and appeal to customs that are accepted by people as legitimate and fair—is favoured by many Papua New Guineans as well as aid project advisors from Australia and elsewhere (see for example, ACFID: 2010). Most writers on the subject make an exception for cases of violence against women and children, stressing the need for a criminal justice approach that protects the victims and punishes the perpetrators.

This attention to criminalising gender violence is in keeping with ideals about having people 'own the project' and implementing international approaches to combating violence against women and children. There is a large body of literature that argues for improvements in police responses to violence; for the establishment of legal aid programs for women who have been assaulted; and for the training of magistrates and judges so that they apply the full force of the law and give sentences that indicate the criminal status of domestic violence. The arguments for restorative approaches come from a different perspective—one which locates problems in the ways that social attitudes diminish the significance of such violence—arguing that domestic violence is contextually different and that imprisoning or punishing men is socially disruptive. In some countries, especially those where 'honour killing' is socially accepted, courts regularly trivialise the suffering and deaths of women (see Ch. 5). But you cannot have it both ways and excepting some forms of violence against people as criminal while dealing with others as minor offences leads back to discriminatory practices.

In PNG the role of the police and the law and justice sector in dealing with domestic violence and sexual offences has been consistently criticised (see Ch. 7; Zorn 2010). At the same time the Australian aid programs aimed at improving their performance and reducing law and order problems generally have given much attention to restorative rather than retributive justice as the most desirable and culturally appropriate way of reducing crime and unrest. These

---

6   For a discussion of this problem as manifest in Vanuatu see Miranda Forsyth 2009; Merry 2006 includes a discussion of this as a general issue in nations where there are dual or multiple systems of administering justice. See Jolly (2011) for a review of Forsyth and the specific problem of gender violence.

approaches stress the need to restore and sustain strong social relations in ways that maintain cohesion within communities. The relationship between husband and wife is recognised as one which is not unitary, involving kin on both sides.

But as Sinclair Dinnen (2002) and others associated with the Law and Justice Project have noted, the restorative justice ideals are in tension with analyses of the problems of female disadvantage and the relative lack of power that women have within Papua New Guinean communities as well as in the pursuit of justice. Qualifying his support for restorative justice, Dinnen writes:

> Retributive justice will always remain an option for dealing with the most dangerous and intractable offenders. In addition, where there are significant imbalances in power between particular groups, as in the case of women appearing before Village Courts, 'restoring' relations may simply serve to reinforce these underlying inequities (2002: 11).

Restorative justice is often represented as the major way that pre-colonial Melanesian people administered justice within and between communities. This is a very partial and highly romanticised image that ignores the historical evidence for widespread tribal fighting (Knauft 2002: 89–156), extremely harsh punishments for crimes and often brutal treatment of women who breached social obligations (see for example Meggitt 1989). As I see it, a major problem in promoting customary forms of conflict resolution is that violence is often a socially-approved response to a grievance, affront or anti-social act. Corporal punishment of children is common in many communities and many people consider beating of a spouse acceptable in certain circumstances. On Lihir, in a study I carried out to see the circumstances in which people accepted or endorsed physical punishment by parents, spouses, police or senior men, I interviewed sixty women and forty men. I listed numerous scenarios: six in which I had observed a parent hit a child (all involving disobedience such as playing truant, or anti-social behaviour such as damaging a fruit tree); one when an older man beat a youth (for stealing betel nut from his basket); several when husbands had hit their wives for failing in their domestic duties and one instance when a woman hit her husband because he had been unfaithful to her. The overwhelming majority considered violence justified in all of the instances I had described. Only two women and one man regarded *any* of the violent acts as inappropriate or morally reprehensible.

In a similar exercise with a group of police women, discussing occasions when they had resorted to violence in their personal lives, the overwhelming majority affirmed that hitting a woman who was the lover of one's husband or boyfriend was justified and acceptable, as was assaulting the offending husband. In fact, many women who had been beaten by husbands suspicious of adultery indicated that their distress was due to the fact that they were innocent rather than the violence itself.

Abby McLeod observes 'violence is also one of many remedies that may be legitimately employed in response to grievance' (2002: 11). James Weiner, in the same paper, describes the ways that failure to resolve conflicts within a group often resulted in a rupture of sociality and refusal to compromise: 'in the Foi social world, it is all or nothing. A quarrel, over property, over adultery, over sorcery accusation, inevitably leads to the departure of one of the disputing parties to another place, especially if powerful men are involved' (Weiner, McLeod and Charles Yala, 2002: 2).

Such uncompromising responses are found in many Papua New Guinean communities where loss of face or public 'defeat' are viewed as intolerable. Most anthropologists who work in villages can give numerous instances where tensions between groups intensify to the point where accusations of sorcery and open arguments reach a point where one group is forced to relocate. Many such stories are attached to historical settlement patterns and land tenure systems. But discussions of restorative justice tend to ignore this long tradition of confrontation, conflict and community fission.

This all-or-nothing approach to conflict resolution is often linked to ideals of masculinity, and uncompromising or vindictive reactions to misfortunes or thwarted desires have been well-documented by anthropologists in a wide range of circumstances. The claim that 'restorative justice' was, or continues to be, the primary resort in village conflicts involving violence is not borne out by either historical or contemporary evidence. Wardlow's essay on the Huli concept *madane* (2005: 57–71) explores the gender implications of violent reactions of men who feel humiliated, envious or resentful because their 'sense of entitlement to something is dashed by another person's refusal to abide by a promise or presumed obligation' (p. 57). *Madane* thus explains (and is used to justify) the murders of Huli women who attempted to divorce husbands without repaying bride wealth, and of prostitutes who refused sex with 'rural, unemployed men' (p. 57) who could not pay them.

While Wardlow confines her argument to the Huli people, the emotional state and the types of violent behaviour it engenders are widespread in PNG. The Tok Pisin terms that I have most often heard for these are *jelas* (jealousy, resentment) and *bel hat* (anger, rage). While these emotions and actions are not confined to men, in discussions of violence and emotions a marked gender difference emerged. When men express resentment in violent rages or destructive acts, people were far more likely to interpret these as 'righteous indignation' and 'justifiable violence'. When women behaved in analogous ways the emotion and the violence was viewed more often as a sign of immature loss of control, undignified and inappropriate (see Ch. 5). Physical fights between women in public places that I have witnessed invariably drew onlookers who expressed amusement and ridicule at the spectacle, whereas assaults on women by men or fights between men did not. In one instance in 2001 when I observed a man assaulting a woman near Goroka market I asked two women standing near me to assist me in trying to help the woman; they refused on the grounds that the violence was so ferocious that the woman 'must have done something really bad'. In village meetings associated with the police project, both men and women regularly explained their refusal to intervene in cases of domestic violence because the man 'must have a reason'. Such responses indicate that there is a continuing belief that violence is justifiable in specific circumstances.

Zimmer-Tamakoshi, in her analysis of violence against women and rape as punitive (1993), elaborates the variety of ways that men justify assault, rape and pack rape in terms of righteous rage following rejection, insult or humiliation by a woman. In the contemporary case studies she includes and the historical examples she draws upon, she demonstrates that 'violence against women has long been accepted in many PNG societies as a *legitimate* means of controlling women and expressing or affecting men's relations with other men' (2001: 574, emphasis added). It is this socially endorsed legitimacy that presents problems for all campaigns aimed at combating violence against women. For it is not only the legitimacy of violence that has to be questioned and rejected, but the deep-seated beliefs about gender relations on which such legitimacy rests. The research conducted in rural and urban areas as part of the Law Reform Commission studies of domestic violence in the 1980s revealed not only its prevalence, but the widespread acceptance of violence by both men and women. There is no evidence that this has dramatically changed in the last two decades in spite of successive campaigns that have attempted to combat the ideology of female inferiority and male entitlement that underpins community acceptance.

Within the police force, where 'awareness' levels are very high, police remain reluctant to prosecute and ambivalent about the criminality of intimate partner violence. Awareness as an aim in itself ignores the fact that this might not actually alter ingrained cultural attitudes. In workshops on gender and human rights that I conducted, the level of awareness and the knowledge of the law that police officers displayed was generally very high. I cannot think of one instance where a police officer did not describe a hypothetical case of domestic violence as anything but 'criminal' or 'illegal'. Yet the majority confessed that when they were confronted by a woman wanting to lay a complaint they would first of all 'counsel' her. As police were not trained to counsel, nor encouraged to mediate between victims and assailants in any context, I invited participants to explain and discuss this strategy. Several explanations were offered. Women were notorious for withdrawing charges or failing to attend court proceedings and police bitterly resented the waste of time and energy they expended in prosecuting to no purpose. In some areas where women's families customarily demanded compensation for injury, women would come and report the crime in order to have leverage in compensation negotiations and once a payment had been made, would withdraw the charge or refuse to follow through—a tactic that was common in rape cases as well (see Forsyth 2009 for an analysis of the ways that people choose a judicial forum strategically). In some instances women did not want charges laid at all—their trip to the police station was simply in order to publicly declare a grievance and so 'shame' assailants. Once police felt able to air their feelings of frustration, the complexity of their responses emerged clearly. Often they were horrified at the injuries inflicted and so tried very hard to collect medical evidence and witnesses. Some were eager to show that they were enforcing the law diligently. But in almost every meeting where the subject came up, police recounted stories of women who repeatedly laid charges and then refused to follow through. These were the cases where police chose to 'counsel', a response which apparently involved giving a sympathetic hearing, driving the woman to the hospital when this was necessary and/or encouraging her to go and stay with relatives until the man 'cooled down'. A few policemen admitted to sending such women away, dismissing their complaints as 'humbug'.[7]

Discussions with hospital staff about treatment of victims of rape and sexual assault revealed that they too were sometimes reluctant to respond in the ways that would assist in providing forensic evidence for criminal prosecutions. In some instances their reluctance was attributable to 'compassion fatigue' as some victims came in repeatedly and yet would take no action against perpetrators. Two nurses explained that they always tried to be sympathetic and supportive but were very conscious of the shame women felt at the prospect of having their injuries made public. They recounted stories about women who had been sexually assaulted in ways that damaged their genitals or caused internal injury and said that they sympathised with the women's reluctance to have details of their injuries presented in court. They were personally appalled at the idea of photographing injuries or collecting forensic evidence from victims.

I have set down these instances from my own experience in order to expose some of the 'on-the-ground' difficulties posed by apparently sensible programs aimed at improving police response and improving medical treatment and the collection of evidence so that prosecutions are more robust. On the face of it, such suggestions appear sensible and relatively easy to implement. Establishing standard procedures for medical treatment, counselling and collection of

---

7   This term, now archaic in Standard English, is used by Papua New Guineans when speaking English and Tok Pisin.

evidence in rape or assault cases at hospitals appears an unremarkable objective. Discussions with relevant people in the Health Department and at various clinics raised no objections and the mood of such meetings suggested full commitment. Yet repeatedly such strategies foundered in practice. The reasons for failure are complex, but at base there is often an acceptance of violence as a justifiable response to behaviour that is considered intolerable. In PNG this allows men to view rape as a justifiable 'punishment' for women whom they consider immoral and for men to assault wives who fail to fulfil marital or domestic responsibilities.[8]

The really difficult task in PNG is therefore similar to that in most countries, one which UNIFEM has described as 'revers[ing] ingrained cultural attitudes to violence against women' (Heyzer 1998: 20). The methods that are usually advocated for effecting this transformation include: 'Media campaigns, radio programs, films, and videos, as well as symbolic "tribunals" featuring personal testimonies of women survivors of violence' (Heyzer 1998: 20). All of these methods have been used in PNG over the past twenty years. Street theatre groups in several major towns, posters, educational programs in villages, awareness programs through women's organisations, training seminars through aid programs and churches have attempted to alter public attitudes and to bring messages about human rights to the 'grassroots' as well as in government departments. Some have failed because they have employed culturally inappropriate images (Eves 2006: 55 and Appendix 9: #88); often the messages are interpreted in ways that are not intended (Macpherson 2008), or even reinforce prevailing notions of masculinity and its entitlements. Eves' study includes several examples where men completely 'misread' a poster. One policewoman told me of a village meeting where men were given a pamphlet that included an image of a man beating a woman and asked to comment on its message. The first four responses were all speculations about the behaviour of the woman that must have provoked the attack and the dominant interpretation was that 'this is a picture of a man who is beating his wife because she must have been unfaithful.'

Many people believe that violence against women is increasing in PNG. In the absence of clear data that demonstrates this, one must retreat to the position that even if it were not, it is still at unacceptably high levels and substantial elements of the population still do not see it as either criminal or breaching women's human rights. This leads us back to the problems posed by the Millennium Development Goal of women's empowerment and the problem of *how* to combat violence against women. To date, many of the programs have been directed at

---

8   Notions of 'immoral' behaviour include failure to defer to men, being single, walking alone, speaking with men who are not relatives and wearing fashionable western clothing or make-up. Any of these things can be interpreted as displaying sexual availability. Within marriage, women reported that refusing sex and failure to have a meal prepared were common excuses for assault (see also Eves 2006: 24; and Spark 2011).

women. They do not have the political or social power to change the behaviour of men. Men are apparently not going to relinquish this power on the basis of arguments put to them about women's rights, especially by women or foreign aid workers. As Eves (2006) and Michael Flood (2002–2003) have argued convincingly, men do not respond well to programs aimed at changing their behaviour when these are forced upon them by law (and one could add, by foreigners through aid programs). Awareness programs do not work well in PNG when men and women are in groups together. To date, most programs aimed at combating domestic violence have been conducted with women as the prime focus for awareness education and directed towards men in similar terms, that is with a view to establishing knowledge about women's rights. There is obviously a need to rethink the assumptions behind this approach.

In exploring the problems specific to PNG, I have concentrated on what I perceive to be major obstacles and blind spots in the development of programs. This is not because I have in mind a fully-developed alternative approach, but because I think that the sorts of changes that need to occur will not really be effected by projects that are specifically focused on violence. Most writers who have tried to come to grips with the problem have regretfully concluded that change will be gradual and slow. Considering what might hasten progress or alter the gender inequalities that underpin violence, I think that the MDGs aimed at empowering women more generally necessarily have to precede campaigns that aim to combat violence.

If we re-examine the 'strategic priorities' outlined by the taskforce, then it is clear that if they were to be implemented in PNG they would have to be programs that were not 'mainstreamed' in broader projects, but were specifically designed to improve the lives of women. Mainstreaming, as Lewis (2006) has pointed out in his discussion of women and AIDS in Africa, does not work. It is a way of reducing costs that has been dressed up in the ideological language of egalitarianism. This would in some instances mean that the 'community' had to wait until women's situation was materially changed. In the area of post-primary education for example, it would require that positive discrimination measures were introduced in order to rapidly increase the numbers of women involved. In health, it would require changes in the policies whereby cuts keep being made to services and recruitment, training and infrastructure. Programs aimed at reducing women's workload, such as water supplies at village level, would have to be privileged over major works such as road building. Altering employment rates and salary differentials in women's favour would require really dramatic changes in the formal and informal systems that prevail in the public service and would also entail specialised training programs.

Figure 9. The NGO, 'Women Arise', demonstrating support for women's rights, Port Moresby, 2006.

Photograph by Christine Stewart.

Affirmative action programs have been controversial in developed countries. I believe that they would encounter considerable opposition in PNG as they would not only challenge current male prerogatives but disrupt established patterns of male patronage based on nepotism, political patronage and *wantokism* (from the TP word *wantok,* meaning relative, person who speaks the same language, compatriot—thus favouritism for one's own kind). In short, the goals are probably unrealistic and do not fit easily into the current development goals of donor nations or the PNG government. They would almost certainly be opposed vehemently by neo-liberals who remain firmly committed to the view that foreign investment and privatisation will ensure economic growth and that this will have 'trickle-down' effects that eventually benefit women. Neo-liberals support the MDG strategy that would 'guarantee women's and girls' property and inheritance rights' as this would provide a means for introducing legislation privatising land. In the current climate, such legislation quite possibly could deprive women of the customary rights they already have in land and benefit men who are better placed to negotiate the formal legal system and register their titles. For, as revealed in the Lihir case, the ways that men dominate discussions over compensation for land in mining negotiations effectively exclude women and deprive them of their rights as citizens. Technically, the law requires equal recognition of women's rights of negotiation, but in practice men 'represent' them in contractual negotiations (see Macintyre 2007). The massive changes required would have to occur in concert to ensure that the desired relationship between the envisaged political gains was attained.

The bureaucratic solution: Monitor, audit, evaluate

The policy and discussion documents that construct the MDGs do acknowledge the massive dimensions of the task, but rather than dealing with problems of inertia, opposition and even obstruction that might occur in developing countries, they posit technocratic and bureaucratic solutions. These, I think, will make the task even more difficult in PNG, where there is already hostility towards forms of tied aid, to the constraints and bureaucratic reporting requirements by aid donors and to the notions of 'accountability' that are attached increasingly to funding. In identifying 'indicators' and quantitative measurement of the success (or otherwise) of aid interventions aimed at achieving the MDGs, the problems of designing, monitoring and evaluating projects will be dramatically increased. In the case of PNG, the lack of data that could provide baselines for the measurement of aid program success means that major research projects would have to precede any project. As all researchers into violence against women in PNG have noted, there is a dearth of reliable information on prevalence, regional variation and demographic factors.

At the conference devoted to the issue of gender indicators and the MDGs discussed above, I outlined the problems involved in accepting the indicator for achievement of the goal of 'combating violence against women' as a reduction in prevalence (Macintyre 2006). The research required to establish a base-line for prevalence would be costly, time-consuming and constitute an invasion of privacy. The difficulties encountered in East Timor by the research team (Hynes *et al.* 2003) engaged in a similar exercise there in 2002 would be compounded in Papua New Guinea. In an era where aid projects are increasingly evaluated in economic terms, the need for thorough research that underpins any project and informs monitoring, evaluation and assessment of its success has finally been recognised. The time and cost involved in getting the sorts of data that allow for such robust and consistent analysis have not.

The criticism of aid programs has escalated. Donor agencies, recipient governments and institutions, development economists and academics have all decried the failure of aid from various perspectives. AusAID is regularly berated for giving 'boomerang aid' (e.g. Aid Watch Website) whereby much of the funding is allotted to the Australian companies who manage projects, or provide services, expert personnel and equipment. Sensitive to such criticisms, eager to demonstrate the success of aid programs and caught up in neo-liberal economic debates about efficiency and effectiveness at the cheapest possible rate, donor governments have increasingly embraced the managerial, corporatist 'solutions': they spend a great deal of money on public relations, generate glossy reports and websites so that the 'taxpayer' can see that money is being judiciously spent and audited.

Two of the major consequences have been the increased emphasis on measurement and on principles of economic efficiency and effectiveness. There are requirements of 'accountability', 'transparency' and outcome measurements that are similar to those imposed on business corporations. Increasingly, projects are required to produce reports that document, measure, evaluate, account for and justify the successes and failures of a project. This is a highly regarded activity by donor agencies as it is thought to provide proof of responsible use of taxpayers' money or supporters' donations and to justify policies and programs by demonstrating their economy.

In Australia (and in many other rich nations), this turn in policy has coincided with 'outsourcing' of aid projects to commercial companies who tender for contracts to deliver the services that are designated under the project agreement with the recipient government agencies. AusAID is therefore the agency that oversees contracts and manages them so that they achieve the goals that have been precisely described in the designs and log-frames that set out the details of a particular project. The processes ensure that an enormous proportion of the budget and time is expended on reporting to AusAID on progress and achievements. Obviously, as the commercial contractors have to maintain their reputations and demonstrate their efficiency, reporting is mainly concerned with showing compliance with the contract and timely presentation of the 'deliverables'. In the case of awareness programs about gender violence, delivery of information and some form of recipient response that illustrates that the message has been received and understood is really all that can be expected.

Advocacy groups and NGOs such as Aid Watch rail against the Australian government programs for simply lining the pockets of consultants and enriching the companies who employ them, as a substantial amount of the cost of a project returns to Australia. This is certainly a matter of concern, but it also means that they carry the burden of accountability in the form of endless reports. In one project that I was involved with, I estimate that about 60 per cent of my time was spent reporting on what I had done. In another project, which entailed meetings and consultations with the intended recipients of the aid project, the proportion of time was similar. But as the travel and meetings had been set up by AusAID to fill eight hours of each day, this meant that the four consultants had to then work until midnight in order to write up the material collected and develop the design of the project so that it reflected the consultations conducted.

In PNG the donors' imposition of these requirements generates great tensions, first, because the doctrines of accountability in the forms of reports, acquittals and completed log-frames are non-negotiable. They are, and are recognised as, displays of bureaucratic mistrust in the competence and reliability of the people working on the project—both the consultants and the Papua New Guineans. They are effectively the donor government's enactment of their power in the relationship and of their distrust in the recipient's capacity to do what the donor wants. Second, they are resented because they demand familiarity with the arcane language of managerialism and so have to be written by the foreign consultants (or advisors) engaged. In short, the Papua New Guineans often feel suspicious of the reporting requirements that effectively silence their participation, contributions and evaluations. This resentment is compounded by the fact that it departs so dramatically from the rhetoric of partnership, participation, 'ownership', 'capacity building' and 'institutional strengthening' that accompanies the negotiations between donor and recipient in the initial stages of any aid project. The experience for all concerned is more often that of working within an alienating hierarchy in which the donor agency is the unseen overseer, the advisors are their agents and the Papua New Guinean 'counterparts' their dependent and untrustworthy recipients of aid that is designed and executed by foreigners.

The underlying rationale is economic. Ultimately, each aid project has to prove that the expenditure has been worthwhile and that it has achieved the goals that were defined in the initial framework. This seems unexceptionable. But when confronted by a goal such as 'Reduce the prevalence of violence against women', most people familiar with the problem would baulk at the task. I have become convinced that 'awareness' and educational projects aimed at women are, or should be, a minor component in the struggle to 'combat violence against women'. It is not because I think there are no ways that this can occur—but because I believe that scrutiny of the numerous studies of such anti-violence awareness programs will reveal that continuing to promote programs *explicitly* aimed at such goals are unlikely to succeed.

The transformation of social and cultural values occurs in ways that are indirect and often tangential to the specific value privileged. Perhaps the best illustration of this is population control. For decades aid programs attempted to reduce population growth by directing campaigns at women. Family planning, contraception, advocating and providing safe abortion and improving access to services were the main ways that women in developing counties were encouraged to manage fertility and reproduction. These programs had limited success and it was discovered that improving girls' access to education had more dramatic effects. But improved economic circumstances and employment opportunities have had an even greater impact on population growth (Sen 1990). In India, the current economic 'boom' has apparently resulted in a discernible drop in the birth rate. I draw attention to this not because it provides an obvious template for changing rates of violence against women (although that might well be the case) but to suggest that 'empowering women' economically is much more likely to have positive effects on their autonomy than educating them about their rights. For, while domestic violence occurs across classes in all societies, prevalence is higher in poorer groups. Poverty remains one of the major reasons why women remain in violent relationships because women perceive, quite accurately, that they will be economically worse-off if they abandon a relationship.

Monitoring, auditing and measuring the effects of aid programs will not improve outcomes, mainly because these processes become ends in themselves. By definition they have to be processes required by the donor agency, so they reassert the unequal power relationship between donor and recipient: accountability becomes confused with accountancy. In 2000, the man who established Canada's major international NGO (CUSO) and for many years was a force in the government aid agency (CIDA) Lewis Perinbaum, criticised this tendency, observing that the managerialist trend effectively stifled innovation and imagination: 'Driven by the "donor-and-recipient" mentality, and trapped by monitoring and control mechanisms that generate bureaucracy instead of productivity and often impede development, CIDA is struggling against overwhelming odds' (the *Globe and Mail* 2008: S12). A recent review of the Australian and Papua New Guinean aid relationship (AusAID 2010) pointed out failures in the ways projects have been implemented in PNG implying an awareness of such matters, but reaffirming the necessity of '[d]eveloping mechanisms to improve reporting, transparency and accountability' (AusAID 2010: 55). While there *are* probably failures of accountability, the failure of projects aimed at reducing violence against women lies in the design of projects and the fact that 'mainstreaming' usually means tagging 'gender' (by which aid agencies usually mean 'women') onto other activities in which gender inequalities persist unchanged and unchallenged.

The Millennium Development Goals are aimed fundamentally at reducing poverty. Many of the strategies and policies are entirely consistent with this aim. But in the Western Pacific, where Australia is the major donor, the goals have become hijacked by neo-liberal economic rationalists and managerialists who lose sight of the goals as they impose more and more constraints on the ways that projects should operate. The ideal of 'productivity', of getting more for less, permeates the aid sector to the point where bureaucrats and others can refer to it as the 'aid industry' without a trace of irony. In the case of reducing the prevalence of violence against women, the research required, the cooperative development of programs that will be effective, the systems of appropriate evaluation and the acceptance of these by Papua New Guinean men and women are going to cost a great deal of money.

As someone who is deeply committed to the ideals of aid being based on sound, thorough research and to the evaluation of projects as well as those of eliminating violence against women I am aware that some aspects of my arguments in this chapter might appear paradoxical or even contradictory. This is partly because I believe that many of the arguments for auditing and monitoring aid are just another way of reintroducing tied aid and of replacing humanist objectives with those of economic rationalism. Contracting aid services to agencies has resulted in the fragmentation of Australia's overall aid strategy into distinct projects so that the integration of strategies aimed at improving women's lives and reducing gender violence is nobody's priority or responsibility. I also believe that the rhetoric of 'win-win' solutions to gender equality in PNG is cynical and ignorant (perhaps both). For women to gain equality in Papua New Guinea, men are going to have to relinquish privileges that are currently maintained by the threat of violence.

References

ACFID (Australian Council for International Development), 2010. Reducing violence and empowering women 2011–12 pre-budget submission, November, Budget Recommendations, Fact Sheet 3.

Aid Watch, 1995–2011. *Aid Watch: Action on Aid, Trade and Debt*. Online: http://www.aidwatch.org.au/. Accessed 27 March 2011.

Astbury, Jill, Judy Atkinson, Janet E. Duke, Patricia L. Easteal, Susan E. Kurrle, Paul R. Tait and Jane Turner, 2000. The impact of domestic violence on individuals. *Medical Journal of Australia* 173: 427–31.

AusAID, 2010. *Review of the PNG – Australia Development Cooperation Treaty (1999)* 19 April 2010.

Bradley, Christine, 2001. *Report to the Family Violence Action Committee of the Consultative Implementation and Monitoring Council*. Discussion paper no. 84, Port Moresby: Institute of National Affairs.

Counts, Dorothy A., 1990. Domestic violence in Oceania: conclusion. *Pacific Studies* 13(3): 225–54.

-------- 1999. 'All men do it': wife beating in Kaliai, Papua New Guinea. In *To Have and to Hit: Cultural Perspectives on Wife Beating*, ed. Dorothy A. Counts, Judith K. Brown and Jacquelyn C. Campbell, 73–86. Urbana: University of Illinois Press.

Counts, Dorothy A., Judith K. Brown and Jacquelyn C. Campbell, eds, 1999. *To Have and to Hit: Cultural Perspectives on Wife Beating*. Urbana: University of Illinois Press.

Creditor Reporting System (CRS) Aid Activity database. Online: http://www. oecd.org/dac/stats/idsonline; or http://www.ausaid.gov.au/keyaid/gender. cfm. Accessed 10 Dec 2007.

Crewe, Emma and Elizabeth Harrison, 1998. *Whose Development?: An Ethnography of Aid*. London: Zed Press.

Dinnen, Sinclair and Allison Ley, eds, 2000. *Reflections on Violence in Melanesia*. Sydney: Hawkins Press and Asia Pacific Press.

Dinnen, Sinclair, 2002. *Building Bridges: Law and Justice Reform in Papua New Guinea*. Discussion Paper 2, State Society and Governance Project, Canberra, Australian National University. Online: http://dspace.anu.edu.au/ bitstream/1885/41088/2/workingpaperdinnen01_3.pdf. Accessed 27 March 2011.

Eves, Richard, 2006. *Exploring the Role of Men and Masculinities in Papua New Guinea in the 21st Century: How to Address Violence in ways that Generate Empowerment for Both Men and Women. Report for Caritas Australia*. Online: http://www.baha.com.pg/downloads/Masculinity%20and%20 Violence%20in%20PNG.pdf. Accessed 28 November 2010.

Flood, Michael, 2002–2003. Engaging men: strategies and dilemmas in violence prevention education among men. *Women Against Violence: A Feminist Journal* 13: 25–32.

Forsyth, Miranda, 2009. *A Bird that Flies with Two Wings: Kastom and State Justice Systems in Vanuatu*. Canberra: ANU E Press. Online: http://epress. anu.edu.au/kastom_citation.html. Accessed 21 January 2011.

Garap, Sarah, n.d. Gender in Papua New Guinea: gender analysis for the Law and Justice Sector Program. Unpublished paper.

Globe and Mail, 2008. Monday 7 January, p. S12.

Grown, Karen, Geeta Rao Gupta and Ashlihan Kes, 2005. *Taking Action: Achieving Gender Equality and Empowering Women*. London and Sterling Va.: Earthscan.

Heyzer, Noeleen, 1998. Working towards a world free from violence against women: UNIFEM's contribution. *Gender and Development* 6(3) (November): 17–26.

Hynes, Michelle, Jeanne Ward, Kathryn Robertson, V. Balaban, M. Koss, Chad Crouse and M. Larson, 2003. *A determination of the prevalence of gender-based violence among conflict-affected populations in East Timor.* Report prepared for Reproductive Health for Refugees Consortium, Centers for Disease Control and Prevention, Division of Reproductive Health and The International Rescue Committee.

Josephides, Lisette, 1985. *The Production of Inequality: Gender and Exchange among the Kewa.* London; New York: Tavistock.

Jolly, Margaret, 1996. *Woman Ikat Raet Long Human Raet O No?*: Women's Rights, Human Rights and Domestic Violence in Vanuatu. In *The World Upside Down: Feminisms in the Antipodes*, ed. Ann Curthoys, Helen Irving and Jeannie Martin, *Feminist Review* 52: 169–90.

Jolly, Margaret, 2011. Flying with two wings? Justice and gender in Vanuatu. In *The Asia Pacific Journal of Anthropology* 12(2): 195–201.

-------- 2000. *Woman Ikat Raet Long Human Raet O No?*: Women's Rights, Human Rights and Domestic Violence in Vanuatu. In *Human Rights and Gender Politics: Asia-Pacific Perspectives*, ed. Anne-Marie Hilsdon, Martha Macintyre, Vera Mackie and Maila Stivens, 124–46. London and New York: Routledge. Updated and expanded version of article first published in *Feminist Review* 52 (1996): 169–90.

Knauft, Bruce M., 1999. *From Primitive to Postcolonial in Melanesia and Anthropology.* Ann Arbor, Michigan: The University of Michigan Press.

Lewis, Stephen, 2006. *Race against Time: Searching for Hope in AIDS-Ravaged Africa.* Toronto, House of Anansi Press.

Macintyre, Martha, 2003. Petztorme women: responding to change in Lihir, Papua New Guinea. *Oceania* 74(1/2): 120–33.

-------- 2006. Indicators of violence against women. *Development Bulletin* 71: 61–63.

-------- 2007. Informed consent and mining projects: a view from Papua New Guinea. *Pacific Affairs* 80(1) (Spring): 49–65.

-------- 2011. Money changes everything: Papua New Guinean women in the modern economy. In *Managing Modernity in the Western Pacific*, ed. Mary Patterson and Martha Macintyre, 90–120. St. Lucia: University of Queensland Press.

Meggitt, Mervyn, 1989. Women in contemporary Enga society, Papua New Guinea. In *Family and Gender in the Pacific: Domestic Contradictions and the Colonial Impact*, ed. Margaret Jolly and Martha Macintyre, 135–55. Cambridge: Cambridge University Press.

Merry, Sally Engle, 2006. *Human Rights and Gender Violence*. Chicago: The University of Chicago Press.

Meyersfeld, Bonita C., 2003. Reconceptualizing domestic violence in international law. *Albany Law Review* 67: 371–426.

OECD, n.d. Development database on aid activities: CRS online. *Development Co-operation Directorate (DCD-DAC)*. Online: http://www.oecd.org/docu ment/0/0,2340,en_2649_34447_37679488_1_1_1_1,00.html. Accessed 27 March 2011.

Sen, Amartya, 1990.   More than 100 million women are missing. In *New York Review of Books,* December 20. Online: http://www.nybooks.com/articles/ archives/1990/dec/20/more-than-100-million-women-are-missing/. Accessed 13 January 2011.

-------- 1992. *Inequality Reexamined*. Cambridge MA.: Harvard University Press.

Sen, Gita, Asha George, Piroska Östlin, 2002. *Engendering International Health: The Challenge of Equity*. Cambridge MA.: The MIT Press.

Spark, Ceridwen, 2011. Gender trouble in town: educated women eluding male domination, gender violence and marriage in PNG. *The Asia Pacific Journal of Anthropology* 12(2): 164–79.

Taylor, John P., 2008. The social life of rights: 'gender antagonism', modernity and *raet* in Vanuatu. In *Changing Pacific Masculinities*, ed. John P. Taylor. Special issue of *The Australian Journal of Anthropology* 19(2): 165–78.

Toft, Susan, 1985. Marital violence in Port Moresby: two urban case studies. In *Violence in Papua New Guinea*, ed. Susan Toft, 14–31. Monograph No. 3. Law Reform Commission, Papua New Guinea.

Toft, Susan and Susanne Bonnell, eds, 1985. *Marriage and Domestic Violence in Rural Papua New Guinea: Results of a Research Project Conducted by the Law Reform Commission and Administrative College of Papua New Guinea*. Port Moresby: Papua New Guinea Law Reform Commission.

United Nations, 2010. What are the Millennium Development Goals? *United Nations Development ProgrammeMillennium Development Goals.* Online: http://www.undp.org/mdg/basics.shtml. Accessed 27 March 2011.

Wardlow, Holly, 2005. Transformations of desire: envy and resentment among the Huli of Papua New Guinea. In *The Making of Global and Local Modernities in Melanesia,* ed. Joel Robbins and Holly Wardlow, 57–72. Aldershott, Hampshire: Ashgate Press.

-------- 2006. *Wayward Women: Sexuality and Agency in a New Guinea Society.* Berkeley: University of California Press.

Weiner, James, Abby McLeod and Charles Yala, 2002. Aspects of conflict in the contemporary Papua New Guinea Highlands. Discussion Paper 4. State, Society and Governance in Melanesia Project, Research School of Pacific and Asian Studies, Canberra: The Australian National University.

Yodanis, C.L., and A. Godenzi, 1999. *Report of the Economic Costs of Violence against Women.* Fribourg, Switzerland: Department of Social Work and Social Policy, University of Fribourg.

Zimmer, Laura, 1990. Sexual exploitation and male dominance in Papua New Guinea. In *Point,* Series No. 14, *Human Sexuality in Melanesian Cultures,* ed. Joel Ingebrittson, 250–67. Goroka, PNG: Melanesian Institute.

Zimmer-Tamakoshi, Laura, 1993. Nationalism and sexuality in Papua New Guinea. *Pacific Studies* 16(4) (December): 61–96.

-------- 1997. 'Wild pigs and dog men': rape and domestic violence as 'women's issues' in Papua New Guinea. In *Gender in Cross-Cultural Perspective,* ed. Carolyn B. Brettell and Caroline F. Sargent, 538–53. Englewood Cliffs, New Jersey: Prentice-Hall.

Contributors

Philip Gibbs from New Zealand is a Catholic priest with the Society of the Divine Word. He first came to Papua New Guinea in 1973 and since then has worked in pastoral ministry and research throughout the Highlands. He has a post-graduate Diploma in Anthropology from Sydney University, and a Doctorate in Theology from the Gregorian University, Rome. Currently he is based in Mount Hagen where he is research advisor for Caritas Australia, and Secretary of the Commission for Social Concerns of the Catholic Bishops' Conference of Papua New Guinea and Solomon Islands. His publications include: (with Marie Mondu), *Sik Nogut o Nomol Sik: A study into the Socio-cultural Factors Contributing to Sexual Health in the Southern Highlands and Simbu Provinces, Papua New Guinea*, Caritas Australia, Sydney, 2010; 'Making Sense of HIV and AIDS: Community Conversation in the Papua New Guinea Context,' in *Catalyst* 2009; 'Sorcery and AIDs in Simbu, East Sepik and Enga,' Occasional Paper 2, National Research Institute, Port Moresby, 2009.

Anna-Karina Hermkens is a cultural anthropologist working as a postdoctoral researcher previously affiliated with the Institute for Religious Studies, Radboud University Nijmegen, Netherlands, and is now an ARC Postdoctoral Fellow on the Laureate Project, *Engendering Persons, Transforming Things*, with Professor Margaret Jolly at The Australian National University. She has been doing research in Indonesia, Papua New Guinea, and Solomon Islands, focusing on material culture, gender issues, and, since 2005, the interplay between religion, gender, conflict and peace-building. She co-edited a volume on Marian pilgrimages, *Moved by Mary*, Ashgate 2009, and has published several articles on the Bougainville conflict in terms of gender, religion, violence and conflict in: *Oceania, Intersections: Gender and Sexuality in Asia and the Pacific*, and *Culture and Religion*.

Fiona Hukula is on study leave from the National Research Institute, Papua New Guinea where she has worked as a researcher since 1998. She is a PhD candidate at the Centre for Pacific Studies, Department of Social Anthropology, University of St Andrews, Scotland, researching gender, violence and urban sociality in an urban settlement. Publications include: *Women and Security in Port Moresby*, Boroko, PNG: National Research Institute (NRI), 1999 and *Rape and Social Identity*, Boroko: NRI, 2005. She is co-author of various community crime surveys conducted by the NRI at various sites around Papua New Guinea.

Margaret Jolly is an Australian Research Council Laureate Fellow and Professor in Anthropology, Gender and Cultural Studies and Pacific Studies in the School of Culture, History and Language in the College of Asia and the Pacific. She is an historical anthropologist who has written extensively on gender in the Pacific, on exploratory voyages and travel writing, missions and contemporary Christianity, maternity and sexuality, cinema and art. Her books include *Women of the Place, Kastom, Colonialism and Gender in Vanuatu*, Harwood Academic Publishers, Chur, Switzerland, 1994; *Sites of Desire, Economies of Pleasure: Sexualities in Asia and the Pacific* (ed. with Lenore Manderson), University of Chicago Press, Chicago, 1997; *Maternities and Modernities: Colonial and Postcolonial Experiences in Asia and the Pacific,* (ed. with Kalpana Ram) Cambridge University Press, Cambridge, 1998; *Borders of Being: Citizenship, Fertility and Sexuality in Asia and the Pacific* (ed. with Kalpana Ram), University of Michigan Press, Ann Arbor, 2001; *Oceanic Encounters: Exchange, Desire, Violence* (ed. with Serge Tcherkézoff and Darrell Tryon), Canberra, ANU E Press, 2009.

Martha Macintyre is currently the editor of *The Australian Journal of Anthropology* and an honorary Research Fellow at the University of Melbourne. She gained her PhD from The Australian National University and has held positions at The Australian National University, Monash University, La Trobe University and the University of Melbourne. She has undertaken research in Papua New Guinea since 1979. Her research interests include historical ethnography, economic anthropology, gender, the social impacts of mining, medical anthropology, fisheries in Melanesia, environmental anthropology and human rights. Her publications include *Human Rights and Gender Politics: Perspectives on the Asia Pacific Region* (ed. with Anne-Marie Hildson, Vera Mackie and Maila Stivens), London: Routledge, 2000; *Women Miners in Developing Countries: Pit Women and Others* (ed. with Kuntala Lahiri-Dutt), Aldershot: Ashgate, 2006; and *Managing Modernity in the Western Pacific* (ed. with Mary Patterson) 2011.

Naomi McPherson is an Associate Professor of Anthropology and Director of Interdisciplinary Graduate Studies at the University of British Columbia, in Kelowna, BC. Naomi is an established scholar, with extensive fieldwork experience in West New Britain (Papua New Guinea). Some of her work on gender issues and women's maternal health include 'Modern Obstetrics in a Rural Setting: Women and Reproduction in Northwest New Britain,' in *Urban Anthropology*, special issue *Women and Development in the Pacific*, 1994; 'Childbirth and Change in West New Britain, Papua New Guinea,' in *Reproduction, Childbearing and Motherhood: A Cross-Cultural Perspective* (ed. Pranee Liamputtong), 2007; and *An Anthropology of Mothering* (ed. with Michelle Walks), 2011. She is currently Editor-in-Chief of *Anthropologica*, the journal of the Canadian Anthropology Society.

Christine Stewart graduated BA (1st Class Hons) from Sydney University in 1966, where she studied Indonesian and Malayan Studies and Anthropology. She first came to PNG in 1968, and gained an LLB from the University of Papua New Guinea in 1976. She has worked in the Papua New Guinea Law Reform Commission, drafting legislation including the original drafts for management of domestic violence, and the Department of Justice and Attorney-General. She spent more than two years in Nauru, drafting legislation there, and subsequently took up consultancy work, the main feature of which was the drafting of the PNG *HIV/AIDS Management and Prevention Act*, 2003 (the 'HAMP Act'). Her PhD at The Australian National University, entitled '*Pamuk na Poofta:* Criminalising Consensual Sex in Papua New Guinea,' has recently been awarded.

Laura Zimmer-Tamakoshi (Bryn Mawr PhD) has often worked in Papua New Guinea since her dissertation research with the Gende people in 1982 and 1983. Her interests include development, inequality, engendered violence, the politics of culture and sexuality, and the Internet as a teaching tool. Notable works include an Internet site *The Anthropologist in the Field*, the first visual media review editor for *Pacific Studies* (1996–2001), and leading roles in the Association for Social Anthropology in Oceania. She has taught at several universities including the University of Papua New Guinea (1986–1990) and been a research associate at several institutions including the PNG National Research Institute. Her publications are many and include *Pulling the Right Thread: The Ethnographic Life and Legacy of Jane C. Goodale* (ed. with Jeanette Dickerson-Putman), University of Illinois Press, 2008; 'Gende Land Management Practices and Conflicts over Land: A Patrilineal Case,' in *Land Management and Conflict Minimisation Projects* (ed. R.J. May), 2007; 'Rape and Other Sexual Aggression,' in *Encyclopedia of Sex and Gender* (ed. Carol and Melvin Ember), Springer, 2004; and editor of *Modern Papua New Guinea*, Kirksville, MO.: Thomas Jefferson University Press, 1998. Most recently, she presented a paper, 'Natural or Unnatural Partners? The Effects of Inequality on Gende Society and their Relations with Mining Companies,' in a workshop Pacific-Asia Partnerships in Resource Development, 2010 and is the author of an illustrated pamphlet on Gende history, *The Gende: People from the High Country of New Guinea*, Marengo Mine Ltd., 2011.

Jean Zorn is Professor Emerita of Law at Florida International University, and is currently teaching at City University of New York (CUNY) School of Law. She has also been a member of the law faculty at the University of Papua New Guinea and the University of the South Pacific (Port Vila). Her particular interests are gender and law, and the relations of custom, customary law and state law in the Pacific, and she has researched and written widely on these topics. Her publications include '"Women's Rights are Human Rights": International Law and the Culture of Domestic Violence,' in *To Have and To Hit: Cultural Perspectives on Wife Beating* (ed. Dorothy Ayers Counts, Judith K. Brown and Jacquelyn C. Campbell), University of Illinois Press, Urbana, 1999; 'Women, Custom and International Law in the Pacific,' Occasional Paper No. 5, University of South Pacific, Port Vila, 2000; 'Women and Witchcraft: Positivist, Prelapsarian, and Post-Modern Judicial Interpretations in PNG,' in

Mixed Blessings: Laws, Religions, and Women's Rights in the Asia-Pacific Region (ed. Amanda Whiting and Carolyn Evans), Martinus Nijhoff, Leiden, 2006 and 'The Paradoxes of Sexism: Proving Rape in the Papua New Guinea Courts,' in *LAWASIA*, 2010.

Carolyn Brewer's primary research interests explore the impact of religion on the construction of gender and sexuality. Her doctoral research (Murdoch University) focused on the impact of Hispanic Catholicism on women's lives in sixteenth- and seventeenth-century Philippines, with special emphasis on the sinking status of female, Animist, spiritual practitioners. She is currently associated with Gender and Cultural Studies in the School of Culture, History and Language, College of Asia and the Pacific at The Australian National University from where she edits the electronic journal *Intersections: Gender and Sexuality in Asia and the Pacific*. Her publications include: *Holy Confrontation: Religion, Gender and Sexuality in the Philippines, 1521–1685*, Manila, Women's Studies Institute, 2001 and *Shamanism, Catholicism and Gender Relations in Colonial Philippines, 1521–1685*, Ashgate, Burlington and Aldershot, 2004. In addition she co-edited with Anne-Marie Medcalf *Researching the Fragments: Histories of Women in the Asian Context*, 2000.

Index

A
abortion, 26, 60, 62, 260
adultery, 3, 56, 58, 65, 142, 145, 251–52
agency, 14
    and empowerment, 12, 17, 27–28, 247
    encompassed, 28, 75, 83, 154
    negative, 27–28, 49, 58, 98
aid, 26–27
    donor agencies, 22, 26, 197, 257–61
    foreign aid, 144, 239–40
    programs for prevention of gender
        violence, xxii, 1, 7, 10, 12, 25–26, 31,
        241–42, 245–46, 248, 250, 254–62
AIDSTOK, 218, 221–22
alcohol, liquor, 8, 10, 20–21, 81, 115, 129,
    132–33, 141, 146, 202, 208–09, 214, 220,
    248
Allen, Bryant, xxi
Allen, Michael, 8
Altman, Jon, xxiii
Amet, Justice Arnold, 178
Amnesty International, xxii, 4, 25, 30
    n18, 107–08, 137 n. 1, 163 n. 1, 218, 228
Anderson, Robin, xx
Association for Social Anthropology in
    Oceania (ASAO), ix–x, 2 n. 4, 32, 137 n.
    1, 163 n. 1, 218, 228
Astbury, Jill, 242
Aufenanger, Heinrich, 110–12, 115, 118,
    123
AusAID, xxii n. 5, 6, 10, 25–26, 143, 215,
    242–43, 245–46, 249–50, 258–61
awareness programs, xxii, 23, 255–56,
    259
B
Bainton, Nicholas A., 198
Banks, Cyndi, 11, 49, 141, 172, 198, 201,
    206, 209
Banks, Glenn, 84
Bariai (people), 3–4, 15, 47, 50–51, 54–55,
    62, 64, 66, 68–69, 145

Barker, John, 15, 137 n. 1, 138
bikhet, 14, 245–7
Billy, Afu, 82
Binder, Lisa A., 172
birth control, contraception, family
    planning, 4, 16, 26, 62–63, 65, 142, 144,
    260
Bismarck Range, 110
Bomana (Port Moresby), xxiii, 20, 23,
    197–99, 216
Bonnell, Susanne, 3, 81, 143, 197, 240 n. 2
Bonnemère, Pascale, xx, 8
Booth, Karen M., 229
Bourke, Michael, xxi
Boroko (Port Moresby), xvii, 213, 217
Borrey, Anou, 3, 20, 82, 143, 173, 198,
    201, 207
Bradley, Christine, 3, 4, 81, 140–41, 143,
    198, 243, 246
Brenneis, Don, xxiii
Brewer, Carolyn, x, 32, 137 n. 1, 163 n. 1
bride price, 6, 9, 14, 31, 74–77, 79, 82–83,
    85, 87–90, 92–99, 110, 113–14, 122,
    127–28, 200, 203, 219, 222
Brison, Karen, 198
Brown, Bernard John, 219
Brown, Hugh, 78
Brown, Judith K., 49, 81, 248, 269
Brown, Paula, 110, 112, 127, 198
Brown, Robert Mcafee, 140–41
Brownmiller, 168, 172
Bruno, Fernanda, 152
Butler, Judith, 5
Butt, Leslie, 22, 141, 145 n. 14
C
Cammack, Diana, xxi
Campbell, Jacquelyn C., 49, 81, 248
Cannings, Justice David, 187–88
Caputi, Jane, 54
Caritas, xxii, 25–26, 31 n. 20, 247
carnal knowledge, 16, 171 n. 6, 204–05
Catholicism, xxi, 15–16, 17 n. 13, 23, 26,
    62, 64, 66, 68, 115, 119, 131, 137–42,
    144–47, 149, 153–54, 203
charismatic, 3, 47, 50–51

and child spacing, 64–65
fundamentalist, 47
and wifely duty, 150–51
Chancer, Lynn Sharon, 230
Chowning, Ann, 49
Christian, xx–xxi, 3 n. 4, 6 n. 8, 51 n. 3,
    119, 131
    beliefs, 15 n. 12, 49, 62, 66, 119–20,
    147
    churches, xvii, xix, xxi, 2–3 n. 4, 8,
    15–16, 23, 28, 31, 62–64, 131, 137 n. 1,
    138–40, 218, 255
    conversion, 3 n. 4, 8, 12, 15–16, 18, 20
    n. 15, 25, 31, 151, 208
    denominations, xxi, 15, 138
    doctrines, 16–17, 138, 146, 151–52
    family, 16, 66, 149–50
    ideals, 15, 22
    love, 62, 147, 150
    moralities, 24, 219, 231
    peace, 15, 149–50
    teaching, 62–66, 152
    values, 11, 16, 138, 150, 152
    wife, women, 8, 27–28, 30–31, 140–41
    n. 10, 146, 150–53, 155, 229
Christianity, 11, 20 n. 15, 31, 138–39, 151,
    208
    anthropology of, 18
    apocalyptic, 23, 146
    evangelical xxi, 8, 15, 3, 138, 151, 219
    see also mission
Clark, Jeffrey, 7, 229
Collier, Richard, 169
colonialism, xxiii, 49, 95, 190, 208
    colonial period, colonial era, xx–xxi,
    5, 15, 64 n. 7, 114–16, 120, 163–64,
    176, 183, 190, 219, 223, 226, 230
    colonial law, 3, 163–64, 169, 223, 225
    colonial power, xix, xxii, 21
    coloniser 3 n. 4, 13, 15
Concilium Legionis Mariae see Mary
condoms, 16–17, 21–24, 62 n. 6, 65,
    141–42, 144–47, 214–16, 218, 220, 229
Conkey, Margaret, 53
Connell, R.W., 154, 168

Connolly, Bob, xx
Constitution, xx–xxi, 15, 19, 29 n. 17, 138,
    182, 189–90, 213, 221, 227, 231
Constitutional and Law Reform
    Commission, 3 n. 4, 119, 223
contraception see birth control
Conway, Jeanette, 141
Coombs, Mary I., 169
cosmology, 47, 51 n. 3, 66
Counts, Dorothy, ix–x, 3, 28, 49, 58, 81,
    163, 198, 228 n. 10, 240 n. 2, 248, 269
Coursen-Neff, Zama, 82
Court, xxiii, 10–11, 18, 21, 68, 87, 92, 121
    n. 19, 124 n. 22, 126, 163–68, 171–72,
    174–75, 177, 179, 180, 182, 184–85,
    215–18, 221, 223–24, 250
    local court, village court, 59–60, 98, 251,
    254
    and sentencing 19–20, 163–92, 199,
    203–06, 250
Crawford, Charles B., 47
Crenshaw, Kimberlé, 175–76
Crewe, Emma, 240, 244, 247, 249
culture xx, xxiii, 1, 5–6, 10, 18, 21,
    25–26, 29–30, 47–51, 61, 68–69, 83, 129,
    141 n. 11, 163–69, 172 n. 7, 175, 192,
    197, 230–31
cultural trait, 5 n. 7, 48
Cummings, Maggie, 16
custom, see kastam
D
Damien, Caspar, 110–12
Dickson-Waiko, Anne, 30, 155, 228 n. 11
Dinnen, Sinclair, xx–xxi, 3, 11, 15, 21–22,
    49, 81–83, 141 n. 11, 197, 217, 251, 228
divination, 14, 129
domestic violence, ix, 6, 28, 49, 55, 62,
    75–76, 87, 132, 139–43, 146–47, 150,
    155, 242–43, 245–46, 248, 250, 253,
    256, 261
domination, male, xxi–xxii, 5, 9, 13, 28,
    50, 54–55, 89, 92, 141, 150, 154–55, 164,
    198, 209, 257
Douglas, Bronwen, 28
Douglas, Mary, 3 n. 4, 229–30

Dowd, Nancy E., 169
Duffield, Lee, 4
Duna people, 2 n. 3, 22, 208
Dundon, Alison, 22, 145
Duratalo, Alimita, 11
Dworkin, Andrea, 172
E
education, xii, xxii, 19, 21, 26, 79 n. 2,
    82, 95, 114, 166–67, 200, 204–05, 209,
    256
        lack of opportunities, 8, 85, 198, 242
        educated elites, xix, 219–20
        and women, 11, 13, 20, 26, 31, 126,
        128, 228, 231, 240–41, 245–47, 256,
        260–61
        Elimbari, Mount (Simbu Province),
        118
        embodiment
        identification with Mary, 17
        of masculinity, 208–09
        of violence, 5 n. 7, 19, 21, 48, 67, 143
empowerment and disempowerment of
    women, 3, 12, 17, 26–28, 31, 49–50–51,
    54, 94, 139 n. 7, 148, 150, 152–55,
    240–43, 246–49, 255–56, 261
engendered violence, 5 n. 7, 11, 15–16,
    18, 48, 51, 67, 69, 73, 75, 81–83, 96–97,
    107–08, 126–27, 133, 163, 269
Epstein, T.S., 99
Errington, Frederick K., 48, 83
Evans-Pritchard, Edward, 109
Eves, Richard, 3, 7, 15, 22–23, 25–26, 31,
    47, 56, 83, 91, 132, 137 n. 1, 141, 143,
    145–46, 151, 198, 248–49, 255–56
F
family planning see birth control
Farmer, Paul, 49
Fiji, xxii–xxiii, 11
Filer, Colin, xxi, 12–13, 29, 84, 219–20
Flanagan, James G., 98
Flood, Michael, 256
Foley, Brian J., 169
Forsyth, Miranda, 3 n. 4, 11, 250 n. 6,
    254
Foucault, Michel, 152, 154, 167

Fountain, Ossie, C., 152
Fraenkel, Jon, xxii n. 4
frustration, rage, 8–9, 20, 76, 87, 96, 115,
    168, 206–07, 210, 248, 252, 254
Fry, Gregory, xxii
G
Galtung, Johan, 4, 47, 49–50, 68–69
Gammage, Bill, xx
Garap, Sarah, xvii n. 1, 6, 28, 81–82,
    97–98, 243
Gavara–Nanu, Justice Les, 191
Gende (people), 6, 9, 11–14, 73–77, 79–99
gender
        equality, equity, inequality, 16, 21–22,
        25–26, 29, 31, 49–50, 69, 89, 114, 150,
        154, 172, 175–76, 183, 185, 189, 209,
        226–27, 231–32, 239–43, 245, 256, 262
        gender violence (expanded definition
        of), x, 5, 7, 73, 75, 82–83, 96–98, 141
        identity, 48
        mainstreaming, 242–43, 249, 256, 261
        relations, 5, 7, 15, 49–51, 69, 73, 75,
        82–83, 107, 109, 112–14, 127, 129–30,
        133, 141 n. 3, 154–55, 197–98, 200,
        209, 241, 243, 253
        see also men and masculinities,
        women
George, Nicole, xxii n. 4
Gerawa, Maureen, 220, 226
Gewertz, Deborah, 48, 51, 83, 228 n. 10
Gibbs, Philip, xxi, 2, 8–9, 14–15, 17 n. 13,
    22, 26, 31, 49, 61, 87, 107, 128, 137–38
Gibson, John, xxi
Ginau, Martha, 4
Glick, Leonard, 109–10
Goddard, Michael, 83, 98, 209, 215 n. 2,
    217
Godelier, Maurice, 8
Godenzi, A., 242 n. 1
Golly, Father Ernest, 17, 23, 139, 144,
    152–55
Gorodé, Déwé, xxiii
Grbich, Judith E., 165
Griffith, R. Marie, 150, 153
Grimshaw, Patricia, 30

Groth, A. Nicholas, 172
Grown, Caren, 3, 240–41, 246
Gupta, Geeta Rao, 3, 240–41, 246
H
Hahn, Scott, 152
Haley, Nicole, xvii n. 1, 2, 22–24, 198, 208
Hammar, Lawrence, 8–9, 22, 24, 49, 137 n. 1, 142, 144, 147, 198, 225, 230
Harris, Bruce, 209
Harrison, Elizabeth, 240, 244, 247, 249
Hawai'i, ix, xiii
Hays, Patricia H., 48
Hays, Terence, 48
Heise, Lori, L., 49–50
Herdt, Gilbert, 7–8, 20 n. 15, 48
Hermkens, Anna-Karina, 8, 15–18, 22–23, 49, 62, 65, 137, 148
Hershey, Christopher, 218, 220
Heyzer, Noeleen, 255
Hilsdon, Anne-Marie, 30
Hinkson, Melinda, xxiii
     HIV, ix, xvii, xxi–xxii, 4 n. 6, 12, 16–17, 22–26, 31, 62 n. 6, 65, 137, 139–47, 213, 215–18, 220–25, 229–31
     and AIDS, xvii, 22–25, 128, 140–42, 144–46, 216, 223, 225, 227, 229, 256
     and violence, 153
     healing, 146
Hogan, Evelyn, 82
hospital records, 107, 124–27, 132
Howell, Philip, 230
human rights, xvii, 12, 22, 26–30, 215, 217–19, 221–22, 231, 239, 242–43, 248, 253, 255
activists, 197
Human Rights Watch, xxii, 6, 215, 218, 222
Hukula, Fiona, 3, 7, 9, 18, 20–21, 61, 92, 173, 197
Huli (people), 6 n. 8, 9, 20 n. 15, 27–28, 129, 145, 206, 252
Hussey, Mark, 47

I
imprisonment, 30 n. 18, 164, 176, 181, 186–88, 250
incest, xvii, xxiii, 20, 60, 199, 203, 205
indecent assault, 20, 199
Individual and Community Rights Forum (ICRAF), 222, 226
inequality (economic and development), 49, 74, 81, 84–85, 94, 97
Inglis, Amirah, xx
Injia, Justice Salamo, 19, 189–92
International Women's Development Agency, xxii, 4, 239
J
jail see prison
Jebens, Holger, xxi, 138
Jenkins, Carol, 84, 141, 198, 217, 220, 222–23
Jolly, Margaret, ix–x, xvii, xxii, 1, 5–7, 11–12, 15–16, 20–21, 28–29, 62, 73, 82, 91, 98, 137 n. 1, 154, 163 n. 1, 229, 231, 240, 250 n. 6
Jorgensen, Dan, 84, 98
Josephides, Lisette, 9, 81, 228, 240 n. 2
judge, 3 n. 4, 11, 18–19, 22 n. 16, 29 n. 17, 163–179, 181, 183–85, 187–92, 219, 250
K
Kabataulaka, Tarcissius Tara, xxii
Kaiku, Patrick, 108
kastam, custom, 10–11, 13–14, 16, 29, 73–74, 76, 82–83, 96, 119, 150, 180–83, 200, 203–05, 207–08, 210, 241, 245, 249–51, 254, 257
Kandakasi, Justice Ambeng, 19, 182–87, 189, 191–92
Kaufman, Michael, 82
Keesing, Roger, 48
Kelly, Angela, 222–23
Kes, Alsihan, 3, 240–41, 246
Kidu, Dame Carol, xvii, xix, xxi–xxii, 107–08, 141, 222–23, 227
Kilby, Patrick, 27
Kimbe (town), 50
kinship, 6 n. 8, 28, 73, 79 n. 2, 82, 84, 183
     new forms of polygyny, 13, 16, 56, 63, 76, 88

nuclear family, 16, 66
and spousal abuse, 47, 49, 56–58, 67–68, 251
Kirriwom, Justice Nicholas, 188
Kleinman, Arthur, 140, 142
Knauft, Bruce, 8, 12 n. 11, 74, 91, 228–29, 251
Kokoda, xx, 4
Konia, Ruth, 217
Krohn-Hansen, Christian, 49
Kuman (people, language), 112–13, 116 n. 16, 126–27, 131 n. 31
kumo
creature, 111–12, 130 n. 27, 132
doctor, 112
person, 111–12, 115, 117–18, 123, 126
witchcraft, 107, 112, 116–23, 125–28, 133
woman, 111, 115, 118, 123, 126–27
Kundiawa (town), 112 n. 10, 119–22, 124–26
Kup (Simbu), 6 n. 8, 97–98
L
Lahiri-Dutt, Kuntala, 13
Langness, Lewis, 6, 198, 229
Law Reform Commission, ix, xxii, 3–4, 10, 119, 140 n. 9, 143, 220, 240 n. 2, 243, 253
landowners, xxi, 12–13, 31, 75, 81–82, 86, 88–90, 93, 96, 99, 245
language, xv, xvii, 3, 24, 30, 50, 230, 256, 260
Austronesian and Papuan languages in PNG (*tok ples*), xx
Bariai people, 52, 55, 65–66
Bislama, 29, 73 n. 1
diversity of indigenous languages, xx, xxiii, 28, 54
English, xvii, xx, 5, 110, 129, 215, 218, 254 n. 7
Gende, 84–85, 94
Kuman, 112, 126
law, language of, 190, 220, 223
Tok Pisin, PNG lingua franca, xvii, xx, 3–4, 6, 9, 13–15, 17, 22, 27 56, 58,

73 n. 1, 94, 97, 114–15, 121, 128, 139, 145, 197, 208, 223, 225, 245, 252, 254 n. 7, 257
legal system, 24, 165–66, 169, 182–83, 219, 226, 231, 257
Legion of Mary (Concilium Legionis Mariae), *see* Mary
Lee, Wendy, 155, 228
Lemonnier, Pierre, xx
Lenalia, Justice Salatiel, 19
Lepani, Katherine, xvii n. 1, xxi, xxv, 22, 24–25, 28–29, 142 n. 12, 198, 221, 230
Lewis, Stephen, 239–40, 243, 256
Ley, Allison, 3, 49, 141 n. 11, 198, 228
Lihir, 13, 244, 251, 257
LiPuma, Edward, 31
Lloyd, Genevieve, 19, 168
love, xvii n. 2, xviii, 17, 62, 119, 147, 149–52, 172, 202–03, 205
Luker, Vicki, xxi, 22
Lulei, Hazel, 82
Lutz, Catherine A., 168, 175
M
Macintyre, Martha, xxi, xxii n6, xxv, 4–6, 9–10, 12–13, 15, 25–29, 31–32, 83–84, 141, 143, 150, 153, 198, 208, 239, 240 n. 1, 244, 247, 258
MacKinnon, Catharine, 171–72
Madang
province, 12, 73–74, 76–79, 81, 85, 88, 110, 138, 180, 188, 201, 204
town, xxiii, 16–17, 23, 76, 80–81, 87–88, 96, 137–41, 143–52, 154–55
male
bachelorisation, 13, 74–76, 85
dominance, 8, 48, 91, 115, 141
identity, 65, 74, 84
initiation, 48, 85–86, 114, 205, 208
privilege, 13, 48, 51, 54, 57, 62–63, 66, 68, 82, 227, 245, 247, 249, 261
male socialisation, *see* socialisation
superiority, 48, 88, 94, 112
Malins, Ian, 152
Mandie, Angela, 228
Mantovani, Ennio, 141

Manuhu, Justice George, 2 n. 4, 119, 188

masculinities, 7–8, 15, 20, 47–49, 55, 57, 74–75, 82–83, 91–92, 117, 154, 168, 191, 198, 207–10, 252, 255
   'troubled' and 'embattled' masculinities, 21, 48, 73–74, 76, 81–82, 84, 89, 99

Marengo Mining, 12, 75–81, 86–90, 96–97

Margry, Peter, 137 n. 2

marriage, 5, 7, 9, 16, 29, 49, 55–59, 62, 74–76, 79–80, 84–85, 87–90, 92, 94, 96, 98–99, 114, 127, 130, 144, 146, 150, 152, 191, 198, 208, 222, 229, 255 n. 8

polygamous, polygynous, 13, 16, 56, 63–64, 76–78, 88

Mary, 17, 137–39, 143, 146–55
   Concilium Legionis Mariae, 147, 148, 151, 156
   Legion of Mary, 17, 23, 137 n. 1, 138–41, 144, 146–47, 149–50, 154–55
   Marianism, 17, 137, 139
   Mother Mary, 137, 145, 148–50, 153

McCaughey, Martha, 47, 50

McDougall, Debra, 16

McLauglin, K. Eleanor, 149, 154

McLeod, Abby, 252

McPherson, Naomi, 3–5, 8, 15–16, 22–23, 25, 47, 53, 62 n. 6, 65, 144–45

Medicins Sans Frontiers, xxii

Meggitt, Mervyn, 8, 127, 198, 251

Merry, Sally Engle, xvii, xxiii, 1–3, 5, 7, 9, 18 n. 14, 25, 29–30, 231, 242 n. 3, 250 n. 6

Meyersfeld, Bonita C., 242

Millennium Development Goals, 1, 3, 26, 239–41, 255, 261

mimesis, 149

mine, mining, xx–xxi, xxiii, 9, 12–14, 28, 31, 75–76, 78–80, 82, 84, 86–90, 99, 244–45, 247, 257

mission, missionaries; missionisation, see also Christianity, xx–xxi, 3 n. 4, 28, 61–62, 73, 114–15, 208, 230

Molisa, Grace Mera, 28, 82

Mondu, Marie, 17 n. 13, 22

Moore, Clive, xix–xx

Mosko, Mark, 17, 151

mothers, 24, 56, 64–65, 78, 92–94, 96, 111, 115, 122, 154–55, 225, 229

Mounier, Emmanual, 140–41

Moutu, Andrew, 227, 232

mythology, 51, 55
   and femicide, 53

N

Naiviti, Rita, 11

National newspaper, 88, 107–09, 119, 129 n. 26, 144, 215–16, 220–21, 226

National AIDS Council, 213, 215, 217–18, 224

National Research Institute, 7, 20, 79 n. 2, 199

Nebilyer Valley (Western Highlands), 6 n. 8

Nelson, Hank, xix–xx, 220

New Caledonia, xxii–xxiii

Nicholas, Isaac, 217

Nilles, John, 112, 127

O

O'Neill, Maggie, 230

O'Neill, Peter, xxi

Ortner, Sherry, 169

P

Papoutsaki, Evangelica, 4

Papua New Guinea Sustainable Development Program, 31

Patterson, Mary, 29, 125 n. 23

Patton, Cindy, 223–26

penetration, sexual, 171, 205

Perinbaum, Lewis, 261

Perkins, Roberta, 223, 230

personhood, 18, 21, 27, 151–52, 171
   see also self

Pflanz-Cook, Susan M., 98

Phillips, Richard, 230

Pilimbo, Peku, 216
   police, ix, xix, xxi–xxiii, 3 n. 4, 9–10, 21–23, 26, 68, 82, 96, 107, 124–27, 131, 143, 174, 175 n. 8, 202, 204, 206, 208,

212, 215–17, 225–27, 229, 241, 243–46, 248, 250–51, 253–54
  community policing, 243–46
  records, 122, 124–28, 132
  violence, 214–15, 217–18, 221, 227, 231
polygyny *see* marriage
Po'o, Tau, 209
Poole, John Fitz Porter, 7, 48
pornography, 19–20, 91, 170–72, 176, 191, 202–03
Poro Sapot Project, 218, 222
Port Moresby, xvii–xxi, xxiii, 20–21, 79 n. 2, 121, 124, 137 n. 1, 140–41, 143, 149, 151, 197–99, 203–05, 213–14, 222, 225, 246–47, 257
postpartum taboo, 59, 64–65, 129
Post–Courier newspaper, 91, 107, 109, 122, 143, 147, 215–16, 218, 220, 225, 227
poverty, xii, 12, 23, 49, 91, 198, 240–42, 244, 247, 261
power, 1, 3, 6 n. 8, 7, 8, 11, 15–17, 21, 25, 28, 49–50, 54–55, 61, 66, 68–69, 75–76, 82, 91, 94, 97, 109–11, 113, 119, 122, 129–33, 137 n. 2, 139 n. 7, 142, 150, 152–55, 172–73, 181, 186, 204–05, 209, 228, 242, 244–45, 247, 249, 251–52, 256, 260
  disempowerment, 13, 49–51, 53–54, 247, 249
  empowerment, 3, 12, 14, 17, 26–28, 31, 51, 94, 148, 150, 152–55, 240–43, 246–49, 255–56, 261
  imbalance, 47, 49, 74
  powerless, 61, 112, 129–33, 172
  relations, 49, 83, 129, 239–40, 250, 261
prison, jail, xxiii, 20–21, 167, 197–99, 201
prisoner, 7 n. 9, 20, 30 n. 18, 138, 167, 185, 199, 203, 205–06
  escape from, 185, 190
  imprisonment, prison sentence, 30 n. 18, 163–64, 166, 173, 175–76, 181, 186–88, 206, 250
  rape of, 7 n. 9, 192
promiscuity, 23, 142, 144–45, 176, 230–31

prostitute, prostitution, 21–24, 83, 91, 213, 215–18, 220, 223–27, 229–32, 252
  female, 215–17, 225–26, 229, 231–32
  male, 22, 142 n. 12, 215, 217, 220, 226–27, 232
protest, ix–x, xvii, xix, xxii n. 7, 218
punishment, 3 n. 4, 10, 53, 60–62, 65, 110, 115, 119, 145, 186–87, 213, 221–22, 227, 231, 241, 249–51, 255
  of children, 68, 251
R
Ram, Kalpana, 137 n. 1, 149
Ramsay, Raylene, xxiii n. 7
Ramu, 77, 81, 86, 110
Ramu Nickel Project, 12, 75, 77–81, 86–88, 96
rape, xii, 3–5, 7, 10–11, 17–21, 24, 27, 29 n. 17, 53–54, 60–61, 65, 69, 73, 81, 91–92, 111 n. 7, 114, 132, 139–40, 146, 153, 163–192, 197–210, 230, 248, 253–55
  and carnal knowledge, 171 n. 6, 204–05
  gang rape, *lainup*, xxiii n. 7, 7, 9–11, 15, 20, 23, 53–54, 253
  and penetration, 171, 205
  prevalence in PNG, 9–10, 19, 183–84
  proof of, 175
  propensity to, 197, 209
real, the, 3 n. 4, 118–19, 169
Read, Kenneth, 7, 12, 17, 198
Reay, Marie, 108
Reed, Adam, 24, 230
Regan, Anthony J., xxi
Reid, Elizabeth, 22, 31, 218
restorative justice, 10–11, 251–52
retribution, 8, 20, 22, 27, 81, 206, 210, 250
Revival Centres of Papua New Guinea, 146
Riches, David, 49
Robbins, Joel, 15, 18, 28, 83, 138, 151–52
Rosi, Pamela, 74, 81, 85, 198
Rudd, Kevin, 4 n. 6
Ruether, Rosemary Radford, 149, 154
Rumsey, Alan, 6 n. 8, 28
rupture, 9, 11, 18, 208, 252

rural, xxi, xxiii, 4, 11, 29, 80–81, 140,
198–99, 220, 223, 247, 252
  and urban, 73, 81, 198–99, 208, 223
  n. 7, 253
  and see village
S
Sahlins, Marshall, 83
Sai, Anastasia, 197–98
Sala, H., 152
Sandy, Larissa, 229
sanguma and *see* witchcraft, sorcery,
  109–10, 121–24, 130–132
Saovana-Spriggs, Ruth, xxi, 11, 28
Save the Children (NGO), xxii, 218
Sawong, Justice Don, 191
Scaletta, Naomi (McPherson), 56 n. 4,
  58, 63
scapegoat, 129–30, 132
Schmidt, Bettina E., 142–43
Schröder, Ingo W., 142–43
Sela, Robyn, 217
self, 17–18, 28, 149, 151–52, 225
  denial, negation, suppression, 17
  self surveillance, 152, 154
  self transformation, 17, 137, 149–53
  see also personhood
Self, Helen J., 223
Semo, Thomas, 20, 199
Sen, Amartya, 26, 239–40, 261
Sen, Gita, 242
Sepoe, Orovu, 155
Sete, Annette, 226
Seville Statement on Violence, 47, 68
Sevua, Justice Mark, 19
sex work *see* prostitution
sexism, 18–19, 164–69, 188, 192
sexuality, 11, 53, 56, 59, 207, 219, 229
  female, 61, 63, 68, 91, 165
sexual jealousy, 16, 54, 56–57, 63, 68
Sikani, Richard, 209
Silverman, Eric Kline, 51
Simbu, xxiii, 2, 4, 8–9, 13–14, 22, 77,
  79–80, 87, 89–90, 97, 107–10, 112–16,
  118–22, 124–25, 127–33, 201
Sipolo, Jully, 82

social hierarchy, 62, 128–29, 133, 172
social panic, 22–23, 143, 213
social structure
  and gender violence, 68
  matrilineal, 13, 28, 197–98, 200, 204,
  207–08, 244–45
  patrilineal, 60, 197–98, 207
socialisation, 3, 5 n. 7, 48, 56, 113, 175,
  197, 199
sociality, 151, 206, 209, 252
Solomon Islands, xxii–xxiii, 73 n. 1, 243
Somare, Michael, xxi
sorcerer, sorcery *and see sanguma*, witch,
  witchcraft, 2, 3 n. 4, 9–10, 13, 49, 68,
  78, 80, 87, 96, 107–10, 118 n. 17, 119,
  122, 125–26, 129 n. 26, 251–52
Spark, Ceridwen, 8, 247, 255 n. 8
Sterly, Joachim, 110–12, 123, 125, 127–28
Stewart, Pamela, 49
Stewart, Christine, ix, xvii, xviii–xix,
  xxii, xxiv, 3 n. 4, 18, 21–24, 32, 137 n.
  1, 163 n. 1, 207, 213–14, 220, 223, 226,
  257
Stoler, Anne Laura, 230
Strathern, Andrew, 49, 82
Strathern, Marilyn, 5–8, 18, 26, 91, 151,
  165
Summers, Anne, 229
T
Taussig, Michael, 149
Taylor, John P., 7, 29, 91, 249
Terry, David, 217, 229
Thèry, Irène, 5
Thomson, Edwina, 15
Thornton, Margaret, 165, 169
Tiwari, Sally, xxii
Toft, Susan, 3–4, 81, 140–41, 143, 198,
  240 n. 2, 247–48
Tolai (people), 98
Tracy, Karen K., 47
tradition, traditional, pre–colonial, 10,
  12 n. 11, 13, 18, 25, 28–29, 66–67, 81,
  83, 85–86, 91, 94, 107, 109–14, 115–16,
  118–20, 128–30, 133, 138, 164, 181–82,

190–91, 197–98, 208–10, 228–31, 245, 250–52

Trompf, Garry, 110

Tuzin, Donald, 8, 48

U

Unage, Michael, 108, 129

UNDP, 240

UNIFEM, 25, 242, 255

urban, xix–xxi, 9, 15, 50, 73–74, 81–82, 92, 95, 138, 146, 153, 166, 168, 198–99, 208, 217, 220–22, 228, 230, 244, 248, 253
    women, 4, 11, 20, 137, 140, 153, 165, 190, 229

USAID, 145 n. 14

V

Valdes, Francisco, 169

Vanuatu, xxii–xxiii, 11, 28–29, 73 n. 1, 249, 250 n. 6

Vaz, Paolo, 152

verifiable, 119, 133

victim, 4, 6–7, 9–10, 17–18, 21, 24, 29, 30 n. 18, 47, 73, 82, 92, 143, 216, 225–27, 242–43, 245, 250, 253
    of rape, 5, 18–21, 24, 146, 163, 165–66, 168–71, 173–82, 188–92, 201–03, 205–08, 254
    of witchcraft, 2, 14, 107, 111, 115, 118–20, 122–23, 124–25, 132
    of witchcraft accusation, witch–killing, 107–08, 118–20, 129, 132

Vinit, Thomas, 147

violence
    acts of, 9, 76, 94, 139–40, 173, 180, 241
    cultural, 2, 5 n. 7, 29, 48–51, 53, 67–69, 82, 91
    domestic, marital, spousal, ix, 6–7, 28, 49, 56–58, 62, 67–68, 73–76, 82, 87, 98, 132, 139–44, 146–47, 150, 155, 198, 222, 228, 241–43, 245–46, 248, 250, 253–56, 261
    emotional, 1, 17, 19, 49, 65, 140, 142, 163–64, 172, 174–75, 189–91, 252

engendered, 5 n. 7, 11, 15, 18, 48, 51, 67, 69, 73, 75, 81–83, 96–97, 107, 126, 163
everyday, 15, 137, 139, 142–43
as genetic trait, 5 n. 7, 47–48
masculine, 49–51, 53–54, 61, 68–69
normative, 153–54
psychological, 1, 49, 164, 169, 174–75, 218, 241, 424 n. 3
spiritual, 8, 12, 15, 49–51
state of, 143, 154
structural, 49–51, 61, 139–41
war, warfare, xxi, 1, 6, 9–11, 15, 28, 53–54, 81, 89, 93, 97–98, 113, 116, 127, 129, 148, 241, 251
    and see rape

W

Wagambie, Commander, 221

Wahgi River (Highlands), 122

Waiko, John, xix

Walker-Morrison, Deborah, xxiii n. 7

Walkowitz, Judith R., 230

Wardlow, Holly, 5, 6 n. 8, 8–9, 11, 14, 18, 20 n. 15, 23–24, 27–28, 31, 49, 58, 83, 98, 100, 128–29, 132, 142, 145, 151, 154, 172 n. 7, 207, 222–23, 229, 248, 252

Watson, Amanda, 4

Weiner, James, 252

West New Britain, 3–4, 25, 47–48, 50, 54, 145

Whitehead, Harriet, 169

Wilde, Charles, 22

Williams, Sarah, 53

witch, witchcraft and see sorcerer, sorcery, sanguma, 2–3, 7, 11, 14, 20, 23–24, 49, 107–112, 118–23, 125, 128–33

witch–killing, accusations of witchcraft, 2, 11, 14, 24, 107–08, 112, 115, 118–33, 203

Wolfers, E.W., xix–xx

women
    bodies, xxiii, 2, 49, 55–56, 61, 147, 153–54, 165, 216, 222, 239–40, 249
    disempowerment see power
    empowerment see power

enculturation process, 47, 60, 68–69
and health, 65, 140–41, 153, 218, 230
n. 14, 240–42, 248, 256
hegemonic femininity, 154
status of, 62, 82, 126–30, 164, 228–29,
241, 246
subordination of, 50, 68, 91, 127,
163–65, 172, 190–91, 228
docility, humility, submission of, 17,
147–50, 153–55,
verbal aggression, 49, 59
white, xx, 7 n. 9, 19, 175
wifely duty, 63, 65

Y
Yadi, Abby, 226
Yala, Charles, 252
Yali, James, 173, 179–81, 187–88
Yiprukaman, Michelle, 215, 217, 220, 227
Yodanis, C.L., 242 n. 1

Z
Zimmer, Laura, 3, 11, 74, 84, 91, 93, 98
Zimmer-Tamakoshi, Laura, 2–3, 6, 9,
11–14, 20, 31, 48, 74, 77, 81–82, 85,
88–89, 93–95, 98, 118 n. 17, 132, 141
n. 11, 164, 172, 198, 209, 228, 240 n. 2,
246, 248, 253
Zocca, Franco, 133
Zorn, Jean, ix, 2–4, 10–11, 18–20, 24, 29
n. 17, 61, 92, 163, 165, 174, 182–83, 250
Zorn, Stephen, 163

www.ingramcontent.com/pod-product-compliance
Lightning Source LLC
Chambersburg PA
CBHW061243270326

41928CB00041B/3383